AQA GCSE

Foundation: Combined Science Trilogy and Entry Level Certificate

Jo Locke
Sam Holyman
Catherine Jones

Ann Fullick
Lawrie Ryan
Jim Breithaupt

CW01496690

Message from AQA

This textbook has been approved by AQA for use with our qualification. This means that we have checked that it broadly covers the specification and we are satisfied with the overall quality. Full details of our approval process can be found on our website.

We approve textbooks because we know how important it is for teachers and students to have the right resources to support their teaching and learning. However, the publisher is ultimately responsible for the editorial control and quality of this book.

Please note that when teaching the AQA Entry Level Certificate or AQA GCSE Combined Science: Trilogy course, you must refer to AQA's specification as your definitive source of information. While this book has been written to match the specification, it cannot provide complete coverage of every aspect of the course.

A wide range of other useful resources can be found on the relevant subject pages of our website: www.aqa.org.uk.

OXFORD
UNIVERSITY PRESS

Contents

How to use this book

Learning objectives

After this topic, you should know:

- Learning objectives at the start of each spread tell you what you will be learning about.

This book has been written by subject experts to match the specifications for *AQA Entry Level Certificate Science and AQA GCSE Combined Science: Trilogy*. It is has lots of features to help you prepare for your course and achieve the very best you can.

Key words are highlighted in the text. You can look them up in the glossary at the back of the book if you are not sure what they mean.

Diagrams are as important as the text for your understanding, so make sure you revise them carefully.

Core Entry Level Certificate topics cover shared topics from the *AQA Entry Level Certificate* and *AQA Combined: Science Trilogy* specifications.

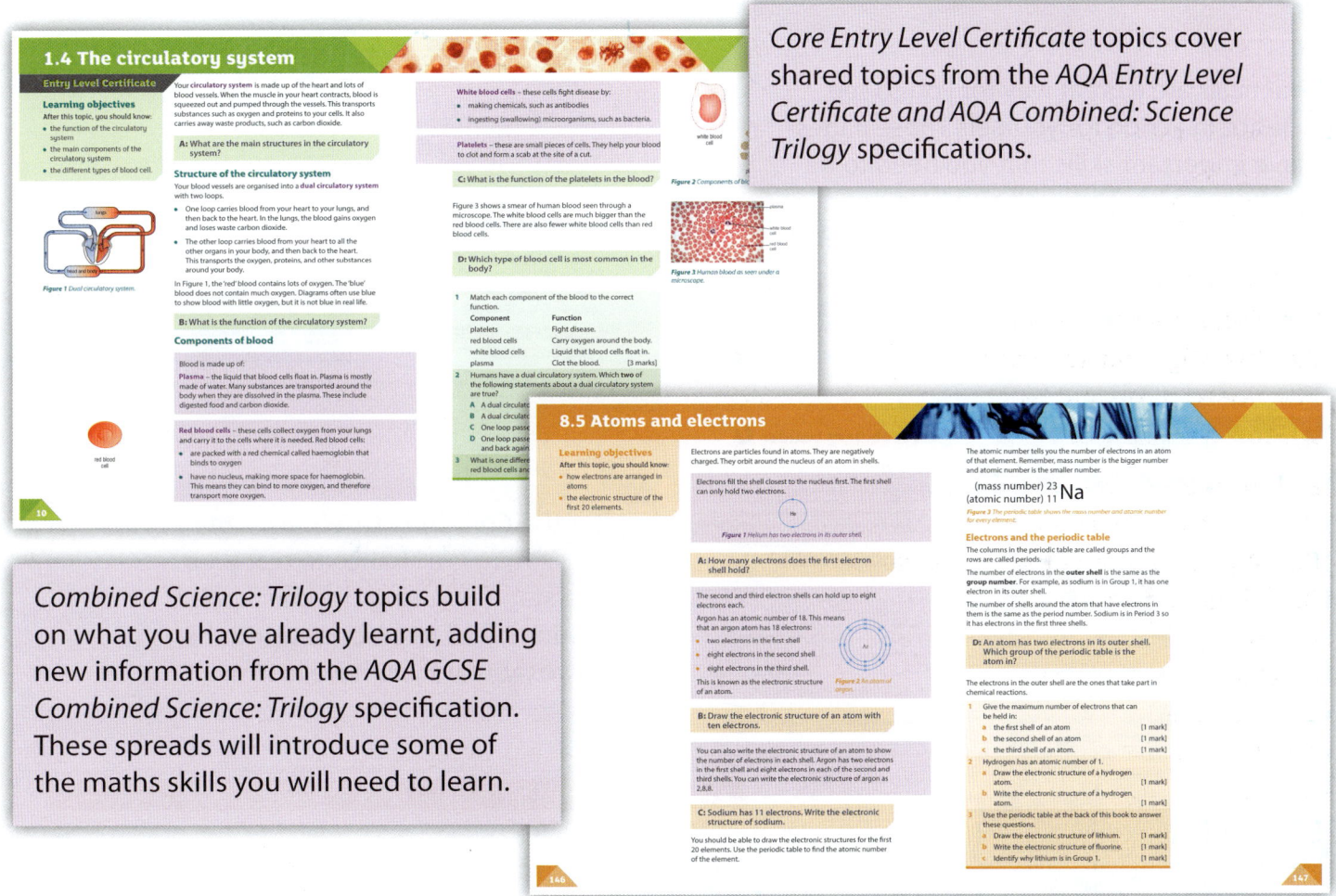

Combined Science: Trilogy topics build on what you have already learnt, adding new information from the *AQA GCSE Combined Science: Trilogy* specification. These spreads will introduce some of the maths skills you will need to learn.

Summary questions

There are summary questions at the end of each topic.

These questions give you a chance to test whether you have learnt and understood everything in the topic.

The questions start off easier and get harder, so that you can stretch yourself.

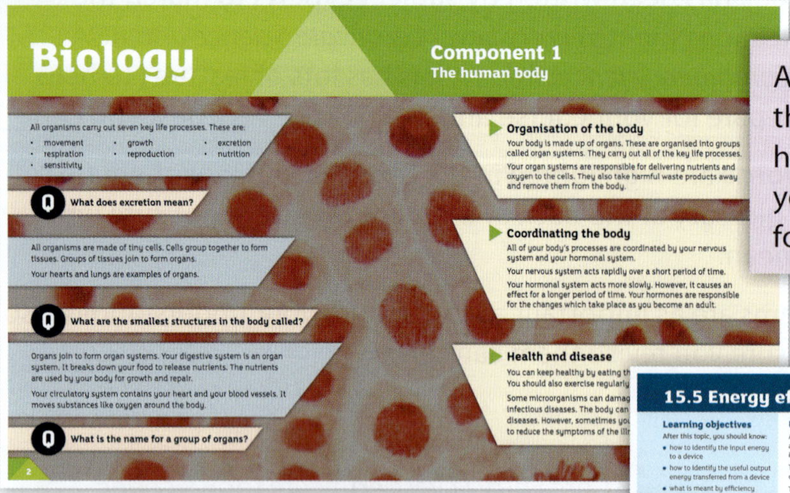

Biology

Component 1
The human body

At the start of each Component there is a summary of what you have already learnt and what you are going to learn in the following chapters.

Practicals are a great way for you to see science in action for yourself. These pages have important skills that you need to be confident with. They will also help your understanding of the rest of the chapter. More information about each practical is available on Kerboodle.

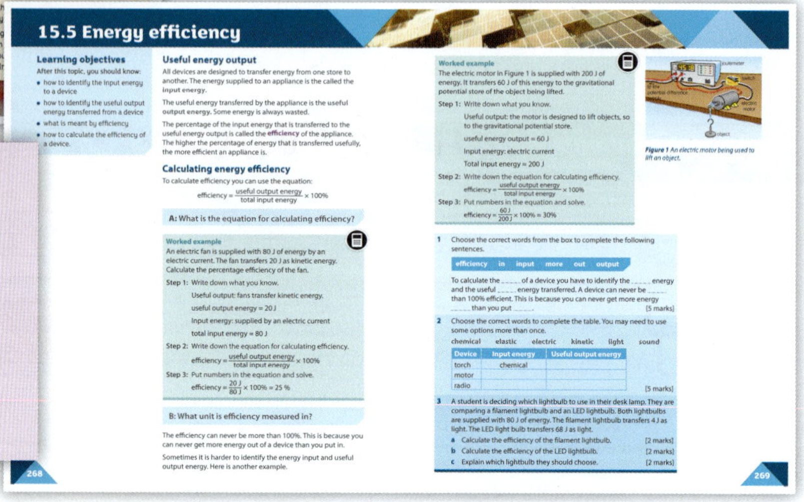

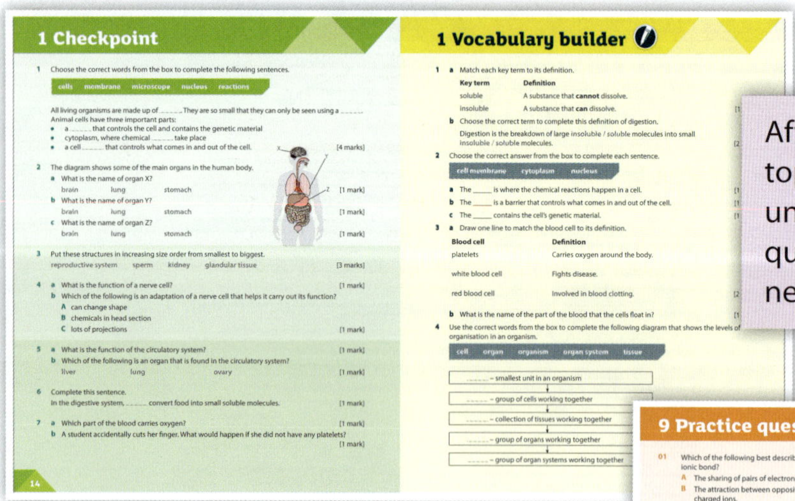

After the *Core Entry Level Certificate* topics, there is a chance to test your understanding using the checkpoint questions, and to practice using the new vocabulary you have learnt.

At the end of every chapter there are practice questions for the whole chapter. These questions will help test whether you have learnt and understood everything in the chapter.

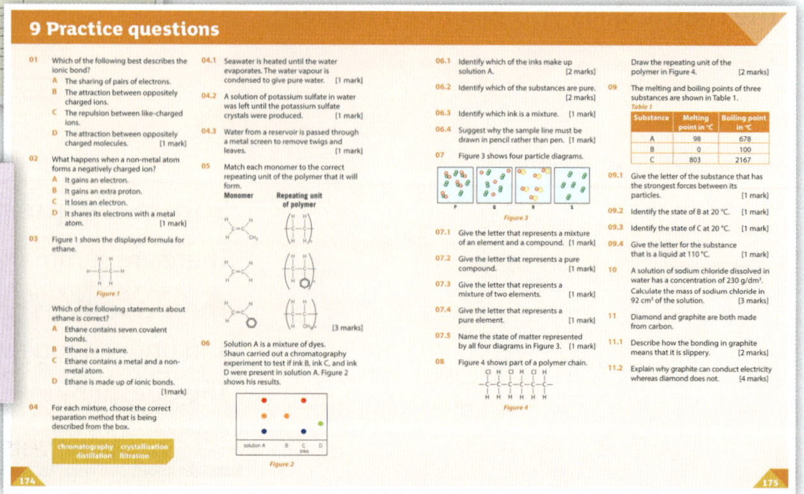

15.5 Energy efficiency

1 Checkpoint

1 Vocabulary builder

9 Practice questions

Kerboodle

This book is also supported by Kerboodle, offering unrivalled digital support for building your practical, maths, and literacy skills.

If your school subscribes to Kerboodle, you will find a wealth of additional resources to help you with your studies and revision, including:

- practicals and follow up activities
- interactive quizzes that give question-by-question feedback
- self-assessment checklists.

Check your own progress with the self-assessment checklists.

Test what you have learnt and find out what to look at again using the interactive quizzes.

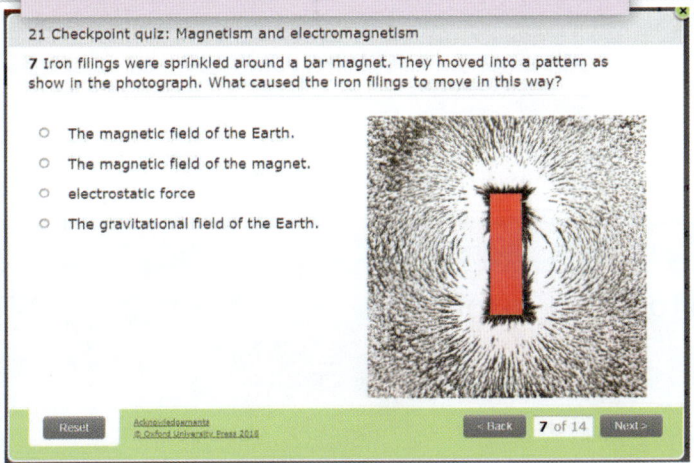

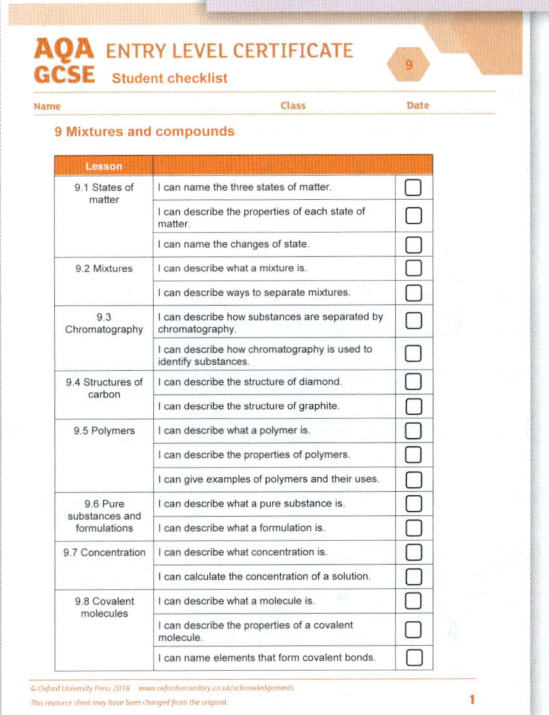

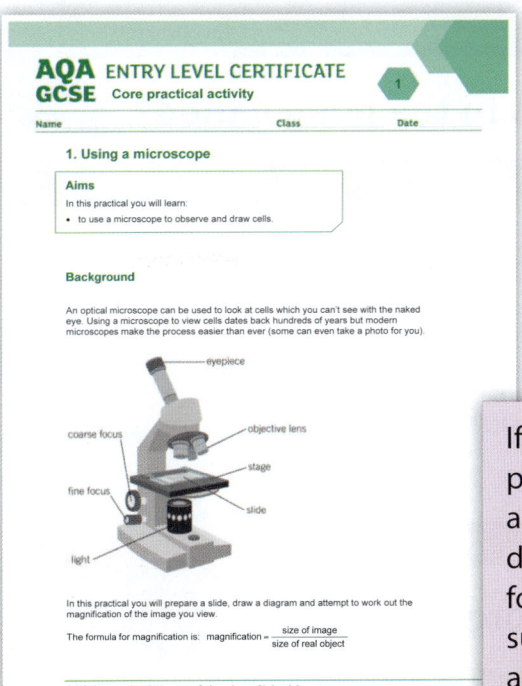

If you are a teacher reading this, Kerboodle also has plenty of practical support, assessment resources, answers to the questions in the book, and a digital markbook along with full teacher support for practicals and the worksheets, which include suggestions on how to support your students at all ability levels.

*AQA only approves textbooks, not any other associated resources.

Biology

All organisms carry out seven key life processes. These are:

- movement
- respiration
- sensitivity
- growth
- reproduction
- excretion
- nutrition

 **Q** **What does excretion mean?**

All organisms are made of tiny cells. Cells group together to form tissues. Groups of tissues join to form organs.

Your hearts and lungs are examples of organs.

 **Q** **What are the smallest structures in the body called?**

Organs join to form organ systems. Your digestive system is an organ system. It breaks down your food to release nutrients. The nutrients are used by your body for growth and repair.

Your circulatory system contains your heart and your blood vessels. It moves substances like oxygen around the body.

 **Q** **What is the name for a group of organs?**

Component 1
The human body

▶ Organisation of the body

Your body is made up of organs. These are organised into groups called organ systems. They carry out all of the key life processes.

Your organ systems are responsible for delivering nutrients and oxygen to the cells. They also take harmful waste products away and remove them from the body.

▶ Coordinating the body

All of your body's processes are coordinated by your nervous system and your hormonal system.

Your nervous system acts rapidly over a short period of time.

Your hormonal system acts more slowly. However, the effects it causes last for a longer period of time. Your hormones are responsible for the changes which take place as you become an adult.

▶ Health and disease

You can keep healthy by eating the right foods in the right amounts. You should also exercise regularly.

Some microorganisms can damage your health by causing infectious diseases. The body can defend itself against some of these diseases. However, sometimes you may need to take medical drugs to reduce the symptoms of the illness and speed up your recovery.

1 What is the body made of?
1.1 Animal cells

Entry Level Certificate

Learning objectives

After this topic, you should know:

- the main parts of an animal cell
- some examples of specialised animal cells
- how the structures in specialised cells relate to their function.

All **organisms** (living things) are made up of **cells**. Cells are the building blocks of life. They are the smallest units found in an organism. Cells are so small you can only see them using a **microscope**.

Structure of animal cells

Most animal cells, including human cells, contain three important parts:

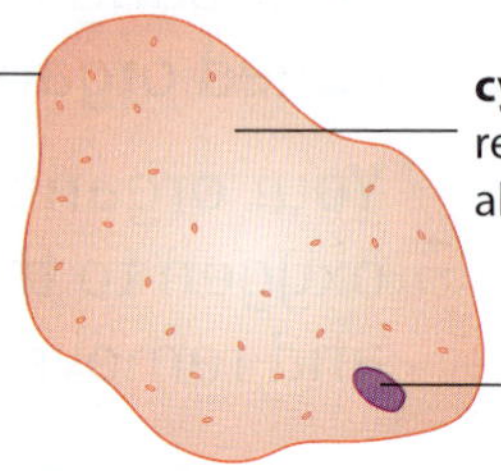

cell membrane – a barrier that controls which substances can pass into and out of the cell

cytoplasm – the chemical reactions that keep the cell alive happen here

nucleus – controls the activities of the cell. It also holds the genetic material

Figure 1 *Parts of an animal cell.*

A: What three parts do all animal cells have?

Specialised animal cells

Most organisms are made up of lots of different cells. Some of these cells are **specialised** to carry out a particular function (job).

A specialised cell has differences to its structure that make it better at carrying out its function. These differences are called **adaptations**.

Some specialised cells work on their own, such as sperm cells. Others such as muscle cells are adapted to work in a group.

B: What are two examples of specialised animal cells?

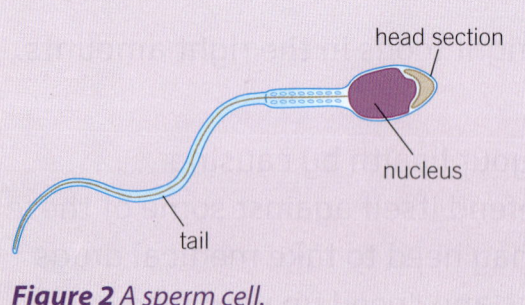

head section

nucleus

tail

Figure 2 *A sperm cell.*

Sperm cells

Sperm cells carry the male genetic material to the egg cell. Some adaptations of a sperm cell are:

- a long tail – moves from side to side to move the sperm cell towards the egg cell
- a head section – contains chemicals that break down the outer layers of the egg, so the sperm cell can join with the egg cell
- a large nucleus – contains the genetic information.

Muscle cells

Muscles pull on bones, making them move. Muscle cells can:

- work together in groups allowing your muscles to contract (shorten) or relax.

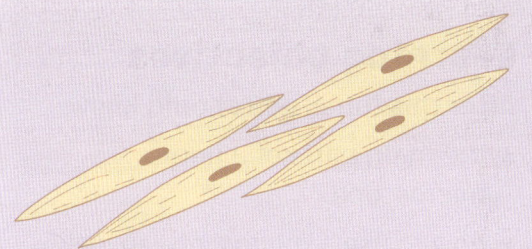

Figure 3 *Muscle cells.*

Nerve cells

Nerve cells carry electrical signals (impulses) around your body. They allow different parts of your body to communicate with each other. Nerve cells:

- are long and thin – so they can carry impulses across large distances

- have lots of projections – these make connections to other nerve cells.

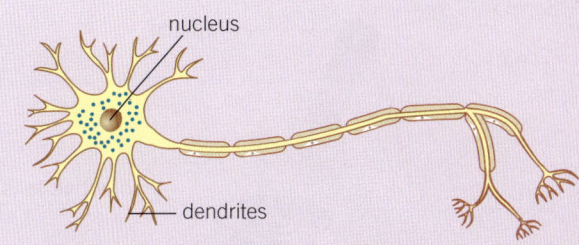

Figure 4 *A nerve cell.*

C: What is the job of a nerve cell in the body?

1   Match each part of the cell to the correct function.

Part of the cell	Function
nucleus	Controls which substances pass in to and out of the cell.
cytoplasm	'Where the chemical reactions take place.
cell membrane	Contains the cell's genetic material. [2 marks]

2   Choose the correct term from the box to complete the sentence.

change shape	send impulses	swim

Muscle cells _____ to cause movement.   [1 mark]

3   A sperm cell has lots of chemicals in its head section. How does this help the sperm cell perform its function?   [1 mark]

1.2 Looking at cells

Learning objectives

After this topic, you should know:

- the main parts of a light microscope
- how to use a microscope to look at a cell
- how to add a magnification scale to a microscope drawing.

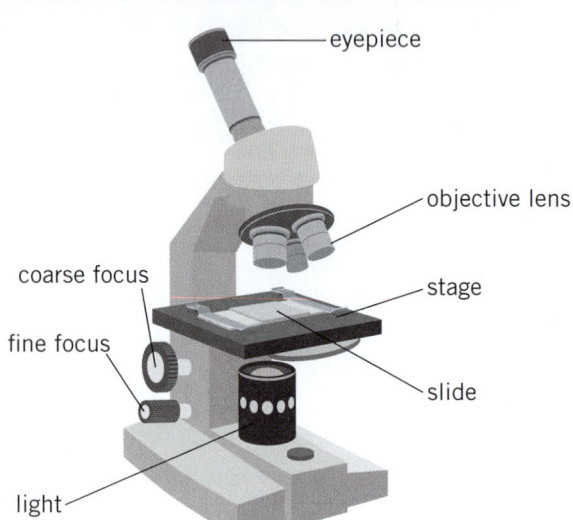

Figure 1 *A microscope.*

eyepiece

objective lens

coarse focus

stage

fine focus

slide

light

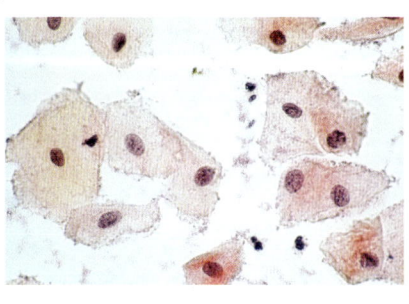

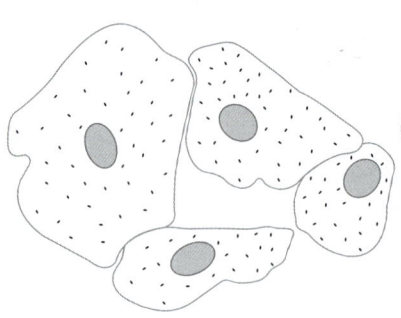

cell membrane

cytoplasm

nucleus

Figure 2 *An example of an observational drawing of cheek cells.*

Cells are so small you can only see them using a microscope. The lenses in a microscope magnify the object you are looking at. This makes it appear bigger.

A: Which part of the microscope magnifies the image?

Using a light microscope

To observe cells under the microscope, follow these steps.

Step 1: Move the stage to its lowest position.

Step 2: Select the objective lens with the lowest magnification.

Step 3: Place the slide, which has cells on it, on the stage.

Step 4: Raise the stage to the highest position possible without the slide touching the lens.

Step 5: Turn on the light and look through the eyepiece.

Step 6: Turn the coarse focus knob slowly to lower the stage until you see the cells.

Step 7: Turn the fine focus knob slowly until the cells come into clear focus.

Step 8: To see the cells in greater detail, repeat using a higher magnification objective lens.

B: Which part of the microscope do you look through?

Making microscope drawings

You can record your observations from a microscope by drawing a picture of the cells you can see. You should always:

- use a sharp pencil
- label the important features
- use a ruler to add label lines
- write the total magnification you used to view the cell.

The magnification of the image is ×200. This means that the image is 200 times bigger than the actual cell. A magnification of ×10 means that the image is 10 times bigger than the object in real life.

Magnification

Microscopes have two lenses, called the eyepiece lens and the objective lens. The lenses have different magnifications.

You can calculate the total magnification of the microscope using:

total magnification = $\dfrac{\text{eyepiece lens}}{\text{magnification}} \times \dfrac{\text{objective lens}}{\text{magnification}}$

Worked example

What is the total magnification of a cheek cell observed using an eyepiece lens of ×10, and an objective lens of ×50?

Step 1: Write down the information you have been given:

eyepiece lens magnification = ×10

objective lens magnification = ×50

Step 2: Put the numbers into the equation and calculate the answer.

total magnification = $\dfrac{\text{eyepiece lens}}{\text{magnification}} \times \dfrac{\text{objective lens}}{\text{magnification}}$

$\qquad\qquad\qquad = \quad 10 \quad \times \quad 50$

$\qquad\qquad\qquad = \quad \textbf{×500}$

---

1   Choose the correct words from the box to complete the following sentences.

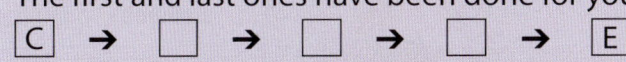

> **lenses   magnification   microscope**

Cells are so small they can only be seen using a _____.
This contains _____ that magnify the object and make it appear bigger.   [2 marks]

2   Arrange the sentences below to describe how you can observe cells under a microscope.
The first and last ones have been done for you

C → ▢ → ▢ → ▢ → E

A Using the coarse focusing knob, move the stage downwards whilst viewing the slide.

B Use the fine focusing knob to bring the image into clear focus.

C Place the slide on the stage.

D Move the stage to its highest position, without touching the lens.

E Repeat using a higher objective lens.   [2 marks]

3   Calculate the total magnification of a microscope with eyepiece lens ×10, and objective lens ×20.
total magnification = objective magnification
                    × eyepiece magnification   [2 marks]

1.3 Levels of organisation

Learning objectives

After this topic, you should know:

- the difference between tissues, organs, and organ systems
- some of the major organs in the human body
- the function of some of the main organ systems in the body.

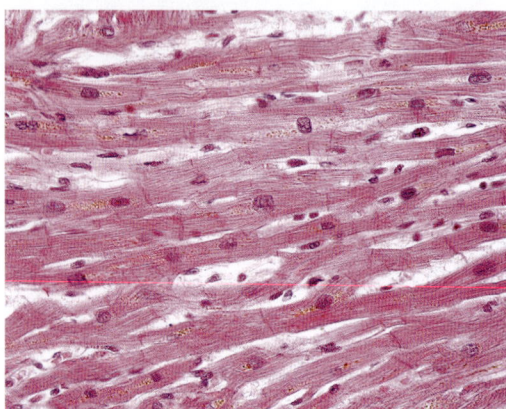

Figure 1 *Muscle tissue contracts. This moves your skeleton.*

You are made up of many cells. Inside your body these cells are organised into different structures.

Tissues

A **tissue** is a group of cells that all have a similar structure and function working together. For example in animals:

- muscular tissue contracts to move bones
- glandular tissue is made up of cells that can make and release special chemicals, such as digestive juices.

These are examples of tissues found in animals.

A: What is one example of an animal tissue?

Organs

An **organ** is made up of several types of tissue that work together to perform a function. For example, the stomach is an organ involved in digestion. It contains:

- glandular tissue – to produce the digestive juices that break down food
- muscular tissue – to mix the food and digestive juices of the stomach together.

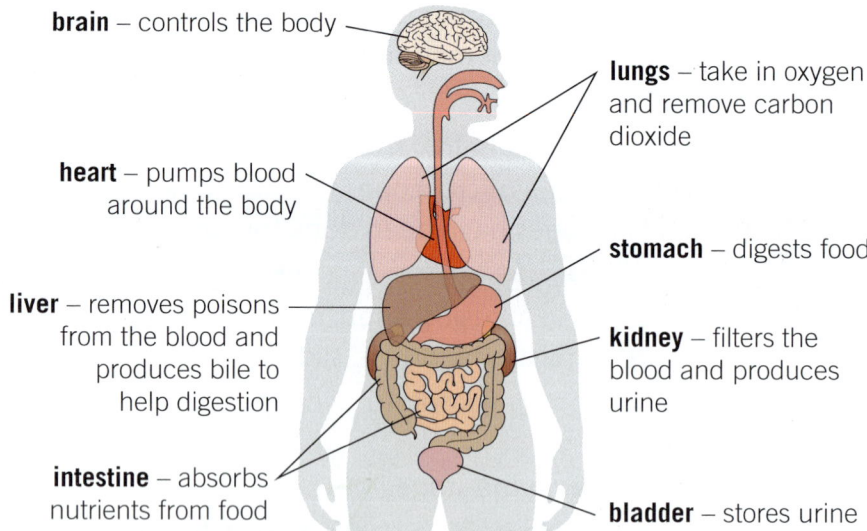

brain – controls the body

lungs – take in oxygen and remove carbon dioxide

heart – pumps blood around the body

stomach – digests food

liver – removes poisons from the blood and produces bile to help digestion

kidney – filters the blood and produces urine

intestine – absorbs nutrients from food

bladder – stores urine

Figure 2 *Some of the main organs in the human body.*

B: Name three organs that are found in the human body.

Organ systems

An **organ system** is a group of organs that work together to perform a function.

Organ systems in the human body include:

- the circulatory system – pumps blood to transport materials around the body

- the digestive system – breaks down food so that it can be absorbed by the body

- the reproductive system – produces offspring.

C: What is the function of your circulatory system?

Levels of organisation

An organism is made up of a number of organ systems working together. Figure 4 shows the levels of organisation in an organism. The cells are the smallest structure and the organism is the largest structure.

1 Look at the list of structures in the human body.

| human | kidney | sperm |

Which structure is:

a an organ? [1 mark]

b a cell? [1 mark]

c an organism? [1 mark]

2 Put the levels of organisation in order of increasing size. One has been done for you.

cell   organ   organism   organ system   tissue

smallest   organism **largest**   [3 marks]

3 **a** What is one example of an organ system? [1 mark]

    b What is one organ that is part of the organ system you have named? [1 mark]

circulatory system

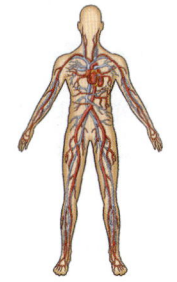

digestive system

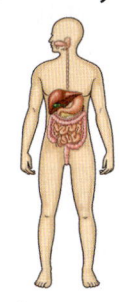

reproductive system

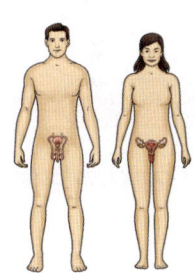

male   female

Figure 3 *Organ systems in the human body.*

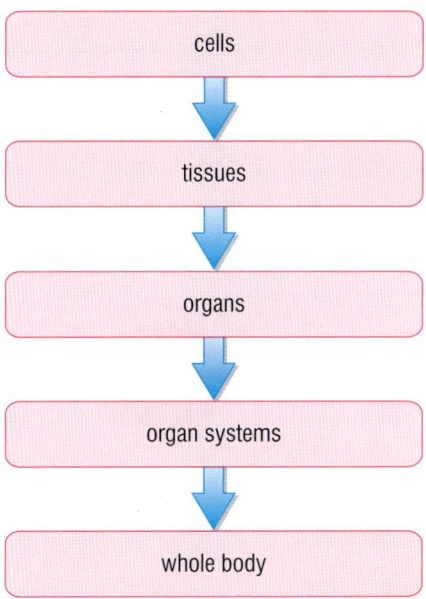

Figure 4 *The levels of organisation in an organism.*

1.4 The circulatory system

Learning objectives

After this topic, you should know:

- the function of the circulatory system
- the main components of the circulatory system
- the different types of blood cell.

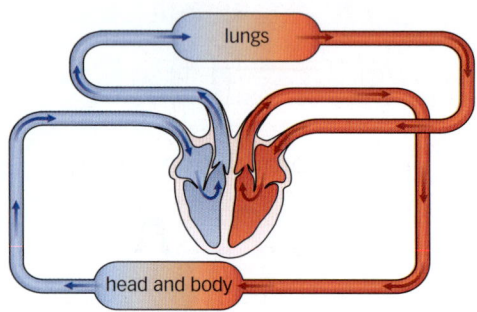

Figure 1 *Dual circulatory system.*

red blood cell

Your **circulatory system** is made up of the heart and lots of blood vessels. When the muscle in your heart contracts, blood is squeezed out and pumped through the vessels. This transports substances such as oxygen and proteins to your cells. It also carries away waste products, such as carbon dioxide.

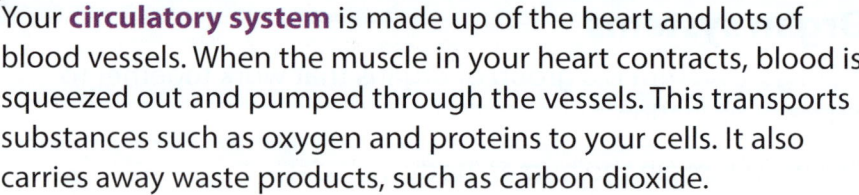

A: What are the main structures in the circulatory system?

Structure of the circulatory system

Your blood vessels are organised into a **dual circulatory system** with two loops.

- One loop carries blood from your heart to your lungs, and then back to the heart. In the lungs, the blood gains oxygen and loses waste carbon dioxide.

- The other loop carries blood from your heart to all the other organs in your body, and then back to the heart. This transports the oxygen, proteins, and other substances around your body.

In Figure 1, the 'red' blood contains lots of oxygen. The 'blue' blood does not contain much oxygen. Diagrams often use blue to show blood with little oxygen, but it is not blue in real life.

B: What is the function of the circulatory system?

Components of blood

Blood is made up of:

Plasma – the liquid that blood cells float in. Plasma is mostly made of water. Many substances are transported around the body when they are dissolved in the plasma. These include digested food and carbon dioxide.

Red blood cells – these cells collect oxygen from your lungs and carry it to the cells where it is needed. Red blood cells:

- are packed with a red chemical called haemoglobin that binds to oxygen

- have no nucleus, making more space for haemoglobin. This means they can bind to more oxygen, and therefore transport more oxygen.

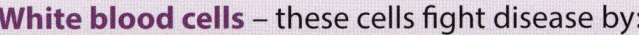

White blood cells – these cells fight disease by:

- making chemicals, such as antibodies
- ingesting (swallowing) microorganisms, such as bacteria.

Platelets – these are small pieces of cells. They help your blood to clot and form a scab at the site of a cut.

C: What is the function of the platelets in the blood?

Figure 3 shows a smear of human blood seen through a microscope. The white blood cells are much bigger than the red blood cells. There are also fewer white blood cells than red blood cells.

D: Which type of blood cell is most common in the body?

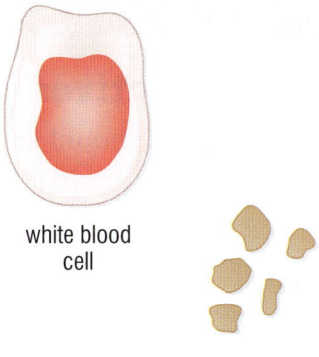

Figure 2 Components of blood.

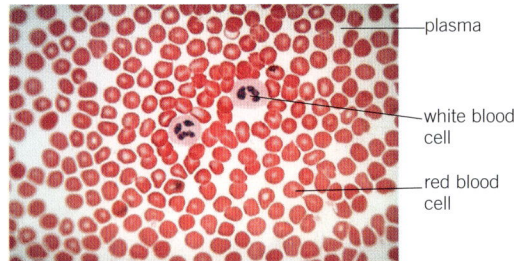

Figure 3 Human blood as seen under a microscope.

1   Match each component of the blood to the correct function.

Component	Function
platelets	Fight disease.
red blood cells	Carry oxygen around the body.
white blood cells	Liquid that blood cells float in.
plasma	Clot the blood. [3 marks]

2   Humans have a dual circulatory system. Which **two** of the following statements about a dual circulatory system are true?

   A   A dual circulatory system has four loops.

   B   A dual circulatory system has two loops.

   C   One loop passes from the heart to the head and back.

   D   One loop passes from the heart to the lungs and back again.   [2 marks]

3   What is one difference in structure between red blood cells and white blood cells?   [1 mark]

1.5 The digestive system

Learning objectives

After this topic, you should know:

- the function of the digestive system
- the main organs of the digestive system
- the role of enzymes in digestion.

The food you eat is made up of large molecules that cannot dissolve in your blood. These molecules are **insoluble**. Your body cannot use these molecules. They need to be broken down (digested) to form smaller molecules that can dissolve in your blood.

These smaller molecules are **soluble** and therefore can be absorbed and used by your cells. The process of **digestion** takes place in your **digestive system**.

A: What happens during digestion?

Your digestive system starts with your mouth and finishes at your anus. In between, there are several different organs that help you to digest food.

B: Write down three of the organs in the digestive system.

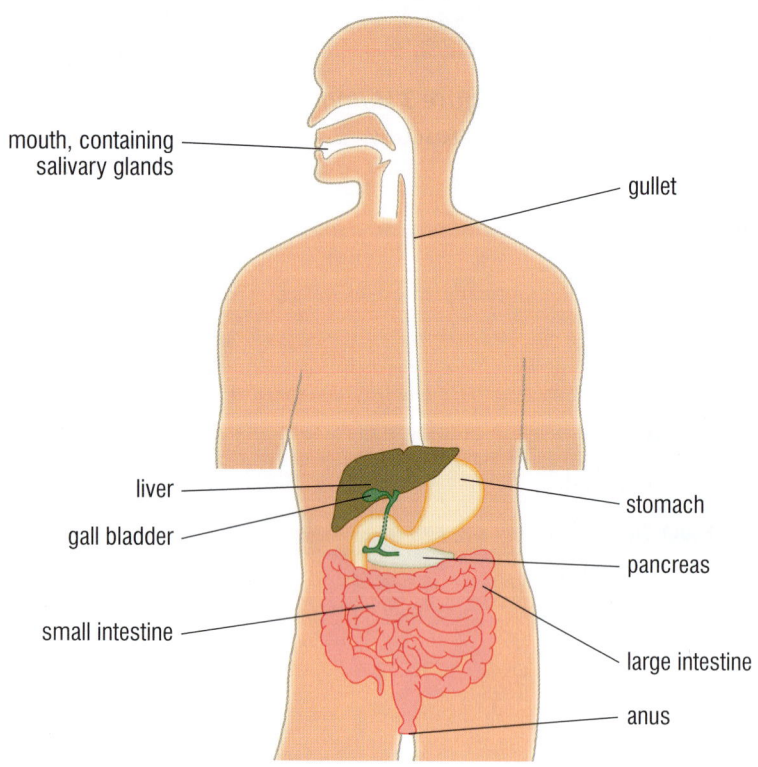

Figure 1 *The main organs in the digestive system.*

Labels: mouth, containing salivary glands; gullet; liver; gall bladder; small intestine; stomach; pancreas; large intestine; anus

Movement of food through the digestive system

Mouth – where food enters the body. Food is chewed to break it into smaller chunks.

Stomach – pieces of food are mixed with digestive juices and acids. The food breaks down more.

Small intestine – the useful small molecules (nutrients) pass through the intestine wall into the bloodstream. This is called absorption.

Large intestine – only food that cannot be digested gets this far. Water is absorbed back into the body. This leaves a solid waste of undigested food. This leaves the body through the anus.

C: What happens to food in your stomach?

Digestive juices

Your digestive system contains glands called the **salivary glands** and **pancreas**. These glands make and release **enzymes**. Enzymes break down large insoluble food molecules into smaller soluble molecules. Your stomach and small intestine makes enzymes too

Your **liver** produces bile. Bile is then stored in the **gall bladder**. Bile makes the food in your small intestine less acidic and also helps to digest fats.

D: Where is bile stored in the digestive system?

1   Match each organ to its correct function.

Organ	Function
liver	Absorbs small soluble food molecules into the bloodstream.
stomach	Absorbs water from undigested food.
small intestine	Produces bile.
large intestine	Breaks down large insoluble molecules. [3 marks]

2   Complete the sequence of organs below to correctly describe the passage of food through the digestive system:

mouth → _____ → _____ intestine → _____ intestine → anus

[3 marks]

3   What is the role of enzymes in digestion?   [1 mark]

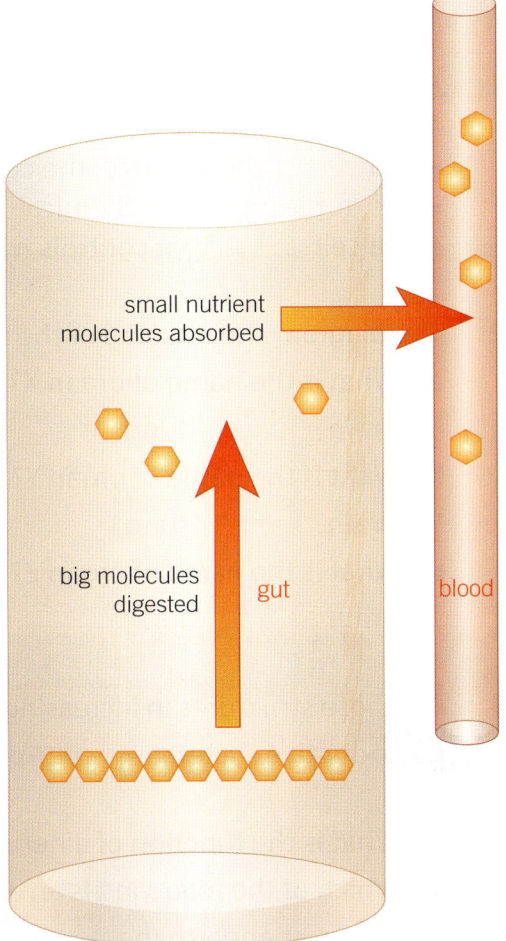

small nutrient molecules absorbed

big molecules digested   gut   blood

Figure 2 *During digestion large insoluble molecules are broken down into small soluble molecules. These then pass into the bloodstream.*

1 Checkpoint

1   Choose the correct words from the box to complete the following sentences.

> cells   membrane   microscope   nucleus   reactions

All living organisms are made up of _____. They are so small that they can only be seen using a _____.
Animal cells have three important parts:
- a _____ that controls the cell and contains the genetic material
- cytoplasm, where chemical _____ take place
- a cell _____ that controls what comes in and out of the cell.   [4 marks]

2   The diagram shows some of the main organs in the human body.
   a   What is the name of organ X?
       brain   lung   stomach   [1 mark]
   b   What is the name of organ Y?
       brain   lung   stomach   [1 mark]
   c   What is the name of organ Z?
       brain   lung   stomach   [1 mark]

3   Put these structures in increasing size order from smallest to biggest.
   reproductive system   sperm   kidney   glandular tissue   [3 marks]

4   a   What is the function of a nerve cell?   [1 mark]
   b   Which of the following is an adaptation of a nerve cell that helps it carry out its function?
       A   can change shape
       B   chemicals in head section
       C   lots of projections   [1 mark]

5   a   What is the function of the circulatory system?   [1 mark]
   b   Which of the following is an organ that is found in the circulatory system?
       liver   lung   ovary   [1 mark]

6   Complete this sentence.
   In the digestive system, _____ convert food into small soluble molecules.   [1 mark]

7   a   Which part of the blood carries oxygen?   [1 mark]
   b   A student accidentally cuts her finger. What would happen if she did not have any platelets?
                                                                                       [1 mark]

1 Vocabulary builder ✒

1   **a**   Match each key term to its definition.

Key term	Definition
soluble	A substance that **cannot** dissolve.
insoluble	A substance that **can** dissolve.

[1 mark]

  b   Choose the correct term to complete this definition of digestion.

Digestion is the breakdown of large insoluble / soluble molecules into small insoluble / soluble molecules.

[2 marks]

2   Choose the correct answer from the box to complete each sentence.

| cell membrane | cytoplasm | nucleus |

  a   The _____ is where the chemical reactions happen in a cell.   [1 mark]

  b   The _____ is a barrier that controls what comes in and out of the cell.   [1 mark]

  c   The _____ contains the cell's genetic material.   [1 mark]

3   **a**   Draw one line to match the blood cell to its definition.

Blood cell	Definition
platelets	Carries oxygen around the body.
white blood cell	Fights disease.
red blood cell	Involved in blood clotting.

[2 marks]

  b   What is the name of the part of the blood that the cells float in?   [1 mark]

4   Use the correct words from the box to complete the following diagram that shows the levels of organisation in an organism.

| cell | organ | organism | organ system | tissue |

_____ – smallest unit in an organism

↓

_____ – group of cells working together

↓

_____ – collection of tissues working together

↓

_____ – group of organs working together

↓

_____ – group of organ systems working together

[5 marks]

1.6 Plant and animal cells

Learning objectives

After this topic, you should know:

- the main parts of plant and animal cells
- the similarities and differences between plant and animal cells
- examples of specialised plant cells.

Your body is made up of animal cells. These contain a nucleus, cell membrane, and cytoplasm.

Parts of animal cells

Animal cells also contain two other structures:

- **mitochondria** – where the chemical reaction **respiration** takes place, this transfers energy for the cell to use
- **ribosomes** – where proteins are made. Proteins are used for growth and repair.

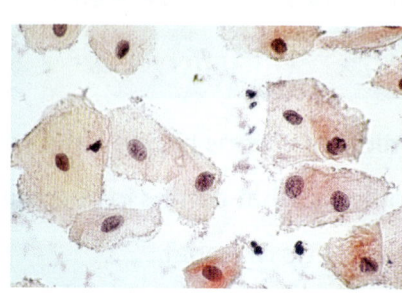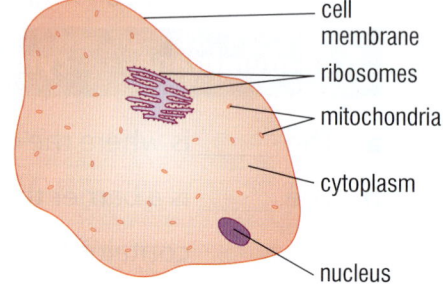

Figure 1 *This photo shows animal cheek cells. The structures in a cell are often easier to see in a cell diagram than in a real image.*

A: Give the function of a ribosome.

Parts of a plant cell

Plant cells have all the structures that an animal cell has. However, plants and animals are very different. Plants make their own food. They also cannot move their whole body from place to place. This means they need extra cell parts. Many plant cells also contain:

- **chloroplasts** – contain the chemical chlorophyll. Chlorophyll absorbs light, which is needed for the chemical reaction photosynthesis. This is how plants produce their food. All plant cells contain

- **permanent vacuole** – full of cell sap. Cell sap is made up of water, sugars, and salts. It keeps the cell rigid (stiff) which helps support the plant

- **cell wall** – surrounds the cell. The cell wall is made of cellulose, which makes the wall rigid. This helps support the cell.

Figure 2 *Parts of a plant cell.*

Figure 3 *These are moss cells viewed through a light microscope ×40.*

B: Name two cell structures that are only found in plant cells.

Specialised plant cells

Like animal cells, plant cells can also be specialised for specific functions.

What parts of a plant cell can you see with a microscope?
Use a microscope to look at a plant cell. What structures can you see?

Root hair cell

Root hair cells absorb water and nutrients from the soil. They have two main adaptations:

- root hair – creates a large surface area for absorbing water

- lots of mitochondria – transfer energy needed to move minerals into the cell

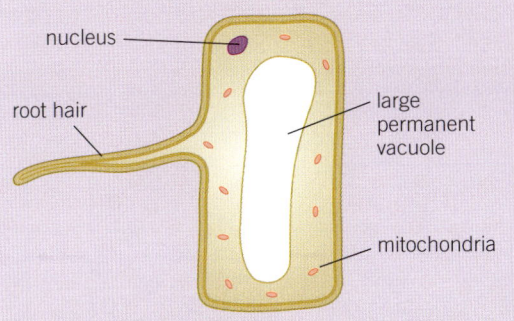

Figure 4 *A root hair cell.*

Xylem cell

Xylem is the transport tissue in plants. It carries water and minerals from the roots to the rest of the plant.

A special chemical called lignin builds up in spirals in the cell walls of xylem cells. The cells then die forming long hollow tubes. This means water can move through easily. The lignin also makes the tubes very strong, which helps support the plant stem.

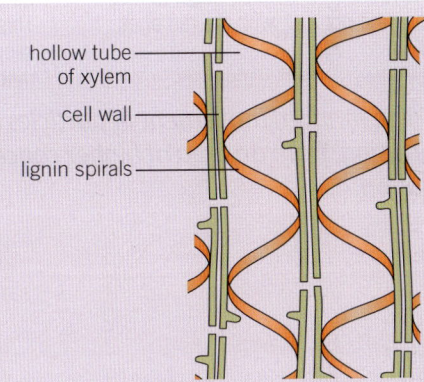

Figure 5 *Xylem cells.*

C: Name two examples of specialised plant cells.

1   From the following list, choose the cell components that are found in **both** plant and animal cells.

   **cell membrane   cell wall   cytoplasm
   nucleus   chloroplasts**   [3 marks]

2   a   Which cell component is **only** found in plant cells?

   chloroplasts   mitochondria   ribosomes   [1 mark]

   b   Describe the function of this cell component.   [3 marks]

3   Explain why a root hair cell does not need chloroplasts.
                                                          [3 marks]

1.7 Transport in cells

Learning objectives

After this topic, you should know:

- the process of diffusion
- the factors that affect the rate of diffusion
- the process of active transport.

Your cells need to take in substances such as glucose and oxygen for respiration. Your cells also need to get rid of waste products such as carbon dioxide. Gases and dissolved substances can move into and out of your cells across the cell membrane. The gases and dissolved substances move mainly by **diffusion**.

A: Name one substance that diffuses into cells.

Diffusion

Diffusion is the movement of gas particles, or substances in a solution. Overall, the particles move from an area where there are lots of particles (**high concentration**) to an area where there are fewer particles (**low concentration**). This causes the particles to spread out.

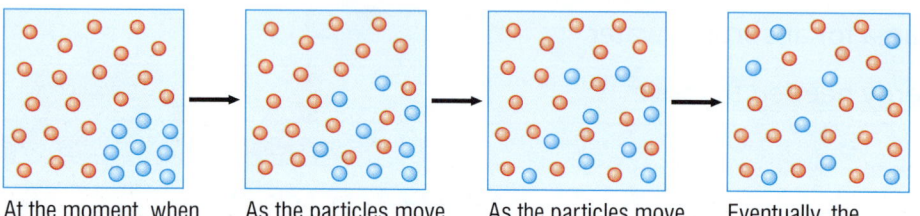

At the moment, when the blue particles are added to the red particles they are not mixed at all

As the particles move randomly, the blue ones begin to mix with the red ones

As the particles move and spread out, they bump into each other. This helps them to keep spreading randomly

Eventually, the particles are completely mixed and diffusion is complete

Figure 1 *The random movement of particles results in substances spreading out, or diffusing, from an area of higher concentration to an area of lower concentration.*

Diffusion takes place because of the random movement of particles. The movement of the particles causes them to bump into each other, and this moves them all around.

Factors that affect the rate of diffusion

The rate of diffusion is how quickly the particles spread out. Three factors that affect the rate of diffusion are:

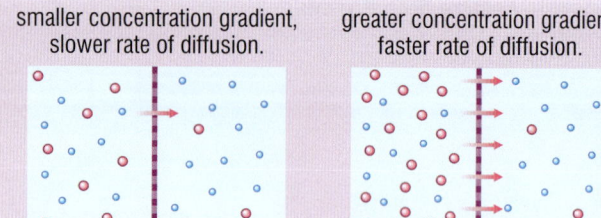

smaller concentration gradient, slower rate of diffusion.

greater concentration gradient, faster rate of diffusion.

Figure 2 *Diffusion happens down a concentration gradient. The greater the concentration gradient, the faster the rate of diffusion.*

Concentration gradient

The difference in the concentration of particles between two areas is called the concentration gradient.

To increase the rate of diffusion you could increase the concentration gradient. This causes more particles to move from the area of high concentration to the area of low concentration, so the rate of diffusion increases.

Temperature

To increase the rate of diffusion you could increase the temperature. The higher the temperature, the faster the particles move, and so the faster the rate of diffusion.

Surface area

To increase the rate of diffusion you could increase the surface area of the membrane that the particles are diffusing across. This allows more particles to move in the same period of time, because there is more space.

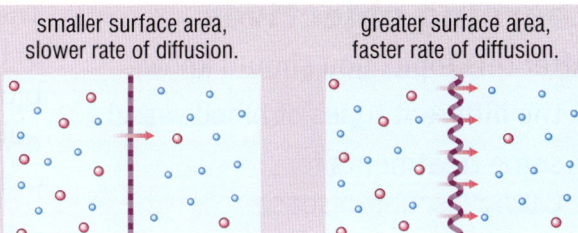

smaller surface area, slower rate of diffusion.

greater surface area, faster rate of diffusion.

Figure 3 *The greater the surface area, the faster the rate of diffusion.*

B: Give **three** ways by which you can increase the rate of diffusion.

Active transport

Sometimes the substances a cell needs have to be moved from an area where there are fewer particles (**low concentration**) to an area where there are more particles (**high concentration**). This needs a special process called **active transport**.

Active transport moves particles **against** the concentration gradient. Energy is needed to do this. Cells that carry out a lot of active transport contain lots of mitochondria. These mitochondria are where respiration happens, transferring the energy the cell needs.

Plants use active transport to take in minerals from the soil. There is a lower concentration of mineral ions in the water surrounding the roots than in the plant. The plant's root hair cells use active transport to move these ions across the cell membrane and into the root cell.

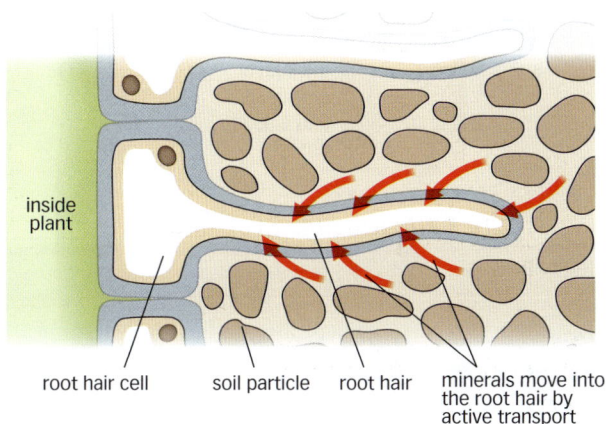

inside plant

root hair cell   soil particle   root hair   minerals move into the root hair by active transport

Figure 4 *Active transport in root hair cells.*

C: Give **one** example of active transport.

1   Choose the correct word from the box to complete the following sentences.

    high   low

    Diffusion is the overall movement of particles from an area of _____ concentration to an area of _____ concentration.   [1 mark]

2   Describe **two** differences between diffusion and active transport.   [2 marks]

3   A student puts one drop of purple dye into a beaker of water. Explain why, several minutes later, all of the water is purple coloured.   [4 marks]

1.8 Blood vessels

The circulatory system carries substances around your body in the blood. Blood moves around the body in in tubes called blood vessels. There are three types of blood vessel – **arteries**, **veins**, and **capillaries**.

A: Name the three types of blood vessel.

Types of blood vessel

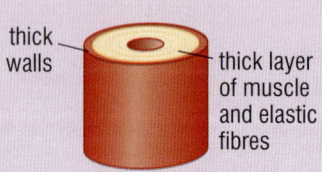

Figure 1 The structure of an artery.

thick walls

thick layer of muscle and elastic fibres

Arteries

Arteries carry blood **away** from your heart to the organs of your body.

When your heart beats, it forces blood into your arteries. This blood is at high pressure. Your arteries stretch as the blood is forced through them. You feel this as a pulse. Arteries have thick walls containing muscle and elastic fibres.

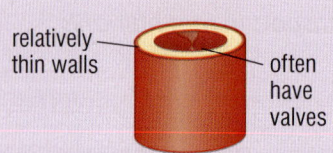

Figure 2 The structure of a vein.

relatively thin walls

often have valves

Veins

Veins carry blood **back to** your heart from the organs around your body.

The blood in veins is at lower pressure than the blood in arteries. Therefore, veins have thinner walls than arteries. They also have valves that open when blood flows through them. These valves close afterwards to stop blood flowing the wrong way.

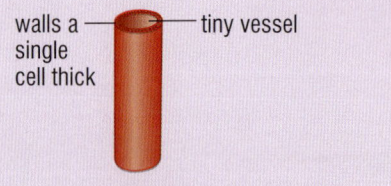

Figure 3 The structure of a capillary.

walls a single cell thick

tiny vessel

Capillaries

Capillaries are very small blood vessels. They make up a large network of tiny blood vessels that link your arteries to your veins.

Capillaries are narrow with very thin walls. This makes it easier for substances to diffuse between your blood and your cells.

Cardiovascular disease

Cardiovascular disease (also known as CVD) is a name for diseases that affect the heart or blood vessels.

If you eat lots of fatty food, layers of fat can build up inside your arteries. This makes it more difficult for blood to flow to your organs. This means that less oxygen is carried to your organs. If this happens in an artery carrying blood to your heart muscle, it can cause a heart attack. This means that some of the heart muscle tissue dies.

C: What substance can block blood vessels?

Treating cardiovascular disease

Doctors can treat blocked arteries by using:

- **Stents**
  A stent is a hollow metal tube. It can be placed in a blood vessel, holding the blood vessel open. This allows blood to flow freely.

- **Bypass surgery**
  In bypass surgery, damaged arteries are replaced with blood vessels that are taken from other parts of the body.

- **Statins**
  Statins are drugs that slow down the rate at which fatty materials are deposited in blood vessels.

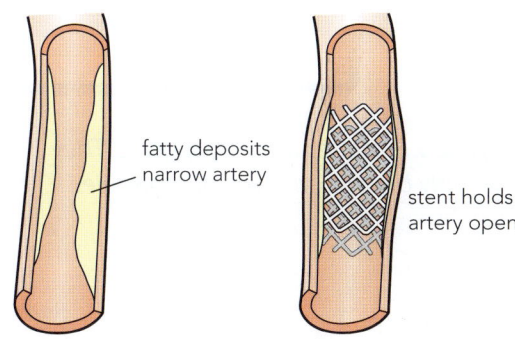

Figure 4 *If an artery has fatty deposits, a stent can hold it open.*

fatty deposits narrow artery

stent holds artery open

1 For each description, choose the correct term from the box.

artery	capillaries	vein

  a has valves

  b has thick walls with muscle tissue

  c form a large network   [3 marks]

2 Describe the differences in structure between an artery and a vein.   [3 marks]

3 Explain why fat building up in an artery could cause a heart attack.   [3 marks]

1.9 Enzymes

Learning objectives

After this topic, you should know:

- the structure of an enzyme
- the three main groups of digestive enzyme
- the function of carbohydrases, proteases, and lipases.

The digestive juices in your digestive system contain **enzymes**. Enzymes are biological **catalysts**. This means they speed up a chemical reaction, but are not used up themselves. When a chemical reaction has finished, an enzyme can be used again to speed up the same type of reaction.

A: Describe what is meant by a catalyst.

The structure of enzymes

Enzymes are large molecules. These large molecules fold to form a shape. Enzymes have an **active site**. The active site is where molecules of other substances bind to the enzyme.

The molecule that binds to the active site of the enzyme is called the **substrate**.

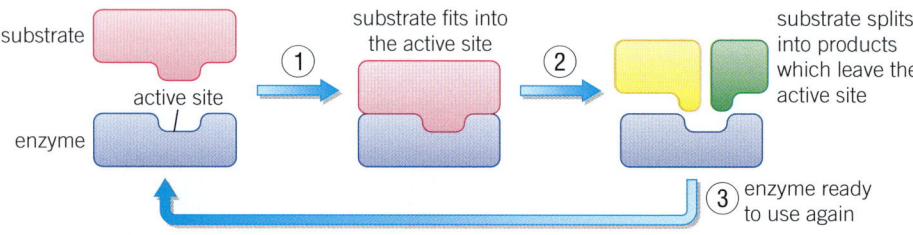

Figure 1 *Enzymes are very specific. They can only bind to one type of molecule.*

The shape of the active site is very important. Each type of an enzyme has an active site with a different shape. This means that the enzyme can only bind to one type of molecule. You can think of it fitting like a lock and key. Once the enzyme and the substrate bind together, the reaction takes place rapidly and the products are released from the enzyme.

B: Name the part of the enzyme that binds to the substrate molecule.

Digestive enzymes

There are three main groups of enzymes in the digestive system – **carbohydrases**, **proteases**, and **lipases**.

Carbohydrases

Carbohydrases break down carbohydrates into simple sugars, such as glucose.

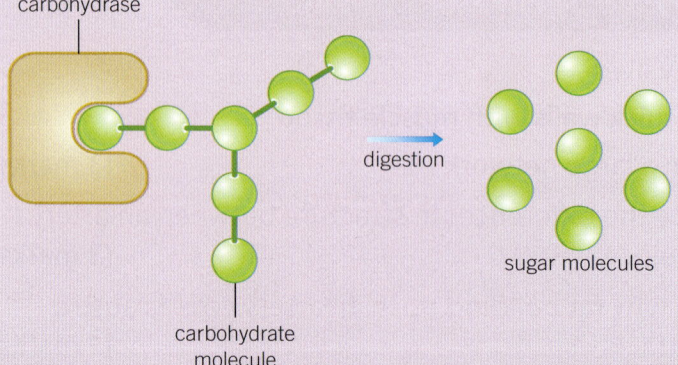

Figure 2 *Carbohydrate digestion – this happens in your mouth and small intestine.*

How are enzymes affected by acids?

Amylase is an enzyme that breaks down starch, a carbohydrate found in bread. Investigate how the presence of an acid affects the ability of amylase to break down starch. You can use iodine to test for starch.

Proteases

Protease enzymes break down proteins into amino acids.

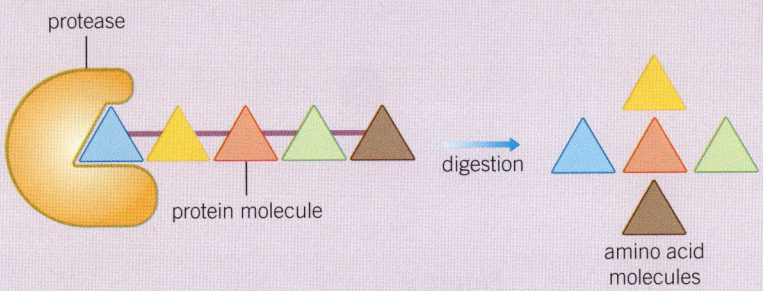

Figure 3 *Protein digestion – this happens inside your stomach and small intestine.*

Lipases

Lipase enzymes break down lipids (fats and oils) into fatty acids and glycerol.

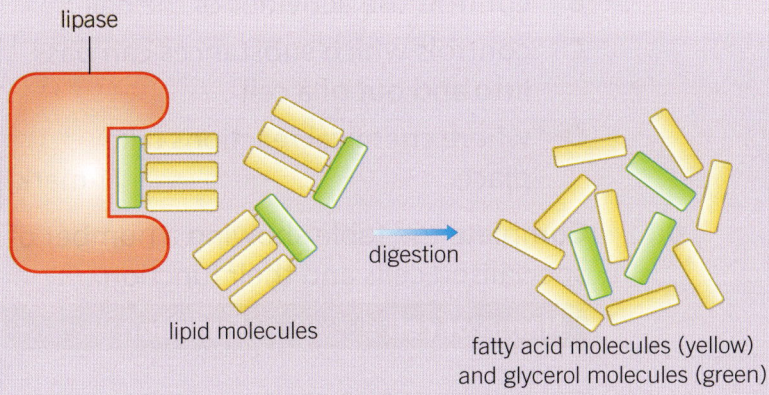

Figure 4 *Lipid digestion – this happens inside your small intestine.*

C: Name the enzyme that breaks down carbohydrates.

1   Match each enzyme to the molecules it breaks down.

Enzyme	Molecule	
lipase	protein	
carbohydrase	lipid	
protease	carbohydrate	[2 marks]

2   Describe the role of enzymes in digestion.   [3 marks]

3   Explain why amylase cannot catalyse the breakdown of a protein molecule.   [3 marks]

1 Practice questions

01 Use the correct words from the box to complete each sentence.

> a cell   an organ   an organism
> an organ system   a tissue

The basic building block of living organisms is called _____.

A group of cells with similar structures and functions is called _____.

The brain is an example of _____.

[3 marks]

02 Figure 1 shows some organs of the male human body.

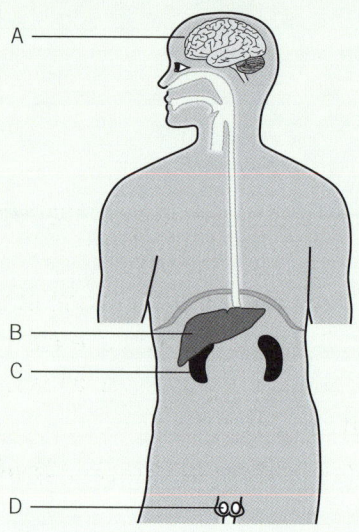

Figure 1

02.1 Name organs A, B, C, and D. Choose one answer for each organ.

A: **brain**   **eye**   **mouth**
B: **liver**   **lungs**   **stomach**
C: **kidney**   **small intestine**   **stomach**
D: **bladder**   **ovaries**   **testes**

[4 marks]

02.2 Which of organs A, B, C, or D is part of the reproductive system?   [1 mark]

03 Look at Figure 2 of an animal cell.

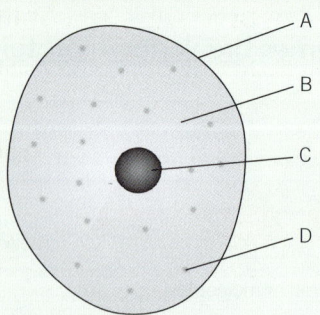

Figure 2

03.1 Choose the correct name for structure C.

cytoplasm   haemoglobin   nucleus

[1 mark]

03.2 Choose the correct function of the cell membrane.

A   contains genetic material

B   controls the activities of the cell

C   controls which substances can pass into and out of a cell

D   where chemical reactions take place   [1 mark]

04 Complete the table showing a number of specialised cells and their function.

Name of cell	Function
sperm	
	change shape to cause movement
nerve	

[3 marks]

05 Figure 3 shows the components of the blood.

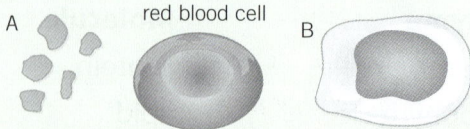

Figure 3

05.1 Name components A and B.   [2 marks]

05.2 Describe **two** ways that red blood cells are adapted to transport oxygen from the lungs to cells of the body.   [2 marks]

06 Which list of cell components can be found in **both** plant and animal cells?

    A cell membrane, cytoplasm, nucleus, vacuole

    B cell wall, chloroplasts nucleus, vacuole

    C cytoplasm, mitochondria, nucleus, ribosomes

    D chloroplasts, cytoplasm, mitochondria, nucleus
                         [1 mark]

07.1 Complete the table using a tick (✓) to summarise the differences between diffusion and active transport.

	Diffusion	Active transport
substances move against the concentration gradient		
energy is needed		
oxygen moved into the blood from the air sacs due to this process		
mineral uptake into plant roots occurs due to this process		

                              [4 marks]

07.2 Give **two** ways you can speed up diffusion.   [2 marks]

08.1 Choose the name of the blood vessel that carries blood away from the heart.

    artery   capillary   vein   [1 mark]

08.2 Give the function of a valve in a vein.   [1 mark]

08.3 The coronary arteries carry blood to the heart muscle cells. In coronary heart disease, layers of fatty material build up inside the coronary arteries. Explain why this could be dangerous.   [3 marks]

08.4 Name one way to treat a blocked coronary artery.   [1 mark]

09.1 Figure 4 shows an enzyme and three possible substrate molecules, A, B, and C.

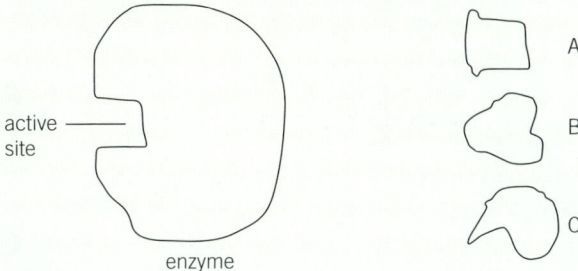

Figure 4

    Select which **one** substrate would bind to the active site.   [1 mark]

09.2 Amylase is an enzyme that breaks down large carbohydrate molecules. Explain why it is unable to break down lipids.   [2 marks]

09.3 Name the type of enzyme that can break down lipids.   [1 mark]

10 A student wanted to observe some cheek cells under a light microscope.

10.1 Name of the part of the microscope that the slide sits on.   [1 mark]

10.2 The microscope has an objective lens with magnification ×40 and an eyepiece lens with a magnification of ×10. Calculate the total magnification of the microscope.   [2 marks]

Learning objectives

After this topic, you should know:

- what the process of respiration is
- the word equation for respiration
- why respiration is needed.

Your body needs energy for everything it does. For example, you need energy to move, to grow, and to keep warm.

You get your energy from the food you eat. Glucose (a sugar from your food) reacts with oxygen to transfer energy to your cells. This reaction is called **respiration**. The waste products carbon dioxide and water are also produced.

The word equation for respiration is:

glucose + oxygen → carbon dioxide + water (+ energy)
    reactants   *products*

A: What is the name of the chemical reaction that transfers energy to cells?

Glucose

During digestion your body breaks down large food molecules. Some large molecules are broken down into small glucose molecules. These molecules can then be absorbed into your bloodstream.

Glucose dissolves in the blood plasma and is transported around your body. When the blood reaches a cell that needs glucose, the glucose moves into the cell by diffusion.

Oxygen

When you breathe in, oxygen fills the air sacs in your lungs. It then diffuses into your blood.

Oxygen binds to the red blood cells, and is carried around your body in the blood vessels. When the blood reaches a cell that needs oxygen, the oxygen diffuses into the cell.

B: Which part of blood transports glucose?

Removing carbon dioxide from your cells

Carbon dioxide is produced during respiration. It is a waste product. If the carbon dioxide remained in your body it would harm you. The carbon dioxide diffuses out of your cells and into your blood plasma. The blood transports it to your lungs where the carbon dioxide then diffuses into your air sacs. The carbon dioxide leaves your body when you breathe out.

How is the air you breathe in different from the air you breathe out?
Investigate how the concentration of carbon dioxide in air breathed out is different from air breathed in using limewater. Limewater is a clear liquid that turns cloudy in the presence of carbon dioxide.

Inside your lungs

Your lungs are full of tiny structures called air sacs. Each one has a good blood supply. Oxygen diffuses into your blood from the air in your lungs. This is exchanged for carbon dioxide, which diffuses from your blood into your lungs.

C: What is the name of the organ where oxygen and carbon dioxide are exchanged?

The need for respiration

When you respire, the energy transferred is used to:

- build up large molecules from smaller ones to make new materials for the cell

- make muscles contract for movement

- keep your body at the same (constant) temperature.

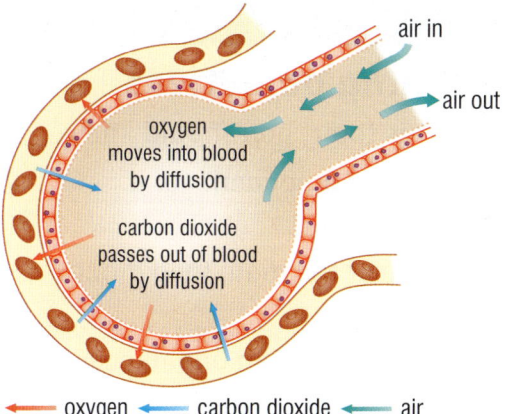

Figure 1 *Your lungs are full of air sacs. This is where gases are exchanged between the blood and the air in the lungs.*

1 Choose the correct words from the box to complete the word equation for respiration.

| carbon dioxide | glucose |

_____ + oxygen → water + _____ (+ energy)   [1 mark]

2 Which **two** of the following are reasons why your body needs to respire?

   A cool down
   B exchange oxygen and carbon dioxide
   C keep warm
   D move muscles   [2 marks]

3 Oxygen is needed for respiration. How does oxygen reach your cells?   [1 mark]

4 The table shows how the percentage of oxygen and carbon dioxide changes between air breathed in and air breathed out.

	Percentage of oxygen	Percentage of carbon dioxide
air breathed in	21	0.04
air breathed out	16	4.00

   a How has the percentage of **oxygen** changed between air breathed in and air breathed out?   [1 mark]
   b By how much has the percentage of **carbon dioxide** increased between air breathed in and air breathed out?   [1 mark]

2.2 Healthy diet

Learning objectives

After this topic, you should know:

- the main components of a healthy diet
- the role of the main food groups in the body
- some effects of an unbalanced diet.

Figure 1 *This food pyramid shows a healthy balanced diet. The largest part of your diet should be carbohydrates. You should only eat very small amounts of fats, oils, and sweets.*

What nutrients do different foods contain?
Use different simple tests to investigate which nutrients are in different pieces of food.

To remain healthy you should eat the right amount of each type of food for your needs. This is called a **balanced diet**.

Types of food

Nutrients are the substances that your body needs to function. There are five types of nutrients.

Carbohydrates

Carbohydrates are your main source of energy. They are found in sugary food, such as fruit, and starchy foods, such as pasta.

Lipids

Lipids are fats and oils. They are a store of energy in your body.

Lipids also help to keep you warm. They are stored under your skin as fat. This also protects your organs. Cheese and butter are sources of lipids.

Proteins

Proteins are needed to repair body tissues and make new cells for growth. Your muscles and organs are mostly made of proteins. Eggs and meat contain a lot of protein.

Vitamins and minerals

Vitamins and **minerals** help you to grow and function normally. Fruits and vegetables are good sources of vitamins and minerals.

Fibre

Fibre provides bulk to your food to keep it moving through the gut. Cereals are good sources of fibre.

Water is also needed in all cells and body fluids.

A: What is the role of fibre in the diet?

Problems of an unbalanced diet

Eating a poor diet can increase your risk of many diseases.

You need energy for everything you do, even sleeping. This energy comes from your food.

Some people do not eat enough food. If the energy in the food you eat is less than the energy you use, you lose body mass. This leads to you being underweight.

Underweight people are more likely to:

- find it harder to fight off disease
- lack energy and feel tired
- be unhealthy as they lack minerals and vitamins.

B: What is one problem of being underweight?

Some people eat too much food, or eat too many fatty foods. If the energy content in the food you eat is more than the energy you use, you gain body mass. This is stored as fat under the skin and around the organs of your body.

Overweight people are more likely to:

- suffer from heart disease
- have a stroke
- develop type 2 diabetes or some cancers.

C: What is one problem of being overweight?

Your lifestyle will affect what your diet should be. The more active you are, the more food you will need to eat. The average person's diet is very different from the diet of an athlete.

How much energy is in a crisp?

Investigate how much energy is released when crisps are burnt by measuring the increase in temperature of a fixed volume of water. You could investigate the difference between a normal crisp and a low-fat crisp.

1 Match each substance to the correct role in the body.

Substance	Role in the body
carbohydrates	Growth and repair.
proteins	Remain healthy.
vitamins and minerals	Provide bulk to food.
water	Source of energy.
fibre	Needed in cells and body fluids.

[4 marks]

2 Complete the sentences.

If you are overweight, you are more likely to _____ .

If you are underweight, you are more likely to _____ . [2 marks]

3 What is meant by a balanced diet? [1 mark]

2.3 Lifestyle and disease

Learning objectives

After this topic, you should know:

- some lifestyle factors that affect health
- the effect that some lifestyle factors have on health.

As well as diet, other lifestyle factors can affect your health. These include:

- exercise
- smoking
- drinking alcohol.

A: What are two lifestyle factors that can affect your health?

Exercise

Doing regular exercise helps you to get fitter. You become healthier because:

- your body mass is likely to become lower. The energy you take in will be used for movement rather than stored as excess fat. This reduces your risk of becoming obese.
- you build more muscle tissue. Your heart gets stronger and you develop bigger lungs. This means you can transport more oxygen around the body for respiration.

People who do not exercise are more likely to be overweight. They are also more likely to have joint problems.

B: What is one way that regular exercise helps you to be healthy?

Figure 1 *People under the age of 18 should do around an hour of physical activity each day. This can be anything from walking to school to playing a sport.*

Smoking

Smoking increases your chances of developing many conditions. Smokers are more likely to die at a younger age than non-smokers.

If you smoke, tar collects in your lungs. Tar is a sticky black material that damages and narrows the airways. It also contains chemicals that cause cancer.

As well as affecting their own health, smokers can also harm other people. Breathing in other people's smoke can cause health problems. This is known as passive smoking.

Alcohol

Regularly drinking more than the recommended amount of alcohol can cause brain damage and liver damage.

Your liver breaks down poisonous chemicals, such as alcohol, into harmless substances. These are then removed from your body. Heavy drinkers often have scarred livers. A damaged liver takes longer to break down alcohol and other chemicals. This can lead to serious health problems and even result in death.

Alcohol also affects your brain. Long term heavy alcohol use damages brain function. This can eventually result in death.

D: What are two health problems caused by drinking alcohol?

1   Match each lifestyle factor to an example of a disease that can be caused by the lifestyle factor.

Lifestyle factor	Disease
drinking alcohol	lung cancer
lack of exercise	liver disease
smoking	obesity [2 marks]

2   Choose the correct words from the box to complete the sentences.

> exercise   heart   liver   lungs   mass   smoking

Regular _____ can help you to remain healthy. This is because it helps to prevent your body _____ becoming too large. It also helps your _____ to become stronger, and your _____ to become bigger.   [4 marks]

3   Complete the following sentence.
Drinking lots of alcohol over a long period of time could cause liver damage and _____ damage.   [1 mark]

2.4 Investigating pulse rate

Learning objectives

After this topic, you should know:

- how to take a person's pulse rate
- how to measure a person's fitness.

When your heart beats, blood is pushed through your blood vessels. This makes your blood vessels bulge as the blood passes. This is what you feel when you take your pulse.

Your pulse tells you how fast your heart is beating. On average, a heart beats around 70 times a minute.

A: What does your pulse measure?

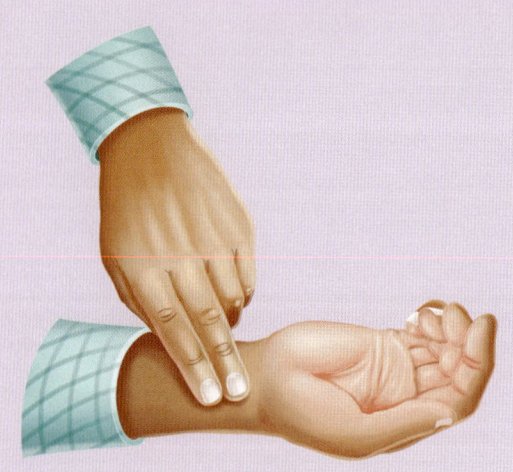

Figure 1 *You can measure your pulse in this position on your wrist.*

Taking your pulse

Your wrist and your neck are good places to measure your pulse.

To take your pulse in your wrist:

Step 1: Hold one of your hands with your palm facing upwards.

Step 2: Put the first and middle fingers of your other hand on the inside of your wrist, as shown in Figure 1. Press your skin lightly until you can feel your pulse.

If you can't feel anything, you may need to press a little harder, or move your fingers around a little.

Step 3: Count the number of 'beats' you can feel in 60 seconds. This tells you how many times your heart beats every minute.

B: Where is one place you can take your pulse?

Measuring fitness

Your heart rate goes up when you exercise. This moves blood around your body faster and delivers more oxygen and glucose to your cells. Your cells can therefore respire more, transferring more energy for movement.

C: What happens to a person's heart rate as they exercise?

Measuring your fitness

You can measure how fit you are by finding out how quickly your pulse rate returns to normal after you have finished exercising. The fitter you are, the quicker your pulse returns to normal.

Step 1: Measure your pulse rate when you are resting.

Step 2: Exercise for one minute, for example, by doing star jumps or press-ups.

Step 3: Measure your pulse rate again, as soon as you stop exercising.

Step 4: Wait for one minute.

Step 5: Measure your pulse rate again.

Step 6: Repeat steps 4 and 5 until your pulse rate returns to normal.

1 Choose the correct words from the box to complete the sentences. Some words can be used more than once.

| heart | pulse | quicker |

Your _____ can be used to measure how many times your _____ beats per minute. The fitter you are, the _____ your _____ rate returns to normal after exercise.

[4 marks]

2 Why does your pulse rate increase when you exercise?

A to deliver more oxygen and glucose to cells

B to make your body fitter

C to make your body move faster   [1 mark]

3 Two students measured how long it took for their pulse rates to return to normal after playing tennis. Student A's pulse rate took 6 minutes to return to normal. Student B's pulse rate took 8 minutes to return to normal.

a Who is fitter – student A or student B?   [1 mark]

b How can you tell from the results that he is fitter?

[1 mark]

2 Checkpoint

1   Use the words from each box to complete the following sentence:

> **balanced   nutrients   proteins   special**

To stay healthy you should eat a _____ diet. This means eating food containing
the right _____ in the right amounts for your needs.   [1 mark]

2   Match each nutrient to the correct use by the body.

Nutrient	Use by the body
carbohydrates	To keep you healthy.
proteins	Give you energy.
vitamins and minerals	For growth and repair.
fibre	To keep the food moving through your gut.

[4 marks]

3   Complete the word equation for respiration using words from the box.

> **oxygen   air   water**

glucose + _____ → _____ + carbon dioxide (+ energy)   [2 marks]

4   What can happen to a person if they eat **more** food than they need to?   [1 mark]

5   Gas exchange takes place inside your lungs.
    Figure 1 shows an air sac from the lungs.
    The air sac is surrounded by a blood vessel.

a   What type of cell is labelled X?   [1 mark]

b   Does **carbon dioxide** diffuse into the blood vessel or
    out of the blood vessel?

c   Does **oxygen** diffuse into the blood vessel or out
    of the blood vessel?   [1 mark]

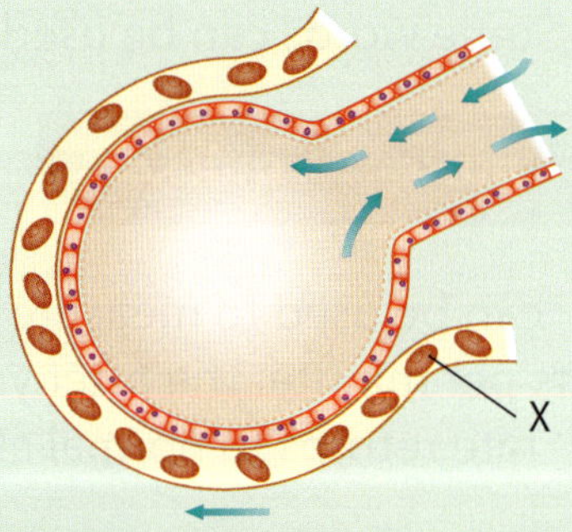

Figure 1

6   a   What is one problem linked to being underweight?   [1 mark]

    b   What is one disease linked to smoking?   [1 mark]

7   Two students are investigating how long it takes for their pulse rate to return to
    normal after exercise. Their results are shown in the table.

	Starting pulse rate	Pulse rate 1 minute after exercise	Pulse rate 3 minutes after exercise	Pulse rate 6 minutes after exercise	Pulse rate 9 minutes after exercise
student A	73	140	98	72	73
student B	81	134	113	96	83

a   Whose pulse rate returned to normal quicker?   [1 mark]

b   Who is fitter, student A or student B?   [1 mark]

2 Vocabulary builder ✏

1   Match each key term with its cause.

Key term	Cause
overweight	When the energy in your food is less than the energy you use.
underweight	When the energy in your food is more than the energy you use.

[2 marks]

2   Match each key term to the correct definition.

Key term	Definition
pulse	Essential substances your body needs to survive.
diet	A way to measure your heat beat.
respiration	Chemical reaction that provides cells with energy.
nutrients	The food a person eats.

[4 marks]

3   a   Choose the correct terms to complete the word equation for respiration.

glucose / sugar + **air / oxygen** → **carbon dioxide / gas** + water   [3 marks]

b   Choose the correct word to complete the following sentence.

Respiration **creates / transfers** energy to cells.   [1 mark]

4   What is being described in this definition?

Eating food containing the right nutrients in the correct amounts for your needs.

ba __ __ __ c __ __ __   d __ e __   [1 mark]

5   Choose the correct word to identify the nutrient that is being described.

a   Your main source of energy. Found in foods like pasta.

carbohydrate   fibre   lipid   protein   [1 mark]

b   Used for growth and repair. Eggs are a good source.

carbohydrate   fibre   lipid   protein   [1 mark]

c   Provides bulk to your food to keep it moving through the gut.

carbohydrate   fibre   lipid   protein   [1 mark]

d   A store of energy and helps to keep you warm.

carbohydrate   fibre   lipid   protein   [1 mark]

2.5 Anaerobic respiration

Learning objectives

After this topic, you should know:

- the differences between aerobic and anaerobic respiration
- the word equation for anaerobic respiration in animals
- the word equation for fermentation.

When you respire, your body uses oxygen and glucose to transfer energy to your cells. This type of respiration is called **aerobic respiration**.

Your muscles need more energy when you exercise. Your breathing rate increases, so you breathe in more oxygen. Your heart rate also increases, so the oxygen is transported to your cells faster. This allows you to respire faster.

During hard exercise, your body needs to transfer energy even faster. Your heart rate may not be able to speed up enough to transport the oxygen you need for respiration. Your body then starts to break down glucose by **anaerobic respiration**.

Anaerobic respiration does not need oxygen to break down the glucose, but it still transfers energy to your cells. Lactic acid is produced. Your body can only respire anaerobically for short periods of time.

The word equation for anaerobic respiration is:

$$\text{glucose} \rightarrow \text{lactic acid (+ energy)}$$
$$\textit{reactant} \qquad \textit{products}$$

When you have finished exercising you keep breathing heavily. The extra oxygen you breathe in is used to break down the lactic acid. The amount of oxygen needed to do this is called the oxygen debt.

A: Name the chemical reaction that transfers energy from glucose **without** using oxygen.

Anaerobic respiration and exercise

Your body normally uses aerobic respiration. It only uses anaerobic respiration when there is not enough oxygen, for example, when you are doing hard exercise.

There are **two** reasons why you normally respire aerobically:

1 Aerobic respiration transfers more energy for every glucose molecule than anaerobic respiration does. This is because the glucose molecule is fully broken down in aerobic respiration. In anaerobic respiration, the glucose molecule is only partially broken down.

2 The lactic acid produced from anaerobic respiration stops your muscles from contracting. This can be very painful.

Anaerobic respiration in microorganisms and plants

Plants and microorganisms also carry out a form of anaerobic respiration, called fermentation. This produces ethanol and carbon dioxide.

The word equation for fermentation is:

glucose $\rightarrow$ ethanol + carbon dioxide (+ energy)
reactant   *products*

In bread making, the carbon dioxide produced creates bubbles that make the dough rise. The ethanol is a waste product and evaporates during baking.

In beer and wine making, the ethanol produced makes the drink alcoholic. The carbon dioxide is a waste product and is released.

Figure 1 *Yeast is the microorganism that carries out fermentation in bread and beer making.*

1. Complete the word equation for anaerobic respiration in animals:

glucose	lactic acid	water

   _____ $\rightarrow$ _____ (+ energy)   [2 marks]

2. a Write the word equation for fermentation.   [1 mark]

   b Name **one** substance that is made using fermentation.   [1 mark]

   c Identify the useful product from fermentation that is used to create the substance you have named.   [1 mark]

3. Explain why sportspeople sometimes get cramp.   [3 marks]

2.6 Increasing the risk of disease

Learning objectives

After this topic, you should know:

- some risk factors of diseases
- the difference between correlation and causation
- how to identify a correlation between a risk factor and a disease.

Some lifestyle factors have been shown to affect how likely you are to develop certain diseases. These are called risk factors.

There are some risk factors that you cannot change. These include the genes you inherit from your parents, and your age. However, some risk factors can be controlled.

A: Describe what is meant by a risk factor of disease.

Risk factors you can control

Risk factors you can control include:

- diet – a low-fat diet reduces the risk of cardiovascular disease (CVD)

- fitness level – being active lowers the risk of CVD. It also reduces the risk of developing joint problems

- maintaining a healthy weight – people who are obese (very overweight) are more likely to suffer from CVD and type 2 diabetes

- alcohol intake – limiting the amount of alcohol a person drinks reduces their risk of liver and brain disease

- smoking – smoking greatly increases the risk of developing lung cancer and other lung diseases

- Sun exposure – limiting your exposure to the Sun reduces your risk of developing skin cancer.

B: Give three risk factors of disease.

Identifying a correlation between risk factors and disease

You can use a scatter diagram to identify a **correlation** between a risk factor and a disease. A correlation is what a link between two variables is called.

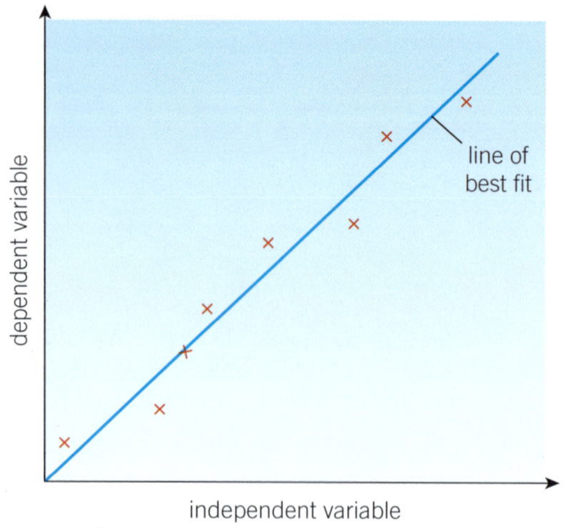

Figure 1 A scatter diagram with a line of best fit.

Reading a scatter diagram

Once you have plotted your data on a graph, you should add a line of best fit. This helps you see if there is a pattern in the data.

Your line of best fit should go through as many data points as possible. It should have the same number of points above and below the line.

You can then identify the type of correlation shown.

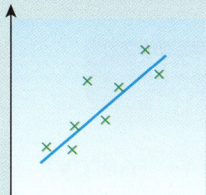 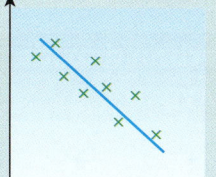 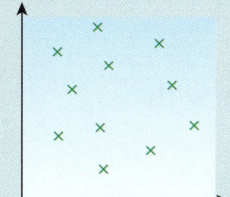

This scatter diagram shows a **positive** correlation. As one variable **increases**, the other **increases**.

This scatter diagram shows a **negative** correlation. As one variable **increases**, the other **decreases**.

This scatter diagram shows **no** correlation. There is **no link** between the variables.

Causation

It is useful to find correlations between lifestyle factors and diseases, but this is only the first step. Two factors may be correlated but this does not prove that one factor causes a change in the other. Doctors and scientists then need to do research to discover if there is a **causal mechanism**. A causal mechanism explains how one factor affects another one.

There is a causal link between smoking tobacco and lung cancer. Tobacco smoke contains toxic chemicals that have been shown to cause cancer. Anyone can get lung cancer, but smoking increases your risk.

1 Sketch a scatter diagram to show:

  a positive correlation   [1 mark]

  b negative correlation   [1 mark]

  c no correlation.   [1 mark]

2 Identify the type of correlation, shown in Figure 2, between the number of cigarettes smoked and the number of cases of lung cancer per 100 000 people.   [1 mark]

3 Describe the difference between causation and correlation.   [2 marks]

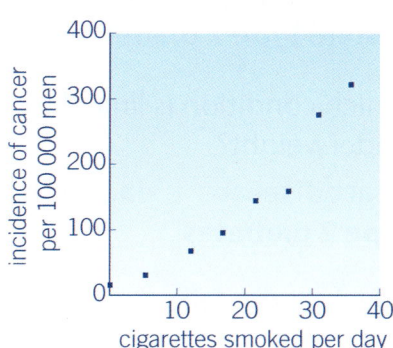

Figure 2

2 Practice questions

01 Identify which of the following is the best description of a healthy diet.

   A a diet containing lots of fruit and vegetables

   B a diet containing mostly protein, with some carbohydrates

   C eating the right foods in the right amounts for your needs

   D eating a diet containing mostly fats and carbohydrates **[1 mark]**

02 For each description, choose the correct nutrient from the box that is being described.

> **carbohydrate   lipid   protein**

02.1 nutrient needed for growth and repair of body tissues _____ **[1 mark]**

02.2 nutrient used as a source of energy and to keep the body warm _____ **[1 mark]**

02.3 nutrient used as the main source of energy in the body _____ **[1 mark]**

03.1 Which condition is linked to being overweight?

lack of energy   poor immune system   type 2 diabetes **[1 mark]**

03.2 Which condition is linked to being underweight?

heart disease   lack of energy   type 2 diabetes **[1 mark]**

04 Which of the following factors is linked to an increased risk of developing lung cancer?

   A alcohol   **B** obesity

   C smoking   **D** sunlight **[1 mark]**

05.1 Use the correct words from the box to complete the word equation for aerobic respiration.

> **carbon dioxide   glucose**
> **oxygen   water**

____ + ____ → ____ + ____ (+ energy) **[3 marks]**

05.2 Complete the following sentence.

When you exercise the amount your body respires _____ . **[1 mark]**

06 Draw one line from each description to show whether it describes anaerobic respiration or aerobic respiration.

Description	Type of respiration
Produces lactic acid.	
	aerobic respiration
Transfers more energy to the cell.	
	anaerobic respiration
Does not produce water.	
Uses oxygen.	**[4 marks]**

07.1 Complete the word equation for anaerobic respiration in microorganisms.

> **carbon dioxide   ethanol**
> **glucose   lactic acid**

____ → ____ + ____ (+ energy) **[3 marks]**

07.2 Name one useful substance made by the process of anaerobic respiration. **[1 mark]**

07.3 Put the sentences in order to describe how oxygen reaches cells for respiration.

   A Air is breathed into the lungs.

   B It diffuses into cells.

   C It is transported by red blood cells.

   D Oxygen in the air diffuses into the bloodstream. **[4 marks]**

08 Alex is an office worker. He spends most of the day sitting at his desk.

Oliver is a builder. He spends most of his day lifting heavy objects.

Oliver needs to eat a lot more food than Alex to have a balanced diet.

Choose the correct statement from the list to explain why.

A Alex is overweight.

B Oliver is healthier than Alex.

C Oliver is more active than Alex, so needs more energy. [1 mark]

09 Doctors claim that regular exercise is good for your heart and lungs.

	Before getting fit	After getting fit
Amount of blood pumped out of the heart during each beat in cm³	64	80
Heart volume in cm³	120	140
Breathing rate in breaths per minute	14	12
Pulse rate in beats per minute	72	63

09.1 Identify what effect getting fit has on heart volume [1 mark]

09.2 Identify what effect getting fit has on pulse rate. [1 mark]

09.3 Describe an investigation you could carry out to measure a person's fitness. [4 marks]

10 The graph in **Figure 1** shows a person's risk of death compared with the amount of alcohol they drink, measured in grams per day.

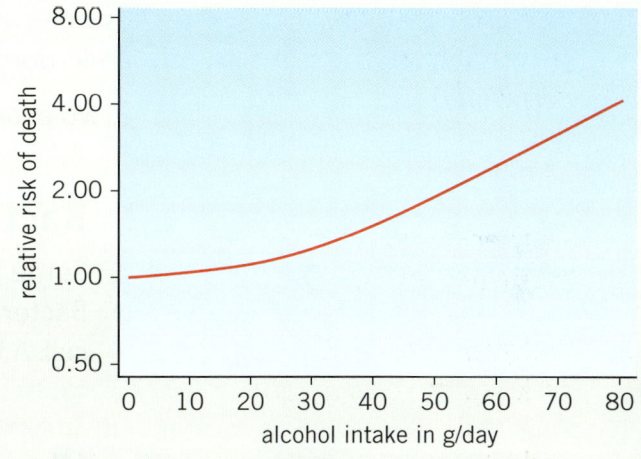

Figure 1

10.1 Identify the type of correlation shown in this diagram. [1 mark]

10.2 Name one health problem that is more common amongst people who regularly drink more alcohol than the recommended amount. [1 mark]

10.3 Explain whether or not this graph **proves** that drinking large amounts of alcohol increases the risk of death. [3 marks]

3 How the body fights disease
3.1 Infectious disease

Learning objectives

After this topic, you should know:

- what a pathogen is
- some examples of pathogens
- how white blood cells prevent disease.

Some diseases can be passed from one person to another. These are called **infectious diseases**. Infectious diseases are diseases that can be spread between organisms.

A: What is an infectious disease?

Infectious diseases are caused by microorganisms. These are organisms that are so small they can only be seen using a microscope. Most microorganisms are harmless. However, some cause disease when they enter your body. These harmful microorganisms are called **pathogens**.

Two examples of pathogens are **bacteria** and **viruses**.

Bacteria

Some types of bacteria are pathogens and can cause diseases. Bacteria are very small organisms. They are made of only one cell. A bacterial cell is much smaller than an animal or plant cell.

Viruses

Viruses are even smaller than bacteria. Because they are so small, they get inside cells. Viruses cause diseases in every type of living organism.

Once a pathogen is in the body, it can reproduce very quickly. Pathogens also produce poisons that make you feel ill. These poisons are called **toxins**. Viruses can also damage cells when they reproduce inside them.

B: What are two types of pathogen?

White blood cells

When a pathogen gets into the body, your **white blood cells** will try to destroy it. This helps to make you better when you get ill, or can stop you getting ill in the first place.

White blood cells protect you from pathogens in two ways.

Ingesting pathogens

Some white blood cells swallow up the pathogen. The white blood cell then digests the pathogen using enzymes. This destroys the pathogen. This is called **ingestion**.

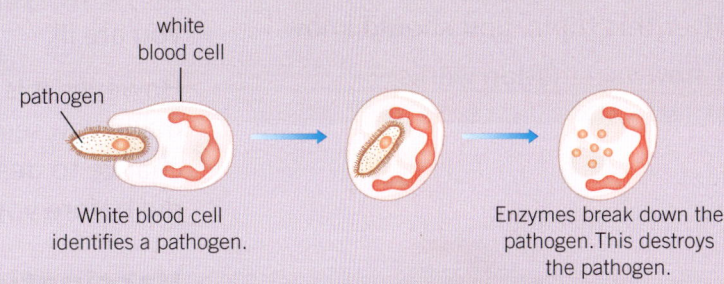

White blood cell identifies a pathogen.

Enzymes break down the pathogen. This destroys the pathogen.

Figure 1 *A white blood cell ingesting a pathogen.*

Producing antibodies

Some white blood cells produce special molecules called **antibodies**. Antibodies attach to pathogens and destroy them.

Each type of antibody will only work against one type of pathogen.

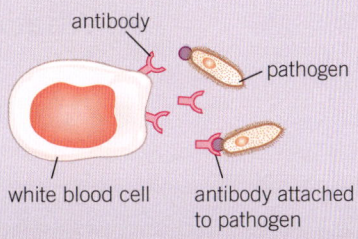

Figure 2 *A white blood cell producing antibodies.*

C: **What is the name of the molecules produced by white blood cells that destroy pathogens?**

1 Use the correct words from the boxes to complete the sentences.

pathogen   spread

An infectious disease is caused by a _____ that can be _____ between people. [1 mark]

antibodies   white blood

_____ can destroy pathogens by ingestion or by producing _____. [1 mark]

2 Choose the pathogens from the following list:

alcohol   bacteria   mosquitos   rats tobacco smoke   viruses [2 marks]

3 What is one way that a pathogen can make you feel ill? [1 mark]

3.2 Vaccination

Learning objectives

After this topic, you should know:

- how vaccination works.

White blood cells destroy pathogens that cause disease when they enter your body. This helps your body to get better when you are ill.

However, it is better not to get ill at all. Some pathogens can make you seriously ill before your white blood cells have a chance to destroy the pathogen. With some diseases, you could die before your white blood cells can respond.

Vaccination

Vaccines contain small amounts of **inactive** or **dead** pathogens. They are put into your body, usually using an injection. This is known as a **vaccination**.

A: What does a vaccine contain?

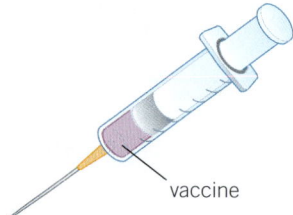

vaccine

Figure 1 *A dead or inactive pathogen is injected into your body.*

These inactive or dead pathogens cannot cause disease. However, they do still cause your white blood cells to make the correct antibodies.

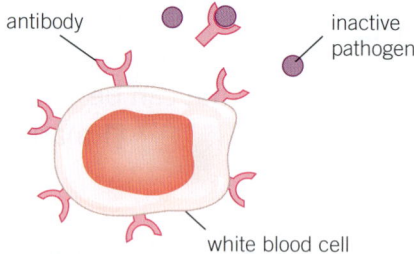

antibody

inactive pathogen

white blood cell

Figure 2 *Your white blood cells produce antibodies that destroy the pathogen.*

Now, if an active form of the pathogen enters your body, your white blood cells can respond faster. They quickly produce the correct antibody. The antibody then destroys the pathogen before it causes the disease.

You are now **immune** to the disease. This means that you cannot get the disease any more.

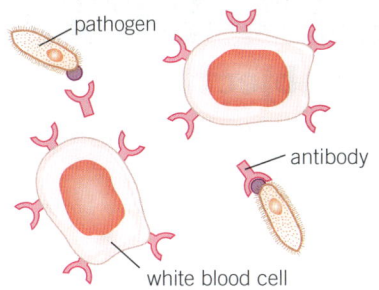

Figure 3 *Your white blood cells can quickly produce the antibody when an active form of the pathogen enters your body.*

B: What does it mean if you are immune to a disease?

During childhood you probably had several vaccinations. These prevent you getting many diseases. The vaccinations also mean that fewer people in the population will have the disease. This means there is less chance of the disease spreading.

1 Match each key word to the correct definition.

Key word	Definition
antibody	injection of dead or inactive form of pathogen into the body
vaccination	produced by white blood cells to destroy a pathogen
pathogen	microorganism that causes disease [2 marks]

2 Why can't the pathogens **in a vaccine** cause disease? Choose one answer.

   A   there are not enough pathogens in the vaccine

   B   the white blood cells stop them from causing disease

   C   they are inactive forms of the pathogen   [1 mark]

3 Put the sentences in the correct order to describe how vaccination works.

   A   If the same type of pathogen later enters the body, white blood cells quickly produce antibodies.

   B   The antibodies destroy the live pathogen before they are able to cause disease.

   C   An inactive pathogen is injected into the body.

   D   White blood cells produce antibodies that destroy the inactive pathogen.   [4 marks]

3.3 Medical drugs

Learning objectives

After this topic, you should know:

- what a drug is
- how antibiotics work
- what is meant by addiction.

Drugs are chemicals that affect how your body works. They change the chemical reactions that take place inside your body.

Medical drugs

Medical drugs are used in medicine. They benefit your health in some way.

There are two main types of medical drugs:

- Some drugs only treat the symptoms of a disease. These are the things you see or feel. For example, you might feel pain. Painkillers reduce the pain that you feel.

- Some drugs cure the disease. For example, **antibiotics** kill bacteria.

Medical drugs are developed and tested before they are given to patients. This makes sure that the drug works and is safe.

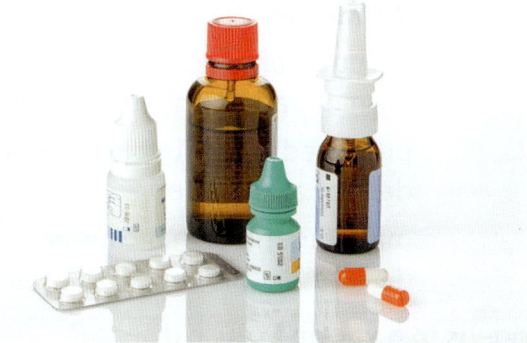

Figure 1 *Medical drugs can come in lots of different forms, including tablets, liquids, sprays, and creams.*

A: What is a drug?

Antibiotics

Antibiotics are drugs that kill bacteria inside your body. These chemicals kill bacterial cells but do not harm your own body cells. Antibiotics can be used to cure diseases that are caused by bacteria. They only kill bacteria and cannot be used to treat diseases that are caused by viruses.

There are lots of different types of antibiotics. One of the most common antibiotics that doctors prescribe is **penicillin**.

B: Write the name of an antibiotic drug.

Drug addiction

Medical drugs can cause harm if they are taken incorrectly. Some drugs also have unwanted side effects.

If your body gets used to the changes caused by a drug, your body may become dependent on the drug. This means that you need to keep taking the drug to feel normal. If this happens, you have an **addiction**.

If someone who is addicted to a drug tries to stop taking it, they may suffer from **withdrawal symptoms**. These can be very unpleasant and make it even harder to give up. Some examples of withdrawal symptoms are headaches, anxiety (nervousness), and sweating.

Doctors have to think about the benefits of prescribing a drug compared with any possible risks.

C: What are **two** examples of a withdrawal symptom?

1 Choose the correct words from the box to complete the following sentences.

| addicted | chemicals | medical | withdrawal |

Drugs are _____ that affect the way your body works. _____ drugs benefit your heath. If you take drugs too often you may become _____ to the drug. When someone who is addicted to a drug stops taking it, they suffer _____ symptoms, making it harder to give up. [3 marks]

2 Which **two** of the following are **medical** drugs?

alcohol   antibiotics   caffeine   painkillers
[2 marks]

3 Flu is caused by a virus. Penicillin is an antibiotic. Why can't penicillin be used to treat flu? [1 mark]

3.4 Testing the effect of antibiotics

Learning objectives

After this topic, you should know:

- the differences and similarities between antibiotics and disinfectants
- how to identify a zone of inhibition on a Petri dish.

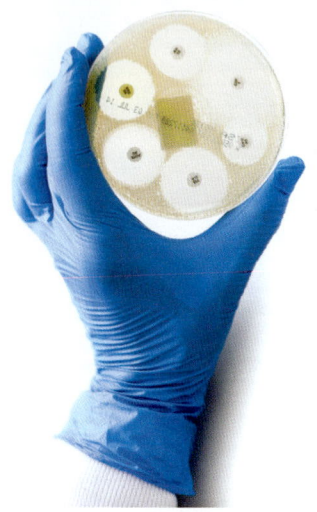

Figure 1 *Bacteria can be grown on a Petri dish.*

Bacteria can reproduce (grow) very quickly. It is very important to stop the growth of harmful bacteria.

Preventing bacterial growth

Chemicals can be used to stop bacteria growing.

Disinfectants are chemicals that can kill bacteria in the environment around us. They cannot be used to treat a bacterial infection inside your body. If you swallowed a disinfectant it would damage your cells and make you ill.

Antibiotics do not damage body cells. These chemicals can be used to kill bacteria inside your body.

A: What are two chemicals that prevent bacteria from growing?

Bacteria can be grown on a Petri dish. We can test different disinfectants and antibiotics, to see how good they are at stopping the growth of bacteria.

In Figure 1, the orange area is where the bacteria have grown.

The grey dots are pieces of paper that have been soaked in an antibiotic or disinfectant.

Around each piece of paper, there is a clear area. This is where the bacteria have been stopped from growing. This area is called the **zone of inhibition**.

B: What is the zone of inhibition?

Investigating the effect of disinfectants and antibiotics

You can measure how well the chemical prevents bacteria growing by working out how large the zone of inhibition is. The larger the zone of inhibition, the more effective the chemical is at stopping the growth of bacteria.

Which antibiotic is more effective?

Step 1: Work out the zone of inhibition for each antibiotic by measuring the area.

Antibiotic	Area of zone of inhibition in cm²
A	7.2
B	8.1
C	3.4
D	5.6

Step 2: Identify which antibiotic has the largest zone of inhibition.

Antibiotic B

Step 3: Use your results to draw a conclusion about which antibiotic is the most effective.

The larger the zone of inhibition, the better the antibiotic is at stopping the growth of bacteria. So antibiotic B is the best at stopping the growth of bacteria.

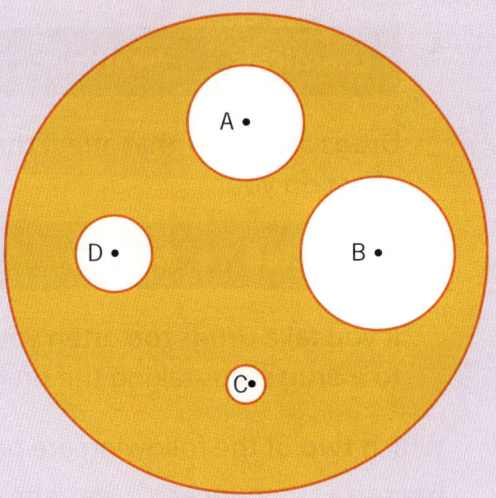

Figure 2

1 Match each chemical to the correct use.

Chemical	Use
antibiotic	Kill bacteria on kitchen surfaces.
disinfectant	Kill bacteria inside the body.

[1 mark]

2 A group of students investigated how well three disinfectants work. Their results are shown in Figure 3.

List the disinfectants in order, from the most effective to the least effective. [2 marks]

3 A student tested the effect of different antibiotics on the growth of bacteria. The following variables were part of the experiment.

- size of bacterial colony
- type of antibiotic used
- volume of antibiotic added

a Which one is the control variable in this experiment? [1 mark]

b One piece of paper soaked in a chemical had no zone of inhibition around it. What does this mean? [1 mark]

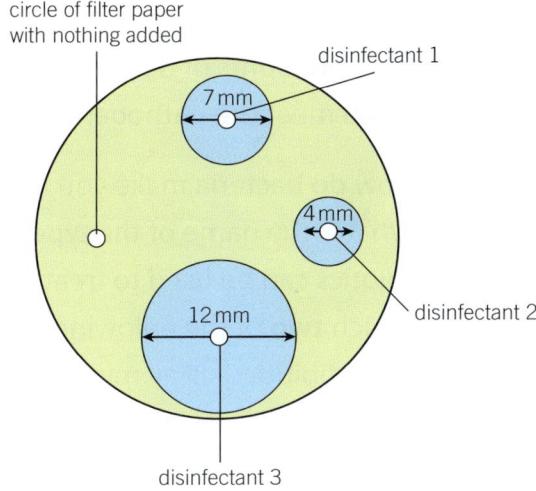

Figure 3

3 Checkpoint

1 Use the correct words from each box to complete the following sentences.

a | chemicals   health   medical   pathogens |

Drugs are _____ that affect the way your body works. _____ drugs have a beneficial effect on your _____. [3 marks]

b | addicted   healthy   withdrawal |

If you take drugs too often you may become _____. When someone who is addicted to a drug stops taking the drug, they suffer _____ symptoms. [2 marks]

2 Which **two** of the following are pathogens?

bacteria   cancer   mushrooms   rats   viruses [2 marks]

3 What is an infectious disease?

A a disease that can be cured with antibiotics

B a disease that is caused by a bad diet

C a disease that can be spread between organisms [1 mark]

4 Put the following sentences in the correct order to explain how vaccination works.

A Antibodies destroy a pathogen before it causes disease.

B White blood cells produce antibodies.

C Small amounts of dead or inactive pathogen are injected into the body.

D If you meet the pathogen again antibodies are produced quickly. [4 marks]

5 a How do bacteria make you feel ill? [1 mark]

b What is the name of the type of blood cell that kills bacteria? [1 mark]

Antibiotics can be used to treat diseases caused by bacteria.

c Which **two** of the following statements about antibiotics are true?

A Antibiotics kill all microorganisms.

B Antibiotics do not damage body cells.

C An example of an antibiotic is penicillin.

D Antibiotics can be used to treat viral infections. [2 marks]

6 a Why does someone who is addicted to a drug need to continue taking it to feel normal? [1 mark]

b Which **two** of the following are examples of withdrawal symptoms?

coughing   headache   infection   sweating [2 marks]

7 Chicken pox is a disease caused by a virus. Penicillin is an antibiotic.
Why can't we use penicillin to treat this disease? [1 mark]

3 Vocabulary builder

1 Match each key word to the correct definition.

Key word	Definition
antibody	A chemical that affects the way the body works.
antibiotic	A chemical that kills bacteria.
drug	A microorganism that causes disease.
pathogen	Produced by white blood cells to destroy a pathogen.

[4 marks]

2 Choose the correct term to complete this definition of ingestion.

Genetic / Infectious diseases are diseases that can be spread between organisms.

They are caused by harmful **animals / microorganisms** called **pathogens / platelets**.   [4 marks]

3 Complete the sentence using the correct word from the box.

> fake   inactive   old

A vaccine cannot make you ill because it contains _____ pathogens.   [1 mark]

4 Sort the following into whether they are **pathogens** or whether they are a **drug**.
antibiotic
bacteria
penicillin
virus   [4 marks]

5 Choose the correct term from each list to identify the key term that is being described.

  a symptoms suffered by a person who tries to stop taking a drug
    unhelpful
    unpleasant
    withdrawal   [1 mark]

  b name given to a person who has become dependent on a drug
    addict
    user
    withdrawal   [1 mark]

6 Complete the sentence.

Organisms that are too small to be seen by the naked eye are called

m _ _ _ _ _ _ _ _ _ _ _ _   [1 mark]

3.5 Bacteria and viruses

Learning objectives

After this topic, you should know:

- how bacteria cause disease
- how viruses cause disease.

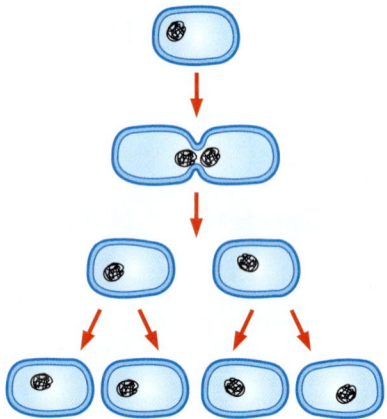

Figure 1 *In ideal conditions, some bacteria divide in two every 20 minutes. Within hours, just a few bacteria will have reproduced to become many thousands.*

Infectious diseases are diseases that are caused by pathogens. They are also known as **communicable diseases**. The pathogens, which include bacteria and viruses, can be passed from one person to another. This spreads the disease.

> **A:** Describe what is meant by a communicable disease.

How bacteria cause disease

Bacteria can produce toxins (poisons) that affect your body and make you feel ill. Sometimes the bacteria directly damage your cells. *Salmonella* is one disease caused by bacteria. *Salmonella* is a type of food poisoning. It is spread by bacteria in, or on, food that has been prepared in unhygienic conditions.

Bacteria reproduce by dividing in two. They can do this quite quickly. Some bacteria can reproduce once every 20 minutes in the right conditions. The more bacteria inside your body the more damage they can cause.

To work out how big the population of bacteria will become after a period of time, you first need to know how long the bacteria take to reproduce. You also need to know the initial population of bacteria.

final population = initial population $\times 2^{\text{number of bacterial divisions}}$

Calculating the number of bacteria

50 bacteria are present in a sample. The bacteria reproduce every 20 minutes. How many bacteria will be present after two hours?

Step 1: Write down the number of bacteria at the start (initial population).

50

Step 2: Work out how many times the bacteria divide.

1 hour = 60 minutes. 2 hours = 60 × 2 = 120 minutes.

$$\frac{120 \text{ minutes}}{20 \text{ minutes}} = 6$$

So, 2 hours = 6 divisions

Step 3: Work out the final population of bacteria.

final population = initial population $\times 2^{\text{number of bacterial divisions}}$

final population = $50 \times 2^6 = 50 \times 64$

= 3200 bacterial cells after 2 hours

How viruses make you feel ill

Viruses take over your body's cells. They live inside your cells and reproduce. This damages and destroys your cells.

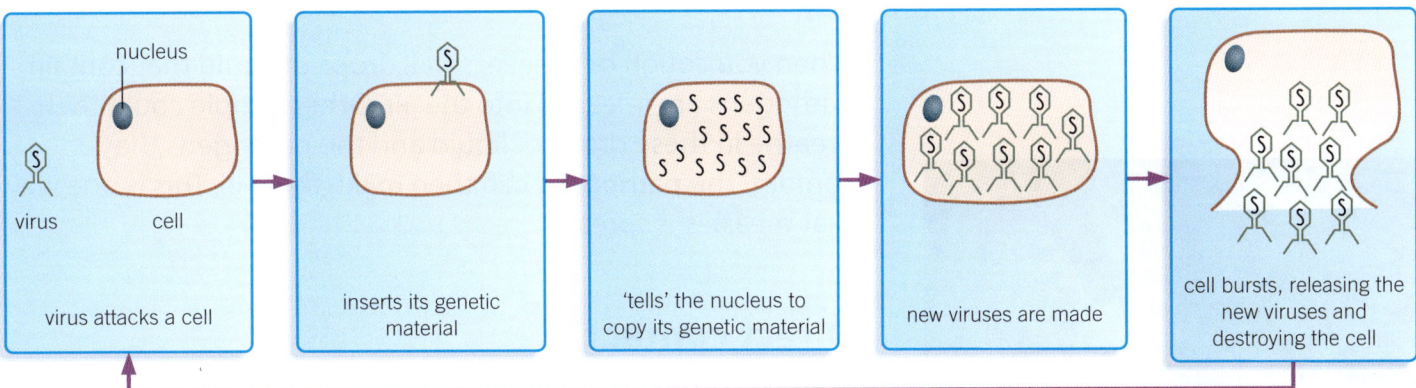

Figure 2 *Viruses reproduce inside your cells.*

Common symptoms of an infectious disease are a high temperature, headaches, and rashes. These happen because of the way your body responds to the damage to your cells and to the toxins produced by the pathogens.

Measles is an example of a disease caused by a virus. It causes fever and a rash. In some cases it can result in death.

C: Name two common symptoms of a disease caused by a virus.

1 Choose the correct words from the box to complete the sentence.

   communicable   pathogen   spread

   A _____ disease is caused by a _____ and can be _____ between people.   [2 marks]

2 Describe how a virus makes you feel ill.   [3 marks]

3 40 bacteria were present in a water sample. In these conditions they divided every 20 minutes.

   a Calculate how many times the bacteria can divide in 5 hours.   [2 marks]

   b Calculate how many bacteria cells there would be after 5 hours. Use the equation:

   final population = initial population × $2^{\text{number of bacterial divisions}}$

                                                                    [3 marks]

3.6 Preventing the spread of disease

Learning objectives

After this topic, you should know:

- some ways that pathogens can be spread
- some methods for preventing or reducing the spread of disease.

Figure 1 *When you cough or sneeze, small droplets of liquid that contain pathogens are released. The pathogens in the droplets could infect other people. This is called droplet infection.*

The pathogens that cause communicable diseases can be spread between organisms.

Ways pathogens are spread

Air

When you cough or sneeze, small drops of liquid that contain pathogens are released into the air. Other people could then breathe in these drops of liquid and the pathogens they contain. The pathogens can then make them ill. This is one way that measles is spread.

Direct contact

When you touch someone, pathogens might be passed between you. This could also happen if you touch an object that an infected person has touched. Gonorrhoea is a disease that is spread by contact during sexual intercourse. Other diseases, such as HIV, can be spread through bodily fluids, such as blood.

Animals

Animals may carry harmful pathogens. If an infected animal scratches or bites you, the pathogens can get into your body. An example is malaria, a tropical disease that is spread by mosquito bites.

Food

Food, especially raw meat, can contain harmful pathogens. These can get into your body if you eat the food. Some of these pathogens cause food poisoning. For example, *Salmonella* food poisoning is caused by bacteria in food.

Water

Untreated water or water containing sewage can have pathogens in it. These pathogens can get into your body if you swallow the water.

Preventing the spread of communicable diseases

You can prevent yourself catching or passing on a communicable disease by:

- covering your mouth and nose when you cough or sneeze

- not touching infected people or objects

- using condoms to prevent bodily fluids being exchanged during sexual intercourse.

Being hygienic can also help to prevent communicable diseases spreading. You should always:

- wash your hands before eating

- cook food through properly. High temperature kills most bacteria

- drink clean water

- protect yourself from animal bites, for example, use insect repellent sprays and mosquito nets.

B: List **three** ways you can prevent yourself catching a disease

1 Match each way a disease is spread to the correct method of preventing the spread.

Way disease is spread	Method of preventing spread
droplets in the air	insect repellent
animal bite	boiling
water	use a tissue [2 marks]

2 Describe how cooking food thoroughly helps to protect you from communicable diseases.   [2 marks]

3 Suggest why a doctor may wear gloves when examining a patient.   [2 marks]

3.7 Testing new drugs

Learning objectives

After this topic, you should know:

- how new medicines are discovered
- the key features of a medical drug
- the main stages in testing new drugs.

Scientists and doctors are trying to find ways of curing more diseases. New medicines are being developed all the time.

Many drugs have come from plants and microorganisms.

- The antibiotic penicillin comes from a type of mould.
- The painkiller aspirin comes from a compound found in willow bark.

New drugs are found in different ways but most new drugs are made in the laboratory.

A: Name an example of a medical drug and its source.

Key features of a drug

A good medicine is:

- effective – it must prevent or cure a disease, or treat the symptoms
- safe – it must not be too toxic (poisonous) or have dangerous side effects
- stable – you must be able to use the medicine under normal conditions and store it for some time
- able to be taken into and removed from your body – it must reach the source of the disease and be cleared from your body once it has done its work.

B: Describe what is meant by an effective drug.

Stages of drug testing

Every medical treatment has to pass several stages of testing before it can be used. This makes sure that it works well and is as safe as possible.

Scientists perform the first tests in the laboratory. They test on cells, tissues, and live animals. This is called preclinical testing.

Drugs that pass preclinical testing can then be tested on humans. This is known as clinical trials.

Drug is tested using computer models and human cells grown in the laboratory. Many drugs fail at this stage because they damage cells or appear not to work.

Drug is tested on animals (nematode worms/fruit flies/mice) to study any side effects.

Drug is tested on a small group of healthy human volunteers to check its safety. Testing drugs on humans is known as clinical trials.

Drug tested on small numbers of volunteer patients who have the illness, to ensure it works.

Drug tested on large numbers of volunteer patients to monitor drug effectiveness, safety, dosage, and side effects.

Drug approved and can be prescribed.

Figure 1 *The main stages of medical drug testing*

C: What is meant by the clinical trials of a drug?

1 Match each feature of a drug to the correct definition.

Feature	Definition
effective	Prevents, cures, or improves symptoms of a disease.
safe	Not too toxic and does not have dangerous side effects.
stable	Able to take and store the medicine under normal conditions. [2 marks]

2 Classify each of the following as a **stage in clinical trials** or a **stage in preclinical trials**.

   a testing on animals in a laboratory [1 mark]

   b testing on human volunteers [1 mark]

   c testing on human tissue in a laboratory [1 mark]

3 Suggest why many potential new drugs are never tested on living organisms. [1 mark]

4 Only 1 in every 10 drugs that undergo clinical trials are approved for use.

   What percentage of drugs are approved for use after clinical trials? [1 mark]

3 Practice questions

01 Choose the correct words from the box to complete the sentences.

> drugs   grow   pathogens
> reproduce   spread   toxins

Infectious diseases can _____ between organisms.

They are caused by harmful microorganisms called _____.

Once inside your body bacteria _____ rapidly.

They may produce _____ that affect your body and make you feel ill. **[4 marks]**

02 Match each disease to the correct way that the disease is spread.

Disease	Way disease is spread
gonorrhoea	Droplet infection in the air.
malaria	Direct contact.
measles	Mosquito bites.
salmonella	Eating contaminated food.

[3 marks]

03.1 Which component of the blood fights diseases?

A   plasma
B   platelet
C   red blood cell
D   white blood cell **[1 mark]**

03.2 Which chemical does the component named in **03.1** produce to kill microorganisms?

A   antibiotics
B   antibodies
C   anticoagulants
D   antiseptics **[1 mark]**

04 Copy and complete the table to match the way a communicable disease is spread with a method of prevention.

Method of spread	Method of prevention
coughing and sneezing	
contaminated meat	
	condoms

[3 marks]

05 *Salmonella* is a type of food poisoning caused by bacteria.

05.1 Describe one way you can prevent *Salmonella* spreading. **[1 mark]**

05.2 Suggest how the bacteria cause disease. **[1 mark]**

05.3 Name a medical drug that could be used to treat this condition. **[1 mark]**

06.1 Describe what a drug is. **[1 mark]**

06.2 Morphine is a drug used to control severe pain.

Explain why a person may find it difficult to stop taking morphine if they have taken it every day for several weeks. **[3 marks]**

07 80 bacteria were present in a meat sample. In these conditions they divided every 30 minutes.

07.1 Calculate how many times the bacteria can divide in 3 hours. **[2 marks]**

07.2 Calculate how many bacteria cells there would be after 3 hours.
Use the equation:
final population = initial population $\times\ 2^{\text{number of bacterial divisions}}$

[2 marks]

08 Figure 1 shows the number of cases of polio in the UK between 1948 and 1968.

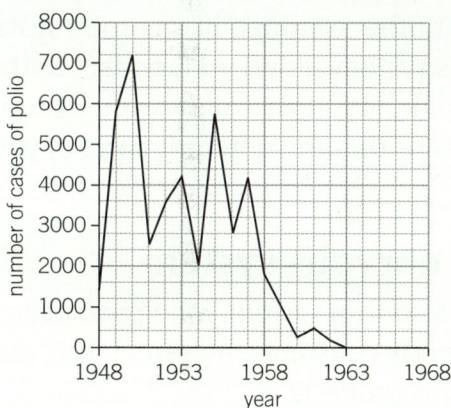

Figure 1

08.1 Which year had the most cases of polio?
[1 mark]

08.2 Describe the trend shown by the graph after 1955. [1 mark]

08.3 A vaccine for polio was introduced in 1955. The vaccine stopped people from getting polio.

Explain how the polio vaccine is used to prevent polio. [3 marks]

09 Lots of research is carried out to develop new medical drugs.

09.1 Give **two** key features of a medical drug.
[2 marks]

09.2 Name **two** ways that a drug is tested, before it is tested on humans. [2 marks]

10 A student is testing the effectiveness of three disinfectants.

She has a Petri dish that has been covered with bacteria. She puts four pieces of filter paper onto the Petri dish. Three of the pieces of filter paper have been soaked in a disinfectant. The other piece of filter paper has been soaked in pure water.

She leaves the Petri dish for a week so that the bacteria can grow. After a week, there are zones of inhibition around the three pieces of filter paper that were soaked in disinfectant.

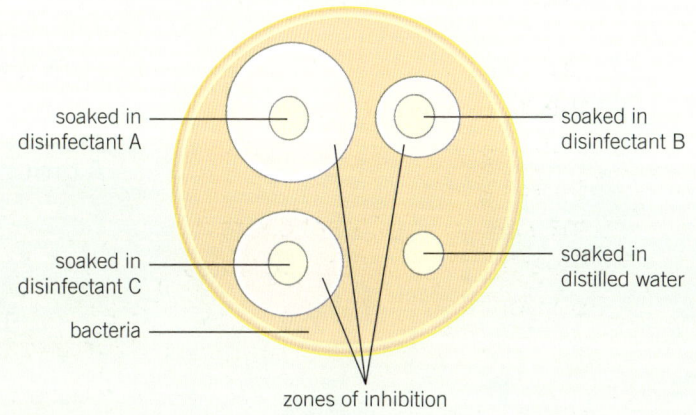

Figure 2

10.1 Identify which disinfectant is most effective at killing bacteria. Give a reason for your answer. [2 marks]

10.2 Suggest why the student included one piece of filter paper soaked in distilled water. [1 mark]

4 How the body is coordinated
4.1 Nervous system

Learning objectives

After this topic, you should know:

- the function of the nervous system
- what reflex actions are.

The nervous system is another example of an organ system in your body. Your nervous system allows you to react to the world around you (your environment). It also allows you to coordinate your behaviour. This means that the different parts of your body can work together.

Functions of the nervous system

Your nervous system is a control system. It helps to keep the conditions inside your body constant (the same). This makes sure that your body works properly.

It is automatic. This means that the whole process happens very quickly because you don't have to think about it.

> A change in your environment is called the **stimulus**.

> A group of specialised cells detect the stimulus. These cells are called **receptors**.

> The receptor cells send a signal to your brain.

> Your brain can then make a response happen.

The response could be making your muscles move or releasing a **hormone**. These are special chemicals that travel around the body to tell an organ how to react.

A: What is one way your body might respond to a stimulus?

Reflex actions

A **reflex action** (also known as a reflex) is a special type of nervous response. Reflex actions are **automatic** and **rapid**. The signal from the receptor does not travel as far because the brain is not involved in a reflex action. This makes them much quicker than a normal nervous response.

B: What are reflex actions?

Examples of reflex actions

Knee-jerk reaction

Doctors test your knee-jerk reflex to check your nervous system is working properly. Tapping a hammer just under the kneecap makes the muscles in your upper leg contract. This makes your lower leg move upwards. This reflex helps you keep your balance.

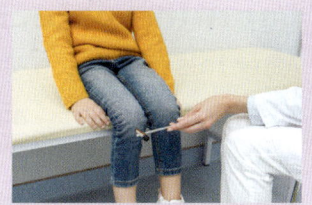

Figure 1 *The knee-jerk reaction.*

Response of your eyes to bright light

The pupil (black circle) in your eye is actually a window. It allows light into your eye. Bright light can damage your eye. In bright light, the muscles around your pupil make your pupil smaller, so that less light enters your eye.

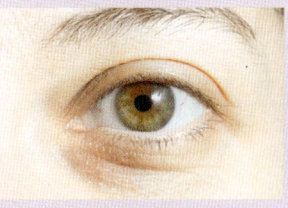

Figure 2 *In bright light, your muscles make your pupil smaller.*

Response of your eyes to dim light

In dim light, the muscles around your pupil make your pupil bigger, which allows more light into your eye.

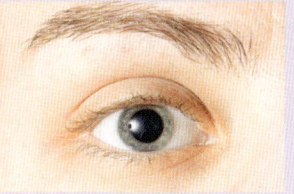

Figure 3 *In dim light, your muscles make pupil bigger.*

C: What is one example of a reflex action?

1   Choose the correct words from the box to complete the sentences.

| brain | hormone | receptor | stimulus |

A change in the world around you is called a _____. This is detected by _____ cells. The _____ decides how to respond to the change. The response could be moving a muscle or releasing a _____.   [3 marks]

2   What are the **two** features of a reflex action?
    automatic   chemical   rapid   slow   [2 marks]

3   Put the sentences in the correct order to describe how the body moves out of the way of a ball.

   A   The receptors send a signal to your brain.

   B   Receptors in your eye see a ball coming towards you.

   C   Your brain then causes your body to move out of the way of the ball.   [3 marks]

4   If something comes near your eye, you blink. You cannot stop your eye from blinking. Is blinking a reflex action?
                    [1 mark]

What are some other examples of reflex actions?
Investigate some other examples of reflex actions, such as the ankle reflex and blinking.

4.2 Testing reactions

Learning objectives

After this topic, you should know:

- some factors that affect human reaction time
- how to measure reaction time.

Reaction time is how fast you can respond to a stimulus.

Human reaction times can be affected by several factors.

- Your reactions get slower as you get older.
- You have slower reactions when you are tired.
- Being distracted will make your reaction time slower. Your body finds it difficult to concentrate on more than one task at a time.
- Some drugs, such as alcohol, slow down reaction times. Other drugs, such as caffeine in coffee, speed up reaction times.

A: What are three factors that affect reaction time?

Comparing reaction times

You can compare your reaction time with other people's by measuring how long it takes you to catch a ruler when it is dropped.

Measuring your reaction time

Step 1: Take a ruler with a reaction time scale on it.

Step 2: One person holds the ruler at the top of the scale and lets it hang vertically.

Step 3: The second person places their thumb and index finger either side of the 0 s mark on the scale. Their fingers shouldn't touch the ruler.

Step 4: Without warning, the person holding the ruler lets go. The second person catches the ruler as it falls.

Step 5: Record the time taken where the top of the second person's finger touches the scale.

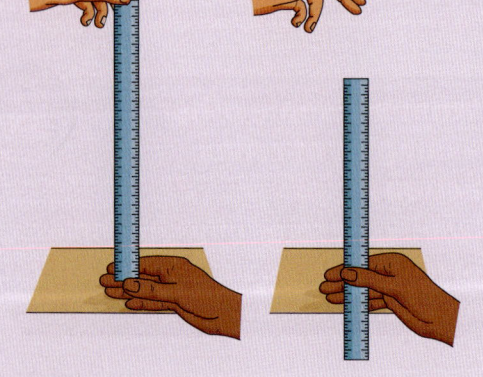

Figure 1

The shorter the distance the ruler travels before it is caught, the faster the person's reflex action. You can use the following table to turn the distance into a reaction time.

Distance the ruler drops before it is caught in cm	Reaction time in seconds
5	0.10
10	0.14
15	0.18
20	0.20
25	0.23
30	0.25

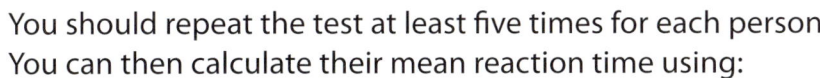

You should repeat the test at least five times for each person. You can then calculate their mean reaction time using:

$$\text{mean} = \frac{\text{add up every result}}{\text{divide by the number of results}}$$

Calculating the mean reaction time

Evelyn measured her reaction time five times. Her results were:

14.0 cm   14.0 cm   13.5 cm   14.5 cm   14.0 cm

Calculate Evelyn's mean reaction time.

Step 1: Add up Evelyn's results.

$$14.0 + 14.0 + 13.5 + 14.5 + 14.0 = 70$$

Step 2: Divide 70 by the total number of results Evelyn had.

Evelyn had 5 results so: $\frac{70}{5} = \mathbf{14\ cm}$

If your results are very similar it means that your results are valid. Any results that are very different are called outliers. These should be repeated to check no mistakes have been made.

How does caffeine affect your reflexes?

Caffeine is found in tea and coffee. Investigate how drinking tea or coffee affects your reaction time.

1 Sort the following factors into those that speed up your reaction time and those that slow down your reaction time.

alcohol   caffeine   old age   tiredness   [4 marks]

2 Choose the correct words from the box to complete this sentence.

catch   drop   faster   slower

The faster you _____ a ruler, the _____ your reaction time.   [2 marks]

3 Two students want to compare their reflex actions. They carry out the ruler-drop experiment. Their results are shown in the table.

Person	Mean distance ruler dropped before it was caught in cm
Evelyn	14
Salma	11

a Who has the faster reaction time, Evelyn or Salma?   [1 mark]

b Why should the tester leave different amounts of time before dropping the ruler?   [1 mark]

4.3 Hormones and the menstrual cycle

Learning objectives

After this topic, you should know:

- what a hormone is
- the main stages in the menstrual cycle.

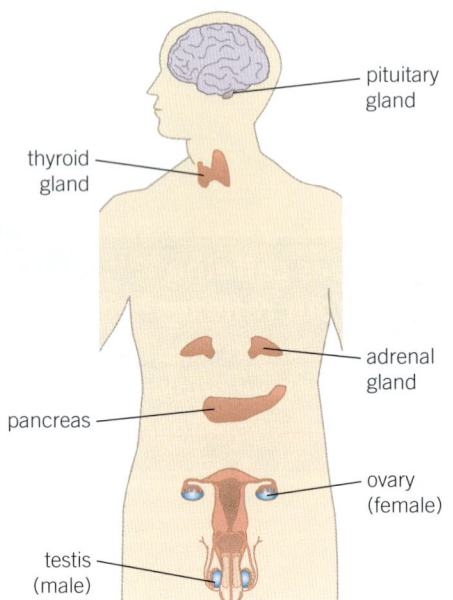

Figure 1 *The position of some glands in the hormonal system.*

Some changes to your body happen quite slowly, and some can affect large parts of your body. These types of changes are controlled by your hormonal system. The hormonal system is another example of an automatic control system. Your hormonal system is made up of lots of glands. These glands release chemicals called hormones.

The hormonal system

Hormones are special chemicals. They are made in your glands and released into your bloodstream. We say that they are **secreted** into the blood. Your blood then transports the hormones to the **target organs**.

A: How are hormones transported around the body?

Hormones control the function of many organs in your body. Hormonal responses are often slow, but can last a long time.

Menstrual cycle

The **menstrual cycle** happens around once a month in teenage girls and women. The menstrual cycle lasts for about 28 days. It is controlled by several hormones, and it prepares the female body for pregnancy.

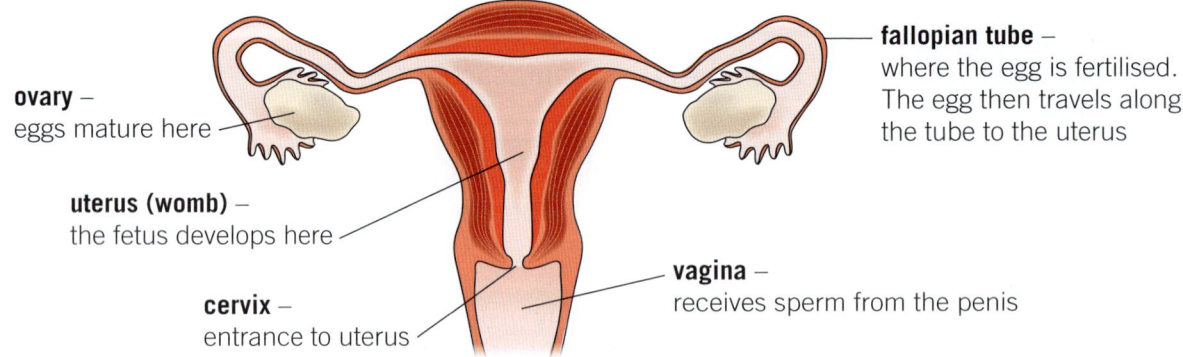

Figure 2 *The female reproductive system.*

B: Roughly how days does the menstrual cycle last?

The main stages in the cycle are shown on the diagram below:

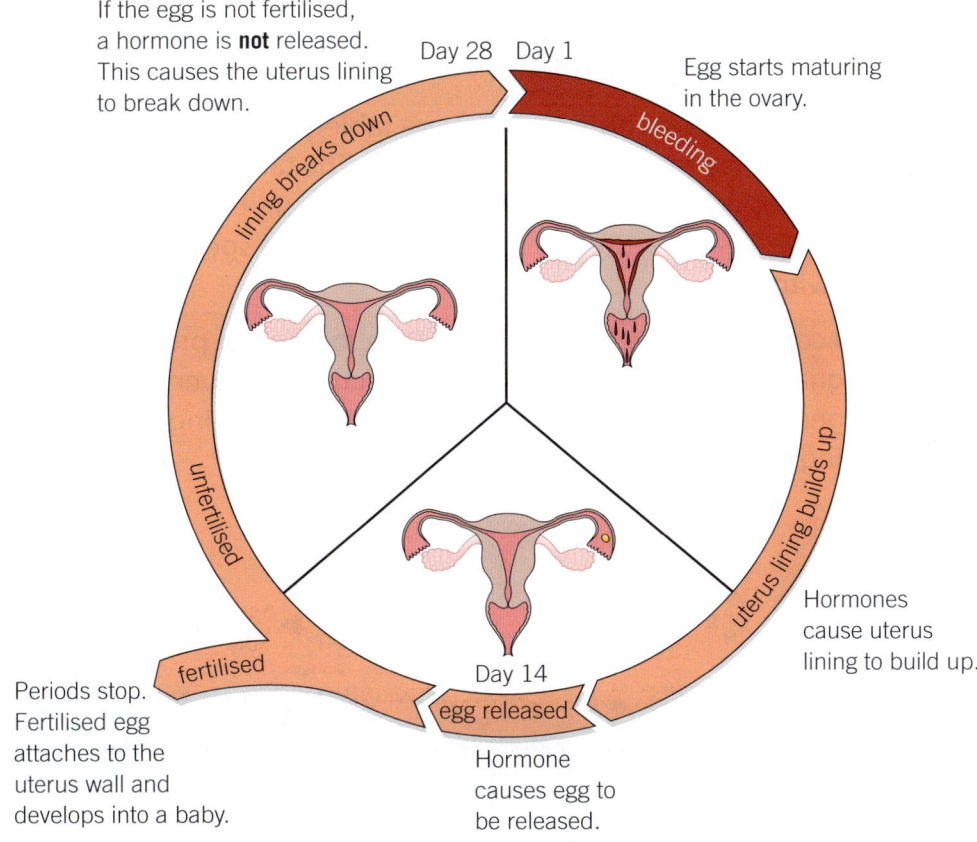

If the egg is not fertilised, a hormone is **not** released. This causes the uterus lining to break down.

Egg starts maturing in the ovary.

Hormones cause uterus lining to build up.

Periods stop. Fertilised egg attaches to the uterus wall and develops into a baby.

Hormone causes egg to be released.

Figure 3 *Hormones control the menstrual cycle.*

1   Match each key term to the correct definition.

Key term	Definition
hormone	organ the hormone has an effect on
target organ	chemical that is secreted by glands
gland	produces hormones and secretes them into the blood [2 marks]

2   Put the stages of the menstrual cycle into the correct order. The first one has been done for you.

 D → ☐ → ☐ → ☐

   A   If the egg is not fertilised, the uterus lining begins to break down.

   B   Hormones cause the lining of the uterus to build up.

   C   A hormone causes an egg to be released.

   D   Broken down uterus lining bleeds out of the vagina.
[2 marks]

3   How are hormones transported to their target organs?
[1 mark]

4.4 Controlling fertility

Learning objectives

After this topic, you should know:

- how hormones are used in contraception
- how hormones are used to treat infertility
- some advantages and disadvantages of using hormones to treat infertility.

When two people are having sexual intercourse, they can take steps to avoid pregnancy. This is called **contraception**. Some contraceptives use hormones.

For example, oral contraceptives are tablets that females swallow. They must be taken every day. The tablets contain hormones that stop an egg from maturing and being released. Pregnancy is prevented as there is no egg for a sperm cell to join with.

Oral contraceptives are a very effective method of preventing pregnancy. They can be up to 99% effective at preventing pregnancy. However, they do not stop diseases being passed on during sexual intercourse.

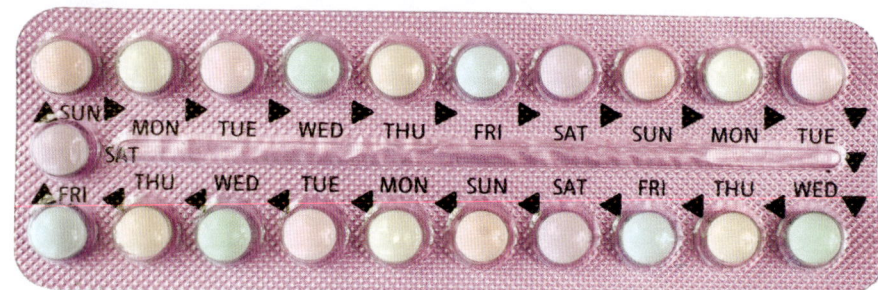

Figure 1 *Oral contraceptives contain hormones. A pill must be taken every day to keep the hormones at the correct level and prevent an egg from maturing.*

A: How does an oral contraceptive prevent pregnancy?

Treating infertility

Some couples have difficulty when trying to have a baby. This is known as **infertility**. Two reasons for infertility are:

- not enough sperm produced in the testes
- not enough mature eggs produced in the ovaries.

Infertility can sometimes be treated. This is called fertility treatment. Females can take a fertility drug that contains hormones that cause more eggs to mature. This increases the chances of getting pregnant as at least one mature egg should now be released every month.

B: What is the type of chemical found in many fertility drugs?

Benefits of fertility treatment

- It allows people to conceive who would not be able to have a baby naturally.

- A female's fertility decreases as she gets older. Fertility drugs can help an older female to be more fertile.

- A female's mature eggs can be collected and stored to be used later. These can be used if a female has to have other medical treatments that damage her eggs.

Possible problems of fertility treatment

- Success rates can be quite low.

- Treatment may result in multiple births (twins, triplets, or more). This can be dangerous for both the mother and the unborn babies.

- Treatment can be very expensive. Not everyone can afford it.

- Fertility drugs can increase some health risks for the female.

1 Choose the correct words from the box to complete the following sentences.

> egg   hormones   pregnancy

An oral contraceptive is a tablet that contains _____. These stop an _____ from being released. Therefore, _____ is prevented as there is no egg for the sperm to join with. [2 marks]

2 Which one of the following can be a cause of infertility?

A not enough sperm produced

B one egg released each month

C sperm that can 'swim' well

D too many sperm produced [1 mark]

3 a What is one advantage of using fertility drugs to treat infertility? [1 mark]

b What is one disadvantage of using fertility drugs to treat infertility? [1 mark]

4 Checkpoint

1 Choose the correct words from the box to complete the following sentences.

> glands hormonal hormones target

The _____ system is made up of _____. They secrete chemicals called _____ directly into the bloodstream. The blood carries the hormone to a _____ organ where it produces an effect.

[3 marks]

2 Which part of the body decides how you should respond to a stimulus?

brain   eyes   muscles

[1 mark]

3 Which **two** of the following are parts of the nervous system?

brain   hormone   receptor   uterus

[2 marks]

4 Which **two** of the following statements about the nervous system are true?

A Nervous responses are quicker than hormonal responses.

B Nervous responses affect a larger area of the body than hormonal responses.

C Reflex actions are a type of nervous response.

D The menstrual cycle is controlled by the nervous system.

[2 marks]

5 Which **two** of the following are examples of reflex actions?

blinking   knee-jerk reaction   running   talking

[2 marks]

6 What type of chemicals control the menstrual cycle?

[1 mark]

7 The pupil in the eye changing size is an example of a reflex response.

   a What type of stimulus causes the pupil to become smaller?   [1 mark]

   b Why is this described as a reflex action?   [1 mark]

8 a How does an oral contraceptive prevent pregnancy?

   A kills the egg

   B kills the sperm

   C stops an egg maturing

   D stops sperm entering the uterus   [1 mark]

   b What is **one** disadvantage of using an oral contraceptive as a form of contraception?   [1 mark]

9 a How can hormones be used to increase the chance of a female becoming pregnant?   [1 mark]

   b What is **one** benefit of using hormones to treat infertility?   [1 mark]

   c What is **one** risk of using hormones to treat infertility?   [1 mark]

4 Vocabulary builder

1 Match each key word to the correct definition.

Key word	Definition
stimulus	cells that detect stimuli
receptors	an automatic and rapid nervous response
reflex	change in the external or internal environment

[2 marks]

2 Choose the correct word to complete the following sentences on the monthly changes to the female reproductive system.

The female cycle that gets the body ready for pregnancy is called the **hormonal system / menstrual cycle**.

The cycle is controlled by **hormones / the nervous system**. These chemicals can also be used to prevent a woman getting pregnant using **contraceptives / plasma**. The chemicals can also be used to help couples have a child in **infertility / fertility** drugs

[4 marks]

3 Choose the correct term to identify the key term that is being described.

   a the part of your nervous system that makes a response happen.

      brain   **nerve cell**   **stimulus**

[1 mark]

   b structure in an animal that releases hormones

      gland   **muscle**   **target organ**

[1 mark]

   c tissue in an animal that transports hormones

      blood   **nerve cells**   **water**

[1 mark]

4 Complete the following sentences on reflex actions.

They are a special type of n _ _ _ _ _ response. They are
r _ _ _ _ and a _ _ _ _ _ _ _ _.

[3 marks]

4.5 The menstrual cycle and contraception

Learning objectives

After this topic, you should know:

- the key events in the menstrual cycle
- different methods of contraception.

After a female has gone through puberty, she is able to get pregnant. In the monthly menstrual cycle, an egg matures and is released. If the egg meets a sperm cell, it may be fertilised and a baby will start to develop.

The menstrual cycle

A female's menstrual cycle lasts around 28 days. It is controlled by several hormones.

A: Give the name of the chemicals that control the menstrual cycle.

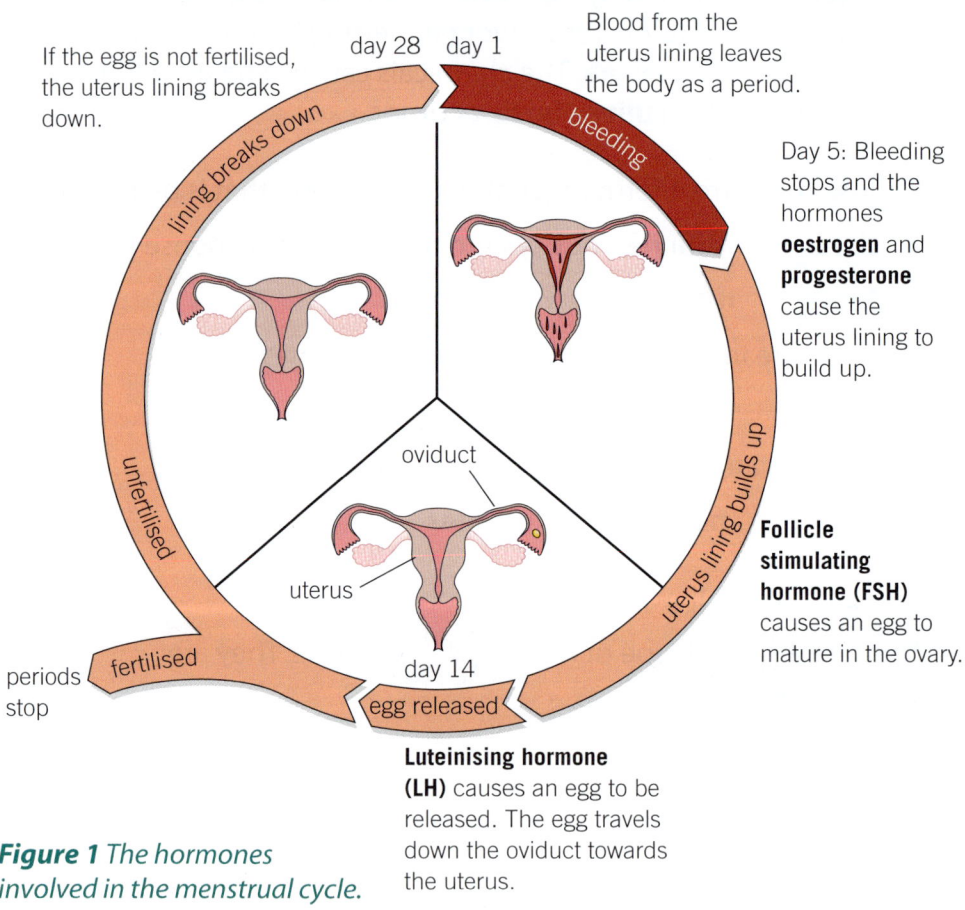

If the egg is not fertilised, the uterus lining breaks down.

Blood from the uterus lining leaves the body as a period.

Day 5: Bleeding stops and the hormones **oestrogen** and **progesterone** cause the uterus lining to build up.

Follicle stimulating hormone (FSH) causes an egg to mature in the ovary.

Luteinising hormone (LH) causes an egg to be released. The egg travels down the oviduct towards the uterus.

Figure 1 *The hormones involved in the menstrual cycle.*

If the egg cell does not meet a sperm cell, the lining of the uterus breaks down. Blood from the uterus lining leaves the body through the vagina. This is known as a **period**, or **menstruation**. The cycle then begins again.

If the egg is fertilised, the uterus lining does **not** break down. The fertilised egg attaches to the uterus wall. The egg is protected and gets nutrients and oxygen from the mother's bloodstream. The woman is now pregnant.

B: Describe what happens if an egg does not meet a sperm cell.

Contraception

Contraception can be used to avoid pregnancy. Two of the most common forms of contraception are condoms and the contraceptive pill.

Condoms

A condom is a thin layer of rubber that fits over an erect penis. It prevents sperm being released into a female's vagina. This is known as a barrier method of contraception.

When used correctly, condoms are a very effective contraceptive. Condoms also prevent the transfer of sexually transmitted diseases (STDs), such as HIV and gonorrhoea.

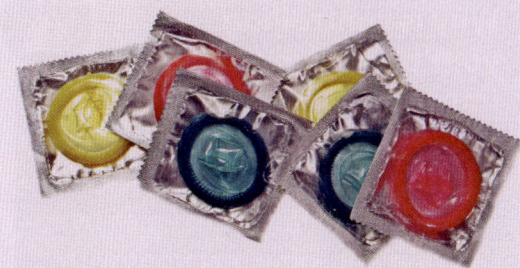

Figure 2 *Condoms are a barrier method of contraception.*

C: Suggest why a condom is called a 'barrier' method of contraception.

Oral contraceptives

The contraceptive pill is a tablet that a female takes every day. The tablet contains hormones that can prevent pregnancy by stopping ovulation (the release of an egg). Some tablets also contain hormones that prevent the uterus lining building up so a fertilised egg cannot attach to it.

The contraceptive pill is a very effective contraceptive. However, it provides no protection against the transfer of STDs.

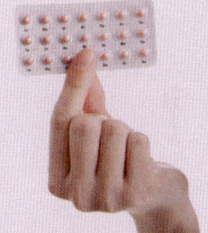

Figure 3 *The contraceptive pill contains hormones that interrupt the normal menstrual cycle.*

1   Describe what is meant by contraception.   [1 mark]

2   Give the role of each of the following hormones in the menstrual cycle.
    a   follicle stimulating hormone   [1 mark]
    b   oestrogen   [1 mark]
    c   luteinising hormone   [1 mark]

3   Explain why a woman is very unlikely to become pregnant before day 10 of her menstrual cycle.   [2 marks]

4.6 Homeostasis

Learning objectives

After this topic, you should know:

- what is homeostasis
- some examples of internal conditions that are controlled
- how blood glucose levels are controlled.

Why is controlling your body temperature important?

To see why your body controls its temperature, investigate how temperature affects enzymes by carrying out some reactions with enzymes at different temperatures.

The conditions inside your body are known as your internal environment. Your organs cannot work properly if this keeps changing. There are many processes going on inside your body that work to keep your internal environment constant. This is called **homeostasis.**

A: Describe what is meant by homeostasis.

Controlling internal conditions

Internal conditions that need to be controlled include:

- the temperature of your body
- the amount of water in your body
- the amount of glucose in your blood.

B: Name one internal body condition that has to be controlled.

Controlling blood glucose levels

It is very important that your cells have a constant supply of glucose. Glucose is used for respiration. The amount of glucose in your blood is called your **blood glucose level**. It can be very dangerous if your blood glucose levels are not kept constant.

After you eat, glucose is released by digestion and passes into your blood. This causes your blood glucose level to rise. If your blood glucose level stays high for a long time it can damage your body's systems.

More glucose is needed when you exercise because your body needs to transfer more energy. This causes your blood glucose level to drop. This can prevent cells from respiring.

C: Give one way you can reduce your blood glucose level.

The role of insulin

Your pancreas is an organ. It senses when your blood glucose level rises. The pancreas then releases the hormone insulin. Insulin causes glucose to move from your blood into your liver cells. It is then converted into glycogen. There is now less glucose in your blood, so your blood glucose level falls.

The glycogen stored in your liver cells can be converted back to glucose if your blood glucose level gets too low.

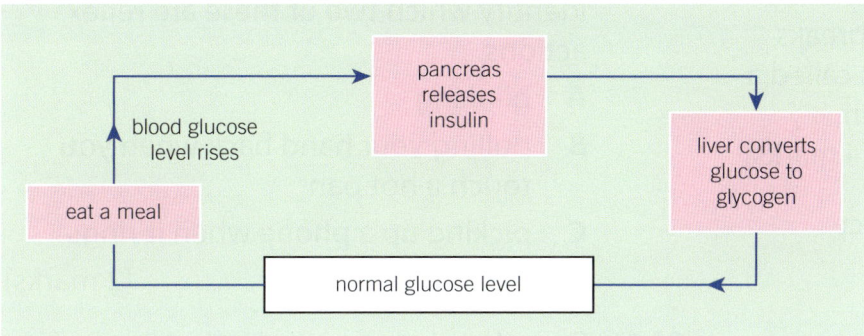

Figure 1 *This flow diagram shows how insulin maintains a constant blood glucose level.*

D: Name the hormone that controls your blood glucose level.

1   Choose the correct words from the box to complete the following sentences.

   | blood   homeostasis   insulin   internal |

   The control of the body's _____ environment is called _____. An example of a condition that is controlled is the _____ glucose level. This is controlled by the hormone _____.   [3 marks]

2   Name the gland that produces insulin.   [1 mark]

3   After you have eaten a meal, your blood glucose level increases. Describe how insulin reduces your blood glucose level.   [3 marks]

4 Practice questions

01 Choose the correct words from the box to complete the following sentences.

> egg   lining   menstrual
> period   28 days

The female reproductive system works in a cycle called the _____ cycle. Around every _____ an _____ is released. If this is not fertilised, the uterus _____ breaks down and leaves the body. This is called a _____. The cycle then begins again.

[4 marks]

02 Match each key term to the correct definition.

Key term	Definition
glands	structure a hormone has an effect on
hormones	chemicals produced in one area of the body of an organism that have an effect on another area
target organ	structures in animals which release hormones [2 marks]

03 Emily walks outside on a sunny day. Choose the correct words from the box to explain how the size of her pupil changes.

> bigger   less   more   muscles
> organs   smaller

In bright light, the _____ around Emily's pupil make her pupil _____, so _____ light enters her eye. This prevents her eye from being damaged.   [3 marks]

04 What is a receptor cell?

  A   a cell that detects a stimulus

  B   a cell that makes a response happen

  C   a cell that makes a muscle move

  D   a cell that releases a hormone

[1 mark]

05 Reflex actions are automatic and rapid. Identify which two of these are reflex actions.

  A   blinking

  B   pulling your hand back when you touch a hot pan

  C   picking up a phone when it rings

  D   talking   [2 marks]

06.1 Describe what is meant by the term homeostasis.   [1 mark]

06.2 Name **two** body systems that have to be controlled.   [2 marks]

07.1 Figure 1 shows the human hormonal system. Label the organs A to C. Choose from the following list:

pancreas   **pituitary gland**

testes   **thyroid gland**

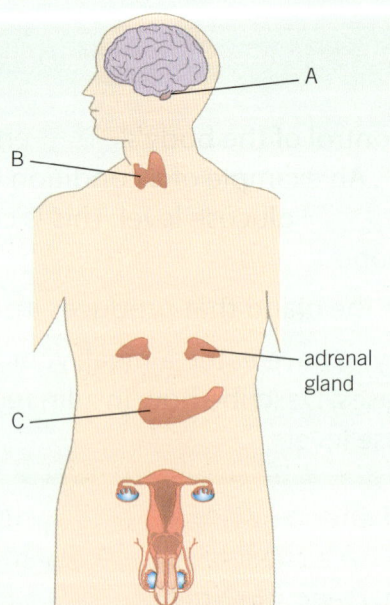

Figure 1   [3 marks]

07.2 Complete the following sentences about homeostasis:

The _____ detects the blood _____ level in your body. If the level rises, _____ is released. This causes glucose to be converted to _____ in your _____. This causes your blood glucose level to fall again. [5 marks]

08 Two students were asked to investigate the effect of drinking caffeine on their reaction times. They use a falling ruler to measure Student A's reaction time. They measured her reaction time before and after drinking a caffeine drink.

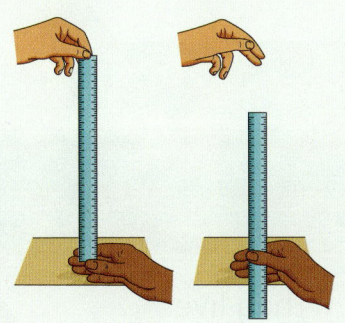

Figure 2

08.1 Put the following steps in order to describe how Will and Sadie should carry out their practical. The first step has been done for you.

A → ☐ → ☐ → ☐ → ☐ → ☐

A Student A places her hand around, but not touching, the base of the ruler. Student B holds the top of the ruler.

B Repeat whole investigation after drinking caffeine drink.

C Repeat five times.

D Student A catches the ruler as it falls.

E Read the distance on the ruler scale. Use a chart to convert ruler distance to reaction time.

F Student B drops the ruler without warning. [4 marks]

08.2 Give **one** variable the students should control. [1 mark]

08.3 The students collected the following data:

	Reaction time in s					
	1	2	3	4	5	Mean
Before drinking caffeine	0.85	0.80	0.82	0.90	0.88	0.85
After drinking caffeine	0.68	0.70	0.84	0.71	0.82	0.75

Suggest what effect caffeine has on the student's reaction time. [1 mark]

09 Figure 3 shows the success rates for fertility treatments in 2010.

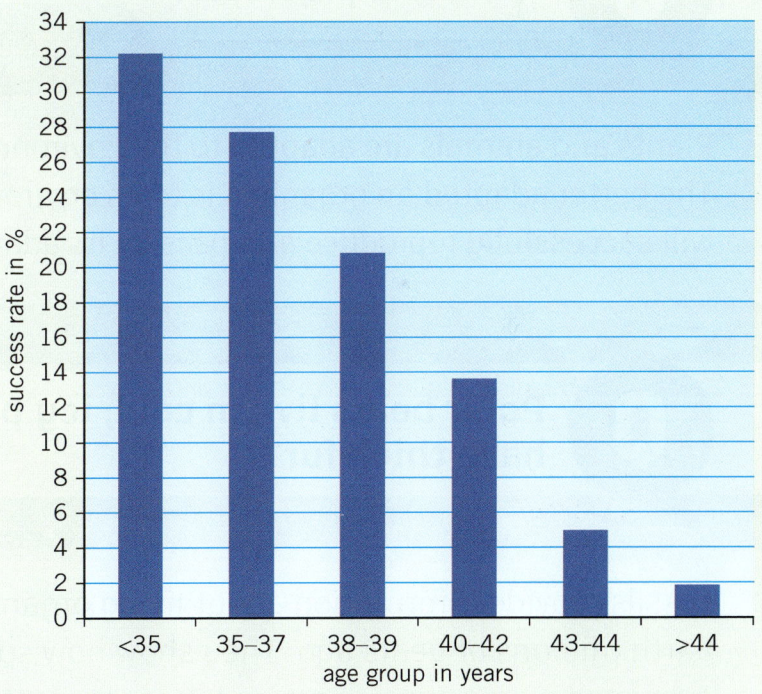

Figure 3

09.1 Which age group has the greatest chance of getting pregnant using a fertility treatment? [1 mark]

09.2 Describe **one** way that hormones can be used to treat infertility. [2 marks]

Biology

Plants are called producers because they make their own food by the process of photosynthesis.

Animals are called consumers because they have to eat other organisms to gain energy.

The feeding relationships between organisms can be represented by a food chain.

Q **What is a producer?**

Plants and animals are adapted to the environment in which they live. The better adapted an organism is to its environment, the more likely it will successfully reproduce and pass on its adaptations to its offspring.

Q **Polar bears live in cold, icy places. Why do they have thick fur?**

Fossils provide information about living organisms that lived on the Earth millions of years ago. They show how species may have changed over time. Some species are no longer present on the Earth today. These species are extinct. They include the dinosaurs.

Q **What does the word extinct mean?**

Component 2
Environment, evolution, and inheritance

▶ Photosynthesis

Plants produce their own food by the process of photosynthesis. They use light energy from the Sun to convert the carbon dioxide and water that they take in into glucose.

All life on earth depends on this process as animals cannot make their own food. They need to eat other organisms to gain energy.

▶ Interaction between organisms

Living organisms are adapted to survive in the environment that they live in.

Organisms interact with one another and their environment in many different ways. For example, plants compete for light and space and animals compete for food and territory.

▶ Evolution

Life on Earth has evolved by the process of natural selection. This has led to the variety of organisms that exist.

The characteristics of living organisms depend on the genetic material they inherit form their parents and the environment in which they live.

5 Feeding relationships
5.1 Photosynthesis

Learning objectives

After this topic, you should know:

- the difference between producers and consumers
- the process of photosynthesis
- the word equation for photosynthesis.

Unlike animals, plants do not have to eat other organisms to survive. They get their energy directly from the Sun.

Producers and consumers

Plants and algae are called **producers** because they make their own food. They use radiation from the Sun to turn materials from their environment into glucose.

Animals are called **consumers**. They have to consume (eat) plants or other animals to gain energy. They break down these organisms during digestion. This releases nutrients, which are then used by the body.

> **A:** What is a producer?

Photosynthesis

Plants and algae make their own food through the process of **photosynthesis**. They take in carbon dioxide and water, and convert it into glucose. Oxygen is also made.

Light from the Sun is needed to make this chemical reaction happen.

Photosynthesis can be represented by the word equation:

$$\text{carbon dioxide} + \text{water} \xrightarrow{\text{light}} \text{glucose} + \text{oxygen}$$

The chemicals that react together are carbon dioxide and water. They are called **reactants**. Glucose and oxygen are the chemicals that are produced by the reaction. They are called **products**.

Oxygen is a waste product and is released back into the air.

Some of the glucose produced is used in respiration. This provides the plant with energy. Lots of the glucose is turned into starch and stored.

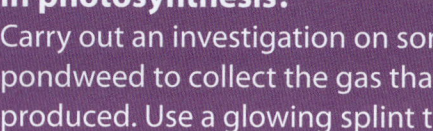

How do we know that plants produce oxygen in photosynthesis?

Carry out an investigation on some pondweed to collect the gas that is produced. Use a glowing splint to show that the gas is oxygen.

> **B:** What is the name of the chemical reaction that plants use to make glucose?

Site of photosynthesis

Photosynthesis happens in the leaves of a plant. The leaves are green because they contain the green chemical called chlorophyll contained in the chloroplasts. Chlorophyll absorbs light from the Sun. This light provides energy for the plant to convert carbon dioxide and water into glucose.

C: Where does the energy for photosynthesis come from?

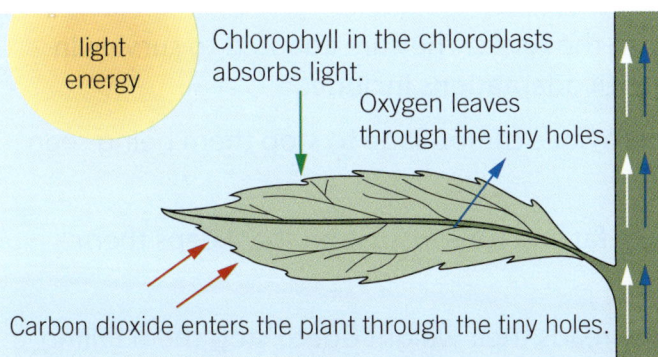

light energy

Chlorophyll in the chloroplasts absorbs light.

Oxygen leaves through the tiny holes.

Glucose is transported to all the parts of the plant. Water is transported from the roots to the stem and leaves.

Carbon dioxide enters the plant through the tiny holes.

Figure 1 *This diagram shows how the substances required for photosynthesis get into a leaf.*

1 Choose the correct words from the box to complete the word equation for photosynthesis.

> oxygen   water

_____ + carbon dioxide → glucose + _____   [1 mark]

2 Sort the following organisms into producers and consumers.

| algae | cats | oak trees | rabbits |

[4 marks]

3 What is the source of energy for all organisms?   [1 mark]

5.2 Adaptations

Learning objectives

After this topic, you should know:

- what is meant by an adaptation
- some examples of animal adaptations
- some examples of plant adaptations.

The area that an organism lives in is known as its **habitat**.

All organisms have special features known as **adaptations**. Adaptations make it possible for an organism to survive the conditions in their habitat.

A: What is meant by an adaptation?

Animal adaptations

Figure 1 *The polar bear is well adapted to live in the Arctic.*

Polar bears live in the Arctic. They are adapted to survive in extreme cold. Their adaptations include:

- white fur – provides camouflage to stop them being seen by their prey
- thick layers of fat and fur – insulation that keeps them warm
- large feet – spreads their weight out to stop them falling through thin ice
- hairs on feet – stop them slipping on the ice
- a greasy coat – sheds water and dries quickly after swimming.

B: What is one adaptation of a polar bear that helps to keep it warm?

Figure 2 *The camel is adapted to live in the desert.*

Some animals are adapted to live in the extreme heat of the desert. These include camels. Their adaptations include:

- large, flat feet – spread their weight to stop them sinking into the sand
- fat store in hump – used for energy, letting them go long periods of time without food or water
- produce very little sweat and urine – reduces water loss
- two rows of eyelashes – keep the sand out of their eyes.

Plant adaptations

The Arctic is cold and windy, with very little rain. Plants in the Arctic:

- grow very close to the ground to avoid the wind

- have small leaves to reduce water loss

- can survive under a layer of snow – the snow acts like a blanket, keeping the plant warm.

Figure 3 *This cereal plant can survive in the tough environment of the Arctic.*

C: **What is one way that plants are adapted to survive in the Arctic?**

Plants in the desert also have a number of adaptations. This helps them to survive with very little water. These include:

- a waxy layer that covers the plant – reduces water escaping from the plant

- stems that store water

- widespread roots – allow the plant to collect water from a large area

- spines instead of leaves – smaller surface area, which reduces water loss.

Figure 4 *Cacti are adapted to live in the desert.*

1 Match each key word to the correct definition.

Key word	Definition
adaptation	The area in which an organism lives.
habitat	Special features that help an organism survive. [1 mark]

2 Which **two** of the following are examples of how a cactus is adapted to prevent water loss?

A can survive under snow   C spines instead of leaves

B grow low to the ground   D waxy layer   [2 marks]

3 a What is **one** adaptation of a polar bear? [1 mark]

   b How does the adaptation you gave in question **3a** help a polar bear survive in its habitat? [1 mark]

5.3 Food chains and food webs

Learning objectives

After this topic, you should know:

- the levels of organisation within an ecosystem
- what food chains show
- what food webs show.

Organisms interact with each other in many ways. For example, some animals eat other animals, and some animals use plants for shelter. They also need to interact with their environment, for example, for water and minerals. All the organisms and physical conditions in an area make up an **ecosystem**.

There are different levels of organisation in an ecosystem.

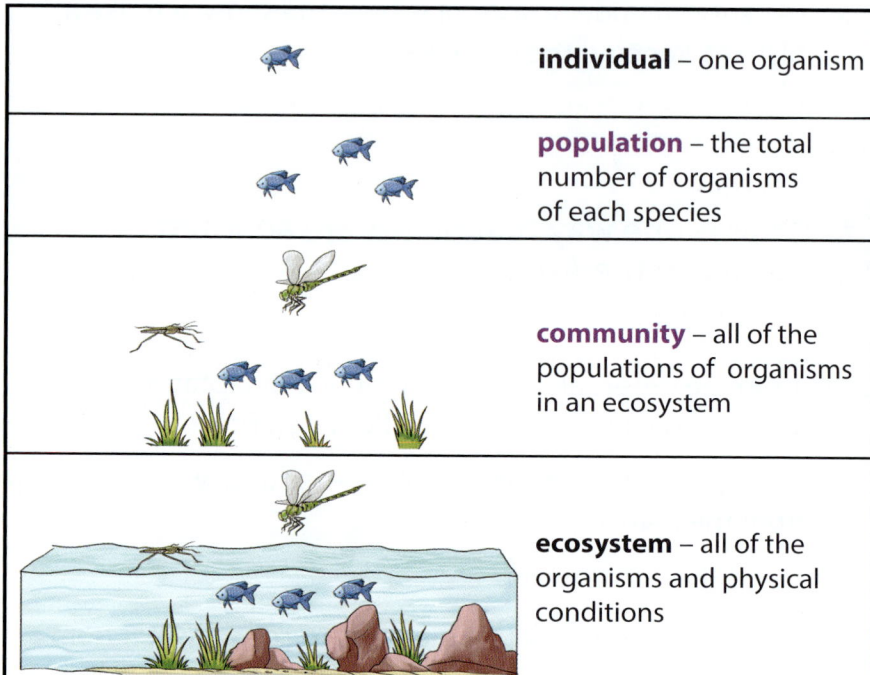

individual – one organism

population – the total number of organisms of each species

community – all of the populations of organisms in an ecosystem

ecosystem – all of the organisms and physical conditions

Figure 1 *The levels of organisation in a pond ecosystem.*

A: What is meant by a community?

Food chains

The feeding relationships in a community can be shown as a food chain. Food chains always start with a producer. An example of a simple food chain is shown in Figure 2.

grass

rabbit

fox

food chains always begin with a producer

a rabbit is a prey organism – it is eaten by another animal

a fox is a predator organism – it eats other animals

Figure 2 *A food chain for open grassland.*

B: What is a food chain?

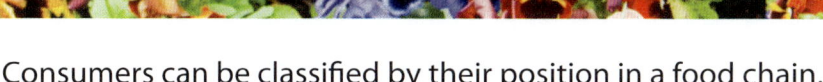

Consumers can be classified by their position in a food chain.

grass is a producer

slugs are **primary** consumers – they eat producers

sparrows are **secondary** consumers – they eat primary consumers

hawks are **tertiary** consumers – they eat secondary consumers

Figure 3 Classifying consumers in a food chain.

Food webs

Food chains only show each species eating one food source. In most communities, animals eat more than one type of food. We can draw **food webs**, like the one in Figure 4, to show this as a series of linked food chains.

The organisms in a food web are all affected by each other. For example, if the number of caterpillars goes up, the number of frogs may also increase because they have more food. However, if a disease kills off lots of slugs, the number of sparrows may decrease because they would have less to eat.

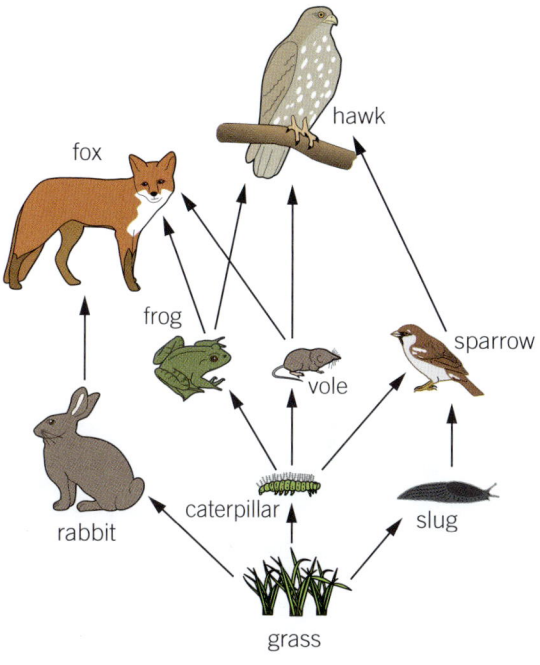

Figure 4 A woodland food web. Food webs show how species depend on each other for food within an ecosystem.

C: What is a food web?

1   Match each key term to the correct definition.

Key term	Definition
ecosystem	Diagram that shows the transfer of energy between organisms.
community	Living organisms and physical conditions in an area.
food chain	The organisms in an ecosystem.

[2 marks]

2   A pond snail eats pondweed. Herons eat fish. Fish eat pond snails.

Draw a food chain using these organisms.

fish   **heron**   **pond snails**   **pondweed**

[3 marks]

3   Look at the food web in Figure 4.

a   What is the name of the producer?   [1 mark]

b   What is the name of a secondary consumer?   [1 mark]

c   What could happen to the population of voles if caterpillars were removed?   [1 mark]

5.4 Decay

Learning objectives

After this topic, you should know:

- what is meant by material cycling
- what is meant by decay
- some of the processes in the decay cycle.

Microorganisms are organisms that are so small they can only be seen with a microscope. Bacteria are examples of microorganisms. When plants and animals die, microorganisms break down their bodies. This releases the materials that they contain back into the environment, where they can be used again by other plants and animals.

Recycling materials

When an organism is alive, it takes in materials from the environment for growth and other processes. For example, plants take mineral ions from the soil that they use to grow. These materials are then passed on to animals when the animals eat the plants.

All the resources on Earth would have been used up a long time ago if these materials were not returned to the environment (recycled).

Fortunately, all the materials that are taken from the environment are returned to the environment, and provide the building blocks for future organisms. Materials are constantly cycling through organisms and the environment.

Materials are returned to the environment when:

- trees and plants lose their leaves
- animals produce droppings
- animals and plants die.

A: What are **two** ways that materials are returned to the environment?

Decay

When animals and plants die, they are broken down. This is called **decay**. The materials that the plants and animals are made up of are released back into the environment. Decay is caused by a group of microorganisms called decomposers. The waste produced by animals and plants also decays because of decomposers.

B: What is a decomposer?

Living organisms are mainly made up of carbon. The carbon needs to be recycled, so it is available for other life on Earth to use.

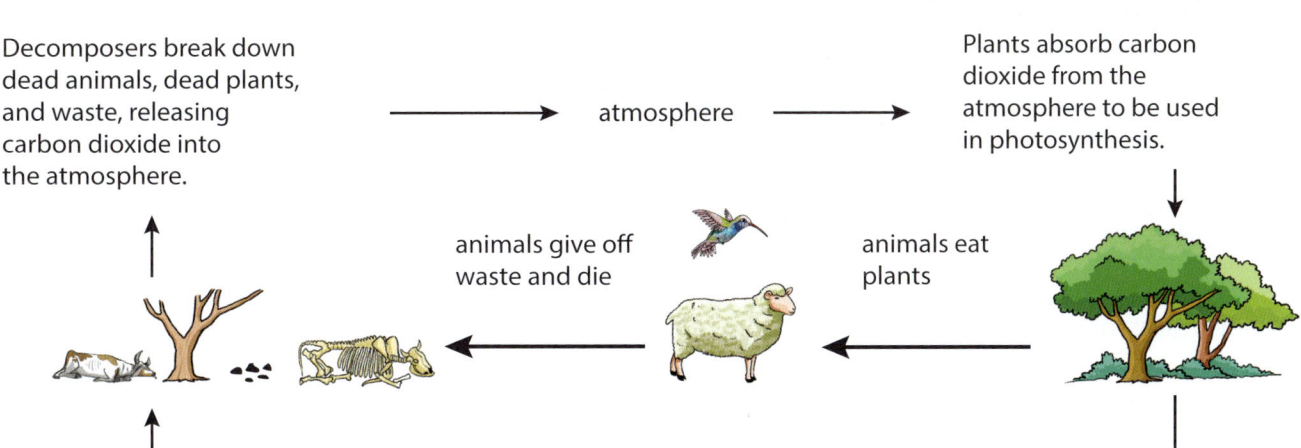

Decomposers break down dead animals, dead plants, and waste, releasing carbon dioxide into the atmosphere.

atmosphere

Plants absorb carbon dioxide from the atmosphere to be used in photosynthesis.

animals give off waste and die

animals eat plants

plants die

Figure 1 *This diagram shows how carbon is cycled through organisms and the environment.*

1 Choose the correct words from the box to complete the following sentences.

materials   microorganisms   recycled

When an organism dies _____ break down its body. This returns _____ to the environment. Materials are constantly being _____ .   [3 marks]

2 Which **two** of the following reasons explain why decomposers are important for the environment?

A make material available for new organisms

B prevent build-up of dead organisms

C produce carbohydrates

D provide shelter   [2 marks]

3 A student wanted to investigate how temperature affects the rate of decay. He took 500 g of moist grass cuttings and kept them at 10°C. After 3 months he measured the mass of grass that was left. He repeated the experiment at four other temperatures: 20°C, 30°C, 40°C, and 50°C . He then plotted a bar chart of his results:

mass of grass left in g

temperature in °C

Which temperature gave the fastest rate of decay?[1 mark]

How does temperature affect how quickly something decays?
Investigate how quickly a piece of food goes mouldy at different temperatures.

5 Checkpoint

1 Choose the correct words from the box to complete the following sentences.

| consumer | cycle | energy | food chain | photosynthesis | producer |

A _____ is a diagram that shows the transfer of _____ between organisms. The first organism is always a _____. It absorbs light from the Sun to make glucose by _____.

The other organisms in the chain are _____. [5 marks]

2 Choose the correct word to complete the word equation for photosynthesis.

| light | oxygen | water |

carbon dioxide + _____ ⟶ _____ + glucose [2 marks]

3 Which **two** of the following are adaptations of a cactus that help it to survive in the desert.

A large leaves   C spines instead of leaves

B small roots   D stems that store water [2 marks]

4 Match each adaptation to the description of how it helps the plant or animal to survive.

Adaptation	How the adaptation helps the organism to survive
covered in thick fur	prevents plant from being eaten
covered in thorns	helps animal to see prey
good eyesight	keeps animal warm

[2 marks]

5 a Which process breaks plants and animals down after they die? [1 mark]

   b Which type of organisms cause this process? [1 mark]

   c What is one material that is recycled? [1 mark]

6 The food web shows the feeding relationships between organisms in an African plain.

   a What is **one** organism that eats impalas? [1 mark]

   b Draw a food chain with four links that exists within the food web. [2 marks]

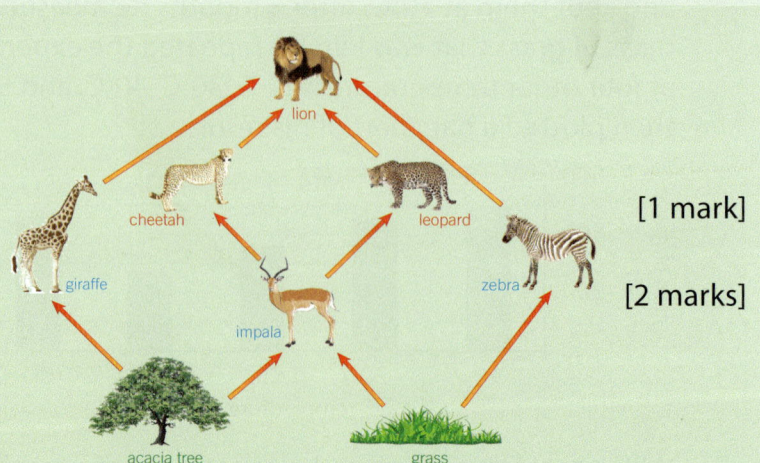

5 Vocabulary builder

1   Match each key word to the correct definition.

Key word	Definition
producer	Animals that eat other organisms to gain energy.
consumer	Microorganisms that break down dead organisms and waste products.
decomposer	Organisms that make their own food by photosynthesis.

[2 marks]

2   Choose the correct term to complete these sentences about producers.

Green plants and algae make their own food by the process of **photosynthesis / respiration**.

These plants and algae are called **consumers / producers**. [2 marks]

3   Look at the diagram below.

oak leaves → caterpillar → blue tit → hawk

Which **two** of the following statements are correct?

A   The diagram begins with a consumer.

B   The diagram begins with a producer.

C   The diagram is an example of a food chain.

D   The diagram is an example of a food web. [2 marks]

4   Choose the correct term from the list to identify the key term that is being described.

a   The number of organisms of one species living in an area.

community   ecosystem   population [1 mark]

b   All the living organisms and physical conditions present in an area.

community   ecosystem   habitat [1 mark]

5   Complete the following sentences about recycling materials.

The process by which waste materials and dead animals and plants break down is called d _ _ _ _. This is caused by a group of microorganisms called d _ _ _ _ _ _ _ _ _ _ _. C _ _ _ _ _ is released back into the environment where it can be used again. [3 marks]

5.5 Interdependence

Learning objectives

After this topic, you should know:

- what is meant by interdependence
- how to interpret the patterns on predator–prey graphs.

Within a community, different species depend on each other for survival. This is known as **interdependence**. If one species is removed it can affect the whole community.

Organisms can affect each other in a number of ways.

Food

Animals rely on plants or other animals for food. For example, foxes depend on eating rabbits for food. Rabbits depend on eating grass to survive.

Plants also depend on animals for nutrients. Plants get nutrients from animal droppings or decayed dead organisms.

Shelter

Some organisms live in, or on, other organisms. For example, squirrels and birds live in trees, fleas live on animals, and some worms live in animals' intestines.

Pollination

Plants need bees to take pollen from one plant to another. This allows plants to fertilise each other. At the same time bees depend on plants for nectar. This is a sugary substance that the bees eat.

Seed dispersal

Some plants need animals to move seeds away from the parent plant. Some seeds are sticky or have tiny hairs that stick to an animal. Other seeds are contained in fruits such as apples. Animal eat the fruits and spread the seeds in their droppings.

A: Give two ways in which squirrels depend upon trees.

A stable community is a community in which all the species and environmental factors are in balance. This means that the population of each species in the community stays around the same size.

Predator–prey cycles

The size of the predator population will directly affect the size of the prey population. Similarly the size of the prey population will directly affect the size of the predator population.

In a stable community the numbers of predators and prey rise and fall in a cycle. One example of a predator–prey cycle is the relationship between Canadian lynx and snowshoe hare. This can be displayed on a predator–prey graph.

Figure 1 Canadian lynx (predator) and snowshoe hare (prey).

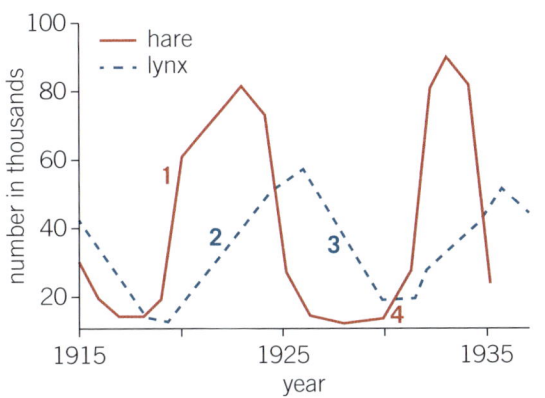

1 If the population of hares increases there is a larger food supply for the lynx.

2 This can therefore support more lynx, so more offspring survive.

3 The growing numbers of lynx eventually reduce the food supply. The number of predators starts to decrease.

4 The prey population starts to increase once more – the cycle then begins again.

Figure 2 The predator–prey cycle between the Canadian lynx and the snowshoe hare.

B: Describe what happens to the size of the lynx population when the hare population becomes very small.

1 Which **one** of the following is a resource that plants may be dependent on **animals** for?

food   **seed dispersal**   **shelter**   [1 mark]

2 Figure 3 shows the predator–prey cycle between foxes and rabbits. Foxes feed on rabbits.

Identify which organism is represented by the dashed green line.   [1 mark]

3 Describe how bees and roses are interdependent on each other.   [2 marks]

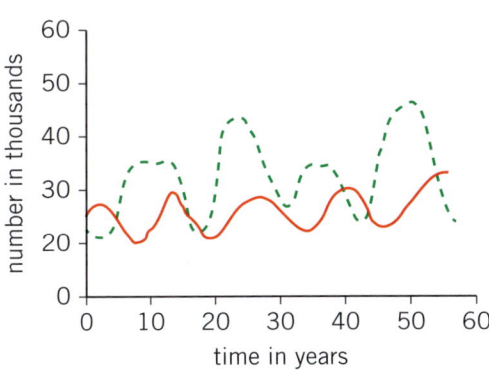

Figure 3

5.6 Factors affecting photosynthesis

Learning objectives

After this topic, you should know:

- some factors that affect the rate of photosynthesis
- the effect of light intensity and carbon dioxide on photosynthesis
- the effect of temperature on photosynthesis.

You may have noticed that plants grow quickly in the summer, yet in the winter they hardly grow at all. How fast a plant grows is affected by how quickly it can photosynthesise.

The word equation for photosynthesis is:

$$\text{carbon dioxide} + \text{water} \xrightarrow{\text{light}} \text{glucose} + \text{oxygen}$$

Factors that limit the rate at which a plant photosynthesises are called **limiting factors**. They include:

- how bright the light is (light intensity)
- concentration of carbon dioxide available
- temperature
- the amount of chlorophyll in the leaves.

A: Name three factors that limit the rate of photosynthesis.

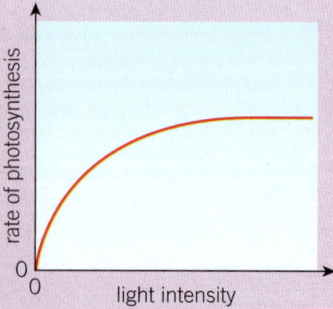

Figure 1 *The effect of light intensity on the rate of photosynthesis.*

Light

As the light intensity **increases**, the rate of photosynthesis **increases**. Photosynthesis does not happen at all in the dark.

At some point, increasing the light intensity does not increase the rate of photosynthesis any further – photosynthesis has reached its maximum rate.

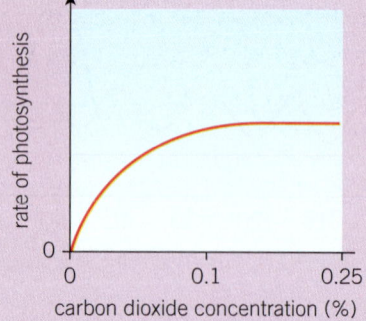

Figure 2 *The effect of carbon dioxide concentration on the rate of photosynthesis.*

Carbon dioxide

Carbon dioxide is one of the reactants for photosynthesis. The greater the carbon dioxide concentration, the faster the rate of reaction.

Eventually, photosynthesis reaches its maximum rate. At this point, increasing the concentration of carbon dioxide does not cause any further increase in the rate of photosynthesis.

Temperature

Up to a certain temperature, increasing the temperature increases the rate of photosynthesis. This is because photosynthesis involves enzymes. The higher the temperature, the faster the enzymes work.

However, if the temperature is too high the structure of the enzymes is damaged. They stop working. This means that photosynthesis no longer happens.

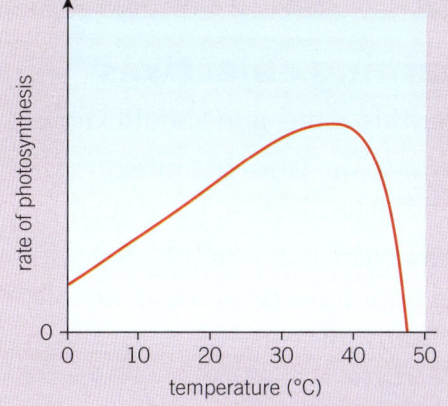

Figure 3 *The effect of temperature on the rate of photosynthesis.*

Chlorophyll

Photosynthesis happens in the **chloroplasts** of a plant cell. Chloroplasts contain a green chemical called **chlorophyll** that absorbs light from the Sun. It is the chlorophyll that makes a leaf green. The less chlorophyll in a plant's leaves, the slower the rate of photosynthesis.

Figure 4 *Some plants have leaves with large white areas. The white areas contain no chlorophyll. These areas of the leaf do not carry out photosynthesis.*

1 Choose the correct words from the box to complete the following sentences.

carbon dioxide	light	limiting	rate

Factors that limit the _____ at which a plant photosynthesises are called _____ factors. These include _____ intensity, temperature, and _____ concentration. [3 marks]

2 Suggest what would happen to the rate of photosynthesis if the weather changed from bright sunshine to cloudy. [1 mark]

3 Explain why increasing the concentration of carbon dioxide affects the rate of photosynthesis. [2 marks]

5.7 Investigating the rate of photosynthesis

Learning objectives

After this topic, you should know:

- how to measure the rate of photosynthesis of pondweed
- how to investigate the effect of light intensity on the rate of photosynthesis.

Figure 1 You can measure how much oxygen is being produced by pondweed by collecting the bubbles of gas.

Rate is a measure of how fast something is happening.

The rate at which a plant is growing can be measured by observing the rate at which it is photosynthesising. The faster a plant is photosynthesising, the faster it will be growing.

A number of factors affect how quickly a plant photosynthesises. These include:

- light intensity
- temperature
- the concentration of carbon dioxide available.

A: Give one factor that affects the rate of photosynthesis.

Measuring the rate of photosynthesis

Oxygen gas is released when plants photosynthesise. The oxygen is not easy to see as it is colourless. However, bubbles of oxygen gas can be seen if you use a plant that lives under water.

B: Why can't you see oxygen gas being given off by plants that live on land?

You can measure the rate at which a plant is photosynthesising by counting the number of oxygen bubbles produced in a set amount of time.

Investigating the effect of light intensity on the rate of photosynthesis

Step 1: Place some pondweed in a beaker of dilute sodium hydrogencarbonate solution. This solution is a source of carbon dioxide for the plant.

Step 2: Place an upside-down funnel over the pondweed.

Step 3: Fill a test tube with water. Place the test tube over the funnel. Oxygen will collect in the test tube.

Step 4: Place the beaker 50 cm away from a light source.

Step 5: Leave for 5 minutes. Then start the stopwatch.

Step 6: Count the number of bubbles produced in 1 minute.

Step 7: Repeat the experiment at different distances from the light source. For example, you could try 10 cm, 20 cm, 30 cm, and 40 cm.

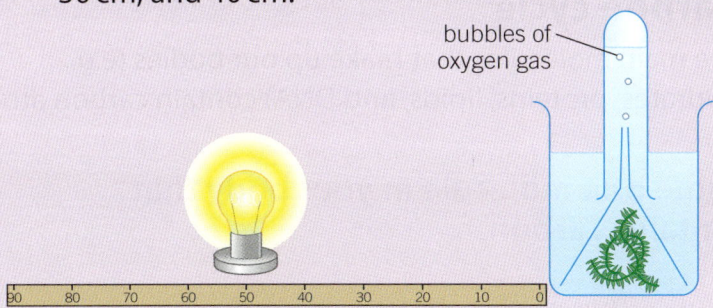

bubbles of oxygen gas

Figure 2 *Apparatus for investigating the effect of light intensity on the rate of photosynthesis.*

Changing the distance between the beaker and the light source will change the light intensity.

C: Identify the independent variable in this investigation.

You can also measure the time taken to produce a fixed volume of oxygen gas by using an upside-down measuring cylinder or a gas syringe.

1   Identify which **two** of the following methods can be used to measure the rate of photosynthesis.

   A   colour change

   B   number of bubbles

   C   temperature change

   D   volume of gas   [2 marks]

2   When investigating how light intensity affects the rate of photosynthesis, you should keep the temperature of the water constant.

   a   What type of variable is the temperature of the water?
                                                            [1 mark]

   b   Suggest why you should keep the temperature of the water the same.   [1 mark]

3   Photosynthesis requires energy from light to happen.
   Predict whether the number of bubbles produced in 1 minute will increase or decrease as the light intensity increases.   [1 mark]

5.8 The carbon cycle

All materials in the living world are recycled to provide the building blocks for other organisms in the future. Carbon is one important material that is recycled.

The carbon cycle

All of the main molecules that make up our bodies (e.g., carbohydrates, proteins, lipids, and DNA) contain carbon atoms.

A: Name **one** molecule in your body that contains carbon.

The amount of carbon on the Earth is fixed (stays the same). It can be transferred from one store to another store in the carbon cycle.

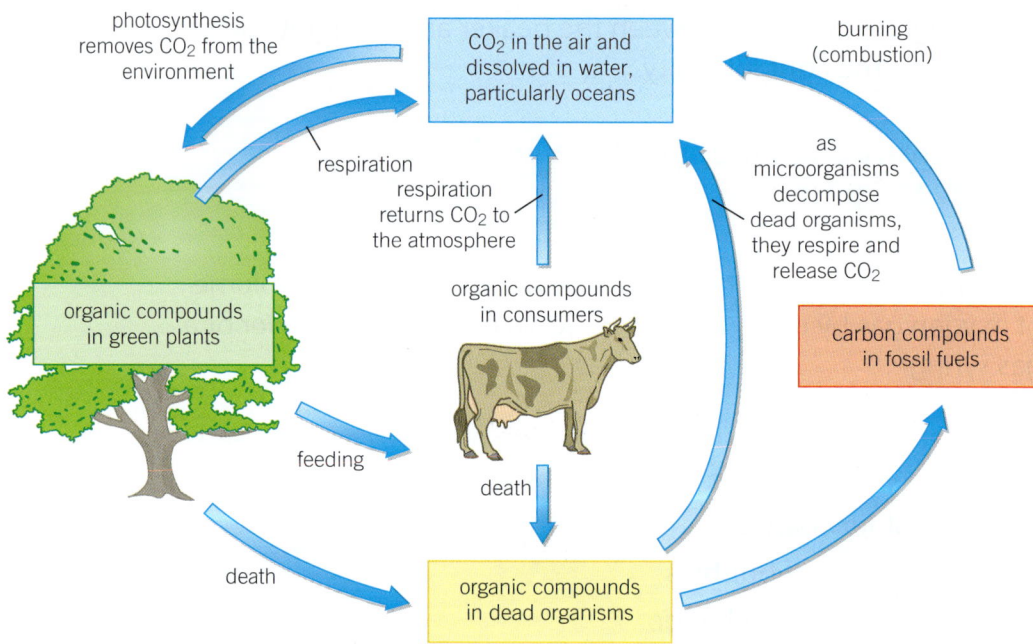

Figure 1 The carbon cycle.

How carbon is released back into the atmosphere

Respiration

All living organisms carry out respiration to transfer energy from chemical stores in food. In the process of respiration, carbon dioxide is produced and released back into the atmosphere.

Decomposition

When organisms die, decomposers break down their remains. This releases carbon dioxide into the atmosphere.

Burning fossil fuels

Some carbon is not easily accessible. It exists in carbon sinks. Fossil fuels are examples of carbon sinks. When we burn fossil fuels, we release carbon dioxide into the atmosphere. The burning of fossil fuels is called combustion.

How carbon is removed from the atmosphere

Plants and algae take in carbon dioxide from the atmosphere during photosynthesis. They use carbon dioxide and water to make glucose and oxygen. The glucose can then be used to make the materials that help plants and algae to grow.

B: Give one way carbon dioxide is removed from the atmosphere.

When animals eat plants, the carbon in the plant is transferred to the animal. Some of this carbon is used to make carbohydrates, lipids, and proteins in the animal's body. This material is then passed on to other animals when they are eaten.

1   Match each key word to the correct definition.

Key word	Definition
respiration	Burning of fossil fuels.
decomposition	Breaking down of dead organisms to release materials.
combustion	Process that transfers energy from chemical stores in food.
	[2 marks]

2   Give **three** ways in which carbon dioxide is released into the atmosphere. [3 marks]

3   Describe how plants take in carbon and then pass it on or return it to the atmosphere. [4 marks]

5 Practice questions

01 Match each key word to the correct definition.

Key word	Definition
community	The place in which an organism lives.
ecosystem	All the living organisms and physical conditions present in an area.
habitat	Group of interdependent living organisms in an ecosystem.
population	The total number of organisms of a species living in an area.

[3 marks]

02 Where in a plant cell does photosynthesis take place?

A chloroplasts

B cytoplasm

C mitochondria

D nucleus   [1 mark]

03 Complete the equation for photosynthesis by selecting the correct answer from each box.

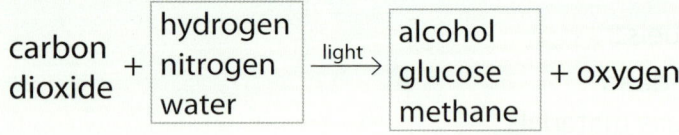

[2 marks]

04 Look at the food chain below.

rose bush → greenfly → ladybirds → spiders

04.1 Name the producer in this food chain.
[1 mark]

04.2 Name the secondary consumer in the food chain.   [1 mark]

04.3 Name the source of energy for this food chain.   [1 mark]

05 Figure 1 shows an Arctic fox.

Figure 1

Describe **two** adaptations of the Arctic fox.   [4 marks]

06.1 Describe what happens to carbon from an animal's body after it dies.   [3 marks]

06.2 Name **one** organism involved in this process.   [1 mark]

07 Figure 2 shows the main stages in the carbon cycle.

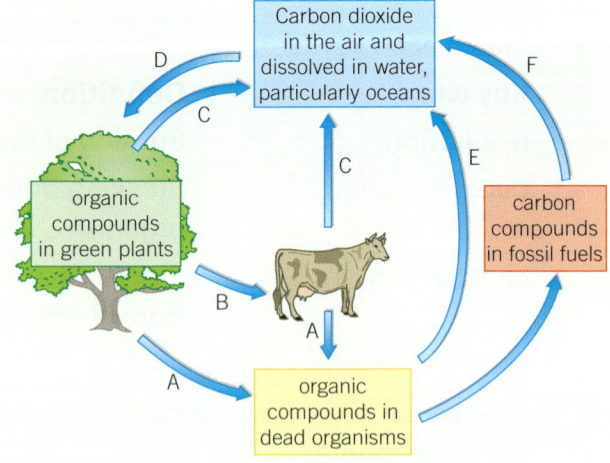

Figure 2

07.1 Which of the labels shows:

   i   death   [1 mark]

   ii respiration   [1 mark]

   iii combustion?   [1 mark]

07.2 Describe how carbon is removed from the atmosphere in the carbon cycle.

                                    [1 mark]

07.3 Name **one** carbon sink.   [1 mark]

08.1 Which graph correctly shows the effect of increasing temperature on the rate of photosynthesis?   [1 mark]

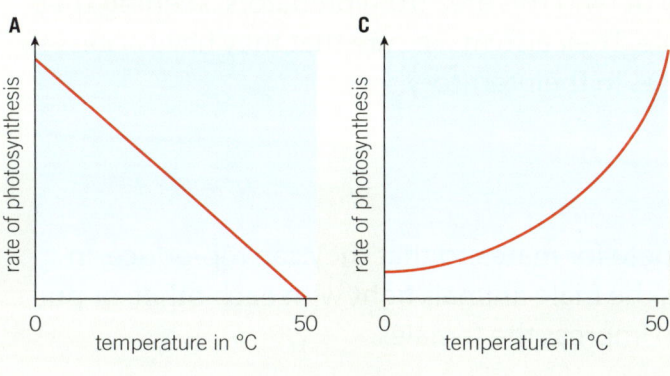

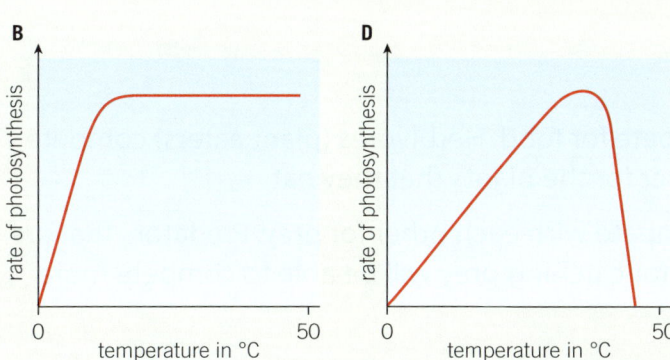

08.2 Explain the shape of the graph you have chosen.   [3 marks]

09 A student investigated the effect of light intensity on the rate of photosynthesis in pondweed. The apparatus she used is shown below.

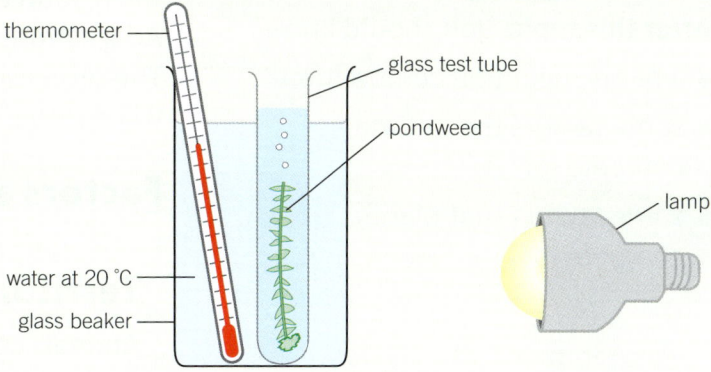

Figure 3

The student placed the lamp at different distances, from the pondweed. She counted the number of bubbles of gas released from the pondweed in one minute for each distance.

She counted the bubbles four times at each distance and calculated the mean value of her results. The student's results are shown below:

Distance in cm	Number of bubbles per minute				
	1	2	3	4	Mean
10	76	81	84	79	80
20	42	42	40	36	40
30	26	27	28	27	27
40	16	19	24	21	

09.1 Calculate the mean number of bubbles released per minute when the lamp was 40 cm from the pondweed.   [1 mark]

09.2 Using the results, suggest the relationship between light intensity and the rate of photosynthesis. Give a reason for your answer.   [3 marks]

6 Organisms and the environment
6.1 Competition

Learning objectives

After this topic, you should know:

- what is meant by competition
- some factors that animals compete for
- some factors that plants compete for.

Plants and animals have to compete with each other for the resources in a habitat. This is known as **competition**. Adaptations help an organism to compete successfully. The organisms that are best adapted to their environment will survive.

Factors animals compete for

Territory

Animals compete for space to live in. This space is called their territory. They defend this area from predators, keeping their population safe. They also make sure that they have access to all the resources in their territory.

Mates

Animals compete for mates so that they can reproduce. In many species, the male animals fight with each other, or put on displays, to impress the females.

Food

Animals compete for food. Herbivores (plant eaters) compete with each other for the plants that they eat.

Predators compete with each other for prey. Predators that are well adapted for catching prey will be able to compete more successfully.

Prey animals compete with each other to escape being eaten. They will compete more successfully if they are better adapted to avoid, escape from, or fight off predators.

Figure 1 *Male peacocks display huge, colourful tail feathers to warn off other males and attract females.*

A: What are **three** things that animals compete for?

Animals can compete with other members of their own species, and animals from other species. Only animals with the best adaptations will compete successfully. They will survive and go on to reproduce.

Factors plants compete for

Light

Trees compete by growing tall so that they can reach more light than other trees. This reduces the amount of light that reaches the plants beneath them.

These plants compete with each other for the available light. Some have very large leaves to make the most of the little light that reaches them. Other plants, such as ivy, grow up the trunks of the trees, giving them access to more light.

Nutrients and water

Plants do not compete for food. They produce their own food by photosynthesis. However, they do need nutrients for healthy growth. They get nutrients and water from the soil through their roots. The plant will be able to get more nutrients and water if its roots are spread further out.

Space

To avoid competition with their own seedlings, plants need to spread their seeds as far as possible. This is so they can gather light, water, and minerals. The seeds will have adaptations to move them away from their parent plant.

Figure 2 *The plants on the ground have to compete for the limited light that passes through the trees.*

How does the space available affect the growth of plants?
Investigate how well some seeds grow when planted close together and far apart.

B: What are four resources that plants compete for?

1 Sort the different resources into whether animals or plants compete for them.

   food   mates   nutrients in soil   space   territory

   [5 marks]

2 Match each adaptation to the resource that it helps a plant compete for.

Adaptation	Resource
Growing taller than another nearby plant.	light
	space
Growing roots deeper into the soil.	
	water [2 marks]

3 Cheetahs and lions eat the same prey species, the gazelle. Cheetahs run faster than lions. Lions are more powerful than cheetahs. Gazelles can move very quickly.

   a Which predator species is likely to be the better competitor for catching gazelles?   [1 mark]

   b Give a reason for your answer.   [1 mark]

6.2 Living and non-living factors

Learning objectives

After this topic, you should know:

- some living factors that affect communities
- some non-living factors that affect communities.

The environment is always changing. This affects the habitats of plants and animals. These changes can be caused by living or non-living factors.

Living factors

Living factors include:

- **new predators arriving**. Organisms with no defences against these predators may be wiped out

- **new competitors arriving**. If a new species arrives in a habitat, the new species may compete for food and space. This may reduce the population of species that are already there

- **food availability**. When there is plenty of food, organisms breed more. When there is little food, animals struggle to survive and often do not breed.

Living factors are also known as biotic factors.

Figure 1 *Grey squirrels are better at competing for food than red squirrels. This means that red squirrels only live in parts of the UK where grey squirrels cannot reach.*

A: What are **three** living factors that can affect organisms?

Non-living factors

Light intensity

Light is needed for photosynthesis. Most plants are more successful at surviving when there is more light available. Some plants are adapted to grow successfully in low light. For example, you often find plants with large leaves in areas of low light intensity.

Temperature

Plants grow faster in warmer temperatures because photosynthesis happens faster. Plants in cold climates tend to be small. This limits the number of animals that can survive by eating them.

Cold-blooded animals such as lizards cannot control their own body temperature. They lie in the Sun to warm themselves up.

Rainfall

Animals and plants need water to survive. If the amount of water available in a habitat changes, this will affect the ability of an animal or plant to survive. For example, a lack of rainfall could cause a drought. This may cause some animals and plants to die. Similarly, a cactus plant can die from too much water if there is a flood in a desert, where there is usually very little water.

Non-living factors are also known as abiotic factors.

B: What are three non-living factors that affect organisms?

1   Sort the following list of factors into living and non-living factors.

   competitors   predators

   rainfall   temperature   [4 marks]

2   Which of the following might happen if a new predator were introduced into a community?

   A   habitat would be destroyed

   B   population of organisms living there would decrease

   C   population of organisms living there would increase

   D   there would be more food available   [1 mark]

3   Grey squirrels are better competitors than red squirrels. What is the effect of introducing grey squirrels to an area containing red squirrels?   [1 mark]

Figure 2 A cactus is adapted to live with little water. If their habitat suddenly had lots of water, the cactus may struggle to survive.

How do you measure some non-living factors?
Use an oxygen meter to measure the concentration of dissolved water in a water-based environment. You can also record rainfall and temperature over a long period of time.

6.3 Plant distribution

Learning objectives

After this topic, you should know:

- how to use a quadrat
- why quadrats can be used to sample living organisms in an area
- how to investigate the distribution of plants in a trodden area and a non-trodden area.

The types and numbers of plants in an area is known as their distribution. You can use a **quadrat** to investigate plant distribution.

A quadrat is a square frame divided into a grid. You place it onto the ground to mark the area you are sampling. You then count the type and number of organisms in each section.

Figure 1 *Quadrats are often used to study the distribution of plants.*

A: What is the name of the piece of equipment you use to study the distribution of plants?

Using a quadrat

To study how the distribution of organisms changes across an area, samples can be taken along a line. This is known as a **transect**. Samples can be taken by placing a quadrat at fixed positions along the line.

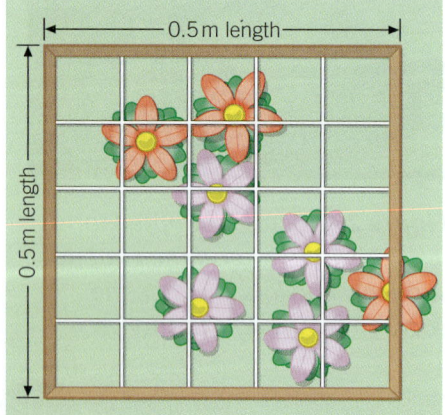

Figure 2 *When using a quadrat, you need to decide whether to count plants that are only partly within the quadrat.*

Before recording your findings, you must decide if plants that are only partly inside the quadrat should be included. For example, in Figure 2:

- if you only count flowers that are fully inside the quadrat, then the quadrat contains 6 flowers
- if you also count flowers that have some parts inside the quadrat, then the quadrat contains 7 flowers.

Whatever you decide, you must use the same rule for your whole investigation.

B: What is a transect?

You can use this method to investigate how the distribution of plants changes between a trodden area, such as a footpath, and a non-trodden area.

Investigating the distribution of plants across a footpath using a transect

Step 1: Lay a tape measure in a straight line, covering a fixed distance either side of a footpath.

Step 2: Choose the regular distance at which you will take your samples. For example, take a sample every metre.

Step 3: Place a quadrat at the first sample site.
Record the number of individual plants in the quadrat and what species they belong to.

Step 4: Record whether the area sampled is trampled, non-trampled or part-trampled.

Step 5: Repeat Steps 2 to 4 for the rest of the sampling sites.

Figure 3 *These students are investigating the distribution of plants along a transect.*

Figure 4 *Lay a tape measure across the footpath. This is your transect.*

1   Choose the correct words from the box to complete the following sentences.

number	quadrat	transect	type

You can investigate the distribution of plants in a field using a _____. You should record the _____ and _____ of plants found in each sample. You can also take samples at fixed points along a line. This is called a _____.

[3 marks]

2   Where would you expect to find a larger number of plants: in a trodden area or a non-trodden area?   [1 mark]

3   The graph in Figure 5 shows how many plants are found at three different sites A, B, and C.

Which sampling site had the greatest variety of plants?

[1 mark]

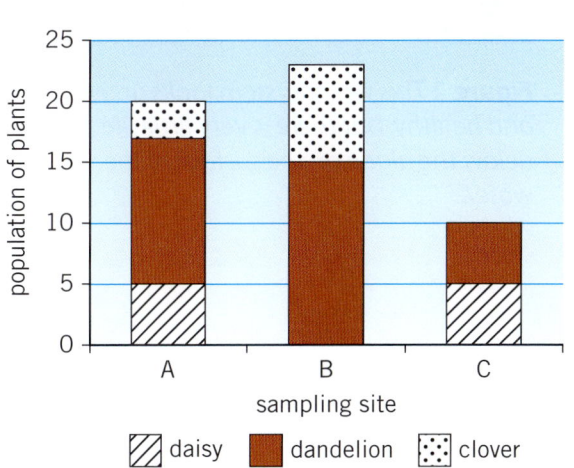

Figure 5

6.4 Pollution

Learning objectives

After this topic, you should know:

- some examples of water, air, and land pollution.

Figure 1 *A large proportion of household and industrial waste ends up in landfill sites.*

The human population is growing rapidly. Because of this, more natural resources are being used, such as foods and fuels. More waste is also being produced. This waste can pollute the land, water, and air if it is not handled properly.

Polluting the land

People can pollute the land in many different ways.

- Most household rubbish is buried in landfill sites. Not all of this material is safe, for example, household batteries contain toxic chemicals.

Many farmers use chemicals to protect their crops.

- **Herbicides** kill weeds that compete with their crops for light and space.

- **Pesticides** kill the insects that might eat the crop.

These chemicals are poisons. They can pass into food chains and kill animals.

A: What are **two** ways that humans pollute the land?

Figure 2 *This water system looks green and healthy, but there is very little life below the algae on the surface of the water.*

Polluting the water

Farmers add fertilisers to the soil. Fertilisers include nutrients that help crops to grow. Nutrients in these fertilisers can be washed into lakes and rivers.

Increased nutrients in the water causes algae and water plants to grow rapidly.

This stops light from reaching below the surface of the water, so plants below the surface die. Oxygen levels fall as the dead plants decompose. This kills other animals living in the water.

Human waste is called sewage. Untreated sewage is sometimes released into water systems. This also increases nutrient levels in water, which causes the algae to grow more.

Toxic chemicals, including pesticides and herbicides, can also be washed into lakes and rivers. These chemicals can poison animals and plants in the water.

B: What are **three** sources of water pollution?

Polluting the air

When some fuels are burnt, they release sulfur dioxide into the air. When sulfur dioxide dissolves in rainclouds, it makes the rainwater acidic. This then falls as **acid rain**.

Acid rain damages the leaves, flowers, and fruit of plants. It can also soak into the soil and damage the roots.

When acid rain falls into lakes, the water becomes slightly acidic. If the concentration of acid gets too high, plants and animals can no longer survive.

Some fuels release smoke into the air. Smoke can cause breathing problems in people.

Figure 3 *These trees have been killed by acid rain.*

How does acid rain affect plant growth?
Investigate how well plants grow in different concentrations of hydrochloric acid.

C: What is the name of the gas that causes acid rain?

1   Complete the following table by ticking the appropriate columns.

Type of pollution	Air pollution	Water pollution	Land pollution
sewage			
fertilisers			
landfill			

[3 marks]

2   Which **one** of the following is an example of a harmful effect of acid rain?

   A   builds up in food chains and causes animals to die

   B   damages tree roots

   C   kills weeds that compete with crop plants

   D   too much growth of algae on the surface of water   [1 mark]

3   What is **one** harmful effect of using pesticides?   [1 mark]

6 Checkpoint

1 Which **three** of the following are non-living factors that affect an environment?

food availability	light intensity	new competitors
new predators	rainfall	temperature

[3 marks]

2 Match each resource plants compete for to its function.

Resource	Function
light	So their leaves can capture enough light.
space	To make the chemicals they need for growth.
minerals	So they can photosynthesise and make food.

[2 marks]

3 Choose the correct word from the boxes to complete the following sentences.

acid	acidic	poisonous	sulfur dioxide	toxic	water vapour

When fossil fuels are burnt, _____ is released into the air and dissolves in the rainwater in clouds. This makes the rainwater _____. The rainwater falls as _____ rain.

[3 marks]

4 Put the following sentences in the correct order to describe how fertilisers can pollute a pond.

A Algae on the surface of the water in the pond grow rapidly.

B Therefore other animals in the pond cannot survive.

C Algae growth blocks light to plants underwater.

D Plants underwater die and microorganisms decompose them.

E Microorganisms use lots of oxygen when decomposing plants.

F Fertilisers are washed from the soil and enter the pond.

[5 marks]

5 Why do plants not need to compete for food? [1 mark]

6 In each of the following examples, what resource are the organisms competing for?

  a In a forest, many plants such as ivy climb up tree trunks. [1 mark]

  b Only foxes that are fast enough can catch their prey. [1 mark]

  c The peacocks with the most impressive tail feathers attract the peahens. [1 mark]

7 One negative effect of human population growth is using more of the Earth's natural resources. What is **one** other negative effect on the environment? [1 mark]

8 **a** What is **one** adaptation that helps an animal to survive a cold environment? [1 mark]

  b What is **one** way an animal could be affected if the temperature of their environment were to suddenly decrease? [1 mark]

6 Vocabulary builder

1   Match each chemical to the correct use of the chemical.

Chemical	Use of the chemical
herbicide	add nutrients to the soil
pesticide	kill insects
fertiliser	kill weeds

[3 marks]

2   Sort the following factors that affect an environment into living factors or non-living factors.

food availability

new predators

rainfall

temperature   [4 marks]

3   Choose the correct word from the list to identify the key word that is being described.

   a   The process by which organisms compete with each other for the resources in the environment.

   adaptation

   competition

   distribution   [1 mark]

   b   Special features that make an organism well suited to its environment.

   adaptation

   competition

   distribution   [1 mark]

   c   Where organisms are found within an environment.

   adaptation

   competition

   distribution   [1 mark]

4   Complete the following sentences about competition.

   Plants and animals compete for different r _ _ _ _ _ _ _ _.

   Animals compete for m _ _ _ _ to reproduce, food, and t _ _ _ _ _ _ _ _.

   Plants compete for l _ _ _ _ for photosynthesis and for n _ _ _ _ _ _ _ for growing.   [5 marks]

6.5 Loss of biodiversity

Figure 1 *A coral reef has a high biodiversity. There are many different species present.*

Biodiversity is a measure of the variety of different species. This could be within a particular ecosystem, or the whole Earth.

All of the species within an ecosystem are dependent on each other. As such, the removal of one species will affect others. For example, the loss of one species could mean the loss of another species' food source.

In general, the greater the biodiversity the more stable an ecosystem is. This is because the species within the ecosystem depend on many different species to survive. Therefore, if the population of one species is reduced, the other populations have other species that they can depend on for survival.

A: Define the term biodiversity.

Human activity can often cause a loss of biodiversity.

Pollution

When pollutants enter the environment, they can have an impact on the number and types of organism in an ecosystem. Generally, the more polluted an area, the fewer the species that can survive there. Biodiversity is **reduced**.

Deforestation

Deforestation is the permanent removal of large areas of forest. Removing forests provides wood for building and fuel. It also creates space for roads, buildings, and agriculture (farming).

Deforestation reduces the number of trees in an area. This in turn reduces the number of animal species. This is because their food source or home has been lost. This then affects the number of predator species that can be supported. Biodiversity is **reduced**.

B: Describe one way that deforestation can reduce biodiversity.

Agriculture

To feed the increasing human population, more land is farmed. This reduces biodiversity by:

- removing hedgerows to allow large machinery to be used. This reduces the number of plant species and destroys the habitat of animals, such as mice and hedgehogs

- using pesticides. This reduces the number of crop pest species, but also kills other insects. This removes the food source for predator species

- using herbicides. This kills plants that grow where they are not wanted. This reduces the number of plant species present in an area. Therefore, fewer animal species can be supported.

C: Give **three** ways that agriculture can result in a loss of biodiversity.

Hunting and fishing

Overfishing has significantly reduced some fish populations. Populations have been lost completely in some areas. Hunting removes a food source for other species. These species may die out as a result.

1 Choose the correct word from the box to complete the sentences.

biodiversity	deforestation	more	reduces

The variety of organisms present in an ecosystem is called _____. The greater the variety present, the _____ stable the ecosystem.

When trees are cleared to create more space for agriculture, this is called _____. This _____ the number of species present in that area. [3 marks]

2 Wolves and cougars are predators that live in Canada.

In one area, wolves prey on two different species. Cougars prey on five different species. Which predator is more likely to survive in this area? Give a reason for your answer. [2 marks]

3 a Give one way that agriculture can result in a loss of biodiversity. [1 mark]

  b Describe how the way given in question **3a** reduces biodiversity. [2 marks]

6.6 Maintaining biodiversity

Learning objectives

After this topic, you should know:

- the difference between an endangered and an extinct species
- how conservation can be used to maintain biodiversity
- how breeding programmes can be used to maintain biodiversity.

The Bengal tiger is an endangered species. It is estimated that there are only 2500 Bengal tigers left in the wild. Their numbers have been reduced by a loss of habitat and poaching.

International efforts by scientists are trying to prevent the Bengal tiger from becoming **extinct**. Extinction means that there are no individuals of this species left anywhere on Earth.

> **A: Describe what is meant by an extinct species.**

Extinction reduces biodiversity. Scientists use several techniques to try to prevent loss of biodiversity, and to increase the number of species in an area. These include **conservation** and **breeding programmes**.

Conservation

Conservation means protecting the natural environment to make sure that habitats are not lost. Protecting a habitat increases the chance that organisms living there will survive. This means the organisms can reproduce and the population can increase.

Figure 1 *The Bengal tiger is an endangered species.*

Nature reserves are areas of habitat that have been selected to conserve wildlife. These sites need to be managed by:

- using controlled grazing. Farmed animals, such as sheep, are only allowed to graze land for limited amounts of time. This gives the plant species time to recover
- restricting human access. Providing paths can help to prevent plants from being damaged by trampling. Restricting access also helps to prevent hunting
- feeding animals. In some habitats the animals are semi-wild and are provided with food. This makes sure that more organisms survive and are able to reproduce
- reintroducing a species into a habitat where it used to live.

> **B: Name two techniques that are used to conserve an organism's habitat**

Breeding programmes

Breeding programmes in zoos and aquariums aim to increase the populations of endangered species.

Scientists working on breeding programmes aim to:

- create a stable, healthy population of a species
- gradually reintroduce the species back into its natural habitat.

Unfortunately there are also problems with breeding programmes.

- Keeping enough genetic diversity can be difficult because there are not many breeding partners available.
- Organisms born in captivity may not be able to survive in the wild. For example, predators bred in captivity may not know how to hunt for food.

Figure 2 *The Wolong National Nature Reserve in China is home to around 150 giant pandas. As of 2016, giant pandas are no longer an endangered species.*

C: Give two aims of breeding programmes.

1   Match each key word to the correct definition.

Key word	Definition
extinct	Protecting a natural environment.
breeding programme	No members of a species are alive anywhere in the world.
conservation	Scheme to increase a species' population in captivity.

[3 marks]

2   Define the term conservation. [1 mark]

3   Give **two** disadvantages of using breeding programmes to maintain biodiversity. [2 marks]

6 Practice questions

01 There is competition between organisms in an ecosystem. Identify which of the following are resources that animals compete for.

food   light   mates
space to grow   **territory**   [3 marks]

02 Match each pollutant to the correct effect the pollutant can have on the environment.

Pollutant	Effect on the environment
sulfur dioxide	growth of algae
pesticide	acid rain
sewage	kills a wide range of insect life [3 marks]

03 Which of the following is an example of an abiotic (living) factor that affects communities?

  A   food availability

  B   light intensity

  C   soil pH

  D   temperature   [1 mark]

04 Suggest what would happen to a population of squirrels if a new predator was introduced into their ecosystem. Give a reason for your answer.   [2 marks]

05 Plants compete with each other for light.

05.1 Describe why plants compete for light.   [2 marks]

05.2 Describe **one** way that plants have adapted to compete in low light levels.   [1 mark]

05.3 Name **one** other factor that plants compete for.   [1 mark]

06 The growth of the human population means more food needs to be produced.

06.1 Suggest **one** other problem with an increasing human population.   [1 mark]

06.2 To increase food production, a farmer uses more pesticides.
Explain why pesticides are used.   [2 marks]

07 Give **two** ways breeding programmes increase the chance of an organism surviving and reproducing.   [2 marks]

08 Which of the following would help to conserve fish stocks in the North Sea?

  A   a ban on fishing during the breeding season

  B   a maximum hole size in fishing nets

  C   increasing the number of fish that are allowed to be caught   [1 mark]

09 Figure 1 shows a food web.

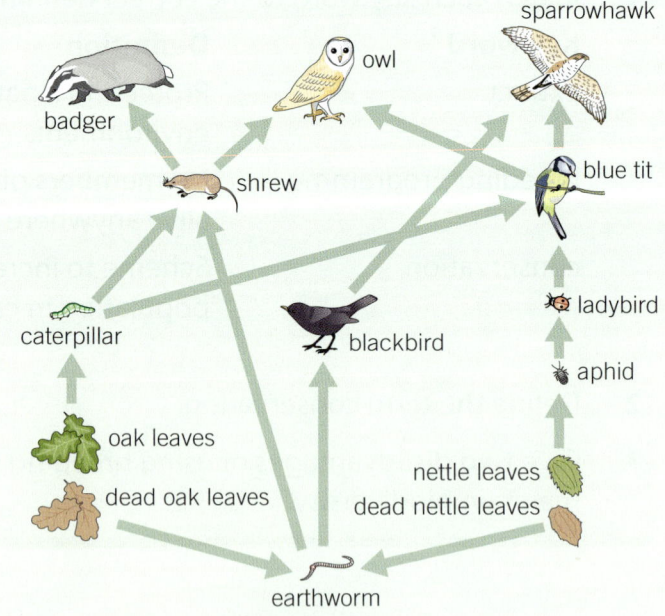

Figure 1

Explain why blue tits are more likely to survive than blackbirds.   [2 marks]

10 A student decided to investigate how the distribution of two types of a plant called plantain varied across a path that she often walked on.

ribwort plantain   greater plantain

Figure 2

The student used a quadrat that was divided into 25 squares. Each square counts for 4% of cover. They can use this quadrat to estimate the percentage cover of each type of plantain.

Figure 3 shows one of the quadrats.

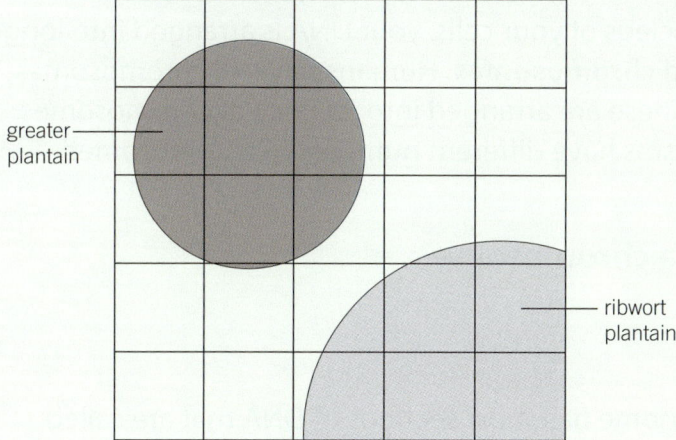

greater plantain

ribwort plantain

Figure 3

The student estimated that the percentage cover of the greater plantain is 20%

10.1 Estimate the percentage cover of ribwort plantain. **[2 marks]**

The student placed the quadrats across the path as shown in Figure 4.

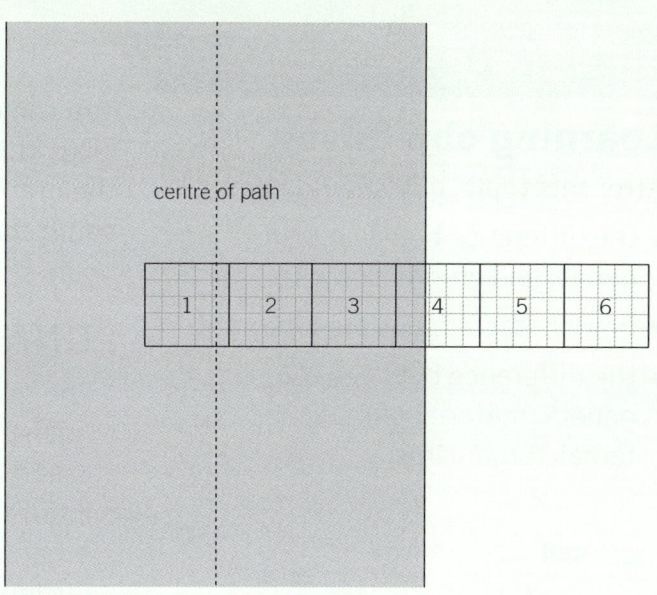

centre of path

1 2 3 4 5 6

Figure 4

10.2 Write down the name of the sampling method that measures changes across a line. **[1 mark]**

10.3 The student's results are shown in the table below. Ribwort plantain grows more on the non-trampled area. Greater plantain grows more on the trampled area.

Percentage cover	Quadrat number					
	1	**2**	**3**	**4**	**5**	**6**
ribwort plantain	2	3	14	20	29	36
greater plantain	30	28	18	5	3	2

Look back at the pictures of greater plantain and ribwort plantain in Figure 2. Greater plantain has flat leaves whereas ribwort plantain has tall leaves.

Suggest why this adaptation would make greater plantain more successful on the trampled area than ribwort plantain.

[2 marks]

7 How life developed on Earth
7.1 Genetic material

Learning objectives

After this topic, you should know:

- the difference between DNA, genes, and chromosomes
- how characteristics are inherited
- the difference between the genetic material of male and female organisms.

You can often tell that people are related because they look alike. This is because they have inherited **genetic material** from their mother and father. This material is mixed, so they gain some characteristics from each parent.

DNA

The genetic material in the nucleus of your cells is a chemical called **DNA**. DNA contains all the information needed to make an organism. DNA is stored in the nucleus of your cells.

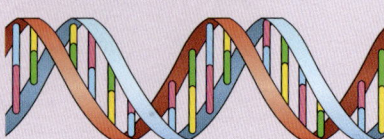

Figure 1 *DNA is a double helix.*

A: What is the chemical that makes up the genetic material in the nucleus of a cell?

Chromosomes

Inside the nucleus of your cells, your DNA is arranged into long strands called **chromosomes**. Humans have 46 chromosomes in each cell. These are arranged into 23 pairs of chromosomes. Other organisms have different numbers of chromosomes.

B: What is a chromosome?

Genes

Each chromosome has short sections of DNA that are called **genes**. Genes control the characteristics of the organism. Each chromosome contains thousands of genes. The combination of genes in an organism controls what the organism looks like and how it functions.

Inheriting genetic material

Inside the nucleus of your cells, the 46 chromosomes are arranged into 23 pairs. One chromosome of each pair comes from your mother, and the other comes from your father.

cell

nucleus containing DNA

cytoplasm

nucleus containing DNA

chromosomes

chromosome

gene

Figure 2 *The nucleus contains chromosomes, and each chromosome contains many genes. Genes are made of DNA.*

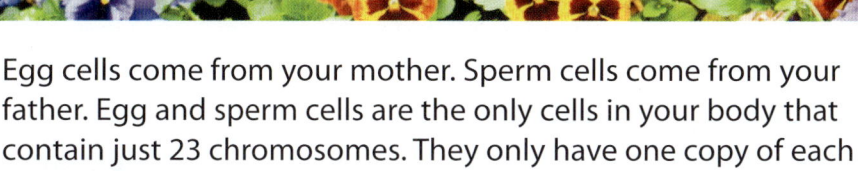

Egg cells come from your mother. Sperm cells come from your father. Egg and sperm cells are the only cells in your body that contain just 23 chromosomes. They only have one copy of each chromosome.

During fertilisation, an egg cell and a sperm cell join together and their chromosomes pair up, producing a fertilised egg cell with 46 chromosomes. This cell will then develop into a baby.

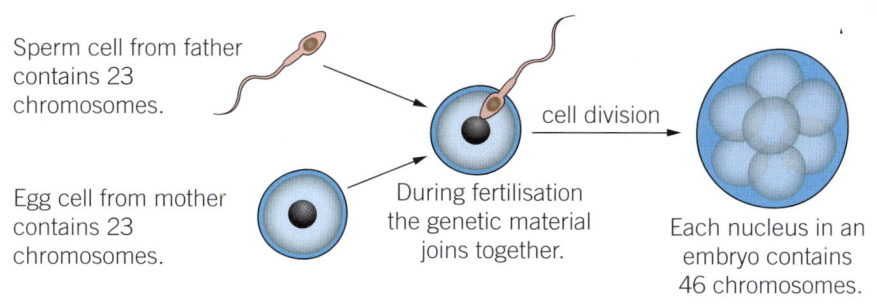

Sperm cell from father contains 23 chromosomes.

Egg cell from mother contains 23 chromosomes.

During fertilisation the genetic material joins together.

cell division

Each nucleus in an embryo contains 46 chromosomes.

Figure 3 *Half your genetic material comes from each parent.*

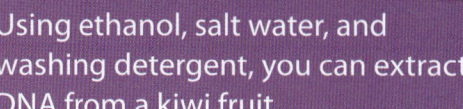

Extracting DNA from kiwi fruit
Using ethanol, salt water, and washing detergent, you can extract DNA from a kiwi fruit.

C: How many pairs of chromosomes are found in the nucleus of a normal human cell?

Sex determination

In humans, the chromosomes in one pair are known as the sex chromosomes. They contain the genes that control whether you will be biologically male or female. If your cells contain two X chromosomes (XX) you are female. If your cells contain one X chromosome and one Y chromosome (XY) you are male.

1 Match each key word to the correct definition.

Key word	Definition
genes	A chemical that genetic material is made from.
DNA	The part of the cell where DNA is found.
chromosome	The parts of a chromosome that control the characteristics of an organism.
nucleus	A long strand of DNA. [3 marks]

2 Arrange the following structures in the correct order of size from smallest to largest.

cell   chromosome   gene   nucleus   [3 marks]

3 What is the sex of a person who has the sex chromosomes XY?   [1 mark]

7.2 Asexual and sexual reproduction

Learning objectives

After this topic, you should know:

- examples of organisms that reproduce asexually and sexually
- the differences between asexual and sexual reproduction.

Figure 1 *Dogs reproduce sexually so there is variation in their offspring.*

Sexual reproduction

Humans and most animals reproduce by **sexual reproduction**. To create new offspring, a sperm cell (the male sex cell) joins with an egg cell (the female sex cell). This mixes the genetic material from the two parents. Their children (offspring) will therefore have characteristics from both parents.

For example, the puppies in Figure 1 are all from the same litter. Different characteristics will be inherited from each parent. Some of these puppies are tan coloured, like the mother shown. The darker coat of the other puppies will have come from the father.

There are three key features of sexual reproduction:

- two parents are needed
- genetic information from the parents is mixed
- offspring share some characteristics with each parent, but they are not identical to their parents. This is called **variation**.

A: How many parents are required for sexual reproduction?

Many plants also reproduce sexually. Pollen (the male sex cell) joins with an ovule (the female sex cell) to create a new seed. The seed will in grow into a plant. Each seed contains a mixture of genetic material. This means that the plant's offspring will each have slightly different characteristics.

Asexual reproduction

In a population of bacteria, all of the bacterial cells are identical. This is because when bacteria reproduce, they produce identical copies of themselves. This is **asexual reproduction**.

B: What is the name of the type of reproduction that is carried out by bacteria?

When bacteria reproduce, they make two copies of their genetic material and then divide in half. There is no mixing of genetic material. Each new bacterial cell has the same genes as the parent cell – the offspring are identical. These identical offspring are called **clones**.

There are three key features of asexual reproduction:

- only one parent is needed
- genetic material is not mixed
- offspring are identical (clones).

Many plants can also reproduce asexually. Spider plants produce long stems, known as runners, with tiny plants (called plantlets) on the end (Figure 2).

A small number of animals can also reproduce asexually, for example sea anemones and starfish.

Figure 2 *Spider plants reproduce using asexual reproduction.*

C: What is meant by a clone?

1 Sort each of the following statements by whether they describe asexual reproduction or sexual reproduction. Tick one box for each row.

	Asexual reproduction	Sexual reproduction
two parents are needed		
the genetic material is mixed		
the offspring are identical		

[3 marks]

2 a Which **one** of the following organisms reproduce asexually?

bacteria   **cats**   **humans**   [1 mark]

b Which **two** of the following organisms reproduce sexually?

bacteria   **cats**   **humans**   [2 marks]

3 Some plants can be grown from cuttings. This means taking a small section from a parent plant and replanting it. The cutting will then grow into a plant that is genetically identical to the parent plant.

Which type of reproduction is taking a cutting an example of? [1 mark]

How similar are plants that have reproduced asexually?
Investigate how similar plants are that are grown from cuttings by comparing their features.

7.3 Investigating variation

Learning objectives

After this topic, you should know:

- what is meant by variation
- some causes of variation
- how to investigate whether two characteristics are linked.

Figure 1 *Differences in characteristics within a species are known as variation.*

All the people in your class will look different from each other. These differences between members of the same species are called variation.

Some variation is inherited from parents, for example, different eye colours.

Some variation is caused by the environment, for example, scars.

Lots of characteristics are affected by the genes you inherit from your parents and by the environment. For example, your height will be partly affected by your genes and partly affected by your diet as you are growing up.

A: What are the two causes of variation?

Some characteristics are linked, for example, height and body mass – generally, the taller you are, the larger your body mass. Other characteristics are not linked, for example, your height is not linked to your hair colour. You can use the method below to investigate a possible link between any two characteristics.

Investigating whether finger length and height are linked

Step 1: Choose at least 10 people to investigate.

Step 2: Select your first person.
Measure the length of their index finger using a ruler. Then measure their height using a scale placed against a wall.

Step 3: Repeat your measurements for each person. Record your results in a table.

Step 4: Look at your results to see if there is a pattern, for example, do taller people have longer fingers?

Some characteristics can be plotted onto a scatter diagram with a line of best fit. This makes it easier to see any patterns.

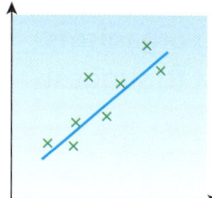

This scatter diagram shows that the two characteristics are linked. As characteristic 1 increases, characteristic 2 increases.

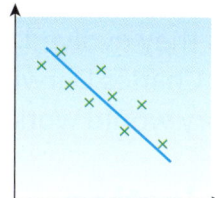

This scatter diagram shows that the two characteristics are linked. As characteristic 1 increases, characteristic 2 decreases.

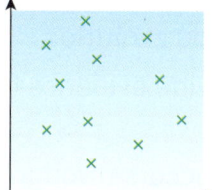

This scatter diagram shows no correlation. This means that there is no link between the characteristics.

Figure 2 *Interpreting scatter diagrams.*

B: **What would the scatter diagram look like if characteristic 1 increases as characteristic 2 decreases?**

1 Choose the correct words from the box to complete the following sentences.

environment	inherits	species	variation

Differences within a _____ are called _____. This can be caused by the genetic material a person _____, or their _____. [3 marks]

2 a Which piece of equipment could be used to measure body mass?

   A ruler   **B** scales   **C** thermometer   [1 mark]

   b Which of the following is a cause of variation in the body mass of people?

   **different arm lengths   different diets
   different hair colour**   [1 mark]

3 A student investigates whether people's height and body mass are linked.

   He finds out that the taller a person is, the greater their body mass.

   Copy the graph in Figure 3 and sketch the shape of the scatter diagram to show how these two factors are linked.   [1 mark]

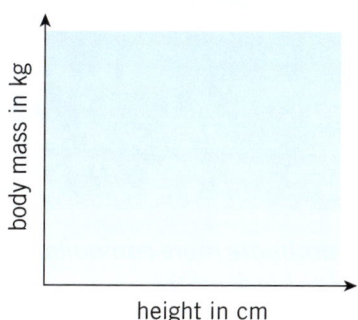

Figure 3

7.4 Evolution and natural selection

Learning objectives

After this topic, you should know:

- what is meant by evolution
- how fossils provide evidence for evolution
- how evolution occurs through the process of natural selection.

The theory of **evolution** states that all species of living organisms have evolved from simple life forms. These simple life forms were organisms made of only one cell. Over the past 3 billion years they evolved to form all of the living organisms we see today. Charles Darwin was the first scientist to suggest how this theory would work.

Natural selection

Evolution occurs because of a process called **natural selection**. In natural selection, the individuals with characteristics most suited to their environment are more likely to survive and breed.

> Within a species there is normally a range of characteristics. This variation is caused by differences in an organism's genetic material.

> The organism with characteristics that are best suited to the environment will survive and breed. Less well-suited organisms die without having bred. This is known as "survival of the fittest".

> The organisms that breed pass on their genetic material to their offspring. The offspring are more likely to have the characteristics that made the parent organism successful.

> The process is repeated many times. Over a long period of time, this can lead to the development of a new species.

Peppered moths

In the past, most peppered moths in Britain were pale coloured. This meant that they were camouflaged against trees. A few moths were black. These were easily seen by birds and so were quickly eaten. The pale moths were therefore more likely to survive and reproduce, so were more common.

In the 19th century, factories started to be built. They burnt fossil fuels and released soot. This soot turned the tree bark black. The black moths were now better camouflaged, so more of them survived. The pale moths now stood out, so were more likely to be eaten.

Figure 1 *Pale moths are more camouflaged on pale bark than black moths.*

After several years, dark peppered moths became more common in urban areas than pale moths. This is an example of natural selection.

A: Which type of peppered moth is most likely to be found in the countryside?

Fossils

Fossils are the preserved remains of animals and plants found in rocks. They provide evidence for the theory of evolution.

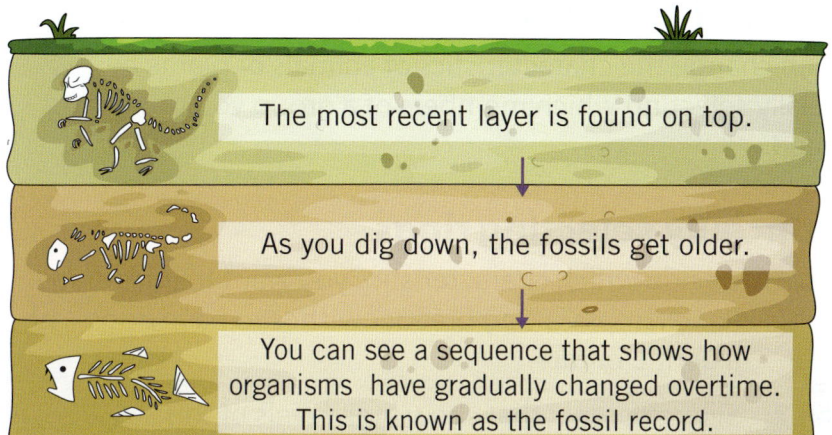

The most recent layer is found on top.

As you dig down, the fossils get older.

You can see a sequence that shows how organisms have gradually changed overtime. This is known as the fossil record.

newest

oldest

Different layers of rock contain fossils of different ages.

Fossils also let us learn about species that no longer exist, such as dinosaurs.

Figure 2 *As trees became covered in soot, black moths became camouflaged and pale peppered moths were easily seen.*

1 Choose the correct words from the box to complete the following sentences.

| billions   evolution   fossils   natural selection |

The theory of _____ states that all living things evolved from simple life forms. This happens by _____. This process has taken _____ of years. _____ provide evidence for evolution.

[3 marks]

2 Which one of the following statements about fossils is correct?

A Fossils are animals or plants that have been trapped in rocks.

B Fossils are the bones of an animal.

C Fossils are the preserved remains of animals and plants.

D Fossils are made from the soft parts of an animal. [1 mark]

3 A population of hummingbirds eats nectar found in long, thin flowers. Some individuals have long beaks and some have short beaks (Figure 3).

After 5 generations, which beak length will be the most common in the population? [1 mark]

Figure 3

7.5 Artificial selection

Learning objectives

After this topic, you should know:

- the process of artificial selection
- some examples of artificial selection.

For thousands of years, people have bred plants and animals to make breeds with particular genetic traits and characteristics.

By repeating the process over many generations, the characteristics of a breed can be changed. This is called **artificial selection**, or **selective breeding**.

A: What is meant by artificial selection?

Process of artificial selection

You can change the characteristics of animals or plants by artificially selecting which members of a group you want to breed.

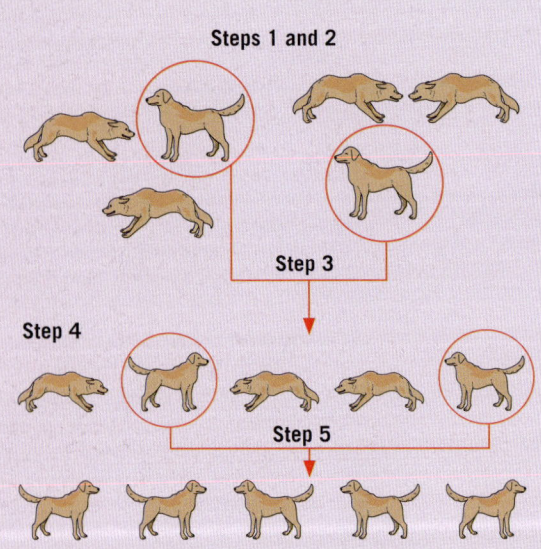

Artificially selecting dogs

Step 1: Decide which characteristics you want to encourage. For example, a dog breeder wishes to have dogs with a gentle nature.

Step 2: Select parents that show high levels of this characteristic. For example, the dog breeder would choose parent dogs that show a gentle nature.

Step 3: Breed these individuals together.

Step 4: Select the offspring that show high levels of this characteristic, and breed them.

Step 5: Repeat for many generations until the offspring all show high levels of the desired characteristic.

Artificially selecting flowers

Plants can also be artificially selected to produce varieties with particular characteristics. For example, roses have been selectively bred to produce large flowers with lots of petals.

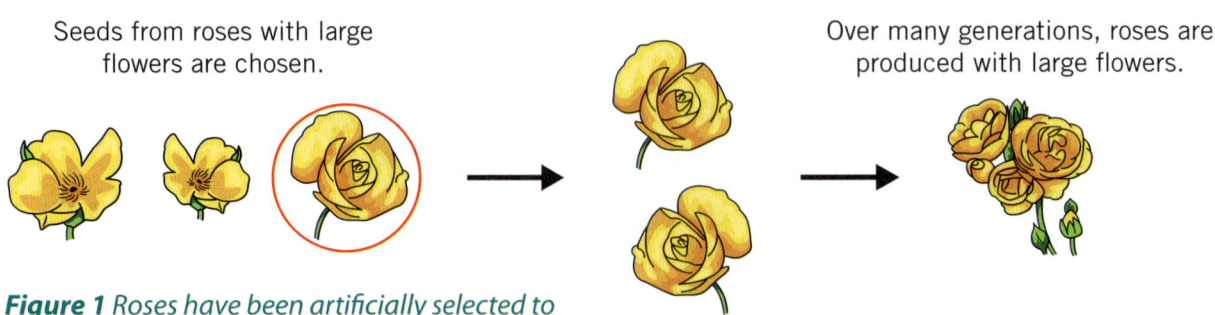

Seeds from roses with large flowers are chosen.

Over many generations, roses are produced with large flowers.

Figure 1 *Roses have been artificially selected to have large flowers with lots of petals.*

Artificially selecting crops

Sometimes an animal or plant with one desirable characteristic will be bred with another individual that has another desirable characteristic. Only the offspring showing **both** of the desired characteristics will be bred again. This allows you to artificially select for two characteristics.

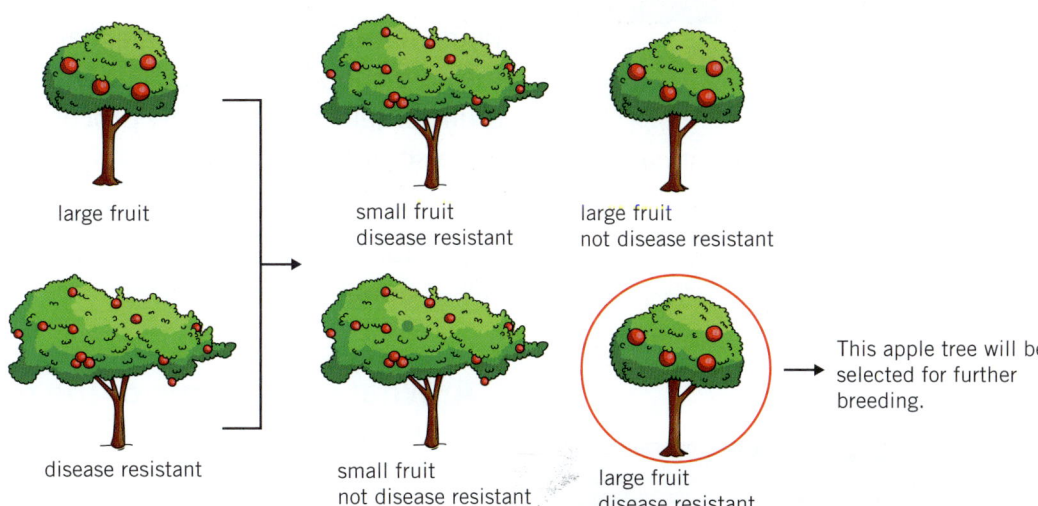

large fruit

disease resistant

small fruit
disease resistant

large fruit
not disease resistant

small fruit
not disease resistant

large fruit
disease resistant

This apple tree will be selected for further breeding.

Figure 2 By breeding plants with two different characteristics, we can produce a plant with both characteristics.

B: What happens after many generations of artificial selection for a characteristic?

1 Choose the correct words from the box to complete the following sentences.

| characteristics | generations | select |

Farmers artificially _____ organisms with desired _____ to breed. This process is repeated over many _____ until all organisms display the characteristic required. [2 marks]

2 Put the statements below into the correct order to describe how dogs might be bred for a gentle nature by selective breeding.

   A Breed the selected dogs together.

   B Select the dogs with the gentlest nature.

   C Repeat for several generations.

   D Select the offspring with the gentlest natures to breed together. [4 marks]

3 The diagram below shows four strawberry plants.

A   B   C   D

Which **two** plants should a strawberry grower breed together to make plants with **lots** of **large** fruit? [2 marks]

7.6 Genetic engineering

Learning objectives

After this topic, you should know:

- how an organism is genetically engineered
- some benefits of genetic engineering
- some risks of genetic engineering.

When farmers artificially select and breed plants and animals, they are choosing particular genes of an organism. However, artificial selection is a slow process that takes many generations. It is also not very accurate.

Scientists are now able to change an organism's genes directly to produce an organism with the desired characteristics. This is called **genetic engineering**.

A: What is the name of the technique that scientists use to change an organism's genes?

Figure 1 *This mouse glows because it has been genetically engineered to contain a gene taken from a jellyfish that glows in the dark.*

Genetically engineering an organism

To create a plant or animal with a desired characteristic, scientists 'cut out' the required genes from an organism that shows this characteristic. These foreign genes are put into cells that are at an early stage of the plant or animal's development. As the plant or animal grows, it will display the characteristics of the foreign genes.

One example of a genetically engineered organism is the frost-resistant tomato plant.

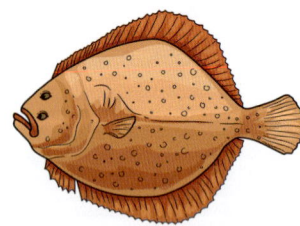

Flounder fish produce a chemical that stops their blood from freezing in the very cold water temperatures they live in.

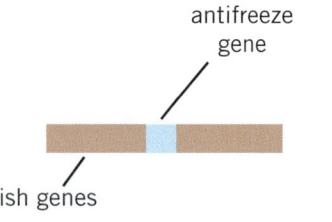

Scientists take the antifreeze gene from the flounder fish...

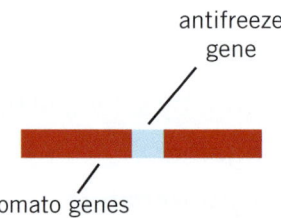

...and insert it into the DNA of tomato cells.

These cells then grow into tomato plants that can survive frost.

Figure 2 *Tomato plants can be genetically engineered to be frost-resistant.*

Benefits of genetic engineering

- Genetic engineering is a very accurate process, as single genes can be taken from one organism and added to a different species.

- It only takes one generation, so it is a quick process.

- Engineered organisms have a specific desired characteristic.

Risks of genetic engineering

- Genetically engineered crops may breed with wild plants. This could introduce foreign genes into the ecosystem. No one knows what effect this could have.

- Genetic engineering is a new science. Some people worry that we do not know what the long-term effects of eating genetically engineered foods might be.

- Some people feel that genetic engineering is unethical. They feel that scientists should not interfere with nature.

B: What is one benefit of genetic engineering?

1 Choose the correct word from the box to complete the following sentences.

characteristics   genes   genetic

Scientists can 'cut out' _____ from one organism and transfer them into the cells of another organism. This will change the organism's _____. This is called _____ engineering. [3 marks]

2 Select **two** advantages of genetic breeding over artificial selection.

less accurate   more accurate   quicker   random   slower
[2 marks]

3 What is **one** disadvantage of genetic engineering?   [1 mark]

7 Checkpoint

1 Which of the following provide evidence for evolution?

decomposers   fossils   soil types   [1 mark]

2 Choose the correct words from the box to complete the following sentences.

| billion   Charles Darwin   complex   Isaac Newton   simple   thousand |

The theory of evolution was developed by _____. It states that all species of living things have evolved from _____ life forms. Evolution has taken place over more than three _____ years.   [3 marks]

3 Complete the diagram by choosing the correct label for each letter.

| chromosome   gene   nucleus |

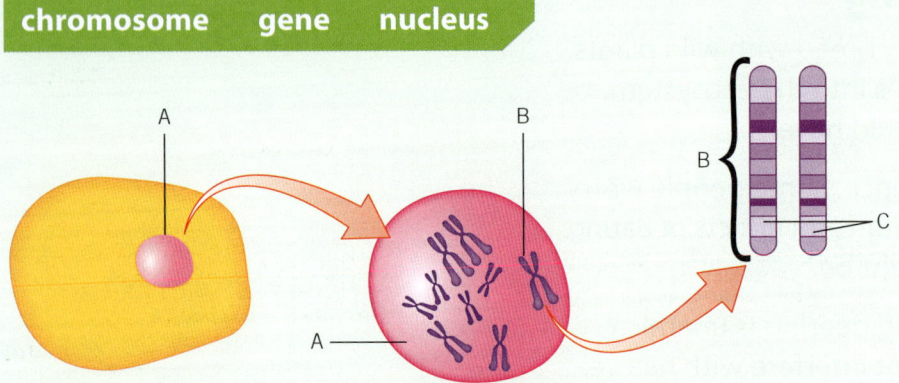

[3 marks]

4 The flow diagram shows how farmers artificially select animals. Choose the correct sentence to complete the flow chart.

> The farmer has many animals that show variation.

    ↓

> A The farmer takes the best genes from their DNA.
> B The farmer chooses animals with the best characteristics.
> C The farmer selects all of the animals.

    ↓

> The animals are bred to produce offspring.   [1 mark]

5 Dogs reproduce sexually. They have 78 chromosomes. How many chromosomes will a male dog's sperm cell contain?   [1 mark]

6 a How many chromosomes are found in a **normal** human body cell?   [1 mark]

  b How many chromosomes are found in a human **sperm** cell?   [1 mark]

  c If you have XX sex chromosomes, are you male or female?   [1 mark]

7 Vocabulary builder

1 Match each process to the correct description.

Process	Description
artificial selection	Organisms that are best suited to the environment are more likely to survive and reproduce.
genetic engineering	Humans only breed organisms with desired characteristics.
natural selection	Genes from one organism are inserted into another organism to give it a desirable characteristic.

2 marks]

2 Choose the correct term to complete these sentences on natural selection.

Natural selection is the process by which **artificial selection / evolution** takes place. The organisms that are most suited to their environment will **die / survive**. When the organisms **breed / evolve**, useful characteristics are passed on to their offspring. After **a few / many** generations, all the offspring will have the desired characteristics.

[4 marks]

3 Do the following statements describe sexual reproduction or asexual reproduction?

Tick one box for each row.

	Asexual reproduction	Sexual reproduction	
two parents needed			[1 mark]
offspring are clones of parents			[1 mark]
offspring have inherited genetic information from both parents			[1 mark]
the runners produced by spider plants use this type of reproduction			[1 mark]

4 Choose the correct term from the list to identify the key term that is being described.

a Plant and animal remains or traces that are preserved in rock

   bones   fossils   skeleton   [1 mark]

b Name given to differences within a species

   mutations   range   variation   [1 mark]

c type of reproduction performed by animals

   asexual   replication   sexual   [1 mark]

5 Complete the following sentences about genetic material.

a A section of DNA that codes for a characteristic is called a g _ _ _.

b A strand of DNA is called a c _ _ _ _ _ s _ _ _.

c DNA is found in the n _ _ _ _ _ _.   [3 marks]

7.7 Dominant and recessive alleles

Learning objectives

After this topic, you should know:

- some dominant and recessive characteristics
- the difference between dominant and recessive alleles
- the difference between homozygous and heterozygous individuals.

Your cells carry two versions of each gene. One version of the gene comes from your mother and the other one from your father. These two copies may be the same, for example, you may inherit two genes for blue eyes. You would therefore have blue eyes.

However, you may inherit two different versions of the eye colour gene. These different versions of a gene are called **alleles**. For example, you may inherit the allele that codes for blue eyes from your mother, and the allele for brown eyes from your father.

A: Define the term allele.

Dominant alleles

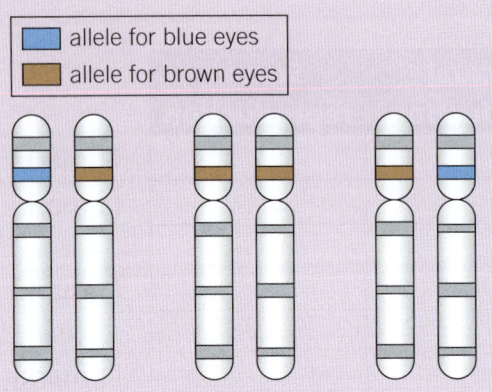

Figure 1 *All these pairs of alleles will give brown eyes.*

Some alleles will always produce a characteristic if they are in an organism's genetic material. These are called **dominant alleles**. Only one copy of a dominant allele is needed for the characteristic to be expressed (shown) in the organism.

The allele for brown eye colour is an example of a dominant allele. If you inherit a copy of this allele you will have brown eyes. It doesn't matter what the other allele is.

Recessive alleles

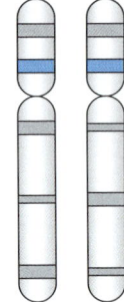

Figure 2 *You will only have blue eyes if you have two copies of the allele for blue eyes.*

The allele for blue eye colour is an example of a **recessive allele**. This characteristic is only expressed if you have two copies of the allele. Therefore, to have blue eyes you must inherit the allele that codes for blue eyes from both of your parents.

B: How many copies of a recessive allele are needed for it to be expressed?

Recording characteristics

Scientists represent different alleles using letters. The dominant allele is shown with a capital letter. The recessive allele is shown using the same letter in lower case.

For example, we use 'B' to represent the dominant allele for brown eye colour and 'b' to represent the recessive allele for blue eye colour.

The combination of alleles present in an organism is known as its **genotype**. The characteristic that an organism displays is known as its **phenotype**.

There are three genotypes for eye colour:

- BB – This individual is **homozygous** for the characteristic. They have two copies of the same allele. Both alleles are for brown eye colour. The individual will have brown eyes.

- bb – This individual is also homozygous. They are homozygous recessive. Both alleles are for blue eye colour. The individual will have blue eyes.

- Bb – This individual is **heterozygous**. They have two different alleles for eye colour. The brown allele is dominant, so the individual will have brown eyes.

C: Identify whether the genotype Bb is homozygous or heterozygous.

1 Choose the correct words from the box to complete the following sentences.

alleles	dominant	recessive	two

Different versions of the same gene are called _____ . _____ alleles will always be expressed if they are present. _____ alleles will only be expressed if _____ copies are present.   [3 marks]

2 Describe the difference between a person who is homozygous for a characteristic and a person who is heterozygous for the same characteristic.   [2 marks]

3 Having freckles (F) is a dominant characteristic. Not having freckles (f) is a recessive characteristic.

Identify whether people with the following genotypes have freckles.

a FF   [1 mark]

b ff   [1 mark]

c Ff   [1 mark]

7.8 Genetic crosses

Learning objectives

After this topic, you should know:

- how to use a Punnett square to show the results of fertilisation
- how to complete a genetic cross to show how sex is inherited
- how to complete a genetic cross to show the likelihood of a characteristic being inherited.

Figure 1 *Will the offspring of these mice be white or black?*

You can work out the possible characteristics of any offspring by looking at how the parents' alleles might combine. You can model genetic crosses using a simple table, called a Punnett square.

A: What is a Punnett square used for?

Using a Punnett square

You can use a Punnett square to work out the possible fur colours of the offspring produced by a homozygous black male mouse breeding with a white female mouse.

Step 1: What is the **phenotype** of both parents?

  black fur (male) × white fur (female)

Step 2: What is the **genotype** of both parents?

Black fur is the dominant characteristic, so white fur is recessive. The male is **homozygous**, so he has two alleles that are the **same**. As the female has white fur, both her alleles must be for the recessive white fur.

  BB × bb

  (male)   (female)

Step 3: Use a Punnett square to work out all the ways that the alleles could pair up in the offspring.

The possible alleles from one parent are written across the top of the square, and the alleles from the other parent are written down the side.

		Father	
		B	**B**
Mother	**b**		
	b		

Step 4: Use the Punnett square to work out all the possible pairings of alleles in the offspring.

		Father	
		B	**B**
Mother	**b**	Bb	Bb
	b	Bb	Bb

Step 5: Work out the proportion of each genotype that is likely to be produced.

All of the possible genotypes are Bb.

130

Step 6: Give the phenotype for each of the possible genotypes.

All of the offspring will have black fur.

Sex inheritance

Sex is determined by one pair of chromosomes. If you have two X chromosomes you are female. If you have one X chromosome and one Y chromosome, you are male.

The genetic cross in Figure 2 shows the likelihood of having a male or a female child.

Table 1 You can also express a probability as a ratio, percentage, or fraction.

Probability	Ratio	Percentage	Fraction
4 in 4	4:0	100%	1
3 in 4	3:1	75%	$\frac{3}{4}$
2 in 4 (or 1 in 2)	1:1	50%	$\frac{1}{2}$
1 in 4	1:3	25%	$\frac{1}{4}$

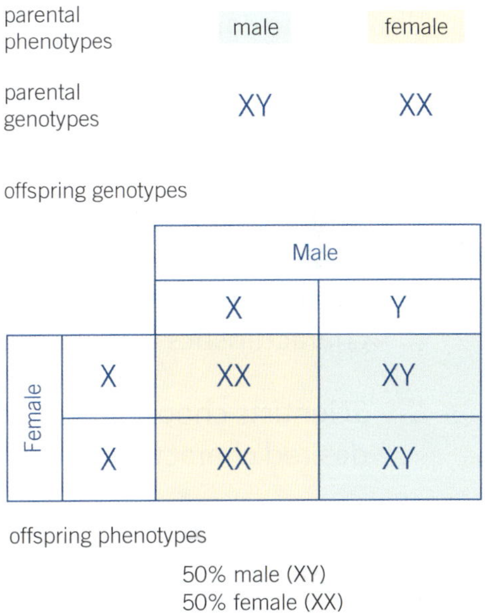

B: What is the likelihood that a couple will have a boy?

1 Match each key word to the correct definition.

Key word	Definition
phenotype	Diagram used to show the possible combinations of alleles.
genotype	The alleles present in an individual for a characteristic.
Punnett square	The characteristic that an organism displays. [2 marks]

2 The allele for freckles is dominant. Two parents have freckles. They are both heterozygous.

a Complete the Punnett square to show the possible combinations of alleles in the offspring of these parents.

		Father	
		F	f
Mother	f		
	f		

[2 marks]

b Write down the genotype of a child who does not have freckles. [1 mark]

c Work out the likelihood that a child of these parents will have freckles. [1 mark]

parental phenotypes   male   female

parental genotypes   XY   XX

offspring genotypes

		Male	
		X	Y
Female	X	XX	XY
	X	XX	XY

offspring phenotypes

50% male (XY)
50% female (XX)

Figure 2 At each pregnancy there is a 50:50 chance of having a boy or a girl. In large populations this will result in equal numbers of boys and girls.

7 Practice questions

01 Choose the correct word from the box to complete the following sentences.

> cell   chromosomes   DNA
> genes   nucleus

Your genetic information is stored on a long molecule called _____. This is arranged into long strands called _____. Small sections of these molecules are called _____, which contain the information to produce a characteristic.

[3 marks]

02 Choose the correct statements to complete the missing stages in the flow diagram describing the process of natural selection.

A All organisms in the species have the well-adapted characteristic.

B Organisms with well-adapted characteristics survive and reproduce.

C Scientists choose the genes for the desired characteristic.

> Organisms within a species show variation.
>
> ↓
>
> [ ]
>
> ↓
>
> Genetic material for this characteristic is passed on to their offspring.
>
> ↓
>
> The process is repeated many times.
>
> ↓
>
> [ ]

[2 marks]

03 Which of the following statements describes variation?
  A altering an organism's genes
  B changes in species over time
  C differences in characteristics within a species
  D when no more individuals of a species are left anywhere in the world [1 mark]

04 Which **two** of the following statements describe sexual reproduction?
  A clones are produced
  B genetic material is mixed
  C identical offspring are produced
  D two parents are needed [2 marks]

05 Genes from bacteria can be put into wheat to make it resistant to insects.

05.1 Name this process. [1 mark]

05.2 Suggest why this is beneficial to the wheat. [1 mark]

05.3 Give one possible risk of this technique. [1 mark]

06 If you dig up a strawberry plant, it will often have many other small strawberry plants attached to it. These are called plantlets. Plantlets can be removed from the parent plant and grown to full sized plants.

06.1 Name this type of reproduction. [1 mark]

06.2 Suggest **one** reason why a farmer may wish to grow strawberry plants from plantlets. [1 mark]

06.3 Strawberry plants can also be grown from seeds.

Suggest **one** reason why a farmer may prefer to grow strawberry plants from seeds. [1 mark]

07 Variation between individuals may be due to inherited genes, environmental factors, or both. Complete the table to show the cause of each type of variation.

Variation	Cause		
	Environ-mental	Inherited	Combination of both
eye colour			
height			
pierced ears			

[3 marks]

08 Normal human body cells contain 23 pairs of chromosomes. The 23rd pair determines the sex of the human.

08.1 Describe the difference between male and female sex chromosomes. [2 marks]

08.2 Complete the Punnett square to show the inheritance of sex.

		Male chromosomes (in sperm cell)	
		X	Y
Female chromosomes (in egg cell)	X		
	X		

[2 marks]

08.3 A couple have three children. They are all boys. Use your Punnett square to predict the probability that their fourth child would be a girl. [1 mark]

09 Wild sheep are small, light, and temperamental. They usually produce one lamb each year. Modern, farmed sheep have different characteristics.

09.1 Name the process that has been used to produce modern sheep from wild sheep. [1 mark]

09.2 Suggest **one** feature that farmers have bred for in modern sheep to make them more useful to us. Describe why this feature is an advantage. [2 marks]

09.3 Describe how farmers produced sheep with the characteristic given in **09.2**. [4 marks]

10 In peas the green phenotype (G) is dominant to the yellow phenotype (g).

10.1 Identify the allele that will always be expressed in this phenotype if it is present. [1 mark]

10.2 Complete the Punnett square for a cross between two heterozygous green pea plants.

	G	g
G		
g		

[2 marks]

10.3 Give the **two** possible combinations of alleles that will result in a green pea plant. [2 marks]

10.4 What is the probability of an offspring being homozygous recessive? [1 mark]

11 On average, a man releases around 250 000 000 sperm cells during sexual intercourse.

11.1 What is this number in standard form?

A 2.5×10^8

B 2.5×10^{-8}

C 25×10^7

D 250×10^6 [1 mark]

11.2 What percentage of these sperm cells will contain an X chromosome? [1 mark]

Chemistry

Every element is made up of only one type of atom. An atom is the smallest part of an element that can exist. All of the atoms in an element are the same as each other, but different to the atoms in a different element.

Q How many elements are in a gold ring?

A mixture contains two or more elements or compounds, but the particles of different substances in a mixture have not joined together. You can change the amount of different substances in a mixture.

For example, pink paint is a mixture of many substances including red and white pigments.

Q Are the elements in a mixture chemically joined?

Two or more elements can join together during a chemical reaction to form a new substance.

You cannot vary the amount of each element in a compound. For example, water is a compound made of hydrogen and oxygen.

Q What must happen to join two elements together to make a compound?

Component 3
Elements, compounds, and mixtures

Elements

Everything in the Universe is made of tiny particles called atoms. There are around 100 different types of atom and each type is called an element.

Elements are shown in the Periodic table.

Mixtures

A mixture is a made of two or more different types of elements or compounds. The different substances that make up a mixture are not joined together.

Mixtures can be separated by several different methods, including filtration, distillation, crystallisation, and chromatography.

Compounds

When two or more elements are joined by chemical bonds they create a new substance. This substance is a compound. Elements are joined together to make a compound during a chemical reaction.

Entry Level Certificate

Learning objectives

After this topic, you should know:

- what an atom is
- what an element is
- what the periodic table is.

All substances are made up of **particles** called **atoms**. Atoms are so small that you cannot see them with your eyes, but you can imagine them. You can picture atoms being like tiny balls, as shown in Figure 1.

Figure 1 *This is a model of a solid. Its atoms are like tiny balls that are all touching and vibrating (shaking).*

A: What do we call the particles that make up all substances?

You are made up of atoms too. Atoms are so small that it takes billions of them to make just one person.

An **element** is a substance that is made of only one type of atom. An atom is the smallest part of an element that can exist on its own. All elements are listed in the **periodic table**. There are about 100 elements that occur naturally.

non-metals

1	2											3	4	5	6	7	0
							1 **H** hydrogen 1										4 **He** helium 2
7 **Li** lithium 3	9 **Be** beryllium 4		key relative atomic mass **atomic symbol** name atomic (proton) number									11 **B** boron 5	12 **C** carbon 6	14 **N** nitrogen 7	16 **O** oxygen 8	19 **F** fluorine 9	20 **Ne** neon 10
23 **Na** sodium 11	24 **Mg** magnesium 12											27 **Al** aluminium 13	28 **Si** silicon 14	31 **P** phosphorus 15	32 **S** sulfur 16	35.5 **Cl** chlorine 17	40 **Ar** argon 18
39 **K** potassium 19	40 **Ca** calcium 20	45 **Sc** scandium 21	48 **Ti** titanium 22	51 **V** vanadium 23	52 **Cr** chromium 24	55 **Mn** manganese 25	56 **Fe** iron 26	59 **Co** cobalt 27	59 **Ni** nickel 28	63.5 **Cu** copper 29	65 **Zn** zinc 30	70 **Ga** gallium 31	73 **Ge** germanium 32	75 **As** arsenic 33	79 **Se** selenium 34	80 **Br** bromine 35	84 **Kr** krypton 36
85 **Rb** rubidium 37	88 **Sr** strontium 38	89 **Y** yttrium 39	91 **Zr** zirconium 40	93 **Nb** niobium 41	96 **Mo** molybdenum 42	[98] **Tc** technetium 43	101 **Ru** ruthenium 44	103 **Rh** rhodium 45	106 **Pd** palladium 46	108 **Ag** silver 47	112 **Cd** cadmium 48	115 **In** indium 49	119 **Sn** tin 50	122 **Sb** antimony 51	128 **Te** tellurium 52	127 **I** iodine 53	131 **Xe** xenon 54
133 **Cs** caesium 55	137 **Ba** barium 56	139 **La*** lanthanum 57	178 **Hf** hafnium 72	181 **Ta** tantalum 73	184 **W** tungsten 74	186 **Re** rhenium 75	190 **Os** osmium 76	192 **Ir** iridium 77	195 **Pt** platinum 78	197 **Au** gold 79	201 **Hg** mercury 80	204 **Tl** thallium 81	207 **Pb** lead 82	209 **Bi** bismuth 83	[209] **Po** polonium 84	[210] **At** astatine 85	[222] **Rn** radon 86
[223] **Fr** francium 87	[226] **Ra** radium 88	[227] **Ac*** actinium 89	[261] **Rf** rutherfordium 104	[262] **Db** dubnium 105	[266] **Sg** seaborgium 106	[264] **Bh** bohrium 107	[277] **Hs** hassium 108	[268] **Mt** meitnerium 109	[271] **Ds** darmstadtium 110	[272] **Rg** roentgenium 111	[285] **Cn** copernicium 112	[286] **Nh** nihonium 113	[289] **Fl** flerovium 114	[289] **Mc** moscovium 115	[293] **Lv** livermorium 116	[294] **Ts** tennessine 117	[294] **Og** oganesson 118

metals

Figure 2 *The periodic table is a table of all the elements. Metals are on the left of the red line and non-metals are on the right.*

Metals are usually grey solids at room temperature, and they look shiny. They are found on the left of the periodic table. Most elements are metals.

Non-metals are found on the right of the periodic table. Non-metals can be solids, liquids, or gases at room temperature.

B: Are most elements metals or non-metals?

Patterns in the periodic table

Each column of the periodic table is called a **group**. Elements in the same group have similar properties to each other. This means that they react in a similar way.

For example, sodium and potassium are both in Group 1. They both react with water in a similar way.

C: What is each column in the periodic table called?

Figure 3 *The Group 2 metals all have similar properties.*

1   Choose the correct words from the box to complete the following sentence.

> **elements   table**

The periodic _____ is a list of all the _____.

[1 mark]

2   Choose the correct words to complete the sentences.
In the periodic table, metals are found on the **left / right** and non-metals are found on the **left / right**. [2 marks]

3   What do elements in the same group have in common?

[1 mark]

8.2 Groups in the periodic table

Learning objectives

After this topic, you should know:

- what a group and a period are in the periodic table
- the names of Group 1 and Group 7
- that elements in the same group have similar properties.

All the elements are listed in the periodic table. The columns in the periodic table are called **groups** and the rows in the periodic table are called **periods**.

Elements in the same group have similar chemical properties to each other. This means they carry out similar chemical reactions.

A: What is a group in the periodic table?

Group 1 elements are called the alkali metals. They are the first column on the left of the periodic table. They are reactive metals and all have similar chemical properties to each other.

Group 7 elements are called the halogens and are found on the right of the periodic table. They are reactive non-metals and all have similar chemical properties to each other.

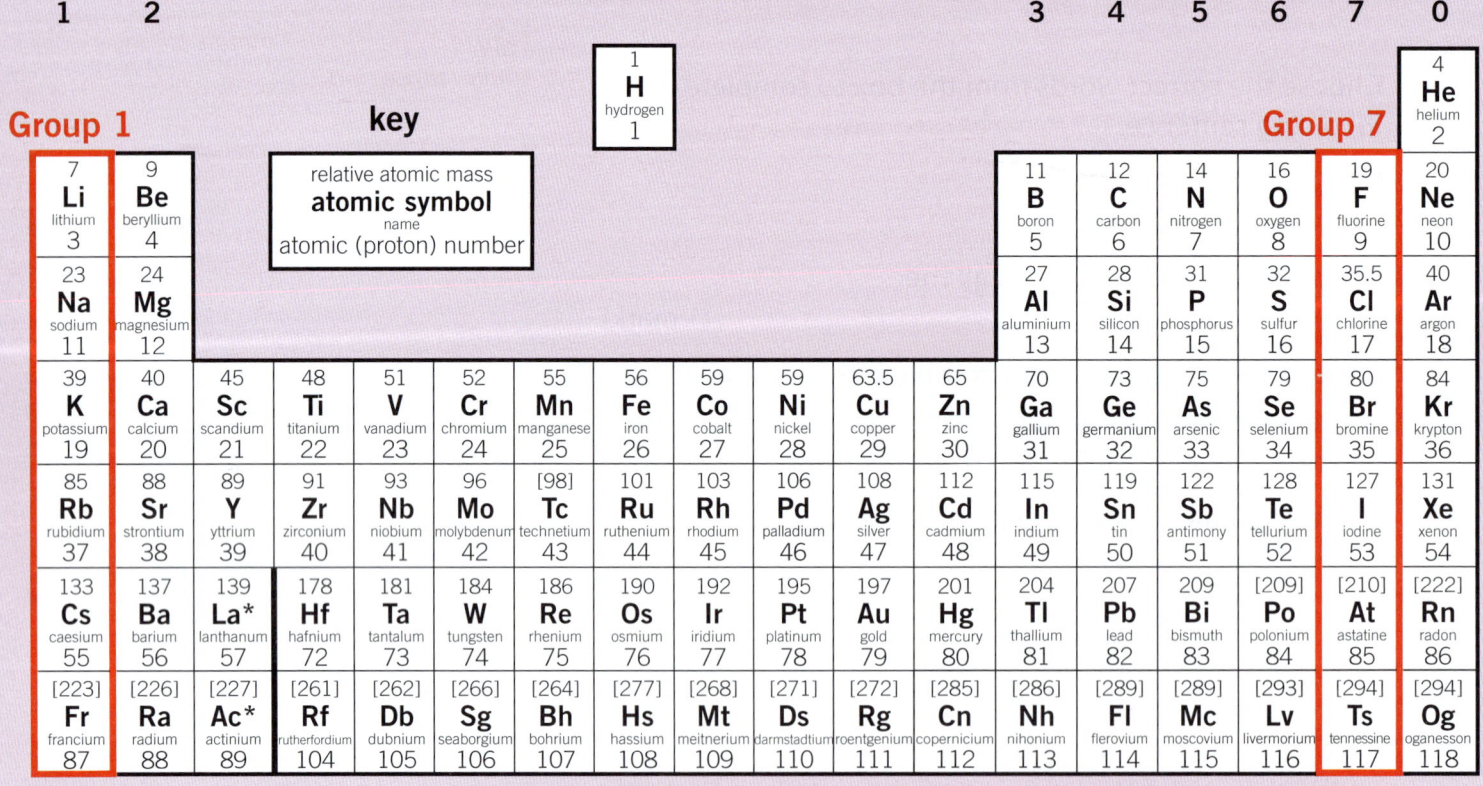

Figure 1 *The vertical columns of the periodic table are called groups. All of the elements in a group have similar properties.*

Lithium and potassium are both metals in Group 1. They react with water to make hydrogen gas. You know a reaction is happening because you can hear fizzing and see bubbles of gas being made. Their reactions are similar but not exactly the same. When potassium reacts with water, it gives off gas a lot more quickly than lithium as it is more reactive.

lithium   **potassium**

Figure 2 Both lithium and potassium react with water in similar ways. However, potassium reacts faster and fizzes a lot more than lithium.

B: What would you see if you put a piece of a Group 1 metal into water?

1   Choose the correct words from the box to complete the following sentences.

   groups   periods   properties

   The columns in the periodic table are called _____. The rows of the periodic table are called _____. Elements in the same group have similar chemical _____ to each other.   [3 marks]

2   Choose the correct words to complete the sentences.

   Group 1 elements are **reactive / unreactive** metals.
   Group 7 elements are reactive **metals / non-metals**.
   Group 7 elements are found on the **left / right** of the periodic table.   [3 marks]

3   Using the periodic table in Figure 1, which three of the following are Group 7 elements?

   **chlorine   iodine   fluorine   sodium
   oxygen   lithium**   [3 marks]

8.3 Making compounds

Learning objectives

After this topic, you should know:

- what a compound is
- the elements that make up a simple compound
- how to describe a chemical reaction.

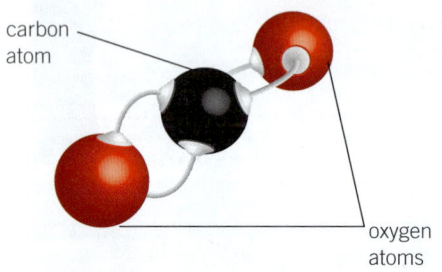

carbon atom

oxygen atoms

Figure 1 *Carbon dioxide is a compound made from carbon joined to oxygen.*

How do different metals react with acids?

Investigate how different metals, such as magnesium, zinc, and copper, react with hydrochloric acid. You could measure how much gas is produced in the reaction.

When atoms of different elements are joined together, they are called **compounds**. Compounds are made in chemical reactions when the atoms of different elements join together.

Some compounds are made from two non-metals reacting together. For example, carbon dioxide is made from carbon and oxygen atoms (Figure 1).

A: Which elements are joined together to make carbon dioxide?

Some compounds are made from a metal and a non-metal joining together. For example, sodium can react with chlorine to make sodium chloride.

B: Which elements are in sodium chloride?

Chemical reactions

Compounds are made in **chemical reactions**. New substances are always made in chemical reactions. The new substance is made because the atoms are rearranged and join together in new ways. The number and types of atoms always stay the same.

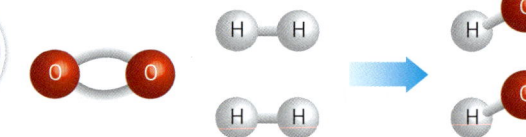

Figure 2 *Water is formed when oxygen reacts with hydrogen. The oxygen atoms and hydrogen atoms are rearranged in the chemical reaction.*

Word equations

Chemical reactions can be described with **word equations**. The starting chemicals are called **reactants**. The new chemical substances that are made are called **products**. The reactants are written first, then an arrow, and finally the products.

reactants → products

For example, lithium reacts with oxygen to form the compound lithium oxide. The word equation for this chemical reaction is:

lithium + oxygen → lithium oxide

C: Hydrogen reacts with oxygen to form water. Write a word equation for this reaction.

Naming compounds

Compounds are named after the elements that they are made up of.

When a compound is made of a metal and a non-metal, you write the name of the metal first. The name of the **metal stays the same** in the name of the compound.

The name of the **non-metal changes** in the compound. The end of the non-metal name will often become **-ide** if it is the only non-metal in the compound. For example, a compound made from magnesium and oxygen would be called magnesium ox**ide**.

Some compounds are made of more than two elements. If an element has a metal, a non-metal, and oxygen, then the end of its name often becomes **-ate**. For example, a compound made from lithium, sulfur, and oxygen would be called lithium sulf**ate**.

So, the name of a compound made from sodium and sulfur would be sodium sulfide. A compound made from sodium, sulfur, and oxygen would be called sodium sulfate.

Table 1 Naming compounds.

Non-metal element(s)	End of name in compound
oxygen	oxide
sulfur	sulfide
chlorine	chloride
bromine	bromide
sulfur and oxygen	sulfate
nitrogen and oxygen	nitrate

D: What is the name of a compound that contains sodium, nitrogen, and oxygen?

1   Match each key word to the correct definition.

Key word	Definition
element	Made of more than one type of atom chemically joined together.
word equation	Made up of only one type of atom.
compound	A summary of a chemical reaction. [2 marks]

2   Which of the following elements are found in magnesium sulfate?

magnesium   nitrogen   sodium   sulfur   oxygen

[3 marks]

3   Complete the word equation for the reaction between sodium and chlorine.

sodium _____ chlorine → _____ _____   [3 marks]

8 Checkpoint

1   Choose the correct words from the box to complete the following sentences.

> **element**　　**group**　　**metals**　　**non-metals**　　**period**

　　a   An _____ contains only one type of atom.　　　　　　　　　　　　　　　[1 mark]

　　b   A _____ is a horizontal row of elements in the periodic table.　　　　　[1 mark]

　　c   The elements in Group 7 of the periodic table are _____.　　　　　　　　[1 mark]

2   Choose the correct words to complete the following sentences.

　　a   Metals are **compounds / elements** that are found on the **left / right** of the
　　　　periodic table. Metals are **dull / shiny** in appearance and are **good / poor**
　　　　conductors of thermal energy and electricity.　　　　　　　　　　　　　　[4 marks]

　　b   Word equations are used to show what happens when the **products / reactants**
　　　　in a chemical reaction form the **products / reactants**. The two sides of the
　　　　equation are linked by the following symbol: = / →.　　　　　　　　　　　[3 marks]

3   The element oxygen is a gas at room temperature.

　　Which **two** statements about oxygen are correct?

　　A   Oxygen is shiny.

　　B   Oxygen is a non-metal.

　　C   Oxygen contains oxygen atoms only.

　　D   Oxygen reacts with other elements to form compounds called bromides.

　　E   Oxygen is found on the left-hand side of the periodic table.　　　　　　　[2 marks]

4   Complete the table.

Name of compound	Elements present
hydrogen bromide	
	lithium and chlorine
magnesium sulfate	

[6 marks]

5   Oxygen reacts with magnesium.

　　a   Complete the word equation for the reaction.

　　　　magnesium + oxygen → _____　　　　　　　　　　　　　　　　　　　　[1 mark]

　　b   Complete the sentence:

　　　　In this reaction, the magnesium and oxygen are called the _____ .　　　　[1 mark]

6   Sodium and lithium are Group 1 metals. Both sodium and lithium react with water
　　to produce hydrogen gas. Sodium is more reactive than lithium.

　　What is a difference you will observe when sodium reacts with water compared with
　　when lithium reacts with water?　　　　　　　　　　　　　　　　　　　　　[1 mark]

8 Vocabulary builder

1   Choose the correct word from the box to complete the sentences.

> **compounds   elements**

Substances made up of only one type of atom are
called _____ .   [1 mark]

2   Match key term to its definition.

Key term	Definition
products	Substances formed in a chemical reaction.
word equation	Substances that take part in a chemical reaction.
reactants	A summary of a chemical reaction.

[2 marks]

3   Choose the correct words to complete the sentences about
the periodic table.

A group is a **column / row** of elements with similar
appearances / properties.
A period is a **column / row** of elements in the periodic table.   [3 marks]

4   Choose the correct words to complete the sentences.

New **compounds / mixtures** are formed in **chemical / physical**
reactions. A new substance is made because the atoms are
created / rearranged. The number of atoms at the end of the
reaction **changes / stays the same**.   [4 marks]

5   Complete the table to show the names of elements and the
compounds they form.

Elements	Name in compound
oxygen	
	sulfide
chlorine	
sulfur and oxygen	
nitrogen and _____	nitrate

[5 marks]

6   Complete the sentences.

a   Group 1 contains r _____ metals.   [1 mark]

b   Group 7 contains n __ __ -m _____ .   [1 mark]

c   All of the elements are listed in the p _____ t _____   [1 mark]

8.4 The model of the atom

Learning objectives

After this topic, you should know:

- the model of the atom
- how to determine the numbers of sub-atomic particles in an atom.

Atoms are so small that you cannot even see them with a microscope – they are only about 0.1 nm wide. Scientists use models of the atom to help explain how chemicals react. Models of the atom also allow scientists to make predictions about the properties of substances.

A: Give two ways that scientists use models of the atom.

The model of the atom

At GCSE, the model of the atom has a very small **nucleus** in the middle.

- The nucleus is where most of the mass of the atom is.
- It is made up of **protons** and **neutrons**.
- It is only $\frac{1}{10\,000}$ of the size of an atom.

Electrons orbit the nucleus in shells. Most of an atom is empty space.

Protons, neutrons, and electrons are types of sub-atomic particle.

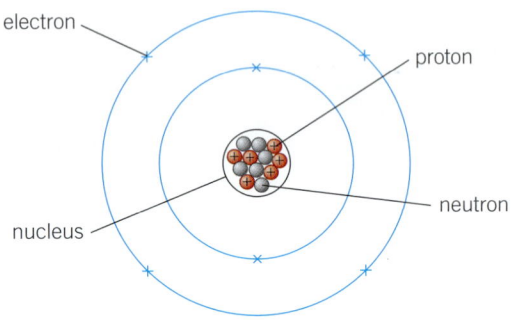

Figure 1 The GCSE model of an atom. The nucleus is made of neutrons and protons. Electrons orbit in shells.

Table 1 The relative charges and masses of sub-atomic particles.

Type of sub-atomic particle	Relative charge	Relative mass
proton	+1	1
neutron	0	1
electron	−1	very small

B: Name the sub-atomic particles found in the nucleus of an atom.

$$^{23}_{11}\text{Na}$$

Figure 2 In sodium there are 11 protons in the nucleus and 11 electrons in the shells. So, there are 23 − 11 = 12 neutrons in the nucleus.

The periodic table can be used to find out how many of each sub-atomic particle are in an atom. Look at sodium in the periodic table.

The lower number tells you how many protons there are in the nucleus of an atom. This is the **atomic number**. In an atom, the number of electrons is the same as the number of protons. So, a sodium atom has 11 protons in the nucleus and 11 electrons orbiting the nucleus.

The higher number is the **mass number**. This tells you the total number of protons plus neutrons in the nucleus.

number of neutrons   =   mass   −   atomic
   in an atom   number   number

Relative mass

The **relative atomic mass** of an element is the number of protons and neutrons in its atom.

You can add up the relative atomic masses of all of the atoms of the elements in a compound to work out the **relative formula mass** of that compound.

Relative atomic mass and relative formula mass do not have a unit.

Isotopes

The atoms of an element all have the same number of protons and so the same atomic number.

Sometimes atoms of the same element have different numbers of neutrons. This means the atoms will have the same atomic number but different mass numbers, and are called isotopes. All isotopes have the same chemical properties.

Worked example

Sulfuric acid has the chemical formula H_2SO_4. This means that it is made up of two hydrogen atoms, one sulfur atom, and four oxygen atoms.

Relative atomic masses: H: 1, S: 32, O: 16 So the relative formula mass of H_2SO_4: $(1 \times 2) + 32 + (16 \times 4)$ = **98**

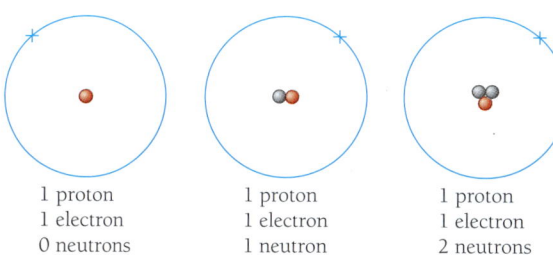

1 proton	1 proton	1 proton
1 electron	1 electron	1 electron
0 neutrons	1 neutron	2 neutrons

Figure 3 *Hydrogen's atomic number is 1 but it has three isotopes.*

1   Match each sub-atomic particle to the correct relative charge.

Sub-atomic particle	Relative charge
proton	−1
neutron	no charge
electron	+1

[2 marks]

2   Lithium's symbol is ^7_3Li.

  a   Give the **mass** number of a lithium atom. [1 mark]

  b   Calculate the number of neutrons in a lithium atom. [1 mark]

3   Chlorine has two isotopes, $^{35}_{17}Cl$ and $^{37}_{17}Cl$. Describe **one** similarity and **one** difference between the two chlorine isotopes. [2 marks]

8.5 Atoms and electrons

Learning objectives

After this topic, you should know:

- how electrons are arranged in atoms
- the electronic structure of the first 20 elements.

Electrons are particles found in atoms. They are negatively charged. They orbit around the nucleus of an atom in shells.

Electrons fill the shell closest to the nucleus first. The first shell can only hold two electrons.

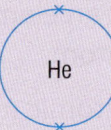

Figure 1 *Helium has two electrons in its outer shell.*

A: How many electrons does the first electron shell hold?

The second and third electron shells can hold up to eight electrons each.

Argon has an atomic number of 18. This means that an argon atom has 18 electrons:

- two electrons in the first shell
- eight electrons in the second shell
- eight electrons in the third shell.

This is known as the electronic structure of an atom.

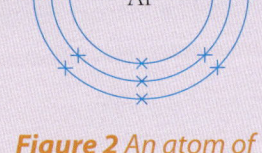

Figure 2 *An atom of argon.*

B: Draw the electronic structure of an atom with ten electrons.

You can also write the electronic structure of an atom to show the number of electrons in each shell. Argon has two electrons in the first shell and eight electrons in each of the second and third shells. You can write the electronic structure of argon as 2,8,8.

C: Sodium has 11 electrons. Write the electronic structure of sodium.

You should be able to draw the electronic structures for the first 20 elements. Use the periodic table to find the atomic number of the element.

The atomic number tells you the number of electrons in an atom of that element. Remember, mass number is the bigger number and atomic number is the smaller number.

(mass number) 23
(atomic number) 11 **Na**

Figure 3 The periodic table shows the mass number and atomic number for every element.

Electrons and the periodic table

The columns in the periodic table are called groups and the rows are called periods.

The number of electrons in the **outer shell** is the same as the **group number**. For example, as sodium is in Group 1, it has one electron in its outer shell.

The number of shells around the atom that have electrons in them is the same as the period number. Sodium is in Period 3 so it has electrons in the first three shells.

> **D: An atom has two electrons in its outer shell. Which group of the periodic table is the atom in?**

The electrons in the outer shell are the ones that take part in chemical reactions.

1   Give the maximum number of electrons that can be held in:
   a   the first shell of an atom   [1 mark]
   b   the second shell of an atom   [1 mark]
   c   the third shell of an atom.   [1 mark]

2   Hydrogen has an atomic number of 1.
   a   Draw the electronic structure of a hydrogen atom.   [1 mark]
   b   Write the electronic structure of a hydrogen atom.   [1 mark]

3   Use the periodic table at the back of this book to answer these questions.
   a   Draw the electronic structure of lithium.   [1 mark]
   b   Write the electronic structure of fluorine.   [1 mark]
   c   Identify why lithium is in Group 1.   [1 mark]

8.6 Metals and the periodic table

Learning objectives

After this topic, you should know:

- what a positive ion is
- the trends in the properties of Group 1 elements.

Most of the elements in the periodic table are metals. They are found on the left and in the middle of the periodic table. All metals have similar properties. They are:

- shiny
- good conductors
- flexible.

All metals are solids at room temperature, except for mercury.

A: Give two properties of all metals.

Metal ions

An atom has no overall charge because the number of positively charged protons is the same as the number of negatively charged electrons.

When a metal reacts, it **loses** electrons from its outer shell. This means that the metal atoms will have more protons than electrons. The metal atom will have a positive charge. Atoms with a charge are called **ions**. Metal atoms always form positive ions when they react.

For example, magnesium is in Group 2. It has two electrons in its outer shell. When magnesium atoms react, they lose the two electrons in their outer shell. They form ions with a 2+ charge.

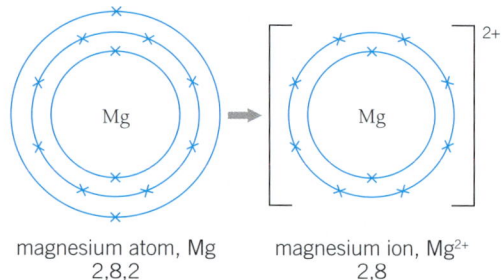

magnesium atom, Mg
2,8,2

magnesium ion, Mg^{2+}
2,8

Figure 1 *Magnesium atoms form 2+ magnesium ions when they react.*

B: Describe what an ion is.

Group 1 metals

Group 1 metals are also called the alkali metals. The properties of the Group 1 metals are:

- soft – they can be easily cut with a knife
- low density compared to other metals
- low melting point compared to other metals.

Each Group 1 metal has just one electron in its outer shell. When a Group 1 metal reacts, it loses one electron and becomes a 1+ positive ion.

Group 1 metals are very reactive. They can react with non-metals.

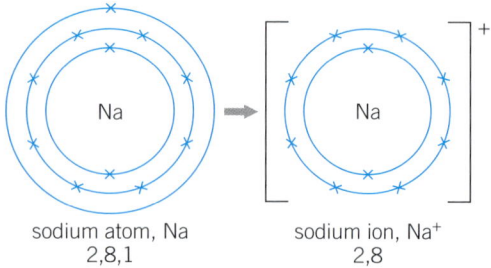

sodium atom, Na
2,8,1

sodium ion, Na^+
2,8

Figure 2 *Group 1 metals lose their outer shell electron and become a 1+ ion.*

C: Give the charge of a sodium ion when it reacts.

As you go down Group 1, the atoms get bigger and it is easier for them to lose their outer shell electrons. This means that their **reactivity** increases.

Figure 3 *The reactivity of Group 1 metals with water increases as you go from lithium, to sodium, to potassium.*

Chlorine

Group 1 metals react with chlorine to form a Group 1 chloride. For example, lithium reacts with chlorine to form lithium chloride. The word equation for this reaction is:

lithium + chlorine → lithium chloride

Oxygen

Group 1 metals react with oxygen to form a Group 1 oxide. For example, sodium reacts with oxygen to form sodium oxide. The word equation for this reaction is:

sodium + oxygen → sodium oxide

Water

Group 1 metals react with water to make a Group 1 hydroxide and hydrogen gas. For example, potassium reacts with water to form potassium hydroxide and hydrogen. The word equation for this reaction is:

potassium + water → potassium hydroxide + hydrogen

D: Identify which element is more reactive – potassium or rubidium?

1 Choose the correct words from the box to complete the following sentences.

    | low | melting point | metals |

    Group 1 elements are _____ . They have a _____ density and low _____ compared to other metals. [3 marks]

2 Choose the correct word to complete the sentence.
    When sodium reacts with **oxygen / water**, sodium hydroxide and hydrogen gas are formed. [1 mark]

3 Write a word equation for potassium reacting with chlorine. [2 marks]

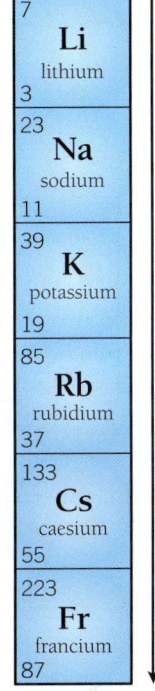

7		
	Li	
	lithium	
3		
23		
	Na	
	sodium	
11		
39		
	K	
	potassium	
19		
85		
	Rb	
	rubidium	
37		
133		
	Cs	
	caesium	
55		
223		
	Fr	
	francium	
87		

Atoms get bigger down the group. Reactivity increases.

Figure 4 *The trend in reactivity of Group 1 metals.*

Non-metal elements are found on the right of the periodic table. Non-metals are dull and brittle when solid, and are normally insulators.

Reactions of non-metals with non-metals

In a chemical reaction, non-metal elements can react together to make compounds. For example, nitrogen and oxygen can react together to make nitrogen dioxide. The word equation for this reaction is:

nitrogen + oxygen → nitrogen dioxide

Reactions of non-metals with metals

Non-metals can also react with metals. When a non-metal reacts with a metal, the non-metal atom **gains** electrons so that there are eight electrons in its outermost shell.

The non-metal atom now has **more** negatively charged electrons than positively charged protons. The non-metal atom will have a negative charge – it will be a negative ion. The name of the non-metal changes to have -**ide** at the end.

For example, chlorine has seven electrons in its outer shell. When it reacts, it gains one electron to give it eight electrons in its outer shell. Chlorine therefore forms an ion with a 1– charge. In the name of the compound, chlor**ine** becomes chlor**ide**.

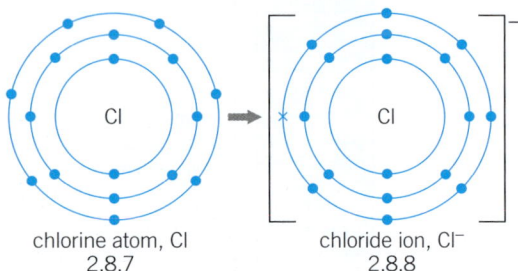

chlorine atom, Cl
2,8,7

chloride ion, Cl⁻
2,8,8

Figure 1 *Chlorine gains one electron and forms an ion with a 1– charge.*

A: Do non-metal ions form positive or negative ions?

Group 7 – the halogens

Group 7 elements are known as the **halogens**. Group 7 elements:

- are non-metals
- have seven electrons in the outer shell
- are found in molecules made of two atoms joined together.

As you go down the group, the mass number of the atoms **increases**. The melting and boiling points also **increase** as you go down the group.

Table 1 *The melting and boiling points of the halogens.*

Group 7 halogen	Melting point in °C	Boiling point in °C
fluorine, F_2	−220	−188
chlorine, Cl_2	−101	−35
bromine, Br_2	−7	59
iodine, I_2	114	184

Reactions of Group 7 elements

Halogens are very reactive elements that can make compounds with non-metals and metals. The reactivity of Group 7 elements **decreases** as you go down the group. Fluorine is more reactive than chlorine, chlorine is more reactive than bromine, and so on. This is because the atoms get bigger, so it is more difficult for them to gain an electron.

Hydrogen

Group 7 elements react with hydrogen to make a hydrogen halide. For example, fluorine reacts with hydrogen to form hydrogen fluoride. The word equation for this reaction is:

hydrogen + fluorine → hydrogen fluoride

Metals

Group 7 elements react with metals to make metal halides. For example, chlorine reacts with magnesium to form magnesium chloride. The word equation for this reaction is:

magnesium + chlorine → magnesium chloride

Displacement reactions

A more reactive Group 7 element will take the place of (displace) a less reactive Group 7 element in a compound.

For example, chlorine is more reactive than bromine. When chlorine is mixed with potassium bromide, chlorine will take the place of bromine in the compound. Bromine and potassium chloride are made. The word equation for this reaction is:

chlorine + potassium bromide → bromine + potassium chloride

Atoms get bigger down the group. Reactivity decreases.

Figure 2 *The trend in reactivity of Group 7.*

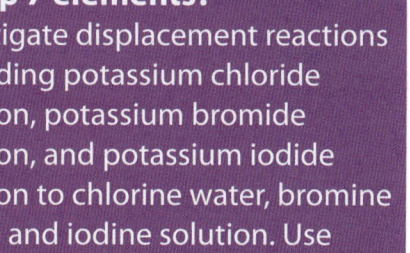

Which Group 7 elements can displace other Group 7 elements?
Investigate displacement reactions by adding potassium chloride solution, potassium bromide solution, and potassium iodide solution to chlorine water, bromine water, and iodine solution. Use cyclohexane to safely see which Group 7 elements are produced.

B: Predict whether chlorine would displace fluorine from hydrogen fluoride.

1 Choose the correct words from the box to complete the following sentence.

   electrons   ion   metal

   When a non-metal reacts with a _____, the non-metal gains _____ to form a negative _____.   [2 marks]

2 Choose the correct word to complete the sentence.
   Bromine will displace **chlorine / iodine** from a compound because bromine is **less / more** reactive.   [2 marks]

3 a Name the product formed when bromine reacts with hydrogen.   [1 mark]

   b Write a word equation for the reaction of bromine with hydrogen.   [2 marks]

8 Practice questions

01 Choose the correct words from the box to complete the following sentences.

> electrons   isotopes
> neutrons   protons

Atoms have a nucleus containing positively charged _____, and _____ with no charge. The shells around the atom contain negatively charged _____.   [3 marks]

02 Lithium is in Group 1 of the periodic table. It has a mass number of 7 and an atomic number of 3.

02.1 How many protons does lithium have? Choose **one** answer.

3   4   7   [1 mark]

02.2 How many electrons does lithium have? Choose **one** answer.

3   4   7   [1 mark]

02.3 How many neutrons does lithium have? Choose **one** answer.

3   4   7   [1 mark]

03 Chlorine is a Group 7 element.

03.1 Name the compound that is made when sodium reacts with chlorine. Choose **one** answer.

chloride sodium

chlorine sodium

sodium chloride

sodium chlorine   [1 mark]

03.2 Give the charge on a halide ion. Choose **one** answer.

1   −1   +1   −2   [1 mark]

04 Choose the correct words to complete the sentences.

The periodic table is a table of all the **compounds / elements**. Elements with similar properties are in the same column or **group / period** of the periodic table. Group 1 elements all have one electron in their **inner / outer** shell. Group 7 elements all have **one electron / seven electrons** in their outer shell.   [4 marks]

05 Group 1 elements are very reactive metals.

05.1 Complete the word equation for the reaction of sodium with water.

sodium + water → ____ + ____   [1 mark]

05.2 Complete the word equation for the reaction that forms lithium chloride.

____ + ____ → lithium chloride   [1 mark]

05.3 Write a word equation for the reaction of potassium with oxygen.   [2 marks]

06.1 Name the part of the atom where most of the mass is found.   [1 mark]

06.2 Name an atom that has no neutrons in its nucleus.   [1 mark]

06.3 Beryllium has an atomic number of 4. Write the electronic structure of beryllium.   [1 mark]

07 When Group 1 metals react, they become ions.

07.1 Sodium has an atomic number of 11. Write the electronic structure of a sodium **atom**.   [1 mark]

07.2 Give the charge of a sodium **ion**.   [1 mark]

07.3 Draw the electronic structure of a sodium **ion**.   [1 mark]

08 The periodic table below shows five different elements. The letters shown are not the symbols of the elements.

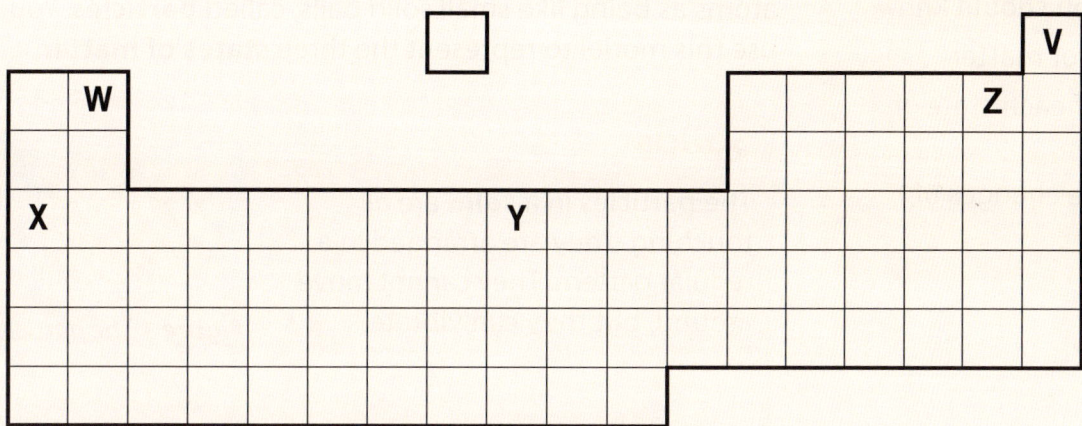

08.1 Give the letter that could be a Group 1 element.

[1 mark]

08.2 Give the letter that could be a Group 7 element.

[1 mark]

08.3 Give a letter that could be a metal.

[1 mark]

08.4 Give a letter that could be a non-metal.

[1 mark]

09 Elements in the same group have similar chemical properties but differ in their reactivity. Use the periodic table to help you answer the following questions.

09.1 In Group 1, which is the most reactive element listed below?

lithium potassium sodium   [1 mark]

09.2 In Group 7, which is the least reactive element listed below?

bromine fluorine iodine   [1 mark]

9 Mixtures and compounds
9.1 States of matter

Learning objectives

After this topic, you should know:

- the three states of matter
- the properties of each state of matter
- the names of the changes of state.

Scientists use **models** of the atom to understand and make predictions about substances. In one model, you can think of atoms as being like small solid balls, called **particles**. You can use this model to represent the three **states of matter**.

Solids

The particles in a **solid** are all touching. They are arranged in a regular pattern. They cannot move around, but they can vibrate.

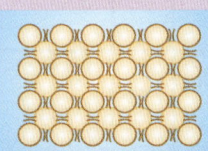

Figure 1 *The particles in a solid.*

Liquids

The particles in a **liquid** are touching but are **not** arranged in a regular pattern. They can move around.

Figure 2 *The particles in a liquid.*

Gases

The particles in a **gas** are moving fast in all directions. There is lots of space between the particles so they are not touching.

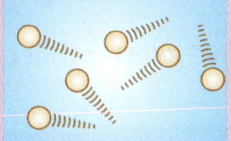

Figure 3 *The particles in a gas.*

A: What are the **three** states of matter?

Changing state

Changing the temperature of substances can cause them to change state. Changing state is a physical change. This means that no new substances are made.

Melting point

At the **melting point**, **melting** and **freezing** can take place.

- Melting happens when a substance is being **heated**. The particles in the solid start to be able to move around, but are still close together. The substance becomes a liquid.

- Freezing happens when a substance is being **cooled**. The particles in the liquid stop being able to move around and become arranged into a regular pattern. The substance becomes a solid.

Boiling point

At the **boiling point**, **boiling** and **condensation** can take place.

- Boiling happens when a substance is being **heated**. The particles in the liquid start to move far apart from each other and begin to move around very quickly. The substance becomes a gas.

- Condensation happens when the substance is being **cooled**. The particles in the gas move closer together until they are touching. They stop being able to move around very quickly. The substance becomes a liquid.

> **B:** Which change of state happens at the melting point when a substance is being heated?

All pure substances have a sharp melting point and a boiling point. These are the temperatures at which the substance changes state. The particles in a solid, liquid, and gas are held together by forces. The stronger the force between the particles, the higher the melting and boiling points will be.

- Substances with **high** melting points and boiling points have strong forces that hold their particles together.

- Substances with **low** melting points and boiling points have weak forces between their particles.

What are the melting points of different substances?
Investigate the melting point of different substances. Draw a conclusion about how strong the forces between the particles of each substance are.

1   Draw particle diagrams for a solid, a liquid, and a gas
    [3 marks]

2   At 100 °C, water changes from a liquid into a gas.
    a   Which change of state is this?
        boiling   condensing   freezing   melting   [1 mark]
    b   What is the name given to the temperature 100 °C for water?   [1 mark]

3   Bromine has a melting point of –7 °C. Gallium has a melting point of 30 °C.
    Which element has stronger forces between its particles, gallium or bromine?   [1 mark]

9.2 Mixtures

Learning objectives

After this topic, you should know:

- what a mixture is
- some ways to separate mixtures.

How does the size of the particles affect how quickly it takes to filter a mixture?

The solid called calcium carbonate can have different-sized particles. Compare how the size of the particles of the solid affects how quickly the solid is filtered from water.

A **compound** is made when the atoms of different elements are chemically joined together. They make a new substance that has different properties from the elements it is made from. The atoms that make up a compound are very difficult to separate.

A **mixture** is two or more substances that are not chemically joined together. The substances in a mixture have the same properties as they do when they are not in the mixture. All of the substances in a mixture can be separated.

   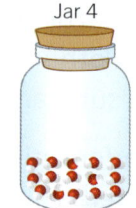

Jar 1 — Oxygen (gas)

Jar 2 — Hydrogen (gas)

Jar 3 — Mixture of oxygen and hydrogen (gas). The oxygen and hydrogen are not joined together. The mixture has the same properties as Jar 1 and Jar 2.

Jar 4 — Compound made from oxygen and hydrogen – water (liquid). The atoms of oxygen and hydrogen are joined together. The compound has different properties from the ones in Jars 1, 2, and 3.

Figure 1 *A mixture is more than one substance not chemically joined.*

A: What is a mixture?

Filtration

Filtration separates solids from a liquid. For example, a mixture of sand and water can be separated by filtration. The sand particles are too big to fit through the filter paper so they stay trapped on the paper. The water **can** pass through the paper and is collected in the flask.

filter paper — sand (the residue)

filter funnel

water (the filtrate)

Figure 2 *Filtration separates solids from liquids.*

B: How can water be separated from sand?

Some solids dissolve in a liquid. This is called a **solution**.

Distillation

Distillation is used to separate and collect a liquid from a solution. The mixture is heated so that the liquid turns into a gas. This gas then passes down a condenser, where it is cooled and turns back into a liquid. The liquid is collected in a different beaker.

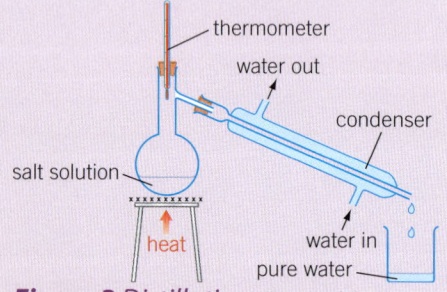

thermometer

water out

condenser

salt solution

heat

water in

pure water

Figure 3 *Distillation separates a liquid from a solution.*

C: What is distillation used to separate?

Crystallisation

Crystallisation is used to separate and collect a solid from a solution. The solution is put in an evaporating dish and gently heated by steam until crystals of the solid start to appear. The heat is removed and the liquid continues to **evaporate**, leaving solid crystals behind.

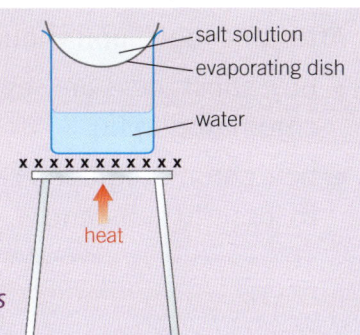

Figure 4 *Crystallisation separates a solid from a solution.*

D: Where does the liquid go during crystallisation?

1   Match each separation method to the mixture that it can be used to separate.

Separation method	Mixture
crystallisation	Solid in a liquid.
distillation	Solid dissolved in a liquid.
filtration	A liquid from a solution.

[2 marks]

2   Choose the correct words to complete the following sentences.

Sand and salt water can be separated by **distillation / filtration**. The salt from salt water can be collected by **crystallisation / distillation**. The water from the salt water can be separated by **crystallisation / distillation**.

[3 marks]

3   Complete the sentence to describe what the diagram shows.

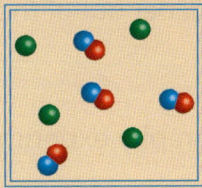

The particle diagram shows a _____ containing one _____ and one compound.

[2 marks]

9.3 Chromatography

Learning objectives

After this topic, you should know:

- how substances are separated by chromatography
- how chromatography can be used to identify substances.

Substances in a solution can be separated by **paper chromatography**.

In paper chromatography, some of the solution is dotted onto a piece of paper. The piece of paper is then dipped into a liquid **solvent**. A solvent is a chemical that something dissolves in.

The solvent soaks through the paper. As it moves up, the solvent carries the different substances in the solution with it. They travel different distances. Water is often used as the solvent in paper chromatography.

A: **What do we call a liquid that can dissolve substances?**

Figure 1 *The solvent moves up the paper and separates the different parts of the solution.*

Paper chromatography

Step 1: Cut out a rectangular piece of filter paper a little bit longer than the height of a beaker. Make sure your paper is narrower than the beaker.

Step 2: Draw a line, in pencil, 1 cm from the bottom of the paper.

Step 3: Put a dot of the solution that you want to separate onto the pencil line. Wrap the top of the paper around a splint.

Step 4: Put a small amount of water into the beaker.

Step 5: Balance the splint on the rim of the breaker. The bottom of the paper should just dip into the water. The pencil line and the sample solution must stay above the water.

Step 6: Leave until the water has soaked up to near the top of the paper.

Then take the paper out of the beaker and leave to dry.

Chromatograms

The result of a chromatography experiment is called a chromatogram.

Each substance in the solution will move up the paper by a different amount. Each substance will make a different spot on the chromatogram. By counting the spots, you can tell how many substances were in the original solution.

B: **What is a chromatogram?**

You can also use chromatography to identify what the substances in a solution are.

- Put a dot of the test solution and dots of the substances that you think are in the solution onto one piece of paper.

- If the dots from the test solution move the same distance as the dots of the known substances, then the test solution contains those substances.

For example, look at the chromatogram in Figure 2.

Solution A is made of two chemicals. The big green dot is the same as the dot for substance B. The small red dot is the same as the dot for substance C.

So, solution A contains substance B and substance C.

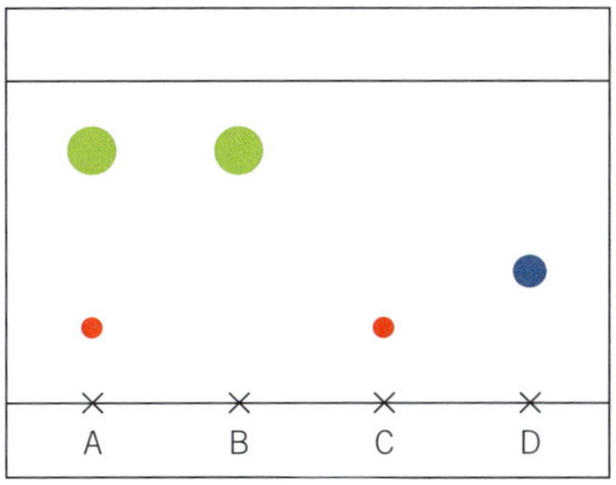

Figure 2 *A chromatogram comparing solution A with substances B and C.*

C: Which substance is **not** in solution A?

1   Choose the correct words from the box to complete the sentence.

| different | similar | solution | solvent |

In chromatography, as the _____ moves up the paper, the different substances in the _____ are carried a _____ distance.   [3 marks]

2   Copy and complete the chromatogram to show a mixture that is made up of three substances.

[1 mark]

3   Look at the chromatogram. Which substances, X, Y, or Z, are found in the solution?

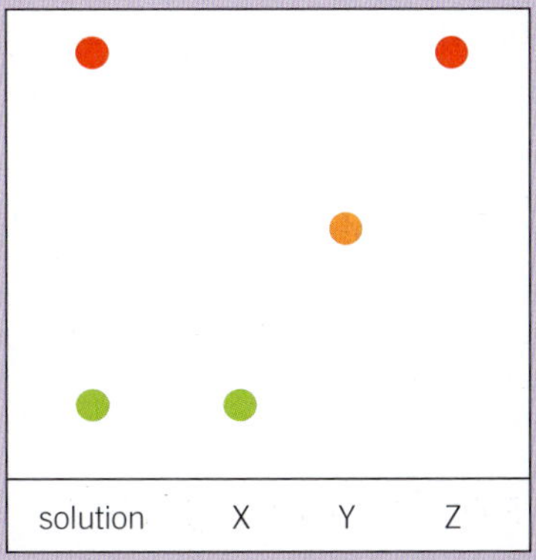

[2 marks]

9.4 Structures of carbon

Entry Level Certificate

Learning objectives

After this topic, you should know:

- the structure of diamond
- the structure of graphite.

Carbon is a non-metal element. Carbon atoms can join up in different ways to make different structures.

Diamond and **graphite** are both made of only carbon atoms. However, they have very different structures that give them very different properties.

Diamond

In diamond, each carbon atom is joined to **four** other carbon atoms by very strong **bonds**. Diamond has a three-dimensional structure. This means that it has width, height, and depth.

Diamond is a very strong and hard material because of the strong bonds between each carbon atom. Diamonds are shiny crystals and do not conduct electricity.

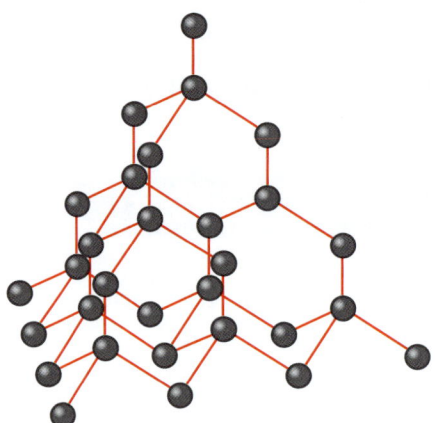

Figure 1 Each black ball is a carbon atom and the red lines are the strong bonds.

Figure 2 Diamonds are strong and hard crystals.

A: How many bonds does each carbon atom in diamond have?

Graphite

In graphite, each carbon atom is joined to **three** other carbon atoms by strong bonds. The carbon atoms are arranged in hexagons that form flat layers.

The different layers of graphite are held together by weaker forces. This means that the layers can easily slide over each other. This makes graphite soft and slippery. Graphite has electrons that can easily move along its layers. This means it can conduct electricity.

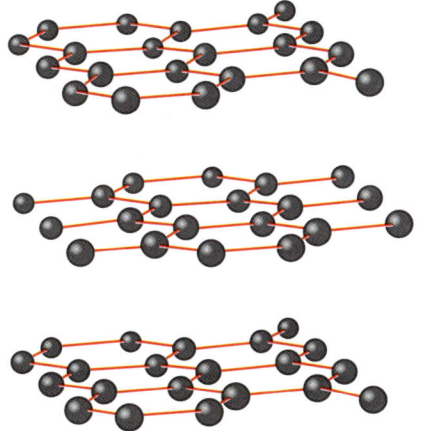

Figure 3 In graphite, the carbon atoms are found in layers.

Figure 4 Graphite is used in pencil leads. The layers slide over each other, which makes graphite soft.

B: How many strong bonds does each carbon atom in graphite have?

Graphite and diamond structures have thousands of atoms. They are called giant molecules.

1   Match each property to the carbon structure it describes.

Property	Carbon structure
Made of flat layers.	
Each carbon has four strong bonds.	diamond
Does not conduct electricity.	graphite
Each carbon has three strong bonds.	[4 marks]

2   Choose the correct words to complete the sentences.

Graphite and diamond are both made **mostly / only** of carbon atoms. In **diamond / graphite** the layers of atoms **can / cannot** easily slide over each other.   [3 marks]

3   Which structure of carbon is hard and strong?   [1 mark]

9.5 Polymers

Learning objectives

After this topic, you should know:

- what a polymer is
- the properties of polymers
- examples of polymers and their uses.

Polymers are very big molecules made of thousands of atoms. Small molecules called **monomers** join up in a chemical reaction to make the polymer. So, the long chain of the polymer is made up from many smaller repeating units.

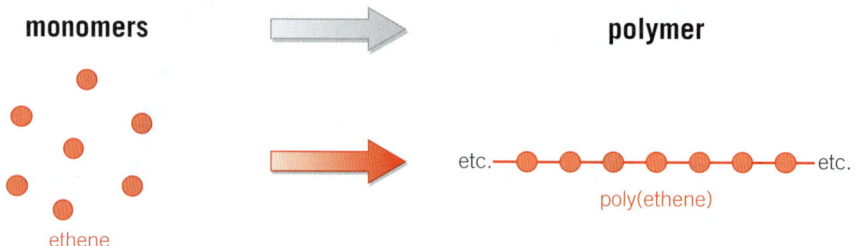

Figure 1 *Monomers join to make polymers.*

A: What is the name of the small molecules that make up a polymer?

A model for a polymer is a necklace made of beads. Each bead is like the repeating unit of the polymer. When the bead is not part of the necklace it is like a monomer.

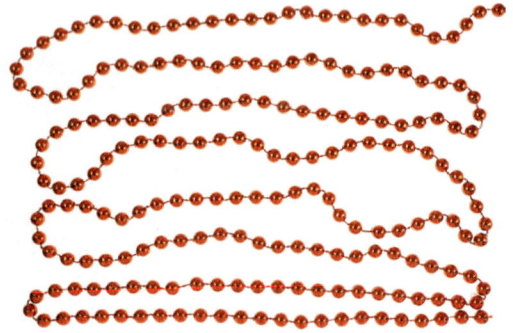

Figure 2 *A beaded necklace is like a polymer. Each bead is like the repeating unit.*

Examples of polymers

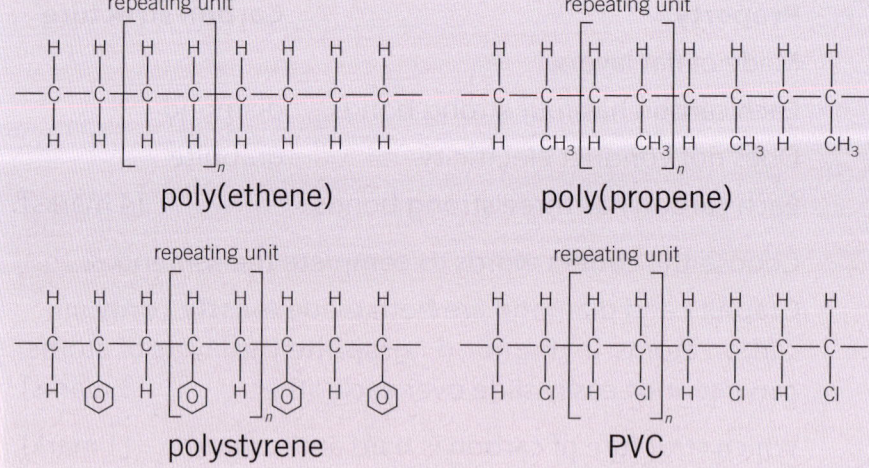

Figure 3 *Part of the chains that make up 4 common polymers shown here. Their repeating units are shown in square brackets.*

Properties of polymers

Polymers are waterproof and can be easily moulded. As such, they are used to make food and drink packaging, and water pipes.

B: What are polymers used for?

Polymers are very unreactive and resistant to chemicals. This makes them hardwearing so they last a long time. Many polymers are not **biodegradable**. This means that they are not broken down by microorganisms. This all makes polymers difficult to dispose of when they are no longer needed.

Most polymers end up in landfill (rubbish tips). Polymers can also be burnt, but this produces air pollution. The more environmentally friendly option is to reduce, reuse, and recycle polymers.

C: Where do most polymers go when they are not used anymore?

1   Match each key term to its definition.

Key term	Definition
monomers	Part of the polymer chain. Small reactive molecules that can join up to make a polymer.
polymers	
repeating unit	Long-chain molecules made from smaller repeating units. [2 marks]

2   Which three of the following are common properties of polymers?

biodegradable   easily moulded   reactive

short molecules   unreactive   waterproof

[3 marks]

3   Copy the part of the polymer chain shown below. Draw square brackets around a repeating unit.

[1 mark]

How does the biodegradability of polymers compare to other materials?
Investigate how the biodegradability of polymers compares to other materials (such as wood, paper, natural fabric, and synthetic fabric), by burying in soil for a period of time.

9 Checkpoint

1 Match each state of matter to the correct description of how the particles move around.

State of matter	Description
solid	The particles are far apart and move around quickly.
liquid	The particles move around but are touching each other.
gas	The particles vibrate.

[2 marks]

2 For each of the following mixtures, what is the correct method to separate them? Choose one answer.

   a   Water from a salt solution.

   chromatography   **crystallisation**   **distillation**   **filtration**   [1 mark]

   b   A mixture of inks.

   chromatography   **crystallisation**   **distillation**   **filtration**   [1 mark]

   c   Salt from a salt solution.

   chromatography   **crystallisation**   **distillation**   **filtration**   [1 mark]

3 Figure 1 shows a separation method. This method can be used to separate solid chalk from water.

   a   What is the name of this separation method?   [1 mark]

   b   Give the correct letter for each of the following labels:
      i   water: [1 mark]
      ii   chalk   [1 mark]
      iii filter funnel   [1 mark]
      iv   filter paper.   [1 mark]

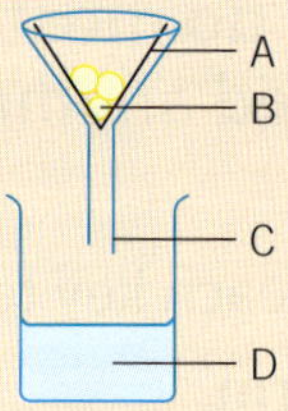

   Figure 1

4 a   Which element are graphite and diamond both made up of?   [1 mark]

   b   Graphite is made up of layers that are held together by weak forces.
       Which property of graphite does this cause? Choose **one** answer.

   conductor   **hard**   **shiny**   **slippery**   [1 mark]

   c   Each atom in diamond is joined to four other atoms by very strong bonds.
       Which property of diamond does this cause? Choose one answer.

   conductor   **hard**   **shiny**   **slippery**   [1 mark]

5 a   Polymers are used to make some water pipes. Which property of polymers make them a good material for this use?   [1 mark]

   b   Polymers are not biodegradable. Why is this a disadvantage?   [1 mark]

   c   Give the general name for the small molecules that react to make polymers.   [1 mark]

9 Vocabulary builder

1 Choose the correct word from the list to identify the key word being described.

   a These contain only one type of atom.

      compounds   elements   mixtures   [1 mark]

   b These contain two or more types of atom that are chemically joined together.

      compounds   elements   mixtures   [1 mark]

   c These contain two or more different substances that are not chemically joined together.

      compounds   elements   mixtures   [1 mark]

2 Choose the correct word to complete the sentences on changes of state.

When a solid **freezes / melts**, it changes from a solid into a liquid. This happens at the **boiling / melting** point of the solid. At the same temperature, the liquid can **freeze / melt** back into a solid. At the **boiling / melting** point, a liquid changes into a gas. At the same temperature, the gas can **condense / freeze** back into a liquid.   [5 marks]

3 Match each separation method to the correct description.

Method	Description
distillation	The liquid from a solution is evaporated off to leave a solid.
filtration	A liquid is evaporated from a solution then condensed and collected in another container.
crystallisation	A mixture is added to paper and separates as a solvent passes up the paper.
chromatography	A liquid mixed with a solid passes through paper to leave the solid as a residue.

      [3 marks]

4 Complete the sentences.

P _ _ _ _ _ _ _ are molecules made up of thousands of atoms. They are made up of many small repeating units called m _ _ _ _ _ _ _. Many are waterproof and are not b _ _ _ _ _ _ _ _ _ _ _.   [3 marks]

5 Choose the correct term to describe the properties of one form of carbon.

In **diamond / graphite**, each carbon atom is joined to three other carbon atoms by strong **bonds / forces**. The carbon atoms are arranged in **layers / rows** that are held together by weak **bonds / forces**.   [4 marks]

9.6 Pure substances and formulations

166

Learning objectives

After this topic, you should know:

- what a pure substance is
- what a formulation is.

A **pure** substance is made of only one chemical. It is not mixed with any other substances. Pure substances can be elements or compounds. All the particles are the same in a pure substance.

Figure 1 *Pure water only has water molecules in it.*

A: Define what a pure substance is.

Melting and boiling points of pure substances

Pure substances have a fixed melting and boiling point – they melt, freeze, boil, or condense at specific temperatures. This can be used to identify them.

For example, pure water melts at exactly 0 °C and boils at exactly 100 °C. If a substance melts at exactly 0 °C and boils at exactly 100 °C then it must be pure water.

Mixtures are made of more than one substance that are not chemically joined together. A mixture will melt and boil over a range of temperatures. The closer the substance is to being pure, the smaller the range.

How is the boiling point of salty water different from the boiling point of pure water?

Add sodium chloride (table salt) into some pure water until no more will dissolve. Then investigate how the boiling point of the salty water is different from the boiling point of pure water using a Bunsen burner and a thermometer.

B: A substance boils at exactly −13 °C. Is the substance pure?

Formulations

A **formulation** is a mixture of substances that makes a useful product. Each part of the mixture is added to do a specific job. This makes the product as useful as possible.

Many of the products you use in everyday life are formulations, such as:

- fuels
- cleaning agents
- paints
- medicines
- alloys
- fertilisers
- foods.

C: Give one example of a product that is a formulation.

1   Match each key term to its definition.

Key term	Definition
melting point	Contains only one element or compound.
pure substance	Mixture of substances that makes a useful product.
formulation	The temperature when a solid becomes a liquid. [2 marks]

2   Identify which of the following is a description of a formulation.

   A   A sample of gas contains only oxygen molecules.

   B   A gold earring is made up of lots of gold atoms joined together.

   C   A painkiller contains aspirin, which is the drug that stops the feeling of pain, and sugar, which makes the tablet taste better.   [1 mark]

3   A substance has a melting point of −2 °C to 0 °C and a boiling point of 101 °C to 102 °C.

   a   Identify if the substance is pure or impure.   [1 mark]

   b   Name the substance.   [1 mark]

9.7 Concentration

Learning objectives

After this topic, you should know:

- what concentration is
- how to calculate the concentration of a solution.

Lots of chemical reactions happen in **solution**. A solution is a type of mixture where a **solute** is dissolved in a **solvent**. A solute can be a solid, liquid, or gas. Solvents are always liquids. For example, coffee is a solution – the coffee granules are the solute, the water is the solvent.

Concentration is a measure of how much solute is dissolved in the solvent. Concentration is the **mass of the solute** in a given **volume of the solvent** – or how many grams (g) of solute are in each cubic decimetre (dm^3) of solvent. The unit of concentration is g/dm^3.

A **concentrated** solution has lots of solute per volume of solvent – it has a high concentration. A **dilute** solution has little solute per volume of solvent – it has a low concentration.

Figure 1 *Coffee is a solution.*

> **A:** Give the unit of concentration.

Calculating the concentration of a solution

You can use the following equation to calculate the concentration of a solution.

$$\text{concentration (g/dm}^3) = \frac{\text{mass of solute (g)}}{\text{volume of solution (dm}^3)}$$

> **Worked example**
>
> 75 g of sodium chloride (the solute) is dissolved in 1.5 dm^3 of water (the solvent).
> Calculate the concentration of the solution.
>
> **Step 1:** Put the numbers into the equation shown above.
>
> $$\text{concentration (g/dm}^3) = \frac{75 \text{ g}}{1.5 \text{ dm}^3}$$
>
> **Step 2:** Calculate the concentration.
>
> $$\frac{75 \text{ g}}{1.5 \text{ dm}^3} = \textbf{50 g/dm}^3$$

> **B:** Write the equation we use to calculate concentration.

If the volume of the solvent is given in cm^3 you need to convert it to dm^3:

$$\text{volume in dm}^3 = \frac{\text{volume in cm}^3}{1000}$$

> **C:** Describe how you convert cm^3 into dm^3.

Calculating the mass of solute in a solution

If you know the concentration of a solution, you can calculate how many grams (the mass) of solute are dissolved in a given volume using the equation:

mass of solute in g = concentration in g/dm^3 × volume of solution in dm^3

Worked example

A solution of sodium chloride in water has a concentration of 70 g/dm^3. Calculate the mass of sodium chloride in 0.5 dm^3 of the solution.

Step 1: **Put the numbers into the equation.**

mass of solute (g) = 70 g/dm^3 × 0.5 dm^3

Step 2: **Calculate the mass of solute.**

70 g/dm^3 × 0.5 dm^3 = **35 g**

D: Write the equation we use to calculate the mass of solute in a solution.

How does the predicted mass of salt in a solution compare to how much is actually in the solution?
Find out how much salt is dissolved in a solution of known concentration. You can do this by measuring the mass of a beaker, adding a sample of the salt solution, heating to evaporate all of the water, and then re-weighing the beaker. Use the concentration to work out how much salt should be in the solution.

1   Match each key word to its definition.

Key word	Definition
solute	A mixture where substances are dissolved in a liquid.
solvent	Substance that is dissolved in a solvent.
solution	Substance that dissolves a solute.
concentration	The amount of a substance dissolved in a given volume. [3 marks]

2   36 g of potassium chloride is dissolved in 1.8 dm^3 of water. Calculate the concentration of the solution. Give the unit.
[3 marks]

3   A solution of magnesium sulfate dissolved in water has a concentration of 360 g/dm^3. Calculate the mass of magnesium sulfate in 55 cm^3 of the solution. Give the unit.
[3 marks]

9.8 Covalent molecules

Non-metal elements can join together by sharing a pair of electrons. One electron comes from each non-metal element involved in the bond, creating a shared pair of electrons. This is a **covalent bond**. Atoms that are bonded together by covalent bonds form **molecules**.

A non-metal element can:

- form one covalent bond to one other atom (e.g., hydrogen)
- form covalent bonds to lots of atoms (e.g., methane).

You can use dot and cross diagrams to show covalent bonds. The dot and the cross each represent an electron – one electron from each atom in the bond.

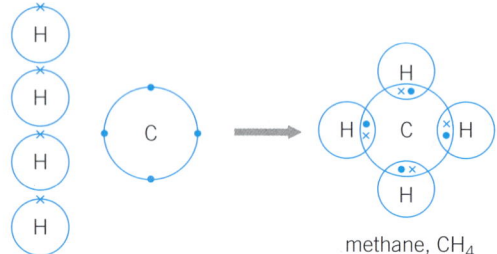

Figure 2 Methane contains one carbon atom that forms four covalent bonds to four hydrogen atoms.

hydrogen atoms   hydrogen molecule, H₂

Figure 1 *Two hydrogen atoms join together with one covalent bond to form a hydrogen molecule.*

A: **Name the type of elements that join together by covalent bonds.**

Covalent bonds can be single bonds, double bonds, or triple bonds. Each bond is made from a shared pair of electrons between the atoms.

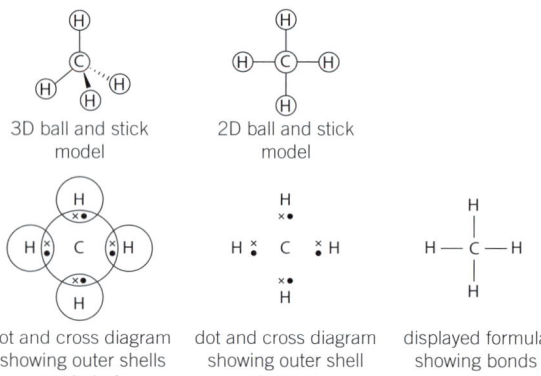

3D ball and stick model   2D ball and stick model

dot and cross diagram (showing outer shells as circles)   dot and cross diagram showing outer shell electrons   displayed formula showing bonds

Figure 4 *There are many different ways you can draw covalent bonds.*

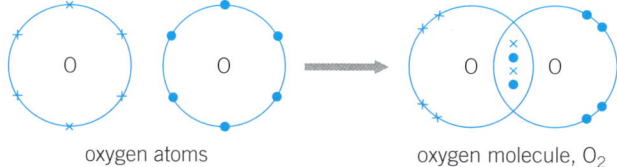

oxygen atoms   oxygen molecule, O₂

Figure 3 *Oxygen atoms join together by a double covalent bond.*

Giant covalent structures

Giant covalent structures are made of many non-metal atoms held together by covalent bonds. These substances have very high melting and boiling points because the strong covalent bonds must be broken to change the state of the substance.

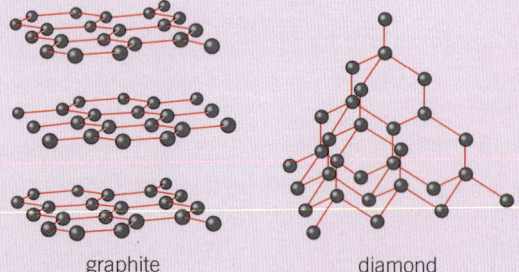

graphite   diamond

Figure 5 *Diamond and graphite are examples of giant covalent structures.*

B: Does graphite have a high melting point or a low melting point?

Small molecules

Small molecules only have a few atoms bonded together with covalent bonds. The bonds holding these atoms together are strong. However, there are also weak forces attracting the molecules to each other. These forces are easy to overcome.

Substances with small molecules have low melting and boiling points. This means they are usually gases or liquids at room temperature. Bigger molecules have higher melting points because the forces between them are stronger.

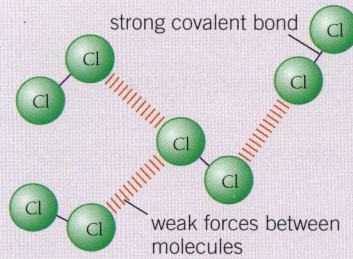

Figure 6 Chlorine atoms are joined by strong covalent bonds within the molecules, but the forces between the molecules are weak.

1   Sort the following properties according to whether they describe small molecules or giant covalent structures.

   gas or liquid at room temperature
   high boiling point
   low melting point
   made of lots of atoms
   solid at room temperature   [5 marks]

2   Identify which **two** of the following are covalently bonded compounds.

   A ammonia, NH_3

   B hydrogen chloride, HCl

   C magnesium oxide, MgO

   D sodium chloride, NaCl   [2 marks]

3   Use the data in the table to identify the structure of substances A, B, and C.

Substance	State at room temperature	Melting point in °C	Boiling point in °C
A	solid	1710	2230
B	gas	−114	−85
C	liquid	−30	174

[3 marks]

9.9 Ionic compounds

Learning objectives

After this topic, you should know:

- what an ionic compound is
- the properties of ionic compounds
- the elements that will form an ionic bond.

Ionic compounds contain **metal** and **non-metal** ions bonded together. They are solids at room temperature as they have high melting and boiling points. Ionic compounds often form crystals that can dissolve in water. They cannot conduct electricity when solid, but can when you dissolve them in water or melt them.

A: Give the types of elements that make up an ionic compound.

Making ionic compounds

Ionic compounds are made in chemical reactions. Electrons from the metal atom are given to the non-metal atom.

- The metal atom will now have a positive charge. It is a positive ion.

- The non-metal atom will now have a negative charge. It is a negative ion.

The oppositely charged ions are attracted to each other. This is an **ionic bond**. They form a compound with no charge.

For example, sodium and chlorine form the ionic compound sodium chloride.

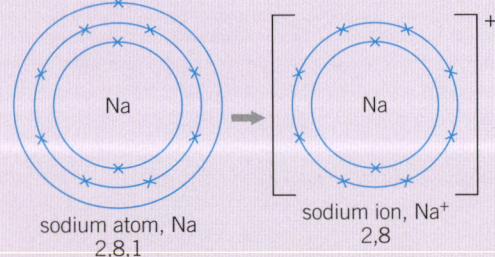

sodium atom, Na
2,8,1

sodium ion, Na⁺
2,8

Figure 1 *Sodium atom loses its outer electron and becomes a 1+ sodium ion.*

Sodium, Na, is in Group 1 of the periodic table. It has one electron in its outer shell. When sodium forms an ionic compound, it loses its outer shell electron and becomes a 1+ sodium ion.

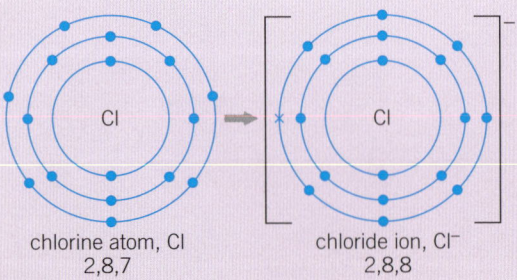

chlorine atom, Cl
2,8,7

chloride ion, Cl⁻
2,8,8

Figure 2 *Chlorine atom becomes a 1– chloride ion by gaining an electron in its outer shell electron.*

Chlorine, Cl, is in Group 7 of the periodic table. It has seven electrons in its outer shell. When chlorine forms an ionic compound, it gains one electron and becomes a 1– ion. Remember that when non-metals become ions, the end part of their name changes. So chlorine becomes a chlor**ide** ion.

The opposite charges of 1+ sodium ion and 1− chloride ion are then attracted to each other and form an ionic bond.

B: Name the type of element that will make a negative ion.

Sodium chloride, NaCl, is an example of an ionic compound. The charges on the ions cancel each other out. Therefore, sodium chloride has no charge.

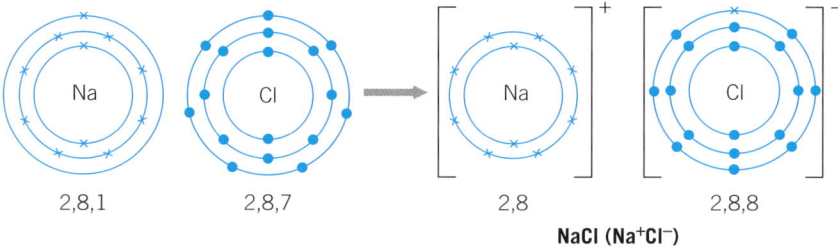

2,8,1   2,8,7   2,8   2,8,8

NaCl (Na⁺Cl⁻)

Figure 3 The positive sodium ion and negative chloride ion are attracted together to form sodium chloride.

Ionic bonds are formed in all directions so ionic compounds make a three-dimensional structure known as a **giant ionic lattice**. An ionic compound can be made up of many thousands of ions.

C: Name the structure made by ionic compounds.

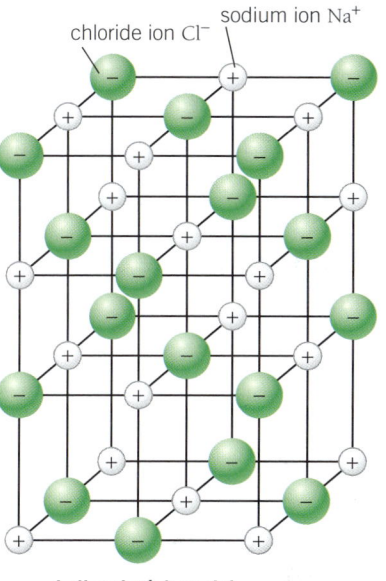

ball and stick model

Figure 4 Giant ionic lattice of sodium chloride.

1   Choose the correct word from the box to complete the following sentences.

> **negatively   positively**

Non-metal atoms form _____ charged ions.
Metal atoms form _____ charged ions.   [1 mark]

2   Identify which of the following ionic compound names is correct. You may need to use the periodic table at the back of the book to answer this question.
chlorine bromide
sodium bromide
sodium magnesium   [1 mark]

3   Magnesium, Mg, forms a 2+ ion. Chlorine, Cl, forms a 1− ion. Give the chemical formula for the ionic compound magnesium chloride.   [1 mark]

9 Practice questions

01 Which of the following best describes the ionic bond?

  A   The sharing of pairs of electrons.

  B   The attraction between oppositely charged ions.

  C   The repulsion between like-charged ions.

  D   The attraction between oppositely charged molecules.   [1 mark]

02 What happens when a non-metal atom forms a negatively charged ion?

  A   It gains an electron.

  B   It gains an extra proton.

  C   It loses an electron.

  D   It shares its electrons with a metal atom.   [1 mark]

03 Figure 1 shows the displayed formula for ethane.

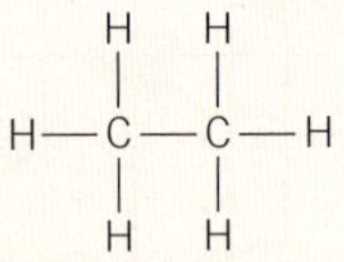

Figure 1

Which of the following statements about ethane is correct?

  A   Ethane contains seven covalent bonds.

  B   Ethane is a mixture.

  C   Ethane contains a metal and a non-metal atom.

  D   Ethane is made up of ionic bonds.   [1mark]

04 For each mixture, choose the correct separation method that is being described from the box.

> chromatography   crystallisation
> distillation   filtration

04.1 Seawater is heated until the water evaporates. The water vapour is condensed to give pure water.   [1 mark]

04.2 A solution of potassium sulfate in water was left until the potassium sulfate crystals were produced.   [1 mark]

04.3 Water from a reservoir is passed through a metal screen to remove twigs and leaves.   [1 mark]

05 Match each monomer to the correct repeating unit of the polymer that it will form.

Monomer   **Repeating unit of polymer**

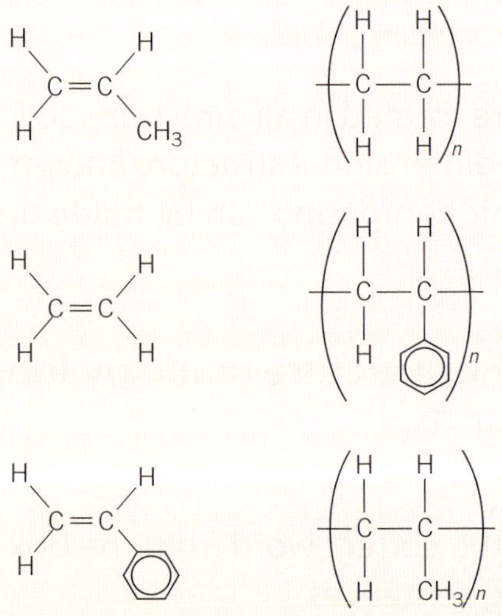

   [3 marks]

06 Solution A is a mixture of dyes. A Student carried out a chromatography experiment to test if ink B, ink C, and ink D were present in solution A. Figure 2 shows his results.

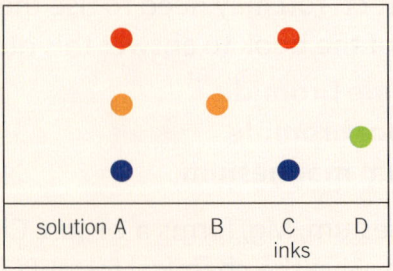

Figure 2

06.1 Identify which of the inks make up solution A. [2 marks]

06.2 Identify which of the substances are pure. [2 marks]

06.3 Identify which ink is a mixture. [1 mark]

06.4 Suggest why the sample line must be drawn in pencil rather than pen. [1 mark]

07 Figure 3 shows four particle diagrams.

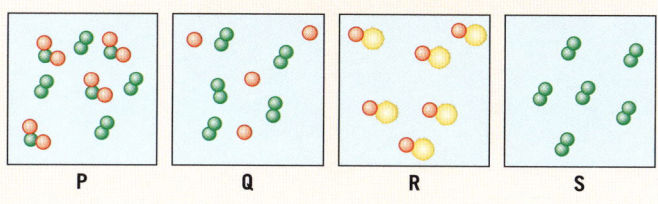

Figure 3

07.1 Give the letter that represents a mixture of an element and a compound. [1 mark]

07.2 Give the letter that represents a pure compound. [1 mark]

07.3 Give the letter that represents a mixture of two elements. [1 mark]

07.4 Give the letter that represents a pure element. [1 mark]

07.5 Name the state of matter represented by all four diagrams in Figure 3. [1 mark]

08 Figure 4 shows part of a polymer chain.

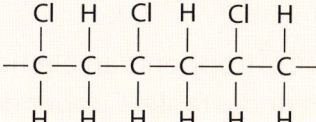

Figure 4

Draw the repeating unit of the polymer in Figure 4. [2 marks]

09 The melting and boiling points of three substances are shown in Table 1.

Table 1

Substance	Melting point in °C	Boiling point in °C
A	98	678
B	0	100
C	803	2167

09.1 Give the letter of the substance that has the strongest forces between its particles. [1 mark]

09.2 Identify the state of B at 20 °C. [1 mark]

09.3 Identify the state of C at 20 °C. [1 mark]

09.4 Give the letter for the substance that is a liquid at 110 °C. [1 mark]

10 A solution of sodium chloride dissolved in water has a concentration of 230 g/dm^3.

Calculate the mass of sodium chloride in 92 cm^3 of the solution. [3 marks]

11 Diamond and graphite are both made from carbon.

11.1 Describe how the bonding in graphite means that it is slippery. [2 marks]

11.2 Explain why graphite can conduct electricity whereas diamond does not. [4 marks]

10 Metals and alloys
10.1 Metals

Learning objectives

After this topic, you should know:

- the structure of metals
- the properties of metals
- uses of copper and aluminium.

Most elements are metals. Metal elements are found on the left of the periodic table.

There are strong bonds between the metal atoms. They are arranged in a regular pattern that forms a giant structure.

Figure 1 *Metals have giant structures made of atoms with strong bonds between them.*

Properties of metals

Most metals have high melting points and are solids at room temperature because of their giant structures. All metals are shiny and are usually grey in colour.

Metals are also good **conductors**. This means that electricity and thermal energy can pass through them easily.

In metals, the layers of atoms can easily slide over each other. This means that metals easily change shape when they are hit or stretched. This makes them good for making into wires.

A: What two things are metals good conductors of?

Copper

Copper's chemical symbol is Cu. Copper is an element and is found in the middle of the periodic table. Copper does not react with air, water, or other chemicals easily. It is unreactive.

Copper is used to make electrical wires as it is easily shaped and is a good conductor of electricity. It is also used to make water pipes as copper does not react with the water.

Figure 2 *Copper has properties that make it useful for electrical wiring.*

B: What are two uses of copper?

Aluminium

Aluminium's chemical symbol is Al. Aluminium is an element and is found in Group 3 of the periodic table. It has a low **density** compared to other metals. This means that a lump of aluminium will feel lighter than a lump of another metal that has the same volume.

When a metal reacts with oxygen in the air, we say the metal **corrodes**. This reaction forms a metal oxide compound.

When aluminium reacts with oxygen in the air, it forms aluminium oxide. A tough layer of aluminium oxide forms on the outside. This layer protects the rest of the aluminium from reacting with oxygen. Aluminium is therefore resistant to corrosion.

Aluminium is used to make drink cans and aeroplanes.

How are the properties of metals different?
Compare the properties of different metals by measuring their conductivity and finding out their density, melting points, and boiling points.

C: What is one property of aluminium?

1   Which three of the following are properties of metals?

   colourless   easily shaped   gases   giant structure
   shiny   soft   [3 marks]

2   Match each use of copper to the property of copper that makes it a good material for that use.

Use of copper	Property of copper that makes it good for that use
	Can conduct electricity.
water pipes	Red coloured.
electrical wires	Does not react with water.
	Can conduct thermal energy.

[2 marks]

3   Metals are used to make cooking pans.
   Which property of metals makes them a good material to make cooking pans from?   [1 mark]

10.2 Alloys

Learning objectives

After this topic, you should know:

- what an alloy is
- some examples of alloys.

Pure metals are often too soft to be useful. Adding other elements to a metal can make it harder. Mixtures that are mainly made from metals are called **alloys**.

The atoms in a pure metal are arranged in regular layers. This makes it easy for the atoms to slide over each other. In an alloy, atoms from the other element break up the regular pattern of layers. As a result, the atoms cannot easily slide over each other. This makes alloys harder than pure metals.

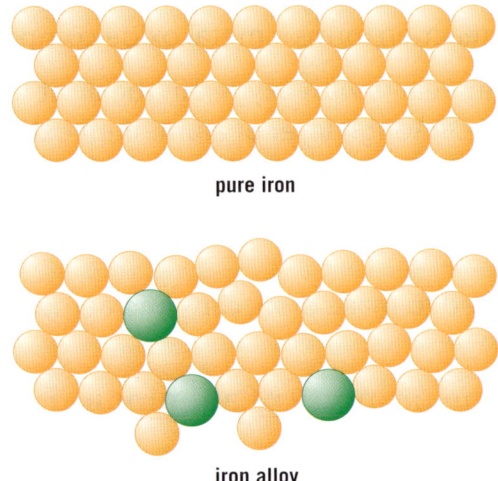

pure iron

iron alloy

Figure 1 *Pure metals are elements so all their atoms are the same. Alloys are mixtures of more than one element.*

A: What is an alloy?

Common alloys

Gold is often used in jewellery. Pure gold is too soft and would be bent or dented easily. Gold is mixed with other metals to make a harder alloy.

Pure aluminium is too soft to be used to make cars and aeroplanes. Aluminium is mixed with other elements to make alloys that are very strong and light.

Steel is mainly made from iron that is mixed with some carbon and sometimes other metals. Steel is stronger and harder than pure iron so is more useful for construction.

B: Why are alloys more useful than pure metals?

Steel

Steel is an alloy of iron and carbon. It is used in many different objects, including cars, buildings, and cutlery. Steels always contain iron and carbon but can also have other elements in them. Different uses of steel need different properties. The other elements are added to produce these properties.

C: Which two elements does steel always contain?

1   Match each key word to its definition.

Key word	Definition
alloy	A substance made from iron and carbon.
steel	A mixture mainly made of a metal. [1 mark]

2   Choose the correct words to complete the sentences.

Impure / Pure metals are usually too soft to be useful. Adding other elements to a pure metal makes an **alloy / compound**.

Alloys are **harder / softer** than pure metals and this makes them **less / more** useful.   [4 marks]

3   Why is it not a good idea to use pure aluminium to make aeroplanes?

[1 mark]

4   The graph in Figure 2 shows the strength of iron and two alloys of iron.

a   What is one advantage of using an alloy of iron instead of pure iron?   [1 mark]

b   Which alloy of iron is stronger: stainless steel or carbon steel?   [1 mark]

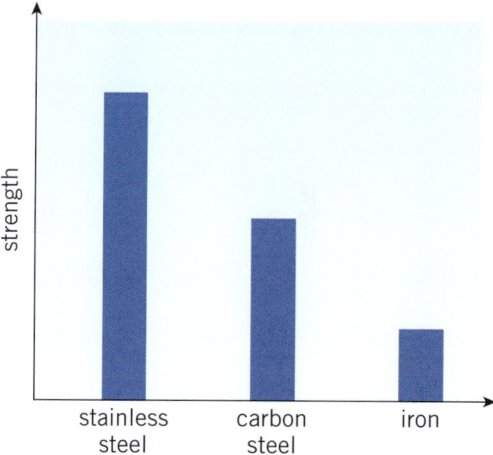

Figure 2

10.3 Extracting metals

Learning objectives

After this topic, you should know:

- how metals exist in nature
- how metals are extracted using carbon.

Some metals do not react easily with other elements. They are unreactive. Gold, silver, and platinum are all unreactive metals. Because they are unreactive, they are found as the metal element itself in nature.

Unreactive metals can be dug up from the earth and rocks, or can be filtered from water. They can then easily be cleaned to make the pure metal.

Figure 1 *Gold is found in rocks as an element – it is not bonded to any other elements in the rock.*

A: What is one example of an unreactive metal?

Reactive metals

Most metals will react with chemicals in the air, soil, or rocks. These metals are found chemically joined to other elements in compounds.

Figure 2 *The element copper is a reddish-brown metal. It is found in rocks bonded to other elements such as oxygen and sulfur.*

These metal compounds can be dug up from the earth. Chemical reactions are then used to remove the metal from the compounds. This process is called **extraction**.

Some metals, like iron, can be extracted by heating their compounds with carbon. Carbon is a non-metal element. During the chemical reaction, the carbon joins to the non-metals in the compound and leaves the iron behind as an element.

Carbon can only be used to extract metals that are **less** reactive than it.

B: Can carbon be used to extract magnesium from a magnesium compound?

1   Choose the correct words from the box to complete the sentences.

   | carbon   extracted   gold   reactive |

   _____ metals like iron are found in compounds. Iron can be extracted by heating with _____.

   Unreactive metals like _____ are found as the metal itself. They do not need to be _____ from a compound. [3 marks]

2   Sort the following metals by whether they can be extracted using carbon or not. Use Figure 3 to help you.

   aluminium   magnesium

   sodium   tin   zinc [5 marks]

3   How can lead metal be extracted from a lead compound? [1 mark]

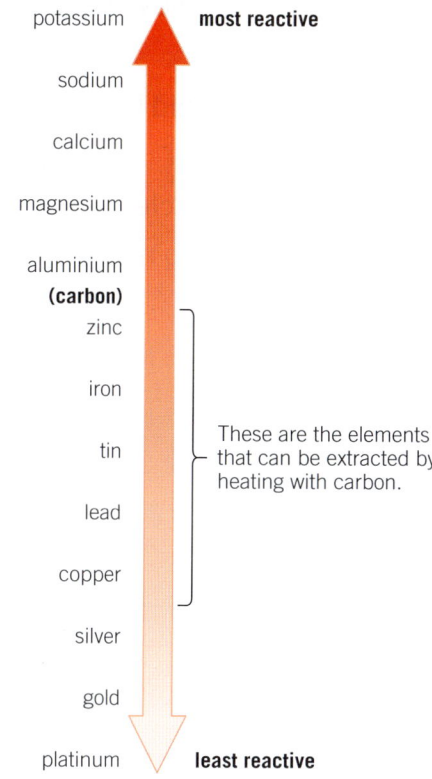

potassium — most reactive
sodium
calcium
magnesium
aluminium
(carbon)
zinc
iron
tin — These are the elements that can be extracted by heating with carbon.
lead
copper
silver
gold
platinum — least reactive

Figure 3 *Only elements that are less reactive than carbon can be extracted from their compounds by heating with carbon.*

10.4 Recycling metals

Learning objectives

After this topic, you should know:

- what ores are
- how metals can be recycled
- the benefits of recycling metals.

Metals are important materials that have many uses, from the zips in clothes to the support beams in buildings.

It takes a lot of time, energy, and money to dig up rocks and extract the metals. **Ores** are rocks or compounds with enough of the metal in them to make it **economical** to extract it. This means that the money made from selling the pure metal is higher than the cost of digging up and extracting it.

Quarries and mines

Ores are dug out of the ground from quarries or mines. A large amount of rock often needs to be dug out to find small amounts of ore.

Figure 1 *Quarries and mines take up large amounts of land. They destroy the habitats of plants and animals, and produce a lot of dust. This quarry removes copper ore from the ground.*

A: How are ores removed from the ground?

Quarries and mines can damage the environment near them. The plants and animals that lived in the area lose their habitat. Eventually, when a mine or quarry is closed, the area can be landscaped and turned back to nature.

Digging out the metal ores makes a lot of dust. This dust can make lung problems, like asthma, worse.

However, quarries and mines need people to work in them, so they create jobs. The roads and services get better near the mines and quarries because there are more people. This improves the standard of living for people who already live in the area.

Recycling metals

There is only so much of each metal that is in or on the Earth. Metals are a **finite resource**. This means that they could all be used up. If we only use metals once we will eventually run out of metal ores and so run out of that metal.

B: What does finite mean?

When a metal object is no longer needed, it can be collected and melted down. The melted metal can be re-shaped and used for a new object. The metal has been **recycled**.

Recycling means that fewer quarries and mines are needed. There is also less waste as the metals are recycled rather than being thrown out. Recycling metals uses less energy than digging up and extracting metals from ores so recycling is better for the environment than extracting and processing metal ores.

C: Does recycling use more or less energy than digging up and extracting metals from their ores?

1. Match each key word to its definition.

Key word	Definition
finite	Melting down and re-using.
recycling	A rock with an economical amount of metal in it.
metal ore	A resource that will run out. [2 marks]

2. Sort the following statements as to whether they are an advantage or a disadvantage of quarries and mines

   destroy habitats   **produce dust**

   produce useful metal   **provide jobs**   [4 marks]

3. Complete the sentence to describe what an ore is.

   An ore is a rock that contains enough metal that it is
   _____ to extract it.   [1 mark]

4. A rock contains some copper. To extract the copper from the rock, it costs £4.50 per 1 kg of copper produced. The 1 kg of copper can be sold for £5.

   Is the original rock an ore?   [1 mark]

10 Checkpoint

1   Choose the correct words from the box to complete the sentences.

> aeroplanes   density   electricity   jewellery   melting point   wires

Copper is a good conductor of _____. It is used to make _____.

Aluminium has a low _____. It is used to make _____.   [4 marks]

2   Which **two** statements about metals are **correct**?

A   They are brittle.

B   They are shiny.

C   They do not allow electricity to flow.

D   They are good thermal conductors.   [2 marks]

3   Choose the correct words to complete the description of alloys.

Alloys are **compounds / mixtures** that are mainly made from
metals / non-metals. Alloys are usually **harder / softer** than the pure metal.
Making alloys makes metals **less / more** useful.   [4 marks]

4   The following list shows the position of carbon and some of the metals in the reactivity series.

calcium → aluminium → **carbon** → iron → copper
←
　　　　　increasing reactivity

a   Name **one** metal that is **less** reactive than carbon.   [1 mark]

b   Name **one** metal that is **more** reactive than carbon.   [1 mark]

c   Can aluminium be extracted from a compound by heating with carbon?   [1 mark]

5   Which **one** of the following statements about ores is correct?

A   Metals that are found as their element and not joined to any other substances are called ores.

B   Ores are rocks that contain enough of a metal that it is economical to extract the metal.

C   Any rock that contains a metal is called an ore.   [1 mark]

6   Why is gold not found combined chemically with other elements?   [1 mark]

7   What is one reason that we should recycle metals?   [1 mark]

8   Metals are dug out of the earth in mines and quarries.

a   Which **one** of the following statements describes an advantage of quarries and mines?

A   produce dust that can cause lung problems

B   old quarries and mines can be landscaped

C   provide jobs   [1 mark]

b   Which **one** of the following statements describes a disadvantage of quarries and mines?

A   quarries and mines destroy habitats of plants and animals

B   metals are a finite resource

C   roads and services around quarries are often improved   [1 mark]

10 Vocabulary builder

1 Match each key word to its definition.

Key word	Definition
element	Two or more substances that are not chemically joined together.
compound	Two or more elements chemically bonded together.
mixture	A mixture made mainly of metals.
alloy	A substance made of only one type of atom.

[3 marks]

2 Choose the correct words to complete the description of an ore.

Most metals are found as **compounds / mixtures**, where they are chemically **attracted / bonded** to other substances. An ore contains enough of the metal to make it **economical / environmentally friendly** to extract the metal.

[3 marks]

3 Choose the correct word to identify what is being described in the sentences below.

a The scientific term for heat.

    conductor   **density**   **electrical**   **thermal**

[1 mark]

b An alloy of iron and carbon.

    iron carbide   **iron carbonate**   **steel**

[1 mark]

4 Choose the correct words to complete the following sentences on metals.

Metals have a **complex / giant** structure made up of lots of atoms. The atoms are joined by strong **bonds / connections**. Most metals have a high melting **point / spot**. Metals are also good **absorbers / conductors** of electricity and thermal energy.

[4 marks]

5 Complete the following sentences about the properties of metals.

Aluminium has a low d _ _ _ _ _ _ compared to other metals.

C _ _ _ _ _ _ _ _ _ is when metals react with oxygen to form the metal oxide.

Metals are good c _ _ _ _ _ _ _ _ _ of electricity and t _ _ _ _ _ _ energy.

[4 marks]

6 Match each key term to its definition.

Key term	Definition
finite	The process where a waste metal is converted into a new product.
recycling	A substance that does not easily join chemically to other substances.
extraction	A resource where only a limited amount is available.
unreactive	Getting a metal from a metal ore.

[3 marks]

10.5 The reactivity series

Learning objectives

After this topic, you should know:

- what the reactivity series is
- how the reactivity series can be used to predict displacement reactions.

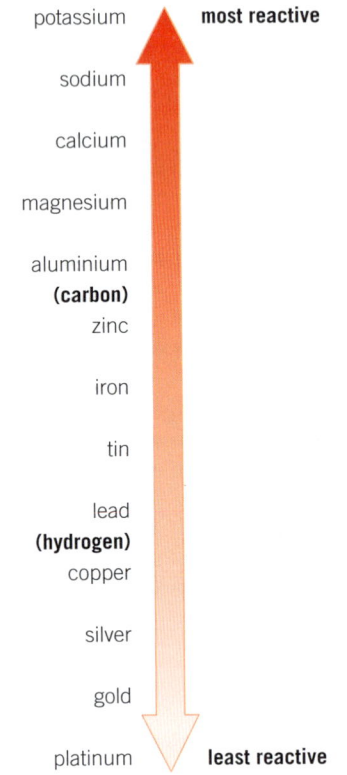

Figure 1 The reactivity series with hydrogen and carbon.

When a metal reacts with other substances, the metal atoms form positively charged ions. The more reactive a metal is, the easier it is for it to become a positive ion.

The **reactivity series** is a list of metals from the most reactive to the least reactive. The list is made from observing the reactions of metals with water and with acid.

Table 1 The reactivity series of metals.

Order of reactivity		Reaction with water	Reaction with dilute acid
most reactive	potassium, K	fizz, give off hydrogen gas, leaving an alkaline solution of metal hydroxide	explode
	sodium, Na		
	lithium, Li		
	calcium, Ca		fizz, give off hydrogen gas, and form a salt
	magnesium, Mg	very slow reaction	
	aluminium, Al		
	zinc, Zn		
	iron, Fe		
	tin, Sn	slight reaction with steam (very hot water)	react slowly with warm acid
	lead, Pb		
	copper, Cu	no reaction	no reaction
	silver, Ag		
least reactive	gold, Au		

Often hydrogen and carbon are added to the reactivity series to help you make predictions.

- Hydrogen is listed between copper and lead. All metals above hydrogen will react with acids.

- Carbon is listed between aluminium and zinc. All metals below carbon can be extracted from their ores by heating with carbon.

A: Identify which metal is more reactive, tin or lithium.

Displacement reactions

In a **displacement reaction**, a more reactive element takes the place of a less reactive element in a compound.

B: Describe what a displacement reaction is.

We can use the reactivity series to predict whether a displacement reaction will happen.

For example, the reactivity series shows that iron is more reactive than copper.

Therefore, if iron was added to copper sulfate solution, the iron **would** take the place of copper in the compound copper sulfate. Iron sulfate solution and solid copper metal would be formed.

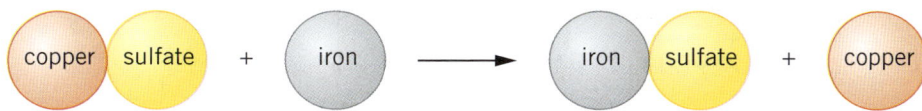

However, if copper was added to iron sulfate, copper **would not** take the place of iron in the compound.

C: Identify whether lead would displace zinc from zinc nitrate.

1 Identify whether the following metals will react with acids.

  A calcium   **B** silver   **C** zinc   [1 mark]

2a Identify which **two** of the following displacement reactions will take place.

  A aluminium + tin chloride

  B copper + magnesium sulfate

  C lead nitrate + iron   [2 marks]

  b Name the metal compound that will be formed by the **two** displacement reactions identified in Question **2a**.   [2 marks]

3 Use the data in the table to put metals X, Y, and Z in order of reactivity.

Metal	Observations from reaction with water	Observations from reaction with acid
X	no reaction	some bubbles given off
Y	no reaction	no reaction
Z	lots of fizzing	explodes

      [2 marks]

10.6 Electrolysis

Learning objectives

After this topic, you should know:

- what electrolysis is
- how electrolysis can be used to extract metals from their compounds.

Ionic compounds are made up of ions of a **metal** and a **non-metal**. They are solids at room temperature and do not conduct electricity. However, when they are molten (melted) or dissolved in water, the ions that they are made up of are free to move. They can then conduct electricity. When ionic compounds are molten or dissolved, they are called **electrolytes**.

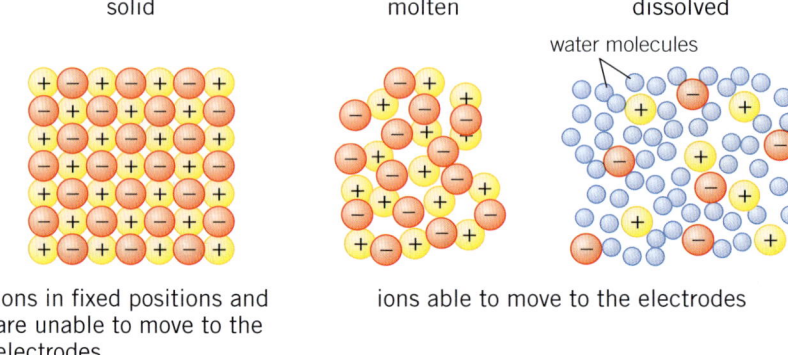

solid   molten   dissolved

water molecules

ions in fixed positions and are unable to move to the electrodes   ions able to move to the electrodes

Figure 1 *Ionic compounds can conduct electricity when molten or dissolved.*

An electric current can be passed through an electrolyte using **electrodes**. As the electric current passes through the electrolyte, the ions of the ionic compound will move towards the electrodes. This process is called **electrolysis**. The ions lose their charge at the electrodes and elements are produced.

A: Give the type of compound that can undergo electrolysis.

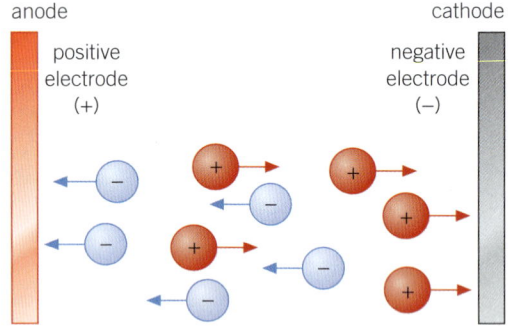

anode   cathode

positive electrode (+)   negative electrode (−)

Figure 2 *The ions move to the electrode with the opposite charge to theirs.*

The positive metal ions are attracted to the negative electrode, which is called the **cathode**. The metal element will be formed at the negative electrode (cathode).

The negative non-metal ions are attracted to the positive electrode, which is called the **anode**. The non-metal element will be formed at the positive electrode (anode).

B: Identify which electrode metal ions go to.

You can write word equations to describe electrolysis reactions. For example, electrolysis can be used to produce zinc and chlorine from zinc chloride.

$$\text{zinc chloride} \rightarrow \text{zinc} + \text{chlorine}$$

Extracting metals

Aluminium cannot be extracted from aluminium ore by heating with carbon. This is because aluminium is more reactive than carbon so cannot be displaced from its compounds by carbon. Reactive metals like aluminium can instead be extracted from their ores by electrolysis.

Aluminium ores contain the compound aluminium oxide. This must be molten but it has a very high melting point. It is mixed with a compound called cryolite, which lowers the melting point.

At these high temperatures, the oxygen that is made reacts with the positive carbon electrodes. This means that they must be regularly replaced because they burn away. The molten aluminium collects at the negative electrode and is removed.

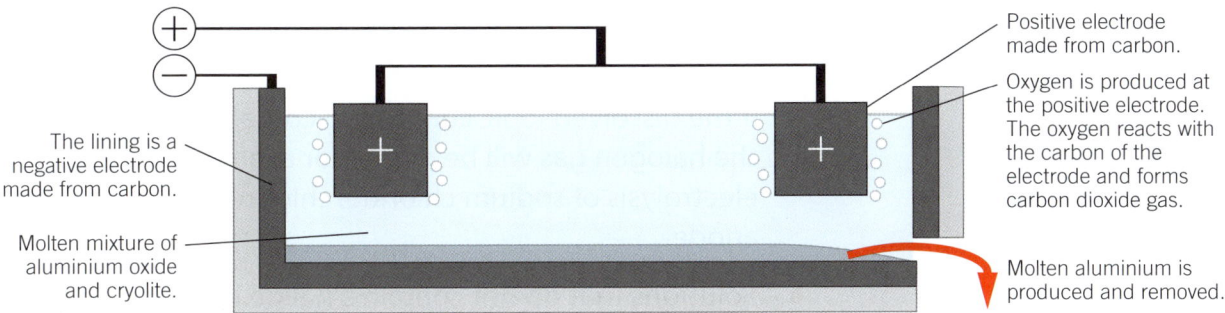

Positive electrode made from carbon.

Oxygen is produced at the positive electrode. The oxygen reacts with the carbon of the electrode and forms carbon dioxide gas.

The lining is a negative electrode made from carbon.

Molten mixture of aluminium oxide and cryolite.

Molten aluminium is produced and removed.

Figure 3 *Aluminium can be extracted from its ores using electrolysis.*

C: Why does the positive electrode need to be replaced regularly?

1   Match each key word to its definition.

Key word	Definition
anode	Process of passing electricity through ionic compounds to form elements.
cathode	Positive electrode.
electrolysis	Molten or dissolved ionic compound.
electrolyte	Negative electrode.

[3 marks]

2   Choose the correct words to complete the sentences.

Aluminium is a **reactive / unreactive** metal. Aluminium ores contain mainly aluminium **oxide / sulfide**. The aluminium oxide is **boiled / melted** and electrolysed. Aluminium is made at the **anode / cathode** and oxygen is made at the anode.

[4 marks]

3   Complete the word equation for the electrolysis of lead bromide.

lead bromide → _____ + _____   [1 mark]

10.7 Investigating electrolysis

Learning objectives

After this topic, you should know:

- how to set up electrolysis
- how to predict the products of electrolysis.

The process of electrolysis uses electricity to break down a compound into simpler substances. Only ionic compounds can undergo electrolysis. They must be melted or dissolved in water so that the ions are free to move.

Ionic compounds are made from a metal and a non-metal. When ionic compounds undergo electrolysis, they are broken down into the metal and non-metal parts.

Predicting the products of electrolysis of a solution

Anode

The **anode** is the positive electrode. Non-metals are produced at the positive electrode.

- If the dissolved ionic compound contains a halide ion then the halogen gas will be made. For example, during the electrolysis of sodium chloride, chlorine is formed at the anode.

- Solutions that do not contain a halide ion form oxygen at the anode. For example, during the electrolysis of sodium sulfate solution, oxygen is formed at the anode.

A: Name the non-metal formed at the anode during the electrolysis of zinc nitrate solution.

Cathode

The **cathode** is the negative electrode.

- If the dissolved ionic compound contains a metal that is **more** reactive than hydrogen, hydrogen gas will be formed at the cathode. For example, during the electrolysis of sodium chloride solution, hydrogen is formed at the cathode.

- If the dissolved ionic compound has a metal that is **less** reactive than hydrogen, then the metal will be made at the cathode. For example, during the electrolysis of silver chloride solution, silver is formed at the cathode.

potassium — most reactive
sodium
calcium
magnesium
aluminium
(carbon)
zinc
iron
tin
lead
(hydrogen)
copper
silver
gold
platinum — least reactive

Figure 1 *The reactivity series.*

B: Name the products formed at the anode and the cathode during the electrolysis of silver chloride.

Investigating the electrolysis of aqueous solutions

Step 1: Half-fill a beaker with the solution to be electrolysed.

Step 2: Put the two electrodes into the solution and connect to the low voltage power supply.

Step 3: Turn on the power supply and observe the electrodes.

Step 4: If you see bubbles, collect the gas in an upside down test tube and test the gas.

   a   If you hear a 'pop' with a lighted splint then you have collected hydrogen.

   b   If a glowing splint re-lights, you have collected oxygen.

   c   If damp blue litmus paper turns red and then bleaches, you have collected chlorine gas.

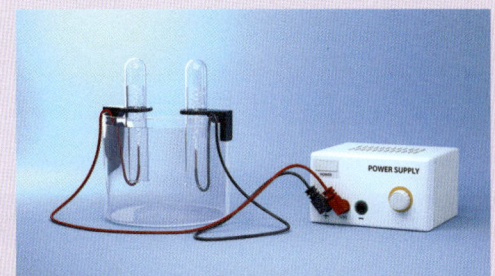

Figure 2 An electrolysis experiment.

C: The gas collected at the anode bleaches damp litmus paper. Identify the gas.

1 Match each gas to the correct test for the gas.

Gas	Test for gas
chlorine	Lighted splint, hear a pop.
oxygen	Damp blue litmus paper turns red then bleaches.
hydrogen	Re-lights a glowing splint.

[2 marks]

2 Predict the products formed at the anode and the cathode during the electrolysis of lithium bromide solution. Choose the correct answer.

  a At the anode:

     bromine   hydrogen   lithium   oxygen   [1 mark]

  b At the cathode:

     bromine   hydrogen   lithium   oxygen   [1 mark]

3 A student electrolysed an unknown ionic compound. He observed a reddish-brown metal forming on the cathode and bubbles of a gas produced at the anode. He tested the gas and found that it bleached damp blue litmus paper.

Name the unknown ionic compound the student electrolysed. [2 marks]

4 A student electrolysed a solution of silver bromide.

Describe what she would observe at the anode and the cathode during the electrolysis of silver bromide solution. [2 marks]

10.8 Sustainability

Figure 1 *Cotton comes from plants. It is a renewable resource.*

Scientists work to improve farming and industrial processes to reduce the amount of energy and resources that we use. This helps us to live more **sustainably**. Sustainable means that we can meet our own needs whilst making sure there are enough resources left to meet the needs of future generations.

A: Describe what we mean by sustainable.

Resources

We use resources from the Earth to make food, for warmth and shelter, and for transport.

Renewable resources can be produced or replaced at the same rate that they are used up. For example, cotton is grown on plants. More plants can be grown to replace the ones we use.

Finite resources can be used up because they cannot be easily produced or replaced. Fossil fuels such as coal, crude oil, and natural gas are all finite resources. We will eventually run out of these resources unless we reduce the amount we use, reuse products, and recycle waste.

B: Describe what a finite resource is.

Life cycle assessment

Life cycle assessments (LCAs) help measure how sustainable a product is. An LCA number is calculated for each product. This is based on how much the environment is affected by making and moving the product. There are four areas to think about:

1. Getting and processing the raw materials.
2. Making the product.
3. Using the product.
4. Getting rid of the product when it is not needed anymore.

Information is collected about each stage of the product's life cycle. A higher number means the impact on the environment is bigger and means the product is less sustainable.

C: Name the four parts of a life cycle assessment.

Reduce

To lower the chances of running out of finite resources, we can reduce the amount of resources that we use. For example, cycling, walking, or getting a bus to school instead of driving reduces the amount of petrol you use. Petrol is a finite resource.

Reuse

Some products can be reused. For example, glass and plastic bottles can be washed and reused.

Recycle

If they cannot be reused, you can recycle products made from materials like glass, plastic, and metals. For example, glass bottles can be melted to make other glass products. Recycling:

- reduces the amount of waste in landfill

- reduces the amount of new resources being used

- uses less energy than making a product from raw materials.

> **D:** List three materials that can be recycled.

1   Match each key word to its definition.

Key word	Definition
renewable	Resources that are being used up faster than they can be replaced.
finite	Resources that can be replaced at the same rate as they are used. [1 mark]

2   The table shows some examples of common resources.

Resource	Source
aluminium	mined and extracted from metal ores
cotton	grown on plants
crude oil	made from crushed remains of organisms from millions of years ago
wood	made from trees

Use the information to sort the resources by whether they are finite or renewable. [4 marks]

3   A coffee shop uses disposable paper cups. However, customers can bring in their own reusable plastic cups.

Paper cups are made from trees. They can only be used once. They can be recycled, but are normally thrown in the bin	Plastic cups are made from crude oil. They can be used on a daily basis for many years. The plastic can often be recycled.

Suggest why plastic cups are considered more sustainable than paper cups, even though they are made from a finite resource. [1 mark]

10 Practice questions

01 Name the metal that is always used to make steel.

A aluminium   **B** cobalt   **C** iron

D magnesium   [1 mark]

02 Which of the following statements about alloys is true?

A Alloys are mixtures of non-metals.

B Alloys always contain carbon.

C Alloys are mixtures of metals.

D Alloys are softer than pure metals.

[1 mark]

03 Which of the following is **not** a property of metals?

A brittle

B good electrical conductors

C good thermal conductors

D shiny   [1 mark]

04 Which of the following is **not** an advantage of recycling metals?

A less quarrying is required

B recycled metal is of a better quality

C energy is saved

D metal ores will last longer   [1 mark]

05 For each solution, predict what would be formed at the cathode and the anode.

05.1 zinc chloride solution   [2 marks]

05.2 potassium bromide solution   [2 marks]

05.3 copper sulfate solution   [2 marks]

06.1 Complete the word equation:

magnesium + zinc oxide →

_____ + _____ _____   [1 mark]

06.2 Explain why this is a displacement reaction.   [2 marks]

07 Match each property of metals to the correct explanation for that property.

Property of metal	Explanation for property
good electrical conductors	Layers of metal atoms can easily slide over each other.
easily shaped	Made of lots of atoms joined by strong chemical bonds.
high melting point	Have electrons that are free to move.

[2 marks]

08 Aluminium is extracted from aluminium oxide using electrolysis.

08.1 Why does the aluminium oxide have to be melted for the electrolysis to take place?   [1 mark]

08.2 Is an aluminium ion positive or negative?   [1 mark]

08.3 At which electrode is the aluminium metal produced?

anode   cathode   [1 mark]

08.4 The electrode where oxygen is produced is made of carbon.

i Explain why this electrode has to be replaced regularly.   [2 marks]

ii Describe a test to prove that oxygen is produced. Include the positive test result.   [2 marks]

09 A student investigated the reactivity of four different metals by reacting them with hydrochloric acid. His method is shown below.

Step 1 Measure 20 cm³ of hydrochloric acid and put into a conical flask.

Step 2 Measure 2 g of the metal powder.

Step 3 Measure the temperature of the acid.

Step 4   Add the metal powder to the acid and leave until the reaction stops fizzing.

Step 5   Measure the final temperature of the solution.

09.1   Name the piece of equipment used to measure the temperature of the solution.
[1 mark]

09.2   The student's results are shown in Table 1. The letters given are not the symbols for the metals.

Table 1

Metal	Starting temperature in °C	Final temperature in °C	Temperature change in °C
W	21	25	4
X	22	45	
Y	21	21	0
Z	21	32	11

Calculate the temperature change for metal X.
[1 mark]

09.3   Put the metals in order of their reactivity. The first one has been done for you.

least reactive   **most reactive**

Y → ☐ → ☐ → ☐
[2 marks]

09.4   The four metals the student used were copper, iron, magnesium, and zinc.

i   Identify which metal is magnesium.

W   X   Y   Z
[1 mark]

ii   Give a reason for your answer to part **i**.
[2 marks]

iii   Identify which metal is copper.

W   X   Y   Z
[1 mark]

iv   Give a reason for your answer to part **iii**.
[2 marks]

10   Solder is an alloy of the metals tin and lead. It is used in making electrical connections. To do this, the solder is melted using a hot metal rod. The liquid solder flows into the required space, and then cools and turns to a solid.

The melting points of tin, lead, and solder are shown in Table 2.

Table 2

Substance	Melting point in °C
tin	232
lead	328
solder	100

10.1   Define the term alloy.
[1 mark]

10.2   Explain why the solder is better suited for its use than the pure metals.
[2 marks]

11   A life cycle assessment assesses the environmental impact of a product during the four stages of its lifecycle.

Suggest why recycling a product will reduce the environmental impact at each stage given below.

11.1   Getting and processing the raw materials to make the product.
[1 mark]

11.2   Getting rid of the product when it is not needed anymore.
[1 mark]

12   Rock A and rock B each contain a different metal. Table 3 shows how much of the metal can be extracted from the rocks, the cost of extracting the metal, and the price that the metal can be sold for.

Table 3

	Cost to extract the metal from the rock in £	Amount of metal that can be extracted from the rock in kg	Price that 100 kg of the metal can be sold for in £
rock A	500	300	180
rock B	450	370	120

Identify which rock is a metal ore. Give a reason for your answer.
[4 marks]

Chemistry

In chemical reactions a new substance is made. The mass at the start and end of the reaction is the same because the atoms are just rearranged.

There are different types of chemical reaction. These include:

- combustion
- thermal decomposition
- oxidation
- displacement reactions
- neutralisation.

Q **What is produced when two chemicals react?**

Indicators change colour in solutions of different pH. Universal indicator changes into lots of different colours and can be used to find the pH of a solution. Acids have a pH of less than 7 and alkalis have a pH of more than 7. A neutral solution has a pH of 7.

Q **A chemical has a pH of 4. Is it an acid or an alkali?**

The air is about 80% nitrogen and 20% oxygen. There is a small amount of other gases including carbon dioxide. One reason carbon dixoide levels are increasing is because humans are burning fossil fuels. This extra carbon dioxide in our atmosphere could lead to climate change.

Q **What is the main gas in air?**

Component 4
Chemistry in our world

▶ ### Reactions of acids

Acids taste sharp and some can be dangerous. They can be found everywhere – from carbonic acid in rain, to citric acid in fruit. Some acids react with metals to make hydrogen gas.

Neutralisation is a chemical reaction between an acid and an alkali.

▶ ### Energy and rate of reaction

Chemical reactions can happen very slowly – like rusting, or very fast – like a firework. The rate of reaction is a measure of the speed of the chemical change.

Energy is transferred during a reaction. If the temperature increases, energy is transferred to the surroundings. If temperature decreases, energy is taken in from the surroundings.

▶ ### Earth's atmosphere

There is a layer of gas around the Earth called the atmosphere. This has changed over the 4.5 billion years the Earth has existed, and continues to change today.

Burning fossil fuels creates acidic gases that can cause problems like acid rain, smog, and asthma. It also makes carbon dioxide, which is a greenhouse gas. This extra greenhouse gas in our atmosphere could be causing more flooding, melting of the ice caps, and increasing world temperatures.

11 Reactions of acids
11.1 Neutralisation

Entry Level Certificate

Learning objectives

After this topic, you should know:

- what an acid and an alkali are
- what happens when an acid meets an alkali
- how to test for carbon dioxide gas.

Figure 1 positioned above the pH scale image

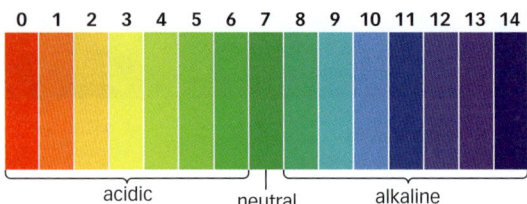

acidic   neutral   alkaline

Figure 1 *The pH scale runs from 0 to 14. Chemicals with a pH value less than 7 are acids. Chemicals with a pH value more than 7 are alkalis. Chemicals with a pH value of 7 are neutral.*

How does the concentration of an alkali affect a neutralisation reaction?

Measure what volume of alkali is needed to neutralise an acid. Investigate how the volume of alkali needed changes when a different concentration of the alkali is used.

Acids

Acids are chemicals that have a pH value less than 7.

Bases

Chemicals that can react with acids are called **bases**. These include:

- reactive metals
- metal hydroxides
- metal oxides
- metal carbonates.

Alkalis

Alkalis are bases that can dissolve in water. They have a pH value greater than 7.

A: A chemical has a pH value of 9. Is it an acid or an alkali?

Neutralisation

Neutralisation is a chemical reaction between an acid and a base. A metal salt and water are always made. Metal hydroxides, metal oxides, and metal carbonates can all react with acids in **neutralisation** reactions.

Metal hydroxides

Metal hydroxides are alkalis because they can dissolve in water.

Sodium hydroxide reacts with hydrochloric acid to form the salt, sodium chloride, and water. This can be described in a word equation:

sodium + hydrochloric acid → sodium chloride + water

Metal oxides

Metal oxides are bases but most are not alkalis as they do not dissolve in water.

Copper oxide reacts with sulfuric acid to form the salt, copper sulfate, and water. The word equation for this reaction is:

copper oxide + sulfuric acid → copper sulfate + water

Metal carbonates

Metal carbonates are bases. Most do not dissolve in water so are not alkalis.

Sodium carbonate reacts with hydrochloric acid to form carbon dioxide, the salt, sodium chloride, and water. The word equation for this reaction is:

sodium + hydrochloric → sodium + carbon + water
carbonate   acid   chloride   dioxide

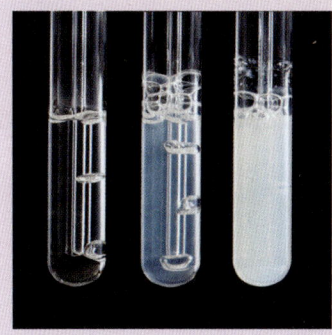

Figure 2 *Test for carbon dioxide with limewater and it will go cloudy. You can use limewater to show that carbon dioxide gas is produced when a metal carbonate reacts with an acid.*

B: What gas is made when a metal carbonate reacts with an acid?

Collecting salts

The salts that are made from a neutralisation reaction will be dissolved in the water. To collect the solid salt, leave the solution out in a warm place. The water will evaporate, leaving the salt behind. This is **crystallisation**.

1   Match each pair of reactants to the correct products of that reaction.

Reactants	Products
zinc carbonate + hydrochloric acid	zinc chloride + water
zinc hydroxide + sulfuric acid	zinc chloride + carbon dioxide + water
zinc carbonate + sulfuric acid	zinc sulfate + carbon dioxide + water
zinc oxide + hydrochloric acid	zinc sulfate + water [3 marks]

2   Classify these chemicals as an acid, base, or alkali.
   copper oxide   hydrochloric acid   sodium hydroxide   sulfuric acid
[4 marks]

3   Complete the word equation for the reaction of calcium carbonate and hydrochloric acid.
   calcium carbonate + hydrochloric acid → _____ + _____ + water   [1 mark]

11.2 Metals and acids

Learning objectives

After this topic, you should know:

- what happens when a metal reacts with an acid
- how to test for hydrogen gas.

Figure 1 *Some metals react with acid to make hydrogen gas and a metal salt.*

Metals like magnesium are reactive. They react with acids. When a metal reacts with an acid you see bubbles and hear fizzing. This is because hydrogen gas is made.

A: What gas is made when a metal reacts with an acid?

When metals react with an acid, they form a metal salt as well as the hydrogen gas. The name of the salt comes from the metal and the acid used.

Table 1 *How to name salts.*

Name of metal	Name of acid	Name of ion from acid	Example of a metal salt
zinc	hydrochloric acid	chloride	zinc chloride
magnesium	sulfuric acid	sulfate	magnesium sulfate
iron	hydrochloric acid	chloride	iron chloride

B: What is the name of the salt formed when iron reacts with sulfuric acid?

When magnesium reacts with hydrochloric acid, bubbles of gas are seen and the pieces of metal get smaller and smaller. The products of the reaction are hydrogen gas and a solution of the salt, magnesium chloride. This word equation for the reaction is:

magnesium + hydrochloric acid → hydrogen + magnesium chloride

When zinc reacts with sulfuric acid, it makes hydrogen gas and a solution of dissolved zinc sulfate. This word equation for the reaction is:

zinc + sulfuric acid → hydrogen + zinc sulfate

C: What is the word equation for the reaction between iron and sulfuric acid?

Testing for hydrogen

You can use the squeaky pop test to show that the gas produced in a reaction is hydrogen.

Step 1: Collect the gas that is given off in the reaction in an upside down test tube.

Step 2: Put a burning splint at the open end of the test tube.

Step 3: If you hear a squeaky pop then the gas is hydrogen.

How does the type of acid affect how much hydrogen is produced?
Investigate the amount of hydrogen produced when different acids react with a metal by collecting the gas produced. Use a lit splint to test that the gas produced is hydrogen.

D: How do you test for hydrogen gas?

1   Choose the correct words from the box to complete the word equation for the reaction.

   sulfuric acid   zinc sulfate

   zinc + _____ → hydrogen + _____   [1 mark]

2   Choose the correct words to complete the sentences.

   When a **reactive / unreactive** metal is put into an acid you will see bubbles. The bubbles show that a **gas / liquid** is made. If the gas is collected and tested with a burning splint, you will hear a **fizzing / pop**. The gas is **hydrogen / oxygen**.   [4 marks]

3   **a**   Complete the word equation for the reaction of iron with sulfuric acid.

   iron + sulfuric acid → _____ + _____   [2 marks]

   b   What is the name of the ion in the salt made that comes from sulfuric acid?   [1 mark]

11.3 Investigating acids and carbonates

Learning objectives

After this topic, you should know:

- how to safely observe reactions between acids and carbonates
- how to make a sample of dry soluble salt.

Metal carbonates can react with acids in a neutralisation reaction. This chemical reaction makes a salt, carbon dioxide, and water.

A: What type of reaction happens between an acid and a metal carbonate?

Reacting acids and carbonates

Step 1: Using a measuring cylinder, measure 20 cm³ of hydrochloric acid into a beaker.
Use a piece of universal indicator paper to measure the pH of the acid. It should be less than pH 7.

Step 2: Stir half a spatula of copper carbonate into the hydrochloric acid. Bubbles of gas will be made.

Step 3: Keep adding half a spatula of copper carbonate until no more bubbles are made. This will mean that all of the hydrochloric acid has reacted.

Step 4: Dip another piece of universal indicator paper into the solution to see what the pH of the solution now is. The pH value should be higher than the pH of the acid in Step 1. This shows it is a neutralisation reaction.

Figure 1 *Add the metal carbonate to the acid until the fizzing stops.*

The carbon dioxide gas produced can be collected and tested with limewater. The limewater goes cloudy, showing that carbon dioxide was made.

B: What chemical do you use to test for carbon dioxide?

The reaction between copper carbonate and hydrochloric acid forms carbon dioxide, water, and the salt, copper chloride. The copper chloride is dissolved in the water. You can separate the salt from the solution.

Separating the salt

Step 1: Filtration
Filter the mixture to remove the unreacted copper carbonate. Keep the liquid.

Figure 2 *Filter the mixture and collect the salt solution.*

Step 2: Evaporation

Pour the liquid into an evaporating dish. Put the evaporating dish over a beaker filled with water. Heat gently until half of the liquid in the dish has evaporated.

Remove from the heat.

Step 3: Crystallisation

Crystals of the copper chloride salt will have started forming.

Leave the solution until all of the water has evaporated and only the copper chloride crystals are left.

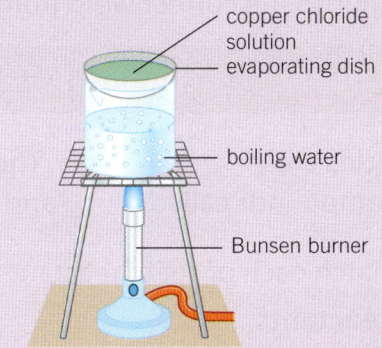

copper chloride solution
evaporating dish

boiling water

Bunsen burner

Figure 3 *Gently heat the salt solution to start to make the crystals.*

C: What are the three separation methods used to separate the salt from the solution?

1 Choose the correct words from the box to complete the following sentences.

| crystals   evaporated   filter   unreacted |

To separate the salt from the solution, first _____ the solution to remove the _____ metal carbonate. Then heat the solution until half of the water has _____. Remove from the heat and leave the solution so that all of the water evaporates and _____ of the salt form.

[3 marks]

2 A student carried out the neutralisation reaction between sodium carbonate and hydrochloric acid. Her results are shown in the table.

Mass of sodium carbonate in g	3	6	9	12	15	18	21	24	27
pH value	3.0	3.5	4.1	5.0	5.9	6.7	7.0	7.0	7.0

What mass of sodium carbonate neutralised the solution of hydrochloric acid? [1 mark]

3 a Complete the word equation for the reaction between calcium carbonate and hydrochloric acid.

calcium carbonate + hydrochloric acid → _____ + _____ + carbon dioxide [1 mark]

b What would you observe during the reaction that shows you that a gas is made? [1 mark]

11 Checkpoint

1 Choose the correct word from the box to complete the sentences.

| bases | neutralised | salts | water |

Acids are _____ by _____ . The products of these reactions are
compounds called _____ and _____ .   [3 marks]

2 Match each of set of reactants to the correct products.

Reactants   **Products**

magnesium + sulfuric acid   magnesium sulfate + carbon dioxide + water

magnesium oxide + sulfuric acid   magnesium sulfate + hydrogen

magnesium carbonate + sulfuric acid   magnesium sulfate + water   [2 marks]

3 a What is the name of the salt formed from the reaction of iron
      and hydrochloric acid?

      iron chloride   **iron chlorine**   **iron hydrochloric**   [1 mark]

   b What is the name of the salt formed from the reaction of zinc
      and sulfuric acid?

      zinc sulfate   **zinc sulfide**   **zinc sulfuric**   [1 mark]

4 a Which gas can be tested for using a burning splint?

      carbon dioxide   **chlorine**   **hydrogen**   [1 mark]

   b If the gas is present, what would you observe happen?   [1 mark]

5 a Which gas is limewater used to test for?

      carbon dioxide   **hydrogen**   **oxygen**   [1 mark]

   b If the gas is present, what would you observe happen?   [1 mark]

6 When zinc carbonate is added to sulfuric acid, three products are formed.

   a What is the name of the salt formed?   [1 mark]

   b Which gas is formed in the reaction?   [1 mark]

   c What is the other product formed?   [1 mark]

7 The compound magnesium oxide is insoluble in water.

   a Is magnesium oxide an alkali or a base?   [1 mark]

   b Complete the word equation for the reaction between magnesium oxide
      and hydrochloric acid.

      magnesium oxide + hydrochloric acid → _____ + _____   [1 mark]

   c How is the salt separated from the solution formed?   [1 mark]

11 Vocabulary builder

1 Match each key word to its definition.

Key word	Definition
soluble	A substance that will dissolve in a solvent.
insoluble	A mixture where a substance is dissolved in a solvent.
solution	A liquid that substances dissolve in.
solvent	A substance that will not dissolve in a solvent.

[3 marks]

2 Choose the correct term from the list to identify the key term being described.

a This type of solution has a pH below 7.

acid   alkali   neutral

[1 mark]

b The type of substance will be formed when an acid is neutralised by a base.

alkali   neutral   salt

[1 mark]

c This type of solution has a pH greater than 7.

acid   alkali   salt

[1 mark]

d This type of substance will neutralise an acid but is insoluble in water.

alkali   base   salt

[1 mark]

3 Choose the correct word from the box to complete the names of the salts in the word equation.

a | chloric   chloride   chlorine |

iron + hydrochloric acid → iron _____ + water

[1 mark]

b | sulfate   sulfide   sulfur |

iron + sulfuric acid → iron _____ + water

[1 mark]

4 Choose the correct words to complete the sentences.

Bases are **chlorides** / **oxides** or **hydroxides** / **nitrates** of metals. They can also be metal **carbonates** / **sulfates**. If a base is **insoluble** / **soluble** in water, it called an alkali.

[4 marks]

5 Complete the sentences below:

The reaction between a base and an acid is called a n _ _ _ _ _ _ _ _ _ _ _ _ reaction. The p _ _ _ _ _ _ _ of the reaction are a s _ _ _ and water.

[3 marks]

11.4 The pH scale

Learning objectives

After this topic, you should know:

- what pH is
- how to identify the particles in acids and alkalis
- how to describe what happens during neutralisation reactions.

The **pH scale** is a measurement of how acidic or alkaline a solution is.

- Solutions with a pH of less than 7 are **acidic**.
- Solutions with a pH of more than 7 are **alkaline**.
- Solutions with a pH of 7 are **neutral**.

A: Give the pH value of a neutral solution.

Universal indicator is a chemical that changes colour to show the pH of a solution. It comes as a liquid that you can add to the solution or a paper strip that you can dip into the solution. To test the pH, add the indicator and compare the colour it changes to against the colour chart.

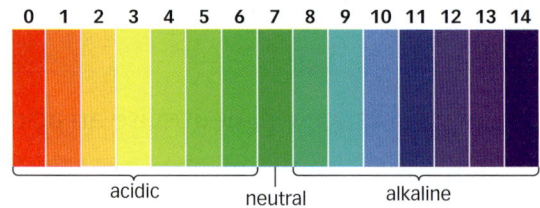

Figure 1 *The pH scale tells you how acidic or alkaline a solution is.*

The pH of a solution can also be measured with a pH probe. Put the end of the probe into the solution and it will accurately show the pH as a number.

B: Give two ways of measuring the pH of a solution.

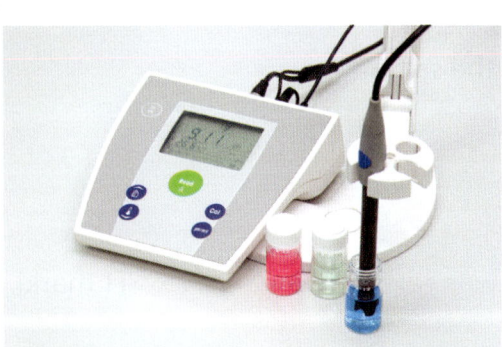

Figure 2 *pH probes can be used to measure pH.*

What are the pH values of different substances?

Measure the pH of lots of different chemicals and substances found around the classroom. You could also measure the pH of some household cleaning products. Are they acidic, alkaline, or neutral?

Acids

All acids can dissolve in water. When acids are dissolved in water they release hydrogen ions, H^+ (aq). This is the particle that makes a solution acidic.

C: Give the formula of a hydrogen ion.

Alkalis

Alkalis are bases that can dissolve in water. When alkalis are dissolved in water they release hydroxide ions, OH^- (aq). This is the particle that makes a solution alkaline.

D: Name the particle that alkalis release when they are dissolved in water.

Neutralisation

When an acid particle and an alkali particle meet, they will always produce water. The acid particles and the alkali particles react with each other and are no longer in the solution.
They turn into new water molecules in the reaction.
This means the pH becomes 7. The solution becomes neutral.
This is a neutralisation reaction.

The word equation for a neutralisation reaction is:

hydrogen ions + hydroxide ions $\rightarrow$ water

You can also write a symbol equation for the reaction:

$$H^+ (aq) + OH^- (aq) \rightarrow H_2O (l)$$

1   Match each chemical to the correct pH value for that chemical.

'<' means less than and '>' means greater than.

Chemical	pH value	
acid	pH = 7	
alkali	pH > 7	
neutral	pH < 7	[2 marks]

2   Identify whether the following substances are acids, alkalis, or neutral.   [4 marks]

Substance	pH of substance
A	3
B	7.3
C	12
D	7

3   Hydrochloric acid can react with sodium hydroxide to make sodium chloride and water.

   a   Name this type of reaction.   [1 mark]

   b   Give the formula of the ions that are reacting in this reaction.   [2 marks]

   c   Suggest the pH of the solution when the reaction is finished.   [1 mark]

11.5 Balanced symbol equations

Learning objectives

After this topic, you should know:

- how to write a balanced symbol equation with state symbols.

Writing symbol equations

A symbol equation shows how the atoms are arranged in the reactants and how they are rearranged to make the products.

The formulas (or formulae) of the reactants are written on the left of the arrow and the formulas (or formulae) of the products are written on the right.

For example, carbon reacts with oxygen to form carbon dioxide. The word equation for this reaction is:

$$\text{carbon} + \text{oxygen} \rightarrow \text{carbon dioxide}$$

The symbol equation for this reaction is:

$$C + O_2 \rightarrow CO_2$$

Oxygen and hydrogen are covalent molecules. They are always written as O_2 or H_2. Look at *9.8 Covalent molecules* to find out more.

Writing a balanced symbol equation

In a chemical reaction, no atoms are made or lost. They are just rearranged to make new substances. When writing a symbol equation, there must be the same number of each type of atom in the reactants and in the products.

Large numbers are put in front of the chemical formula to balance a symbol equation.

> **A: Describe what happens to atoms in a chemical reaction.**

To write a **balanced symbol equation**, start by writing the word equation for the reaction. Then write the formula for each chemical underneath. Count the number of each type of atom in the reactants and the products.

For example, hydrogen reacts with oxygen to make water.

Word equation:	hydrogen + oxygen $\rightarrow$ water	
Symbol equation:	H_2 + O_2 $\rightarrow$ H_2O	
Atom count:	$2 \times H$ $2 \times O$ $\rightarrow$ $2 \times H$ $1 \times O$	

There are more oxygen atoms on the reactant side than there are on the product side. This equation is not balanced. By putting a 2 before the water, the number of oxygen atoms on both sides of the equation becomes the same.

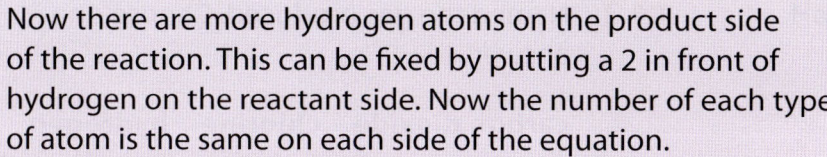

Now there are more hydrogen atoms on the product side of the reaction. This can be fixed by putting a 2 in front of hydrogen on the reactant side. Now the number of each type of atom is the same on each side of the equation.

Balanced symbol equation: $2H_2 + O_2 \rightarrow 2H_2O$

Atom count: $\quad 4 \times H \quad 2 \times O \rightarrow 4 \times H \quad 2 \times O$

The equation is balanced.

You should never change the small numbers after a chemical symbol to balance an equation. You should only ever add large numbers in front of the chemical symbols.

B: Give the formula for two hydrogen molecules.

State symbols

State symbols tell us if the chemical is a solid, liquid, gas, or dissolved in a solution. A state symbol is a lower-case letter in brackets after the chemical formula.

So for the reaction between hydrogen and oxygen, the balanced symbol equation with state symbols is:

$$2H_2(g) + O_2(g) \rightarrow 2H_2O(l)$$

Table 1 State symbols for symbol equations.

State symbol	State of chemical
(s)	solid
(l)	liquid
(g)	gas
(aq)	aqueous solution (this means dissolved in water)

1. Choose the correct terms from the box to complete the table.

State symbol	State of substance
(g)	_____
(____)	solid
(____)	dissolved in water
(____)	_____

[4 marks]

aq   g   gas   l   liquid   s

2. Solid carbon completely burns in oxygen to form carbon dioxide. Add the state symbols for the reaction shown.

$$C + O_2 \rightarrow CO_2 \qquad \text{[1 mark]}$$

3. Magnesium metal can burn in oxygen gas to make a white powder of magnesium oxide.
   a. Write a word equation for this reaction. [1 mark]
   b. Balance the symbol equation below for this reaction:
   $$Mg(s) + O_2(g) \rightarrow MgO(s) \qquad \text{[2 marks]}$$
   c. Name the gaseous reactant. [1 mark]

01 Match each chemical to the correct pH value.

Chemical	pH
alkali	12
neutral	2
acid	7

[2 marks]

02 Which of the following pairs of reactants would produce carbon dioxide?

A   water and calcium carbonate

B   sodium hydroxide and sodium carbonate

C   hydrochloric acid and sodium oxide

D   hydrochloric acid and sodium carbonate [1 mark]

03 Choose the correct words from the box to complete the following sentences.

> acidic   alkaline   H⁺   OH⁻

Hydroxide ions have the symbol _____ and are found in _____ solutions.

Hydrogen ions have the symbol _____ and are found in _____ solutions.

[3 marks]

04 A student adds some magnesium to hydrochloric acid. A gas is produced.

04.1 Describe what the student would observe. [1 mark]

04.2 Named the gas produced. Choose one answer.

carbon dioxide   chlorine   hydrogen oxygen [1 mark]

04.3 Describe how the student would test the gas. Give the result of the test. [2 marks]

04.4 Complete the equation for the reaction using the correct words from the box.

> chlorine   hydrogen
> magnesium chloride
> magnesium chlorine
> magnesium hydroxide   water

magnesium + hydrochloric acid →

_____ + _____

[1 mark]

05 A student tested some common household chemicals using a pH probe and some universal indicator paper. Her results are shown in Table 1.

Fill in the gaps in the table.

Table 1

Substance tested	pH of solution	Colour of universal indicator paper	Is the solution acid, alkali, or neutral?
oven cleaner	14		
battery acid	1		acid
water		green	
washing soda	10		

[7 marks]

06.1 Complete the symbol equation for the reaction of the ions between an acid and an alkali.

$$H^+ (aq) + OH^- (aq) \rightarrow \underline{\hspace{2cm}} (\underline{\hspace{1.5cm}})$$
[2 marks]

06.2 What does (aq) represent in the symbol equation? [1 mark]

06.3 Name the type of reaction shown in this equation. [1 mark]

07 Sodium hydroxide reacts with hydrochloric acid. The products of the reaction look exactly like the reactants.

07.1 Describe how you could use a pH probe to tell when the solution is neutral. [1 mark]

07.2 Describe how you could use universal indicator paper to tell when the solution is neutral. [1 mark]

08 The symbol equation for the reaction between magnesium and hydrochloric acid is:

$$Mg + HCl \rightarrow MgCl_2 + H_2$$

08.1 Balance the symbol equation for the reaction of magnesium and hydrochloric acid. [1 mark]

08.2 Add state symbols to the balanced symbol equation. [1 mark]

09 A student wanted to prepare a solution of sodium sulfate using sodium carbonate and an acid.

09.1 Name the acid that he should use. [1 mark]

09.2 Complete the word equation for the reaction.

sodium carbonate + \underline{\hspace{2cm}} $\rightarrow$
sodium sulfate + \underline{\hspace{1.5cm}} + \underline{\hspace{1.5cm}}
[1 mark]

09.3 Describe how the student could get the solid salt from the solution. [2 marks]

09.4 Sodium carbonate will neutralise acids and it is soluble in water.
Name the type of substance that sodium carbonate is. [1 mark]

10 A student investigated the reactivity of three different metal carbonates.
She measured the volume of gas produced in 1 minute. Her results are shown in Table 2.

Table 2

Metal carbonate	Volume of gas produced in 1 min in cm³
magnesium carbonate	50
sodium carbonate	76
zinc carbonate	23

10.1 Identify which carbonate is the most reactive. [1 mark]

10.2 Give one control variable from the student's investigation. [1 mark]

12 Energy and rate of reaction
12.1 Energy transfers

Learning objectives

After this topic, you should know:

- how energy transfers in a reaction can affect the temperature.

Energy is what makes everything happen. When chemical reactions or physical changes happen, energy is transferred between the reaction and the surroundings.

- The system is the substances that are reacting or undergoing a physical change (such as melting).

- The surroundings are the area around the system.

Energy transfers to the surroundings

In some chemical reactions, energy is transferred **to** the surroundings. This means that the temperature of the surroundings **increases**. Examples of reactions where energy is transferred to the surroundings are:

- oxidation reactions

- combustion (burning)

- neutralisation.

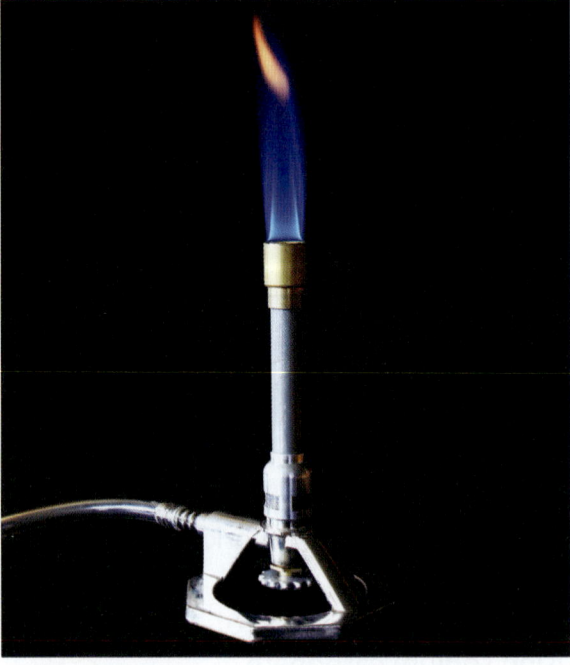

Figure 1 *A Bunsen burner involves a combustion reaction. Combustion reactions transfer energy to the surroundings.*

A: What happens to the temperature of the surroundings when energy is transferred to them?

Energy transfers to the system

Some reactions take in energy **from** the surroundings. This means that the temperature of the surroundings **decreases**. Examples of changes where energy is transferred from the surroundings are:

- dissolving ammonium chloride in water

- citric acid reacting with sodium hydrogencarbonate.

The test tube gets colder in both of these changes.

Figure 2 *Sherbet sweets feel cold in your mouth. This is because when citric acid and sodium hydrogencarbonate react, energy is transferred from the surroundings.*

B: Give one example of a chemical reaction where energy is transferred from the surroundings.

1 Choose the correct word from the box to complete the following sentence.

> from   to

When energy is transferred _____ the surroundings, the temperature of the surroundings increases.   [1 mark]

2 Sort the following changes based on whether energy is transferred to the surroundings or from the surroundings.

citric acid and sodium hydrogen carbonate

combustion

dissolving ammonium chloride in water

oxidation   [4 marks]

3 A student is investigating some chemical reactions. He has recorded his observations in the table below.

Experiment	Temperature at the start of the experiment in °C	Temperature at the end of the experiment in °C
A	23	11
B	23	32
C	23	25

Which of experiments A, B, and C transfer energy to the surroundings, and which take in energy from the surroundings?   [3 marks]

What energy transfers are involved in different reactions?
Investigate the energy transfers involved in different reactions by measuring the temperature changes that occur during the reaction.

12.2 Rate of reaction

Entry Level Certificate

Learning objectives

After this topic, you should know:

- how to increase the rate of a chemical reaction.

Chemical reactions happen at different speeds. Some reactions happen very fast. For example, the chemical reactions in fireworks happen very quickly. Some reactions are very slow. For example, rust is formed when iron reacts with oxygen in the air very slowly. This reaction causes a bike or a car to rust over many years.

The speed of the chemical reaction is called the **rate of reaction**. The more time it takes for a reaction to happen, the slower the rate of the reaction.

A: What is the rate of a reaction?

Speeding up

Chemical reactions happen when the particles of the substances that are reacting hit each other. These hits are called **collisions**. You can increase the rate of a reaction by making the particles collide with each other more often.

Increase the temperature. This makes the particles move faster so they are more likely to collide with each other more often. They also collide with more energy, which helps the particles to react.

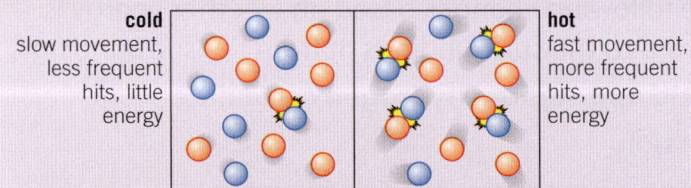

cold
slow movement, less frequent hits, little energy

hot
fast movement, more frequent hits, more energy

Figure 1 *Increasing the temperature of a reaction often increases the rate.*

B: Should you use a high or low temperature for a faster rate of reaction?

Increase the concentration. A **concentrated** solution will react faster than a **dilute** solution. This increases the number of reacting particles in the same space, so there is more chance they will collide.

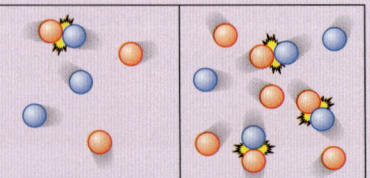

low concentration

high concentration

Figure 2 *Increasing the concentration of the reactants increases the rate of reaction.*

Increase the surface area. If you use a powder rather than a solid lump, more particles are on the surface, so more particles of the reactants can collide with each other at the same time.

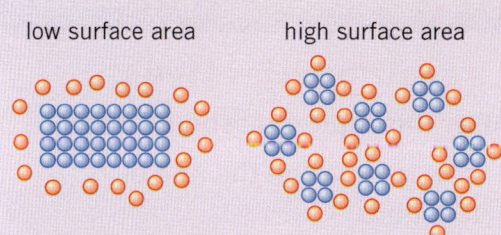

low surface area   high surface area

Figure 3 Increasing surface area increases the rate of reaction.

C: Should you use powder or lumps for a faster rate of reaction?

A **catalyst** is a chemical that helps a reaction to happen faster but is not used up itself. It lowers the amount of energy that the particles need to collide with for a reaction to happen. The number of collisions does not change, but more of them are successful so the rate of reaction increases.

D: What effect does a catalyst have on the number of collisions?

How can you increase the rate of a reaction?
Investigate how the surface area of magnesium or the concentration of hydrochloric acid affect the rate of reaction between dilute hydrochloric acid and magnesium ribbon by measuring the volume of hydrogen produced in a given time.

1   Use the correct words from the box to complete the sentences.

| catalysts | collisions | increased | speed | surface area |

The _____ of a chemical reaction is called the rate of reaction. The rate of reaction can be _____ by increasing the temperature, concentration, and _____. Increasing these reaction conditions increases the frequency of _____ between the particles. _____ can also be used to increase the rate of reaction.   [4 marks]

2   A reaction between a solid reactant and a solution is carried out under three different conditions.

Reaction	Temperature	Concentration of solution	Solid lump or powder?
A	low	high	solid lump
B	high	high	powder
C	high	low	powder

    a   Which reaction will have the fastest rate?   [1 mark]

    b   Which reaction will have the slowest rate?   [1 mark]

3   A solution of sodium hydroxide was reacted with a solution of hydrochloric acid. What is one way that the rate of this reaction could be increased?   [1 mark]

12.3 Monitoring rate of reaction

Learning objectives

After this topic, you should know:

- how to measure the rate of reaction.

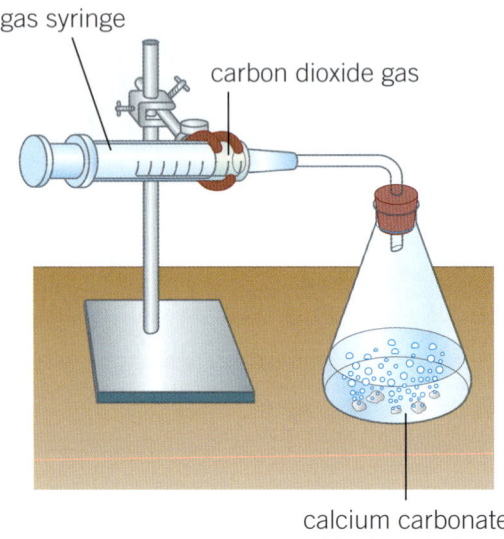

calcium carbonate and hydrochloric acid

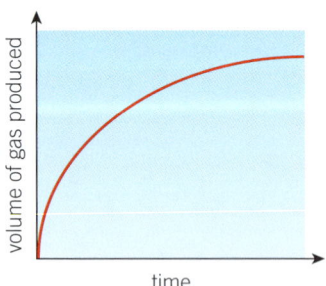

Figure 2 *As the reaction happens, the volume of gas in the syringe will increase. A graph of volume against time shows how the volume of gas produced increases as the reaction happens.*

You can tell how quickly a chemical reaction is happening by measuring:

- how quickly the reactants are used up
- how quickly the products are made.

You can use different experimental methods depending on what the reactants and products are.

Measuring the mass of a reaction mixture

When a solid reacts to produce a gas, you can use a top-pan balance to monitor the rate of the reaction. If the conical flask is left open, the gas leaves the conical flask. This makes the mass drop because there are fewer particles left in the conical flask. The faster the mass is lost, the faster the rate of reaction.

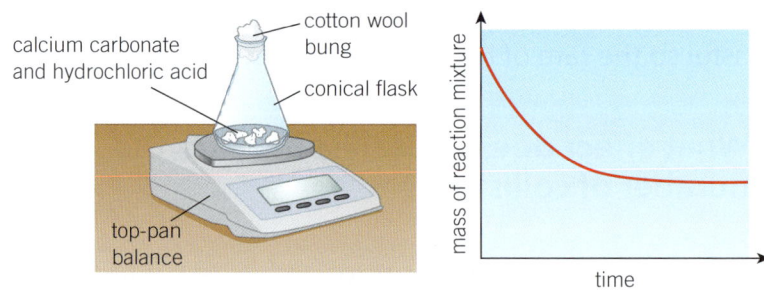

Figure 1 *The mass on the balance will decrease as the reaction happens. A graph of mass against time shows how the mass of the reaction mixture decreases as the reaction happens.*

A: What causes the decrease in mass shown by the reading on the balance?

Measuring the volume of gas

Some chemical reactions make a gas that you can collect. You can then measure the volume of gas produced in a given amount of time. The more gas that is produced in the given amount of time, the faster the rate of reaction.

Measuring the time for a solution to become opaque

Some chemical reactions become cloudy as a solid is made. You can measure the rate of the reaction by timing how long it takes until you can no longer see a cross through the reaction mixture. The faster the time it takes for the cross to 'disappear', the faster the rate of reaction.

Figure 3 When enough yellow solid is produced, you will no longer be able to see the cross on the paper.

A more accurate way is to use a data logger and light sensor to measure how much light can pass through the liquid. The results from a data logger can be plotted on a graph.

B: Why does the cross 'disappear'?

1 Choose the correct word from the box to complete the following sentence.

| decreases | increases |

The faster the mass reading on the balance _____, the faster the rate of reaction.   [1 mark]

2 Magnesium reacts with sulfuric acid to make magnesium sulfate and hydrogen gas.

Which method could be used to measure the rate of this reaction?

A measure the time taken for a cross to no longer be visible

B measure the change in the amount of liquid

C measure the change in mass   [1 marks]

3 A student is investigating the reaction between hydrochloric acid and sodium thiosulfate. She measures the time it takes for the cross under the conical flask to disappear. Her results are shown in the table below.

Reaction	Temperature in °C	Concentration of sodium thiosulfate in g/dm³	Time taken for the cross to disappear in s
A	20	12	25
B	20	24	10
C	40	12	13

Which reaction conditions give the fastest rate of reaction?   [1 mark]

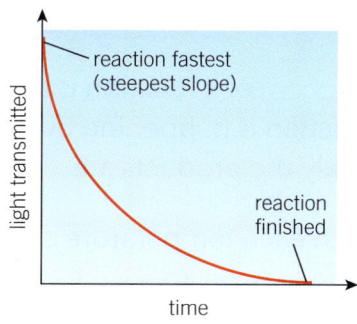

Figure 4 The results from a data logger can be used to plot a graph of light transmitted (passing through) against time.

12 Checkpoint

1   Choose the correct words from the box to complete the following sentences.

> formed   rate   used up

The _____ of a reaction is the speed at which a reaction happens. You can monitor how quickly
a reaction is happening by measuring how quickly the reactants are _____ or by measuring how
quickly the products are _____.   [2 marks]

2   Match each temperature change of a reaction to the correct transfer of energy.

Temperature change	Transfer of energy
temperature increases	energy transferred to the surroundings
temperature decreases	energy transferred from the surroundings [1 mark]

3   Which reaction will have a greater rate of reaction?

   A   solid lump of sodium hydrogencarbonate and citric acid

   B   powdered sodium hydrogencarbonate and citric acid   [1 mark]

4   Which reaction will have a greater rate of reaction?

   A   sodium hydroxide and sulfuric acid at 40 °C

   B   sodium hydroxide and sulfuric acid at 30 °C   [1 mark]

5   The two graphs show the rate of a reaction with a catalyst and without a catalyst. Which graph shows
the reaction with a catalyst?   [1 mark]

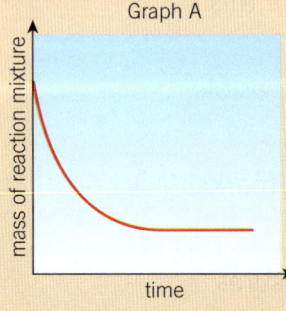
Graph A

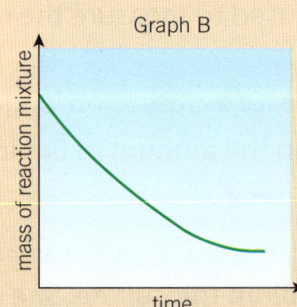
Graph B

6   A student was investigating the effect of concentration on the rate of reaction. The reaction
produced an insoluble solid. She used the following disappearing cross method to measure the rate
of reaction:

   Step 1 Draw a cross on a white piece of paper and put a conical flask on top of the cross.

   Step 2 Add the reactants to the conical flask and start the stopwatch.

   Step 3 When the cross is no longer visible, stop the stopwatch.

   a   The student carried out her experiment with a concentrated solution and a dilute solution.
       Which solution would have a higher rate of reaction?   [1 mark]

   b   What is one other way that the rate of this reaction could be increased?   [1 mark]

12 Vocabulary builder

1 Choose the correct words to complete the following sentences.

When energy is **released / transferred** to the surroundings, the temperature increases.

When energy is **absorbed / taken in** from the surroundings, the temperature decreases.　[2 marks]

2 Match each piece of equipment to what it measures.

Equipment	What it measures
top-pan balance	temperature
light sensor	change in mass
stopwatch	cloudiness of liquid
thermometer	volume of gas
gas syringe	time

[4 marks]

3 The particle diagrams show two solutions with different concentrations.
Use the words in the box below to label each diagram.

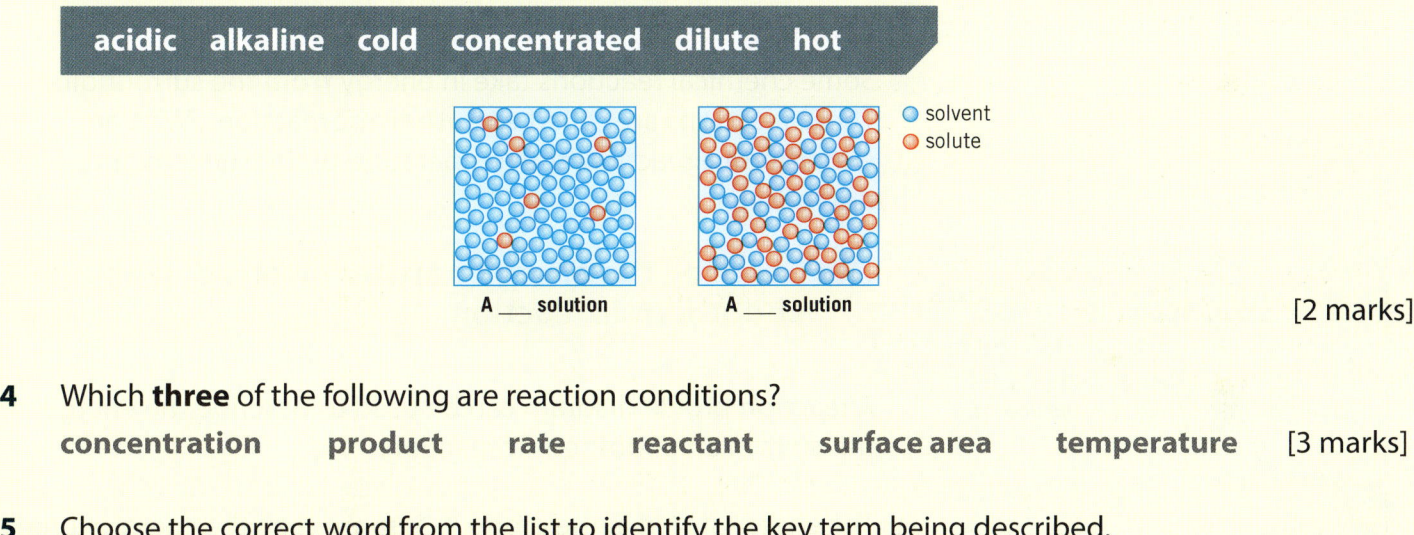

acidic　alkaline　cold　concentrated　dilute　hot

A ___ solution　　A ___ solution　　[2 marks]

4 Which **three** of the following are reaction conditions?

concentration　　**product**　　**rate**　　**reactant**　　**surface area**　　**temperature**　　[3 marks]

5 Choose the correct word from the list to identify the key term being described.

a Another word for burning.

　combustion　　**neutralisation**　　**oxidation**　　[1 mark]

b Reaction where oxygen is added.

　combustion　　**neutralisation**　　**oxidation**　　[1 mark]

c Reaction between an acid and an alkali.

　combustion　　**neutralisation**　　**oxidation**　　[1 mark]

6 Complete the sentences.

a A chemical that increases the rate of reaction without being used up is called a
　c _ _ _ _ _ _ _ _ .　[1 mark]

b In order for two particles to react, they must c _ _ _ _ _ _ .　[1 mark]

12.4 Reaction profiles

Learning objectives

After this topic, you should know:

- what exothermic and endothermic reactions are
- how to describe a reaction in a reaction profile diagram
- what a catalyst is.

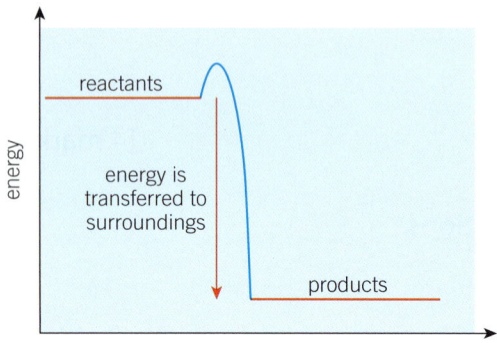

Figure 1 *The reaction profile of an exothermic reaction.*

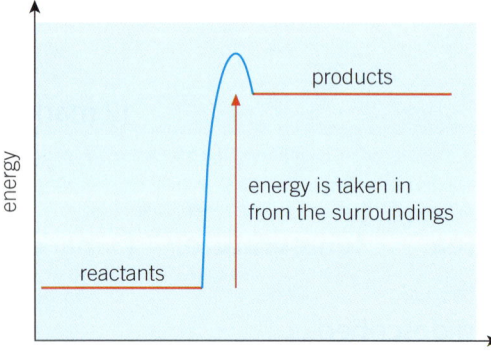

Figure 2 *The reaction profile of an endothermic reaction.*

Figure 3 *The activation energy of an exothermic and an endothermic reaction.*

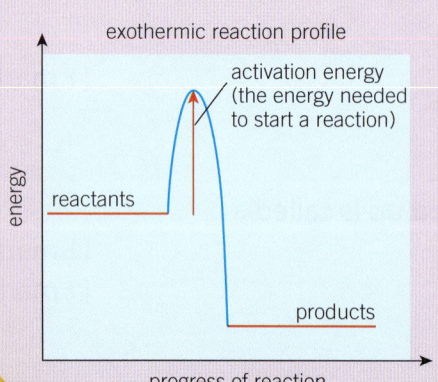

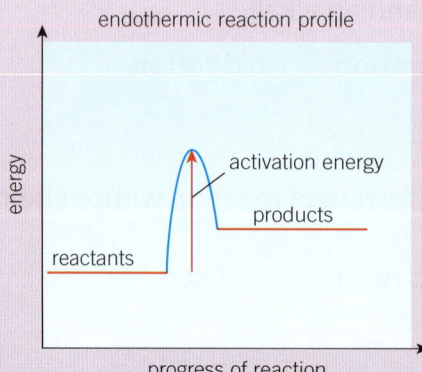

Exothermic reactions

Some chemical reactions transfer energy **to** the surroundings. These reactions are called **exothermic** reactions. An exothermic reaction makes the temperature of the surroundings **increase**. Combustion reactions and oxidation reactions are examples of exothermic reactions.

A: Describe the energy transfer involved in an exothermic reaction.

You can show these energy transfers on a **reaction profile** diagram.

The energy stored in the products is **less** than the energy stored in the reactants. This is because some energy has been transferred to the surroundings.

Endothermic reactions

Some chemical reactions take in energy **from** the surroundings. These reactions are called **endothermic** reactions. With an endothermic reaction, the temperature of the surroundings **decreases**.

B: Describe the energy transfer involved in an endothermic reaction.

A reaction profile diagram can be used to describe the energy transfers in an endothermic reaction.

The energy stored in the products is **more** than the energy stored in the reactants, This is because some energy has been transferred from the surroundings to the reacting chemicals. Thermal decomposition reactions are examples of endothermic reactions.

Activation energy

Reactions can only happen when the reacting particles collide with enough energy. This minimum amount of energy is called the **activation energy**. It can also be shown on a reaction profile diagram.

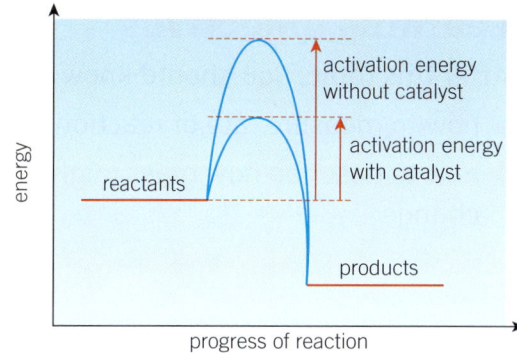

Figure 4 A catalyst lowers the activation energy and increases the rate of reaction.

Catalysts

Catalysts increase the rate of reaction without being used up. They do this by providing a different reaction pathway for the reaction that has a lower activation energy. This means that the reaction can happen more easily.

1   Match each key term its correct definition.

Key term	Definition
exothermic	minimum amount of energy to start a reaction
endothermic	reaction that transfers energy to the surroundings
catalyst	reaction that takes in energy from the surroundings
activation energy	chemical that increases rate of reaction

[3 marks]

2   a   Copy and complete the diagram below to show a reaction profile for an exothermic reaction.

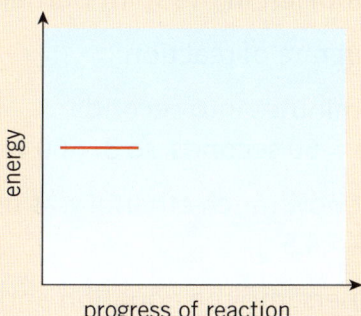

[3 marks]

   b   On your diagram, draw the activation energy for the same reaction in the presence of a catalyst.   [1 mark]

3   When calcium carbonate is heated, it breaks down into calcium oxide and carbon dioxide.

   a   Write a word equation for this reaction.   [2 marks]

   b   The reaction is endothermic. Draw a reaction profile diagram for this reaction.   [3 marks]

Learning objectives

After this topic, you should know:

- how to measure rate of reaction
- how to describe how mass might change.

The rate of reaction is how fast a chemical reaction happens. You can measure the rate of reaction by:

- measuring the volume of a gas produced
- measuring the change in mass
- timing how long it takes for a solution to become cloudy.

The units of rate of reaction are:

- grams per second (g/s) if you are monitoring how the mass changes
- centimetres cubed per second (cm^3/s) if you are monitoring how much gas is being made.

The mean rate of reaction can be calculated by:

$$\text{mean rate of reaction} = \frac{\text{amount of reactant used or product made}}{\text{time}}$$

A: Give the units for rate of reaction if you are measuring the volume of gas produced.

Worked example

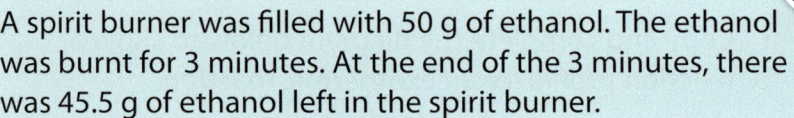

A spirit burner was filled with 50 g of ethanol. The ethanol was burnt for 3 minutes. At the end of the 3 minutes, there was 45.5 g of ethanol left in the spirit burner.

Calculate the mean rate of reaction.

Step 1: Convert minutes into seconds.
1 minute = 60 seconds, so $3 \times 60 = 180$ seconds

Step 2: Work out how much ethanol was used.
$50 - 45.5 = 4.5$ g

Step 3: Put numbers into the equation and calculate the mean rate of reaction.

$$\text{mean rate of reaction} = \frac{\text{amount of reactant used}}{\text{time}}$$

$$= \frac{4.5 \text{ g}}{180 \text{ s}} = 0.25 \text{ g/s}$$

Drawing graphs of rate of reaction

You can use graphs to show how the rate of reaction changes during a reaction. The steeper the graph, the faster the rate of reaction.

Graph of change in mass of reaction mixture against time

As the reactant is used up, and the gas product is released, the mass of the reaction mixture decreases. The graph is steep at the start. This is when the reaction is fastest. As the reaction progresses, the graph levels off until all of the reactants have reacted. The reaction is finished when the line is completely level.

Graph of volume of gas produced against time

As the gas product is produced, the volume increases. The graph starts off steep. This is when the reaction is fastest. As the reaction progresses, the graph levels off until all of the reactants have reacted. The reaction is finished when the line is completely level.

The rate of reaction only affects how fast the products are made – not the amounts that are made. So graphs showing the same reaction at a fast rate and a slow rate would both eventually level off at the same height.

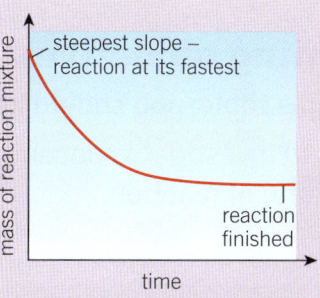

Figure 1 *A graph showing how the mass of the reactants decreases during the reaction.*

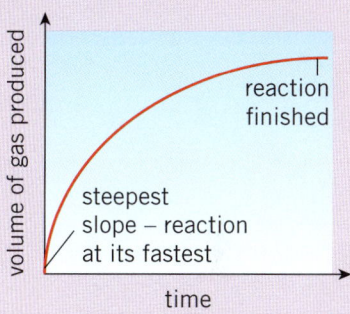

Figure 2 *A graph showing how the volume of gas produced increases during the reaction.*

B: Describe how the gradient of a graph changes with the rate of reaction.

1   What is the equation used to calculate the mean rate of a reaction? [1 mark]

2   A student reacts zinc with hydrochloric acid to form zinc chloride and hydrogen gas.

   a   Write a word equation for the reaction. [1 mark]

   b   In her reaction, she collects 60 cm³ of hydrogen gas in 10 minutes.

      Calculate the mean rate of reaction. Give the correct units for the rate of reaction. [3 marks]

3   A student is investigating the reaction between iron and sulfuric acid. He carries out two experiments with:

   1   iron and dilute sulfuric acid

   2   iron and more dilute sulfuric acid.

   He measured the decrease in the mass of the reaction mixture.

   Experiment 1 had a faster rate of reaction than experiment 2.

   Sketch a graph to show the rate of reaction for both experiment 1 and experiment 2. [3 marks]

12.6 Investigating rate of reaction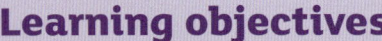

Learning objectives

After this topic, you should know:

- how to investigate concentration and rate of reaction.

Rate of reaction is a measure of how fast a chemical change is happening.

You can measure the rate of reaction by finding out how quickly the reactants are used or the products are made. The faster the reactants are used or the products are made, the faster the rate of reaction.

Many factors affect how quickly a chemical reaction happens, for example:

- surface area of a solid reactant
- temperature
- adding a catalyst
- concentration of reactants in solution.

A: Give one factor that affects the rate of a chemical reaction.

Measuring the rate of a chemical reaction

Some chemical reactions produce a gas. Bubbles will be seen and fizzing will be heard. The gas can be collected and this can be used to find the rate of reaction.

There are two ways that you can measure the rate of a reaction by collecting the gas:

- measuring the volume of gas made in a set time
- measuring the time it takes to make a set volume of gas.

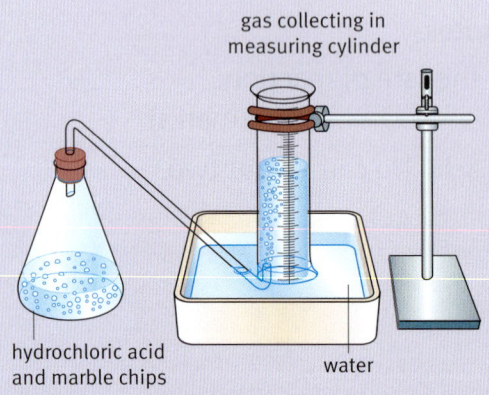

Figure 1 *Apparatus for investigating the effect of changing concentration on the rate of reaction.*

Investigating the effect of changing concentration on the rate of reaction

Step 1: Fill the water trough and measuring cylinder with water and use a clamp to hold the measuring cylinder upside down in the water trough. Wear eye protection.

Step 2: Add 50 cm³ of 80 g/dm³ hydrochloric acid and 1 g of marble chips into the conical flask.

Step 3: Quickly put the bung back into the flask and start the stopwatch.

Step 4: Record the time taken to collect 25 cm³ of gas.

Step 5: Repeat for 40 g/dm³, 20 g/dm³, and 10 g/dm³ concentrations of hydrochloric acid.

Once you have collected results, you can plot them onto a graph. The concentration of acid goes on the *x*-axis and the time taken goes on the *y*-axis.

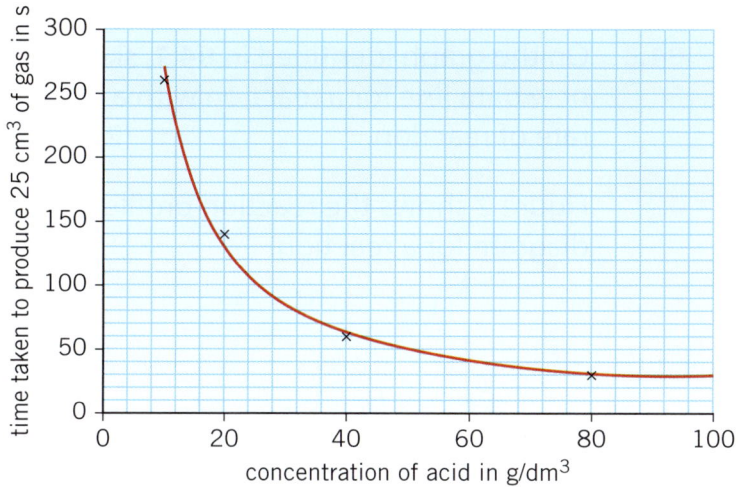

Figure 2 *You can plot a graph of time against concentration.*

1   Choose the correct words from the box to complete the following sentences.

   products   quickly   reaction

   Rate of _____ is how quickly a chemical reaction happens. This can be measured by observing how _____ the reactants are used or the _____ are made.   [2 marks]

2   Sort the following variables by whether they are the independent variable, the dependent variable, or a control variable for the investigation of the effect of concentration of rate of reaction.
   concentration of acid
   surface area of calcium carbonate
   temperature
   time to produce 25 cm³ of gas
   volume of acid used   [5 marks]

3   A student investigated the effect of concentration on the rate of reaction between magnesium carbonate and hydrochloric acid. She measured the volume of carbon dioxide gas produced in 1 minute. Her results are shown in the table.

   Draw a graph of the student's results.

Concentration of hydrochloric acid in g/dm³	Volume of gas produced in 1 min in cm³
80	65
60	43
40	20
20	9

[4 marks]

12 Practice questions

01.1 Match each key term to its definition.

Key term	**Definition**
exothermic	energy is taken in from the surroundings
endothermic	energy is transferred to the surroundings

[1 mark]

01.2 Give the temperature change of the **surroundings** for an exothermic reaction and an endothermic reaction. [1 mark]

02 Which one of the following is always exothermic?

A combustion

B melting

C photosynthesis

D thermal decomposition [1 mark]

03.1 Choose the correct words from the box to complete the paragraph.

| activation | available | decreases |
| increases | reaction | used up |

A catalyst is a substance that _____ the rate of reaction because it lowers the _____ energy for the reaction. The catalyst is not _____ by the reaction. [3 marks]

04 Figure 1 show the results from two different reactions.

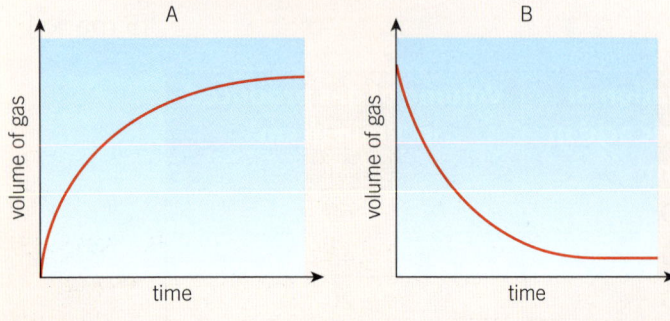

Figure 1

04.1 Which graph shows a reaction where the volume of gas **increases** with time? [1 mark]

04.2 Name a piece of equipment that can be used to measure the volume of gas. [1 mark]

04.3 On the graph identified in **04.1**, sketch a new data line for a reaction with a slower rate of reaction. [2 marks]

05 Figure 2 shows the reaction profile diagram for a reaction.

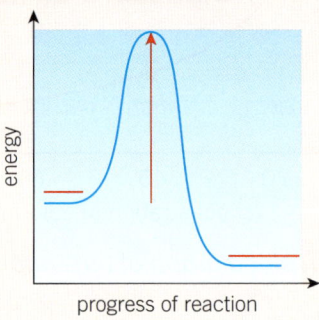

Figure 2

05.1 Complete the graph with the following labels.

activation energy   products reactants [3 marks]

05.2 Identify whether the reaction is exothermic or endothermic. [1 mark]

05.3 Explain what is meant by the activation energy of a chemical reaction. [2 marks]

05.4 On the graph, sketch the curve you would expect if a catalyst was used. [3 marks]

06 Two substances were tested to see if they could be used as catalysts for a reaction.

The results are shown in Table 1.

Table 1

Substance	Effect on rate of reaction	Mass of substance at start of reaction in g	Mass of substance at end of reaction in g	Appearance at start of reaction	Appearance at end of reaction
X	increases	0.2	0.01	blue solution	red solid
Y	increases	0.2	0.2	red solid	red solid

Identify which substance can be used as a catalyst. Explain your answer.

[3 marks]

07 The graph in Figure 3 shows how the volume of gas produced changes during a chemical reaction.

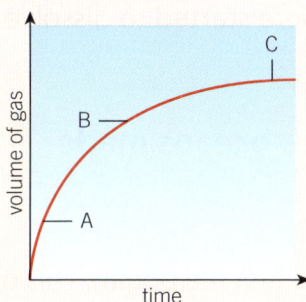

Figure 3

07.1 Give the letter that points to the time of the reaction where the reaction is at its quickest. [1 mark]

07.2 Give the letter that points to the time of the reaction where the reaction has stopped. [1 mark]

07.3 96 cm³ of gas was produced in 12 seconds. Calculate the mean rate of reaction in dm³/s. [3 marks]

08 The three diagrams in Figure 4 show methods used to follow how quickly a reaction is happening.

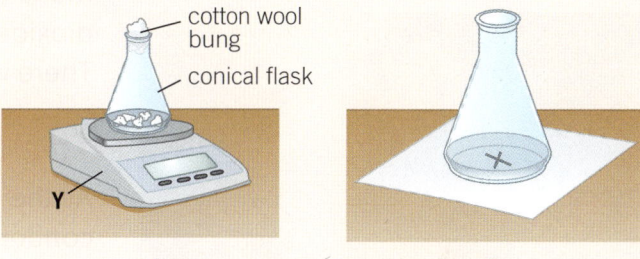

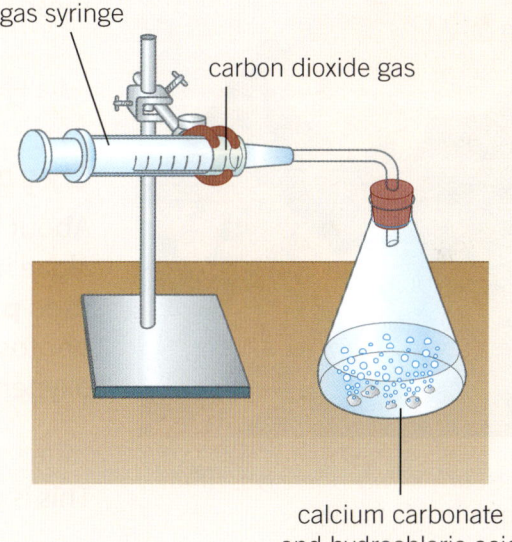

Figure 4

i Which method would you use to measure the volume of gas produced? [1 mark]

ii Which method would you use to measure how the mass of the reaction mixture changes? [1 mark]

iii What is the name of the piece of equipment labelled Y? [1 mark]

13 Fuels and the atmosphere
13.1 Development of the atmosphere

Learning objectives

After this topic, you should know:

- what the atmosphere is made of
- how the atmosphere has changed over time.

***Figure 1** The early atmosphere was formed by volcanoes.*

Do plants produce oxygen?

Use pondweed or another underwater plant and collect the gas that is produced. Use a glowing splint to test whether this gas is oxygen.

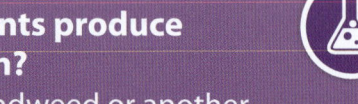

There is a blanket of gas around the Earth called the **atmosphere**. The gases that make up the atmosphere have changed over billions of years.

The early atmosphere

When the Earth first formed there were a lot of volcanoes. For Earth's first billion years, the volcanoes let out gases that made the first atmosphere. This atmosphere was mainly carbon dioxide, a little bit of water vapour, and some other gases. There was no oxygen.

The oceans

As the Earth cooled, the water vapour in the early atmosphere condensed into liquid water. This formed oceans. Carbon dioxide in the early atmosphere started to dissolve into these oceans.

A: How were the Earth's oceans made?

Oxygen

About 3 billion years ago, the first life began. This early life was algae in the sea and later plants on land. The algae and plants used **photosynthesis** to make their own food. The process of photosynthesis turns carbon dioxide and water into glucose and oxygen. The word equation for the reaction is:

$$\text{carbon dioxide} + \text{water} \rightarrow \text{glucose} + \text{oxygen}$$

This is where the oxygen in the atmosphere comes from.

B: What is the source of oxygen in the atmosphere?

Carbon dioxide

In the early atmosphere, the amount of carbon dioxide gas was much higher than it is now.

It began to decrease due to:

- being used by plants in photosynthesis

- dissolving in the oceans

- becoming trapped in fossil fuels and rocks called carbonates.

This is what happened to most of the carbon dioxide.

C: Where was most of the carbon dioxide trapped?

The atmosphere today

Today, the atmosphere is made of about 80% nitrogen and 20% oxygen, with a very small amount of other gases. Less than 1% of the atmosphere is the noble gas called argon (see Group 0 in the periodic table).

D: Which gas makes up the largest part of our atmosphere?

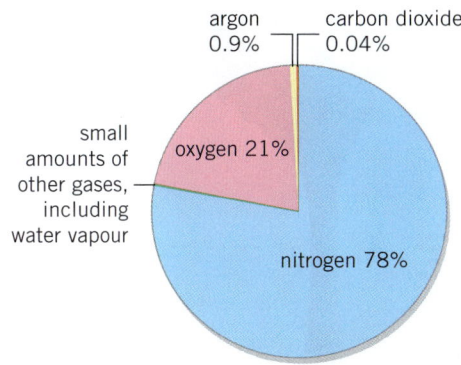

Figure 2 *The atmosphere today is about four-fifths nitrogen and one-fifth oxygen.*

1   Choose the correct words from the box to complete the following sentences.

> **carbon dioxide   nitrogen   oxygen**

Today's atmosphere is about 80% _____ and 20% _____.
It contains a small amount of other gases, including _____, argon, and water vapour.   [2 marks]

2   Choose the correct words to complete the following sentences.
The early atmosphere was made from volcanic **gases / liquids**. The water vapour cooled and **condensed / evaporated** to make the oceans. The oceans then **dissolved / melted** some of the carbon **dioxide / monoxide**.   [4 marks]

3   Green plants carry out photosynthesis. The word equation for the reaction is:

carbon dioxide + water → glucose + oxygen

During photosynthesis:

a   which gas is taken in from the atmosphere?   [1 mark]

b   which gas is given out into the atmosphere?   [1 mark]

13.2 Crude oil

Learning objectives

After this topic, you should know:

- what crude oil is
- how crude oil can be separated.

Crude oil is a type of fossil fuel. It is a brown liquid made up of a mixture of lots of chemicals. It is made from tiny dead animals from millions of years ago.

Crude oil is a finite resource (it can run out) that is found underground. Most of the crude oil that we use in the UK comes from the oil fields in the North Sea.

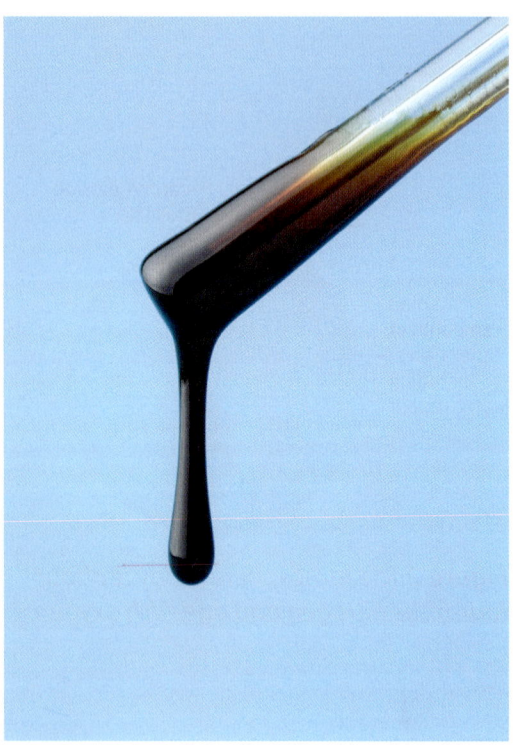

Figure 1 *Crude oil is a mixture of a lot of chemicals. Most crude oil in the UK comes from under the North Sea.*

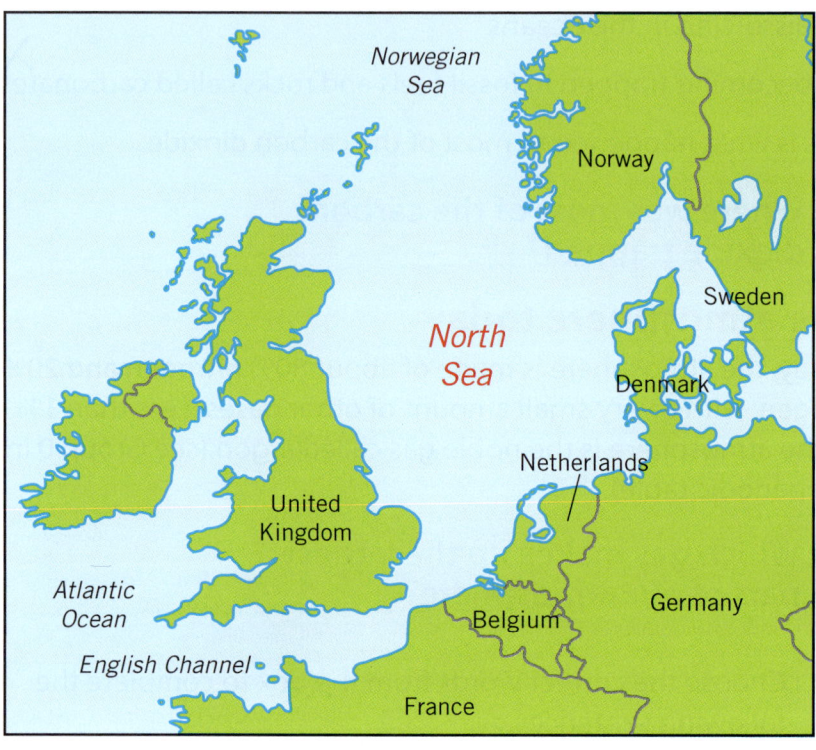

A: Where does the UK get most of its crude oil from?

How do the properties of the different fractions of crude oil differ?

Record your observations on the viscosity (how runny the substance is) of different fractions from crude oil. How does it change as the size of the molecules in the fractions increases?

Separating crude oil

Crude oil itself does not have many uses. However, the chemicals that make up crude oil are very useful as fuels, such as petrol and diesel, and oils. An oil refinery separates the chemicals that make up crude oil.

Fractional distillation

Fractional distillation is used to separate the useful chemicals that crude oil is made up of. Each group of chemicals that is separated is known as a **fraction**. The chemicals that make up each fraction have similar boiling points. This is what allows them to be separated from the other fractions.

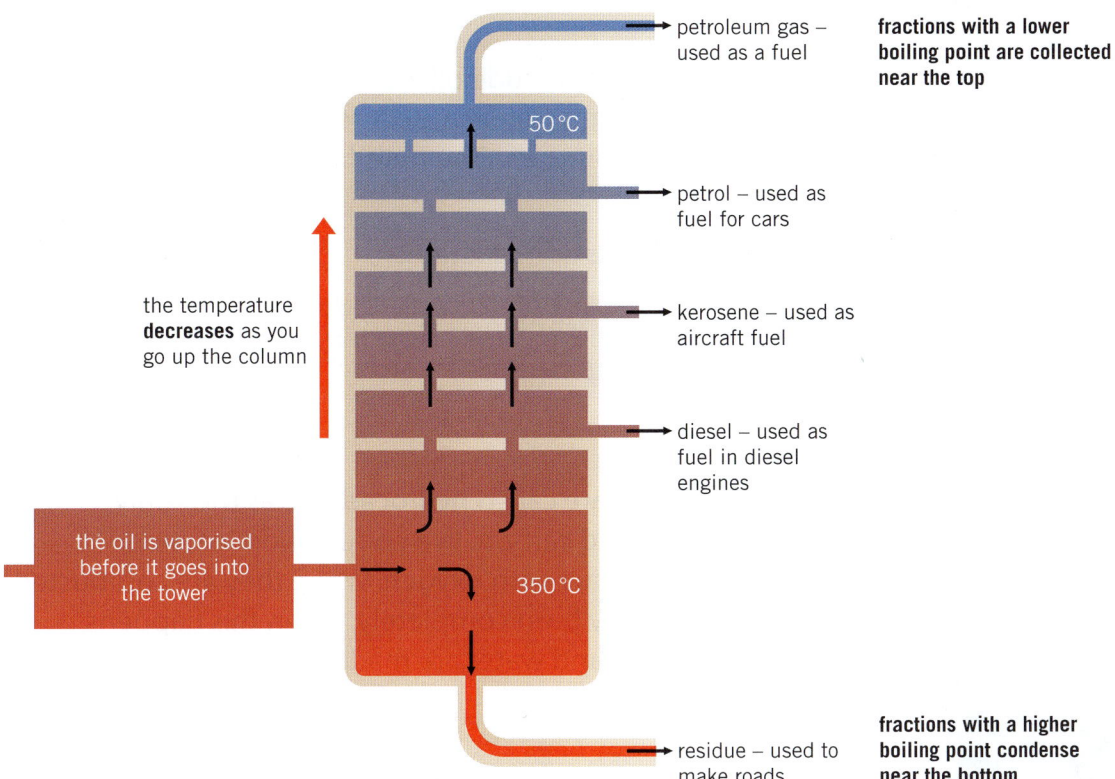

petroleum gas – used as a fuel

fractions with a lower boiling point are collected near the top

50 °C

petrol – used as fuel for cars

the temperature **decreases** as you go up the column

kerosene – used as aircraft fuel

diesel – used as fuel in diesel engines

the oil is vaporised before it goes into the tower

350 °C

residue – used to make roads

fractions with a higher boiling point condense near the bottom

Figure 2 *Fractional distillation is used to separate crude oil into more useful chemicals.*

B: How do we separate crude oil?

1   Match each key term to its definition.

Key term	Definition
crude oil	the process used to separate crude oil
fractional distillation	a group of chemicals with similar boiling points
fraction	a mixture of chemicals that are useful as fuels and oils

[2 marks]

2   Which **two** statements about crude oil are true?

  A   Fractional distillation of crude oil takes place in a refinery.

  B   Petrol and diesel are fractions separated from crude oil.

  C   Crude oil is made up of one chemical that can be broken down into lots of different chemicals.

  D   Each fraction is made up of only one chemical.   [2 marks]

3   Where is crude oil found?   [1 mark]

13.3 Fuels and combustion

Learning objectives

After this topic, you should know:

- the products of complete combustion
- the products of incomplete combustion.

Fuels

Some of the fractions of crude oil are **fuels**, for example, petrol and diesel. We use fuels to make electricity, heat our homes, cook food, and fuel our cars. The fuels from crude oil are known as **fossil fuels**.

Fuels burn in **combustion** reactions.

A: What are two fractions found in crude oil that can be used as fuels?

Combustion

Fuels from crude oil are called hydrocarbons as they only contain hydrogen and carbon. In a combustion reaction, hydrocarbon fuels react with oxygen. When they are combusted in lots of oxygen they burn completely. When this happens, only carbon dioxide and water are made. This is **complete combustion**.

B: What are the two products of complete combustion?

If there is a limited supply of oxygen, not all of the fuel will burn. When hydrocarbon fuels burn incompletely, carbon **di**oxide, carbon **mon**oxide, and solid bits of carbon called soot are produced, as well as water. The soot makes the flame 'dirty'. This is **incomplete combustion**.

Investigating complete and incomplete combustion

Bunsen burners use a hydrocarbon called methane as their fuel. The methane can undergo complete combustion and incomplete combustion.

- If the air hole of the Bunsen burner is open, the flame is blue – this is complete combustion. The word equation for the complete combustion of methane is:

  methane + oxygen → carbon dioxide + water

- If the air hole is closed, the flame is yellow – this is incomplete combustion. One of the word equations for the incomplete combustion of methane is:

  methane + oxygen → carbon dioxide + carbon monoxide
  + carbon (soot) + water

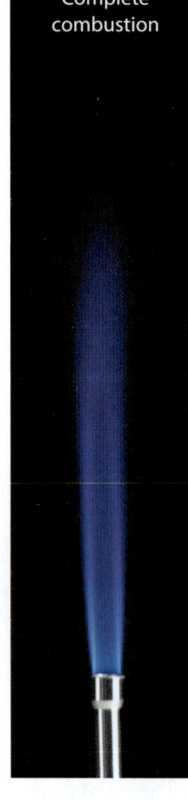

Incomplete combustion

Complete combustion

Figure 1 *The safety flame is incomplete combustion and the heating flame is complete combustion. The collar on the Bunsen burner can turn and add different amounts of oxygen to the flame.*

Investigating the products of combustion

Step 1: Set up a tripod on a heatproof mat with a ceramic evaporating dish on the tripod.
Fill the evporating dish with water.

Step 2: Make sure the air hole on the Bunsen burner is closed. Turn on the gas tap and light the Bunsen burner using a lit splint.

Step 3: Open the air hole to get a blue flame. Put the Bunsen burner underneath the evaporating dish and heat for 3 minutes.

Step 4: Close the air hole and remove the Bunsen burner.

Step 5: Leave the evaporating dish to cool. Once it has cooled, look at the bottom of the dish. Use tongs to handle to evaporating dish. The evaporating dish should be clean.

Step 6: Put the evaporating dish back onto the tripod and fill with water again. Place the Bunsen burner back underneath. Leave the air hole closed so that the flame is yellow. Heat for 3 minutes.

Step 7: Remove the Bunsen burner and leave the evaporating dish to cool. Once it has cooled, look at the bottom of the dish. Use tongs to handle to evaporating dish. The evaporating dish should be covered in soot.

---

1 Match each key term to its definition.

Key term	Definition
incomplete combustion	burning in lots of oxygen
complete combustion	a chemical that is burnt to transfer energy
fuel	burning in limited oxygen [2 marks]

2 Sort the following substances according to whether they are products for complete combustion, incomplete combustion, or both.

carbon dioxide   **carbon monoxide**   **carbon (soot)**   **water**   [4 marks]

3 Diesel is a hydrocarbon fuel.

  a Complete the word equation for the **complete combustion** of diesel.

    diesel + _____ → carbon _____ + water   [1 mark]

  b Complete the word equation for the **incomplete combustion** of diesel.

    diesel + _____ → carbon _____ + carbon _____ + water + carbon (soot)   [1 mark]

13.4 Air pollution

Learning objectives

After this topic, you should know:

- what air pollution is
- the problems that air pollution causes
- how air pollution can be reduced.

Figure 1 *Acid rain can kill trees and wear away stone buildings and statues.*

Air **pollution** is when human activities release chemicals into the air at levels that would not normally be there.

Acid rain

Fossil fuels from crude oil always have a little sulfur in them. When the fuels are burnt, the sulfur reacts with oxygen to make sulfur dioxide. This acidic gas is then released into the atmosphere. Sulfur dioxide can dissolve into rain water and make **acid rain**.

Car engines are very hot and have high pressure inside. This makes the nitrogen and oxygen in the air react to make oxides of nitrogen. The oxides of nitrogen can also dissolve into rain water to make acid rain.

Acid rain can increase chemical weathering, kill trees, and change ecosystems. Acid rain can also cause breathing problems.

A: Which two chemicals can make acid rain?

Incomplete combustion

When fuels undergo incomplete combustion, the products can be harmful.

Carbon monoxide

If a fuel does not have enough oxygen, it will undergo incomplete combustion. This produces carbon monoxide. Carbon monoxide is a colourless, odourless, and poisonous gas. Breathing in too much carbon monoxide can cause death.

Some household boilers use methane fuel, the same fuel used by Bunsen burners. It is important that boilers are regularly checked to make sure they get enough oxygen. Each year, around 25 people die from carbon monoxide poisoning caused by incomplete combustion in boilers.

Solid particles

Some cars and other engines use diesel fuel. Incomplete combustion of diesel fuels releases solid soot particles into the atmosphere. These small particles block sunlight in the atmosphere and so reduce the amount of light that reaches the surface. This is **global dimming**.

These tiny particles can also be breathed in by people. This can cause health problems like coughs, asthma, and possibly cancer.

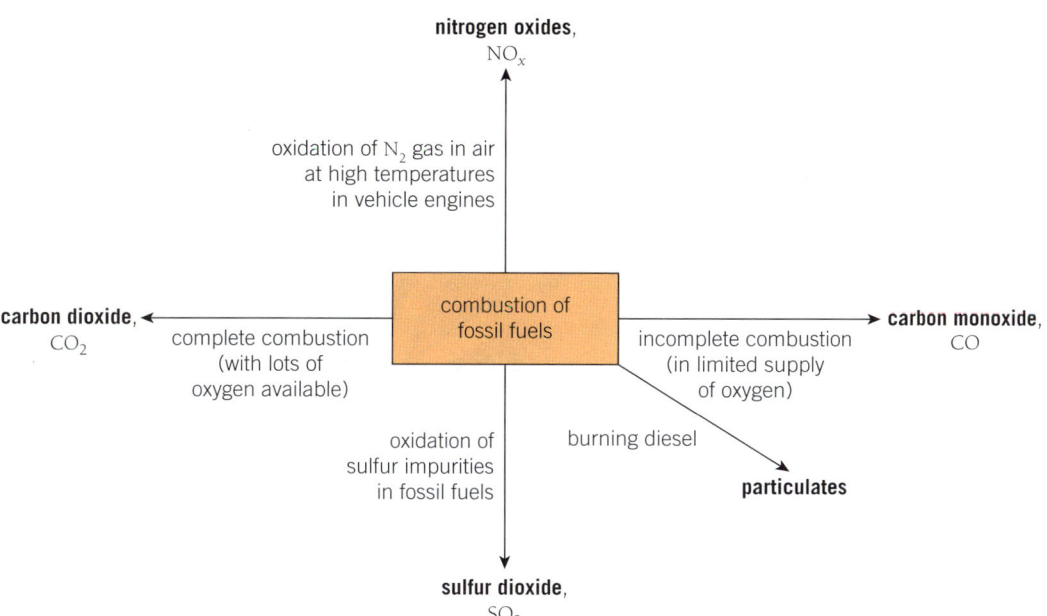

Figure 2 *Summary of air pollutants.*

1   Match each substance to the correct harmful effect it can have.

Substance	Harmful effect
sulfur dioxide	toxic
carbon monoxide	global dimming
solid particles	acid rain [2 marks]

2   Which **two** of the following are effects of acid rain?

   A   cancer

   B   global dimming

   C   kills trees

   D   weathered buildings   [2 marks]

3   Complete the sentence to describe where carbon monoxide comes from.

   Carbon monoxide is formed from _____ of fuels.   [1 mark]

13.5 Climate change

Learning objectives

After this topic, you should know:

- what the greenhouse effect is
- how human activities have increased the amount of greenhouse gases in the atmosphere
- what global climate change is.

The greenhouse effect

Greenhouse gases in the atmosphere trap energy from the Sun. This helps keep the Earth warmer than it would be without the atmosphere. However, some human activities have increased the amount of these greenhouse gases in the atmosphere.

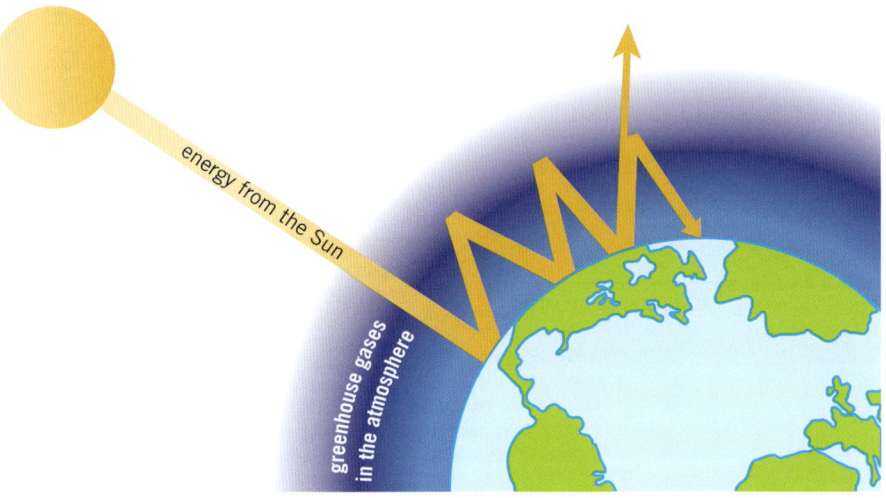

energy from the Sun

greenhouse gases in the atmosphere

Figure 1 *Greenhouse gases trap heat in our atmosphere. The amount of greenhouse gases in our atmosphere is increasing and this could lead to global climate change.*

Greenhouse gases

Carbon dioxide is a greenhouse gas. It is made when hydrocarbon fuels are combusted (burnt).

Methane is another greenhouse gas. Methane is made when rubbish in landfill sites breaks down. It is also produced by cows on cattle farms.

A: What are **two** greenhouse gases?

The amount of carbon dioxide and methane in the atmosphere has increased a lot in the past hundred years. This is because the human population has increased a lot. We now burn more fuels, throw away more rubbish, and raise more cattle.

We have also cut down lots of trees. Trees carry out photosynthesis, which removes carbon dioxide from the atmosphere. By cutting them down, we have reduced the amount of carbon dioxide that is removed from the atmosphere.

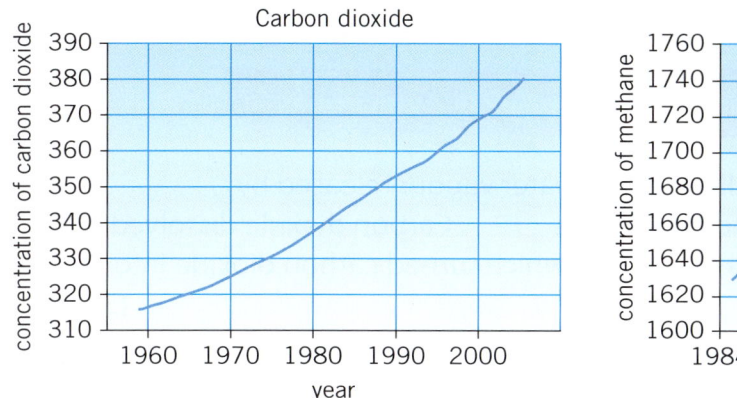
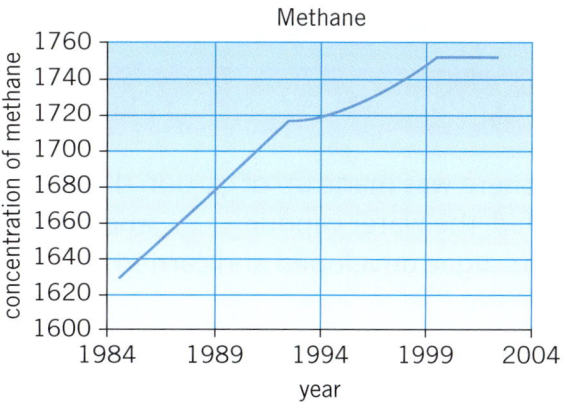

Figure 2 *The concentrations of carbon dioxide and methane in the atmosphere have changed in the last seventy years*

The increase in the amount of greenhouse gases means that more energy from the Sun could be trapped in the atmosphere. This may have caused the average global temperature to increase. This leads to global climate change.

Effects of global climate change

- Polar ice caps melt – animals like the polar bear lose their habitats.

- Sea levels rise – increase in flooding around the coast.

- More extreme weather – more tropical storms that are more powerful and droughts (no rain) last longer.

- Desert areas get hotter and drier, and grow in size.

B: What is one possible effect of global climate change?

1   Choose the correct words from the box to complete the following sentences.

> **climate   combusted   greenhouse**

When fossil fuels are _____ they release carbon dioxide. Carbon dioxide is a _____ gas and could cause global _____ change.   [2 marks]

2   Which **one** activity increases the amount of carbon dioxide in the atmosphere?

   A burning fossil fuels
   B cattle farming
   C rubbish breaking down in landfill sites
   D using aerosol sprays   [1 mark]

3   What is **one** reason that the increase in the global human population has led to an increase in the concentration of greenhouse gases in the atmosphere?   [1 mark]

13 Checkpoint

1 Choose the correct words from the box to complete the following sentences.

The early atmosphere was made up of carbon dioxide and water vapour released by _____.
As the Earth cooled, the water vapour _____ and formed the _____. Carbon dioxide dissolved in the oceans. Plants and algae developed and carried out _____, which turned carbon dioxide into _____.

[5 marks]

2 Match each substance to the correct harmful effect it can have.

Substance	Harmful effect
sulfur dioxide	acid rain
carbon monoxide	global dimming
solid particles	poisonous

[2 marks]

3 Crude oil is a mixture that can be separated into different fractions.

  a Which method is used to separate the fractions of crude oil?

    chromatography   crystallisation   **fractional distillation** [1 mark]

  b What is the name of one of the fractions found in crude oil?

    carbon dioxide   fossil fuel   petrol   sulfur dioxide [1 mark]

4 The pie chart shows the composition of the atmosphere today. Complete the pie chart using labels from the box.

15%   21%   60%   78%   **carbon dioxide**
nitrogen   oxygen   water vapour

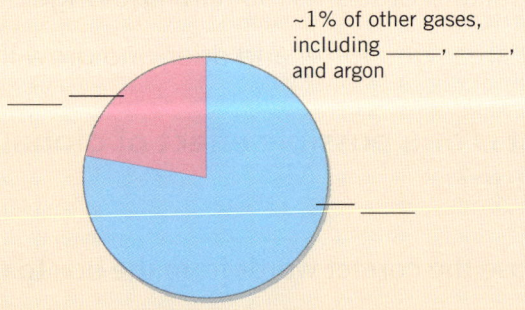

~1% of other gases, including _____, _____, and argon

[4 marks]

5 **a** Complete the word equation below for the **complete** combustion of methane.

    methane + _____ → carbon dioxide + _____ [1 mark]

  b What two substances can be formed in **incomplete** combustion but not in complete combustion? [2 marks]

  c Methane is a greenhouse gas. What is one human activity that increases the amount of methane in the atmosphere? [1 mark]

6 What is one effect of global climate change?

  desert areas get colder   more pollution   **rising sea levels** [1 mark]

13 Vocabulary builder

1 Match each process its definition.

Process	Definition	
combustion	how the oceans formed from water vapour in the atmosphere	
photosynthesis	how crude oil is separated	
condensation	scientific term for burning	
fractional distillation	process by which plants make their food	[3 marks]

2 Carbon monoxide is a colourless, odourless, and poisonous gas.
Choose the correct term that each statement is describing.

   a Can cause illness or death in people.

     colourless   **odourless**   **poisonous**   [1 mark]

   b Substance has no smell.

     colourless   **odourless**   **poisonous**   [1 mark]

3   **a** Match each type of combustion to its definition.

Type of combustion	Definition	
complete combustion	burning in a limited supply of oxygen	
incomplete combustion	burning in excess supply of oxygen	[1 mark]

   b Sort the following substances according to whether they are a product of complete combustion, incomplete combustion, or both.

     carbon (soot)   **carbon dioxide**   **carbon monoxide**   **water**   [4 marks]

4 Choose the correct words to complete the sentences on crude oil.
Crude oil is a **compound / mixture** of **carbohydrates / hydrocarbons**. Fractional **distillation / evaporation** is used to separate the crude oil into its different **compounds / fractions**.   [4 marks]

5 Complete the sentences.
M _ _ _ _ _ _ and carbon dioxide are examples of g _ _ _ _ _ _ _ _ gases. These gases contribute
to g _ _ _ _ _ c _ _ _ _ _ _ change.   [4 marks]

13.6 Cracking

Learning objectives

After this topic, you should know:

- what cracking is
- why cracking is done
- what the products of cracking are.

The fractions of crude oil that contain shorter molecules, like petrol, are more useful than those that contain longer molecules, like fuel oil. Long-chain hydrocarbons can be broken down into smaller, more useful hydrocarbons using **cracking**.

Cracking uses heat to break down the molecules. This is an example of thermal decomposition. There are two ways that hydrocarbons can be cracked.

- Steam cracking – long-chain hydrocarbons are mixed with steam and heated to a high temperature.
- Catalytic cracking – long-chain hydrocarbons are passed over a hot catalyst.

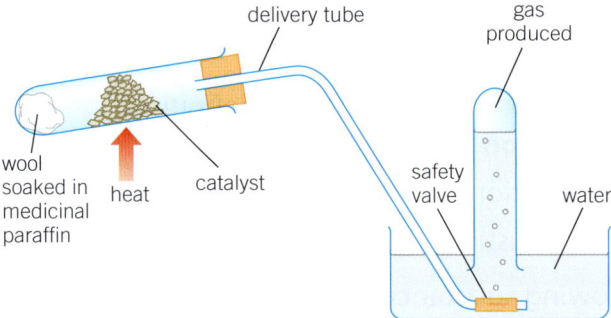

Figure 1 Cracking a long-chain hydrocarbon in the lab by catalytic cracking.

A: Describe the two types of cracking.

Products of cracking

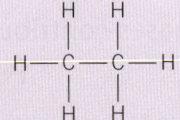

Figure 2 *Ethane is an alkane. All of the bonds are single bonds.*

Cracking makes two types of short-chain molecules – **alkanes** and **alkenes**.

Alkanes are hydrocarbons that only have single bonds. They are used as fuels.

B: Name the family of hydrocarbons that only contain single bonds.

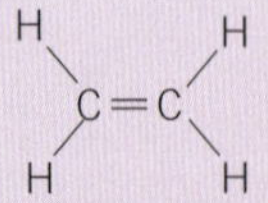

Figure 3 *Ethene is an alkene. It has a double bond between the two carbon atoms.*

Alkenes are hydrocarbons that have a carbon carbon double bond, C=C. This double bond makes them more reactive than alkanes. They are a starting material for making many new chemicals, including polymers.

C: Describe why alkenes are more reactive than alkanes.

For example, decane, $C_{10}H_{22}$, is a hydrocarbon made of ten carbon atoms. It can be cracked to form pentane (an alkane) and two alkenes called propene and ethene. The word equation for the cracking of decane is:

$$decane \rightarrow pentane + propene + ethene$$

You can write a balanced symbol equation for this reaction.

$$C_{10}H_{22} \rightarrow C_5H_{12} + C_3H_6 + C_2H_4$$

Testing for alkenes

Alkenes are more reactive than alkanes. Alkenes react with bromine water whereas alkanes do not. Bromine water is orange. When bromine water is mixed with an alkene they react and the mixture becomes colourless. When bromine water is mixed with an alkane there is no reaction so the mixture remains orange.

Figure 4 *Bromine water becomes colourless with an alkene (hexene) but not an alkane (hexane).*

1 Choose the correct words from the box to complete the sentences.

> **alkanes**   **alkenes**   **thermal**

Cracking is the _____ decomposition of long-chain hydrocarbons. Cracking can make _____, which are used to make polymers. It also makes shorter-chain _____, which are used as fuels.   [2 marks]

2 a What colour is bromine water?   [1 mark]

b When substance A is mixed with bromine water, the mixture turns colourless.

Name the type of hydrocarbon that substance A is.   [1 mark]

3 Octane can be cracked to form an alkane and an alkene.

a Complete the balanced symbol equation for the cracking of octane.
$$C_8H_{18} \rightarrow C_5H_{12} + \underline{\hspace{2cm}}$$ [1 mark]

b List two conditions needed to carry out steam cracking.   [2 marks]

13.7 Carbon footprint

Learning objectives

After this topic, you should know:

- what a carbon footprint is
- how carbon footprint can be reduced.

The **carbon footprint** is one way to measure the effect that a product, service, or event has on the environment. The carbon footprint is the total amount of carbon dioxide and other greenhouse gases made during the entire life cycle of the product, event, or service.

As greenhouse gases are linked to global climate change, it is important to reduce our carbon footprint so that less greenhouse gas is released.

> **A:** Define the term carbon footprint.

Reducing carbon footprints

A carbon footprint can be reduced if less greenhouse gas is released into the air over the lifecycle of a product, event, or service. Some ways that the carbon footprint can be reduced are:

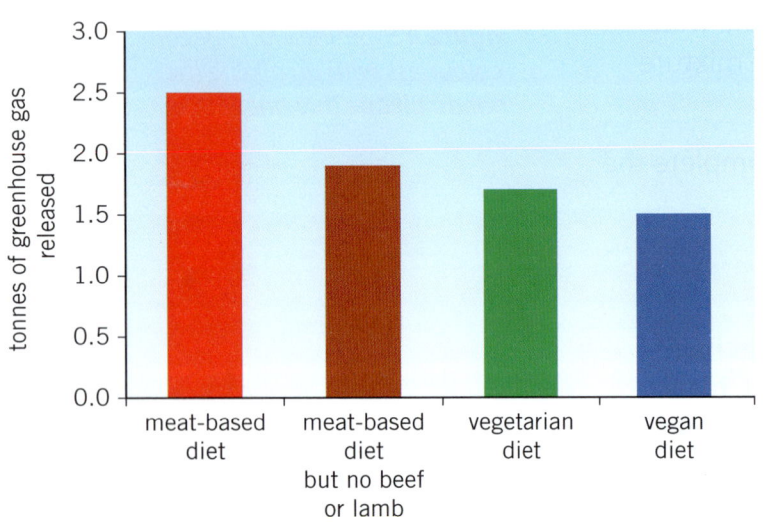

Figure 1 *Meat farming produces more greenhouse gases than plant farming. As such, the more meat you eat, the greater your carbon footprint.*

- Reducing the energy used to make a product, service, or event.

- Using alternative fuels that do not produce carbon dioxide, for example, using solar power or wind power to generate electricity rather than fossil fuels.

- Reusing and recycling to reduce waste and methane produced at landfill sites.

- Eating a lower-meat diet – raising fewer cows means less methane is released into the air. Fewer resources are needed to grow vegetables than are needed to farm animals for meat-based diets.

- Collect and store the greenhouse gases in rocks. This is called carbon capture.

> **B:** List two ways that the amount of methane being released into the atmosphere can be reduced.

Everyone can reduce their own carbon footprint by reducing:

- the energy they use – for example, by riding a bike rather than driving a car

- the waste they make – by recycling packaging rather than throwing it in the bin.

Challenges to reducing carbon footprints

Not everyone thinks that greenhouse gases released by human activity are causing global climate change. This makes international agreement difficult on how to cut carbon footprints.

Money is needed to reduce carbon footprints, as new, more efficient ways need to be found to make, use, and dispose of products. Alternative processes and fuels are often more expensive to set up and are not as reliable as traditional fuels yet.

As countries become more developed, their carbon footprints increase. If the same restrictions were put on every country, less developed countries might not be able to access the high quality of life in more developed countries.

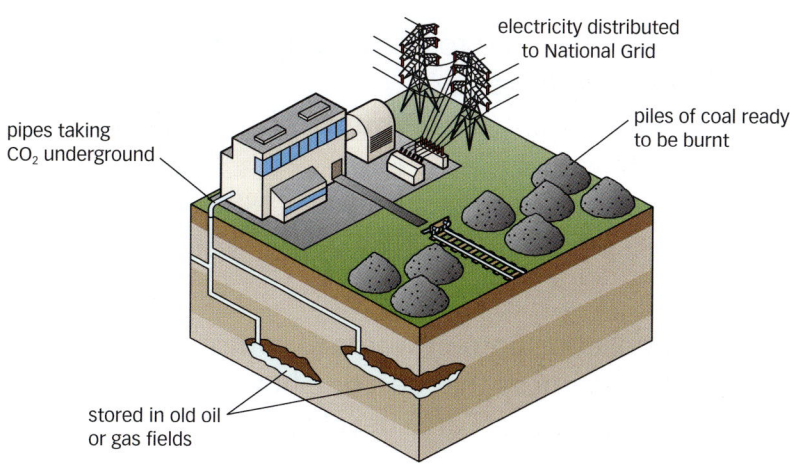

electricity distributed to National Grid

pipes taking CO₂ underground

piles of coal ready to be burnt

stored in old oil or gas fields

Figure 2 *Carbon dioxide produced when generating electricity can be stored underground to stop it entering the atmosphere.*

C: Give one reason why it is difficult to reduce our carbon footprint.

1 Choose the correct words from the box to complete the following sentences.

> carbon   greenhouse   methane

_____ footprint is a measure of the amounts of _____ gases released over the life cycle of a product, service, or event. It can be reduced by reducing emissions of carbon dioxide and _____.   [2 marks]

2 Which one of the following would reduce the carbon footprint of a country?

A burning landfill waste to generate electricity

B using wind and solar power to generate electricity

C burning only methane to generate electricity   [1 mark]

3 Explain why reducing the amount of meat you eat reduces your carbon footprint.   [2 marks]

13 Practice questions

01 Match each gas to its proportion in the atmosphere today.

Gas	Proportion
argon	78%
oxygen	just under 1%
nitrogen	21%

[2 marks]

02 Choose the correct words to complete the sentences that describe how the atmosphere of Earth developed.

For Earth's first **billion / million years**, **combustion / volcanoes** released gases that formed the early atmosphere. This atmosphere was made up of **carbon dioxide / oxygen** and water vapour. The water vapour **condensed / melted** to form the oceans. [4 marks]

03.1 Choose the correct number of years ago that plants and algae developed on Earth.

3 million   4.6 million
3 billion   4.6 billion   [1 mark]

03.2 Name the process by which plants turn carbon dioxide into oxygen and another product. [1 mark]

03.3 Complete the word equation for the process named in Question 03.2.

carbon dioxide + _____ →

oxygen + _____
[1 mark]

03.4 Describe **two** other ways in which the amount of carbon dioxide in the atmosphere **decreased**. [2 marks]

04 Heptane and hexane are hydrocarbons.

04.1 Name the elements that hydrocarbons contain. [1 mark]

04.2 Heptane is an alkane. Hexene is an alkene.

Identify which of the following images shows heptane and which shows hexene.

A

B   C

[2 marks]

04.3 Complete Table 1 to show what happens when hexene and heptane are added to bromine water.

Table 1

Chemical	Observation when added to bromine water
heptane	
hexene	

[2 marks]

05.1 Name the **two** gases that react to produce oxides of nitrogen. [2 mark]

05.2 Describe the conditions under which oxides of nitrogen are formed. [3 marks]

06 Propane is used as a fuel that undergoes combustion.

06.1 Name **two** substances that might be formed during the **incomplete** combustion of propane but not during the **complete** combustion of propane.

[2 marks]

06.2 Which of these products is poisonous? [1 mark]

06.3 Balance the symbol equation for the **complete** combustion of propane.

$$C_3H_8 + O_2 \rightarrow CO_2 + H_2O$$ [1 mark]

07 Decane is an alkane. Its chemical formula is $C_{10}H_{22}$. Decane can undergo cracking to form two alkanes and an alkene.

07.1 Describe the conditions needed for steam cracking. [2 marks]

07.2 Complete the symbol equation for the cracking of decane.

$$C_{10}H_{22} \rightarrow C_4H_{10} + C_3H_8 + \underline{\hspace{2cm}}$$ [1 mark]

07.3 Give one use of the alkene produced in the cracking of decane. [1 mark]

07.4 The alkane C_4H_{10} is called butane. Write a word equation for the complete combustion of butane. [2 marks]

08 Describe how petrol and diesel are separated from crude oil. [4 marks]

09 A man wants to reduce his carbon footprint. He drives to work every day. Suggest one way he could change his lifestyle to reduce his carbon footprint. [1 mark]

10.1 Explain why reducing the amount of beef consumed would reduce the production of greenhouse gases. [2 marks]

10.2 Suggest one negative effect of reducing the amount of beef consumed. [1 mark]

11 Boilers burn fuel to heat houses. If a house is poorly ventilated, carbon monoxide can build up.

11.1 Explain why carbon monoxide is formed in poorly ventilated houses. [2 marks]

11.2 It is recommended that houses have a carbon monoxide alarm fitted. They detect when carbon monoxide is being produced.

Explain why we need a carbon monoxide alarm to detect carbon monoxide, rather than using our senses. [2 marks]

14 Water for drinking
14.1 Drinking water

Learning objectives

After this topic, you should know:

- how to make drinking water.

Water that is safe to drink is also known as **potable water**. It is not pure water as it will have small amounts of substances dissolved in it. It may also have a small number of **microbes** in it. Microbes are living organisms that are too small to be seen without a microscope. It is important that the water only has low levels of microbes as high levels could make you ill.

A: What is potable water?

Making potable water

Fresh water is water that does not have salt in it. Fresh water can be found in lakes, in rivers, and in the ground. Potable water is often made from fresh water. The fresh water is filtered to remove all the solids. It is then **sterilised** to kill microbes. This is how most potable water in the UK is made.

B: What is fresh water?

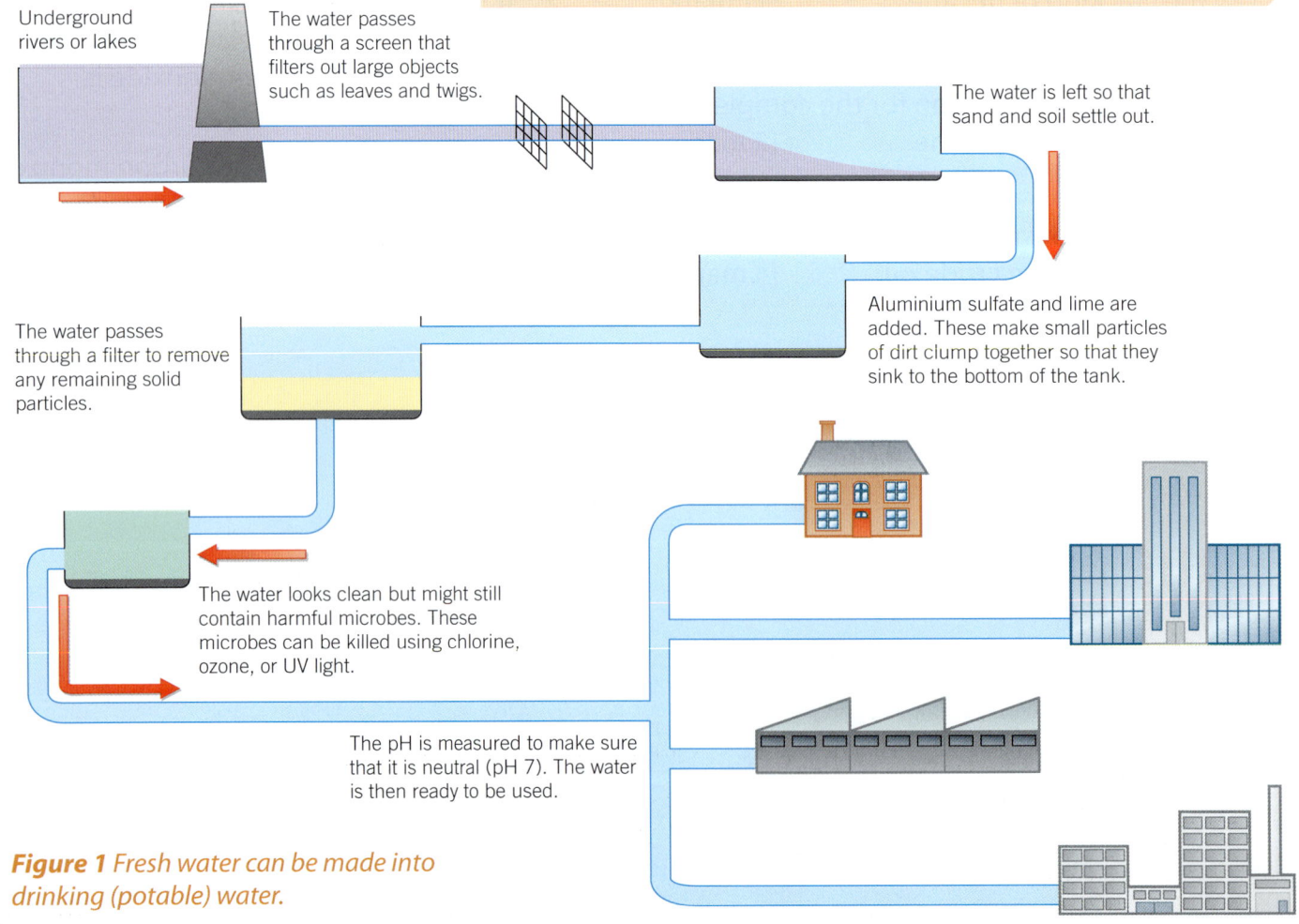

Underground rivers or lakes

The water passes through a screen that filters out large objects such as leaves and twigs.

The water is left so that sand and soil settle out.

Aluminium sulfate and lime are added. These make small particles of dirt clump together so that they sink to the bottom of the tank.

The water passes through a filter to remove any remaining solid particles.

The water looks clean but might still contain harmful microbes. These microbes can be killed using chlorine, ozone, or UV light.

The pH is measured to make sure that it is neutral (pH 7). The water is then ready to be used.

Figure 1 Fresh water can be made into drinking (potable) water.

If there is no fresh water, sea water can be used to make potable water. Sea water is very salty. Distillation can be used to remove salt from salty water. However, this needs a lot of energy as the water has to be heated to turn it into a vapour. This makes distillation expensive.

C: How can sea water be made into drinking water?

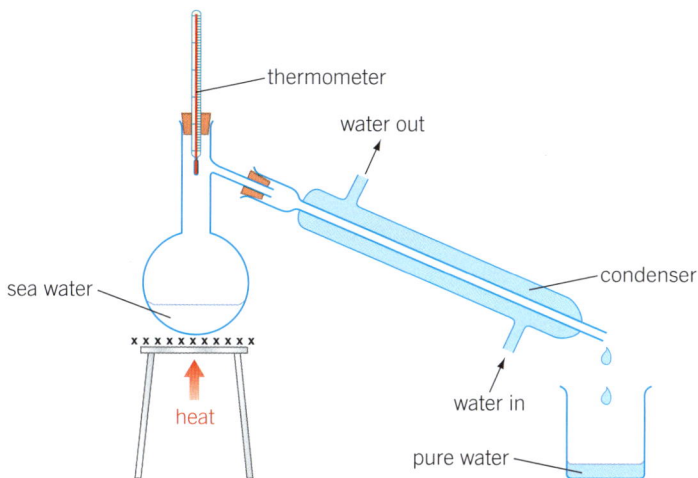

Figure 2 *Distillation can be used to make potable (drinking) water from salty water.*

1 Match each key term to its definition.

Key term	Definition	
potable water	water with salt dissolved in it	
fresh water	water with no salt dissolved in it	
sea water	contains only water molecules	
pure water	drinking water	[3 marks]

2 Choose the correct words to complete the sentences.

In the UK, **drinking / fresh** water is made from **fresh / salty** water. The fresh water is **boiled / filtered** to remove the solids and then **chlorine / lime** is used to kill microbes and **distil / sterilise** the water. [5 marks]

3 Potable water can be produced from fresh water and from salty sea water.

  a Which processes are used to produce potable water from fresh water?

    distillation   filter and sterilise   no treatment needed [1 mark]

  b What is the name of the process used to make salty water potable? [1 mark]

  c What is one disadvantage of using the process in question 3b to create potable water? [1 mark]

14.2 Investigating water

Learning objectives

After this topic, you should know:

- how to separate the solids in a solution
- how to measure the amount of solids dissolved in water
- how to measure the pH of water.

Pure water only has water molecules in it. It has no smell or taste.

Most water is a mixture with some dissolved chemicals. When the water is evaporated, the dissolved solids are left behind. The mass of these solids can be measured using a top-pan balance.

A: What is pure water?

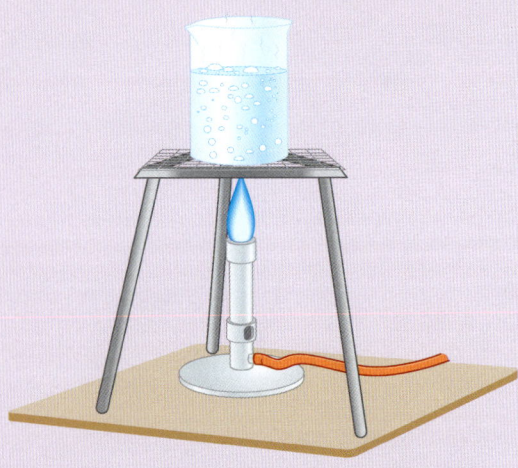

Figure 1 *Apparatus for investigating the solids dissolved in samples of water.*

Investigating the amount of dissolved solids in water

Step 1: Use a top-pan balance to record the mass of an empty 100 cm³ beaker.

Step 2: Using a measuring cylinder, add a 50 cm³ sample of water into the beaker.

Step 3: Set up a Bunsen burner, tripod, and gauze in the centre of a heat-proof mat.

Step 4: Put the beaker on the top of the gauze and move the Bunsen burner under the beaker.

Step 5: Using the blue flame of the Bunsen burner, heat the water until all of it boils away.

Step 6: Turn off the Bunsen burner and let the beaker and contents cool down.

Step 7: Measure the new mass of the beaker.

Calculate the mass of the solid by:

mass of the solid = mass of beaker at the end – mass of beaker at the start

You should see some solid left in the beaker. You can test samples of water from different places to see if the amount of solid dissolved in the water changes.

B: The mass of a beaker at the start was 52 g and the mass of the beaker at the end was 55 g. What was the mass of solid dissolved in the water?

Measuring the pH of a water sample

You can also compare the pH of water from different places. Pure water has a pH of 7. When water has chemicals dissolved in it, the pH may change.

The pH can be measured by:

- Using a pH probe

- Using universal indicator and comparing to a colour chart.

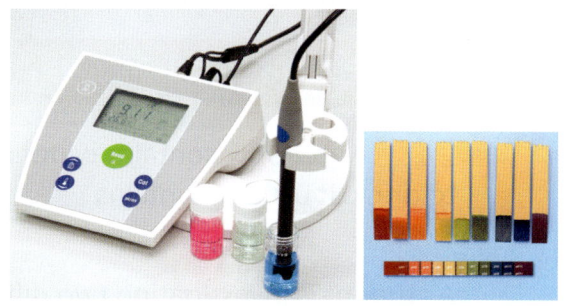

Figure 2 *You can use universal indicator or a pH probe to measure pH.*

C: How can you find the pH of a sample of water?

1   Which **two** methods can be used to measure the pH of a sample of water?

   A   pH meter

   B   thermometer

   C   top-pan balance

   D   universal indicator   [2 marks]

2   A student investigated the amount of solids dissolved in tap water taken from three different houses. Her results are shown on the graph.

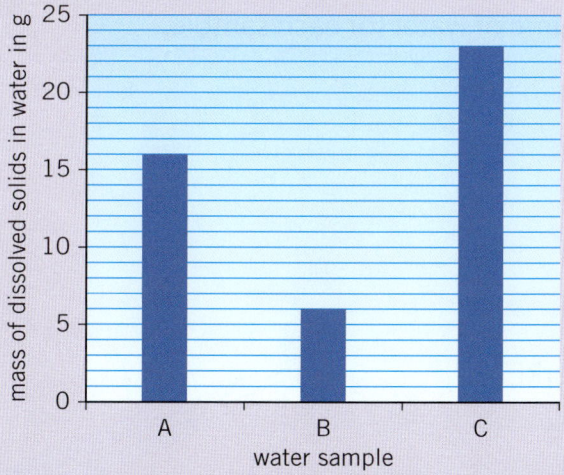

   a   How much was dissolved in water sample A?   [1 mark]

   b   Which water sample had the most solids dissolved in it?   [1 mark]

3   You should keep the volume of the water sample constant when investigating how much solid is dissolved in a sample.

   a   What type of variable is the volume of the water?   [1 mark]

   b   Why should you keep the volume of the water the same?   [1 mark]

14 Checkpoint

1 Choose the correct words from the box to complete the following sentences.

_____ water only contains water molecules. _____ water is water that is safe to drink. It usually contains _____ amounts of substances _____ in it.   [4 marks]

2 A student is investigating two different sources of water. First he measures the amount of solids dissolved in his samples. He uses the following method.
Step 1: Measure the mass of a beaker.
Step 2: Put 50 cm³ of the sample water into a beaker.
Step 3: Heat until all the water has evaporated.
Step 4: Measure the mass of the beaker.

Table 1 shows his results.

Table 1

Sample	Mass of beaker at the start in g	Mass of beaker at the end in g	Mass of dissolved solids in g
A	53	56.5	3.5
B	53	55.4	

a What mass of solid was dissolved in sample B?   [1 mark]
b Which sample contained the most dissolved solids?   [1 mark]
c The student made sure he used the same volume of water for each sample. What type of variable is this?
control   dependent   independent   [1 mark]

3 Figure 1 shows the equipment used to produce drinking water.

a What is the name of this separation method?
chromatography   crystallisation
distillation   evaporation   [1 mark]
b What is the name of the piece of equipment labelled Y?
beaker   condenser   conical flask
evaporating dish   [1 mark]
c What is the name of the piece of equipment labelled X?   [1 mark]
d Is this method used to produce drinking water from fresh water or salt water?   [1 mark]

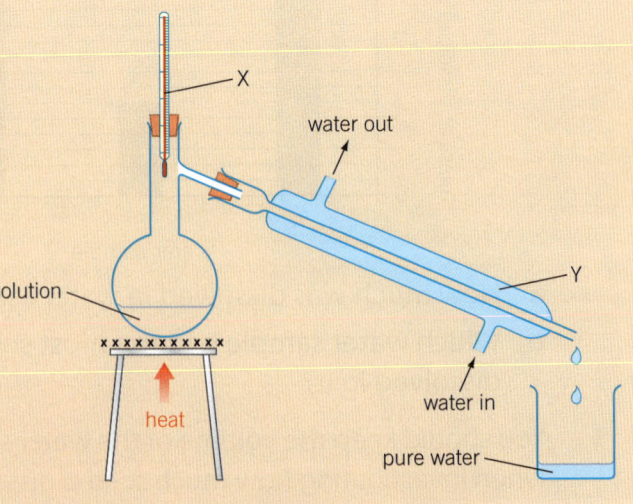

Figure 1

14 Vocabulary builder ✏

1 Match each type of water to its description.

Type of water	Description	
pure water	water from rivers or lakes	
sea water	only contains water particles	
potable	water that contains salt	
fresh water	water suitable for drinking	[3 marks]

2 Choose the correct words to complete each sentence.

a **Lakes / Seas** are a source of fresh water. [1 mark]

b Fresh water contains very little **microbes / salt**. [1 mark]

c The **concentration / pH** of drinking water should be 7. [1 mark]

d Fresh water is **distilled / filtered** to remove solids. [1 mark]

e Water is **condensed / sterilised** to kill microbes. [1 mark]

3 Water that is safe to drink contains small amounts of substances dissolved in it.
Choose the correct words from the box to complete the sentences below.

solutes	solution	solvent

Water is a _____ because substances can be dissolved in it.

The dissolved substances are the _____.

Drinking water is type of mixture called a _____. [2 marks]

4 Choose the correct word for each description of a stage in the treatment of water.

a Method used to produce drinking water from salty water.

distillation   **filtration**   **sterilisation** [1 mark]

b Water passes through a grid that separates out twigs and leaves.

distillation   **filtration**   **sterilisation** [1 mark]

c Process by which microbes are killed.

distillation   **filtration**   **sterilisation** [1 mark]

5 Complete the sentences.

P _ _ _ _ _ _ _ water is water that is safe to drink. It may still contain small amounts of
d _ _ _ _ _ _ _ _ substances or m _ _ _ _ _ _ _. [3 marks]

14.3 Waste water treatment

Learning objectives

After this topic, you should know:

- what waste water is
- how waste water is treated.

We use water every day for washing, cleaning, drinking, and flushing the toilet. Industries use a lot of water to make the products and services that we use. When we have used the water, it is called **sewage** and is taken away in drains. This water must be treated before it can be put into rivers and streams.

All waste water will have some organic matter in it. Waste water from homes and farms will also have harmful microbes. The waste water from farms and industry will have harmful chemicals in it.

A: Name two substances that are removed from waste water from a farm.

Treating sewage

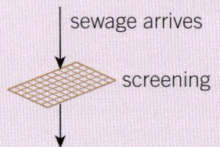

Screening

When waste water comes into the plant, it is passed through a metal grid that filters out the large solids.

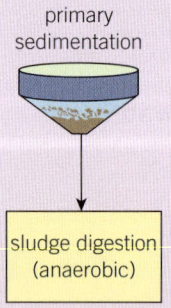

Sedimentation

The water is then left to settle. The smaller solid substances that passed through the metal grid sink to the bottom of the tank. The solid and liquid parts are separated. The solid is called **sludge**. The liquid is called **effluent**. The effluent flows into another tank.

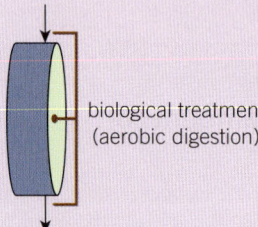

Aerobic digestion

The water of the effluent may still contain harmful microbes and organic matter. Non-harmful bacteria are added to the water and oxygen is bubbled through so that the bacteria can break down the organic matter and the microbes. This is called aerobic digestion.

The useful bacteria are separated from the water, and the water can now be released back into rivers and lakes.

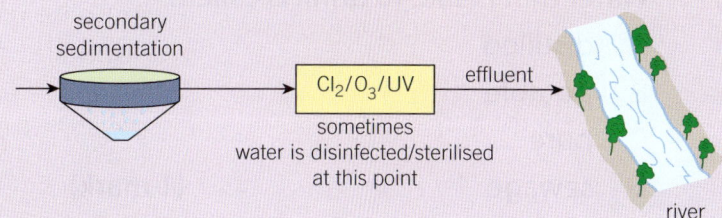

secondary sedimentation → Cl$_2$/O$_3$/UV → effluent → river

sometimes water is disinfected/sterilised at this point

B: Name the stage of waste water treatment where solid substances settle out of the water.

Sludge

The sludge produced during sedimentation undergoes further treatment. It is broken down by microbes without oxygen (anaerobically). The sludge can then be turned into fertiliser to help crops grow or made into a biofuel.

sludge digestion (anaerobic) → fertiliser, biogas, solid fuel, landfill sites } → generate electricity

C: Give two uses for sludge.

1   Match each stage in waste water treatment to the correct description.

Stage in waste water treatment	Description
screening	remove solid particles
aerobic digestion	remove large solids
sedimentation	remove microbes and organic matter
anaerobic digestion	break down sludge

[3 marks]

2   Name **two** substances that need to be removed from **industrial** waste. [2 marks]

3   Describe how sewage can make a fuel. [3 marks]

14 Practice questions

01 Water that is safe to drink is called:

   A distilled

   B potable

   C pure

   D sewage   [1 mark]

02 Which separation technique is used to remove twigs and leaves from water?

   A condensation

   B crystallisation

   C distillation

   D filtration   [1 mark]

03 Complete the table to show what industrial and agricultural material waste water contains.

Table 1

	Organic matter	Harmful microbes	Harmful chemicals
industrial waste water			
agricultural waste water	✓		

[3 marks]

04.1 Put the following statements in the correct order to describe how drinking water is produced from fresh water.

Two have been done for you.

☐ → D → ☐ → B → ☐

   A Aluminium sulfate and lime are added causing small dirt particles to clump together.

   B Water is filtered again to remove any remaining solid particles.

   C Water is sterilised to kill any microbes.

   D The water is left so that sand and soil settle out.

   E Water is filtered to remove leaves and twigs.   [2 marks]

04.2 What is **one** disadvantage of using distillation to produce drinking water?   [1 mark]

05 For each of the following substances, describe what role they have in treating waste water.

05.1 ozone   [1 mark]

05.2 aluminium sulfate   [2 marks]

05.3 oxygen   [1 mark]

06 During the process of treating waste water, sludge is produced.

06.1 Describe the treatment that sludge undergoes.   [2 marks]

06.2 Name the gas that must not be used in this process.   [1 mark]

06.3 The treatment of sludge produces methane. Why is methane useful?   [1 mark]

06.4 Give one other use of sludge after it has been treated.   [1 mark]

07 Label the particle diagrams X and Y to show which represents pure water and which represents potable water.

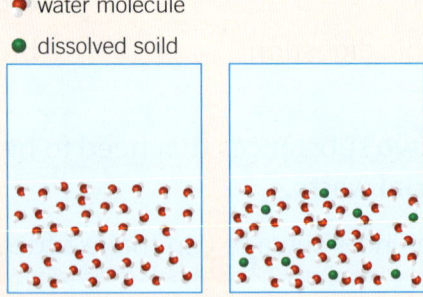

🔴 water molecule

🟢 dissolved soild

X   Y   [1 mark]

08 A student investigated three samples of water to find the amount of dissolved solids in each sample. His results are shown in Table 2.

Table 2

Sample of water	Mass of beaker at the start in g	Mass of beaker at the end in g	Mass of dissolved solids in g
A	53	61.4	
B	53	56.7	3.7
C	53	54.2	1.2

08.1 Calculate the the mass of dissolved solids in sample A. [1 mark]

08.2 One of his samples of water came from the sea. The other two came from fresh water sources. Identify which sample of water is the sea water. [1 mark]

08.3 Use the axes below to plot the student's results onto a bar chart.

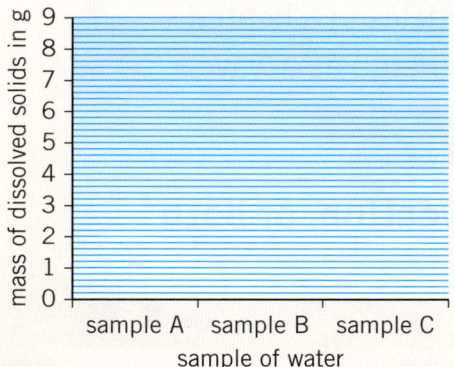

09 A student knows that drinking water has to have a pH of 7. This means that the water is neutral.

Some water she tests has a pH of 9. It is alkaline. To neutralise the solution, she adds hydrochloric acid 5 cm³ at a time and measures the pH using universal indicator paper.

Her results are shown in Table 3.

Table 3

Volume of acid added in cm³	Colour of universal indicator paper
5	
10	
15	
20	
25	
30	
35	

09.1 Which volume of acid gave a neutral solution? [1 mark]

09.2 The hydrochloric acid reacts with the alkali in the water to form sodium chloride. Sodium chloride is a salt. It dissolves in the water to form salty water.

Name the method that can be used to separate the water from the salt water solution. [1 mark]

10 Tablets can be added to water taken from a river to make it safe to drink. These tablets release chlorine when added to the water.

10.1 What do they remove from the water? [1 mark]

10.2 Student A thinks that the tablets have purified the water. Student B thinks that the water is still not pure.

Who is right about the tablets? Give a reason for your answer. [2 marks]

11 Two towns need to build a new factory for producing potable water. Town A is near a lake. Town B is near the coast.

11.1 How can each town produce potable water? [2 mark]

11.2 What is one disadvantage of using the processes in 11.1 to create potable water? [1 mark]

Physics

There are several different energy stores:

- thermal energy store
- chemical energy store
- kinetic energy store
- gravitational potential energy store
- elastic energy store.

Energy can be transferred between stores.

Q **What type of energy store is a battery?**

Thermal energy is transferred from hot to cold objects. The energy can be transferred by conduction, convection, or radiation.

Conduction is the transfer of thermal energy by the vibration of particles. Convection is the transfer of thermal energy when particles in a heated liquid or gas rise. Radiation is the transfer of thermal energy as a wave.

Q **Does a kettle use conduction, convection, or both to heat water?**

Force can change the shape of an object, or the speed or direction an object is moving in.

Forces are measured in newtons. There are different kinds of forces, including friction, tension, compression, and weight.

Q **What can forces do to an object?**

Component 5
Energy, forces, and the structure of matter

▶ **Energy stores and transfers**

Energy cannot be created or destroyed but it can be stored in many different ways. Energy can be transferred between the different stores of energy.

When energy is transferred between stores, only part of the energy is usefully transferred. The rest of the energy is transferred in less useful ways. This energy is called wasted energy.

▶ **Forces and work**

Forces are pushes and pulls. Forces are divided into contact forces and non-contact forces.

If a force causes an object to move then work is done and energy is transferred. The bigger the force or distance moved, the greater the work done.

▶ **Nuclear radiation**

Energy can be released from atoms. In the centre of an atom is a nucleus, which contains smaller particles called protons and neutrons.

Some atoms are unstable and will break down to produce radiation.

15 Energy
15.1 Changes in energy stores

Learning objectives

After this topic, you should know:

- the ways energy can be stored
- how energy can be transferred between stores.

Energy stores

Here are some examples of **energy stores**.

Energy store	Description	Example
chemical	the energy stored in food, fuels, or chemicals found in batteries.	fuel, food
kinetic	the energy stored in the movement of an object	a moving car, a planet
gravitational potential	the energy stored in an object when it has been raised above the ground	a book on a shelf
thermal	the energy stored in an object because of its temperature	a hot cup of tea
elastic (strain)	the energy stored in an object when it is squashed or stretched	a stretched spring

A: What are three examples of an energy store?

Energy transfers

Energy can be **transferred** between stores.

As a coal fire burns, the chemical store decreases, and energy is transferred to the thermal store of the room. This **energy transfer** increases the thermal store of the room, making it warmer.

As a skydiver falls, their speed increases. Their gravitational potential energy store decreases, and their kinetic energy store increases.

B: A tennis ball is thrown into the air. What are the changes to the energy stores as the ball moves upwards?

There are four ways energy can be transferred between stores:

- electrically

- mechanically (for example, lifting a book onto a shelf or pushing a box along the floor)

- by heating

- by light or sound.

When you boil a kettle, the electric current in the heater transfers energy to the thermal store of the water and the kettle. You can show these transfers using an energy transfer diagram.

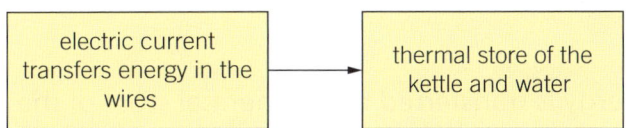

Figure 1 *An energy transfer diagram for a kettle.*

How do everyday appliances transfer energy?
Investigate the way that devices you use regularly transfer energy. Draw energy transfer diagrams for them.

C: What are the ways that energy can be transferred between energy stores?

1   Choose the correct words from the box to complete the following sentences.

> **decreases   gravitational   increases
> kinetic   potential   thermal**

A car driving along a road has energy in its _____ store. If the car drives faster this store _____. If the car drives up a hill, energy is transferred to its _____ store. If the car brakes, the kinetic store _____.   [3 marks]

2   Choose the correct energy stores to show the changes in the energy stores when a brick is dropped to the floor.

**chemical store   gravitational potential store
kinetic store   thermal store**

_____ → _____ → _____   [3 marks]

3   How is energy transferred in each of these situations?

   a   From the battery of a fan to the kinetic store of the fan blades.   [1 mark]

   b   From the wood in a fire to the thermal energy store of the room.   [1 mark]

   c   From your muscles to the gravitational potential store of a box you are lifting.   [1 mark]

15.2 Energy conservation

Learning objectives

After this topic, you should know:

- that energy cannot be created or destroyed
- how to identify useful energy transfers
- what is meant by wasted energy
- how to reduce wasted energy.

Conservation of energy

When a hairdryer is switched on, energy is transferred by the electrical current to the thermal store of the heater and the kinetic store of the fan. **All** of the energy is transferred. This is because energy **cannot be created or destroyed**.

Although all the energy is transferred, not all of it is transferred usefully.

Useful energy: energy transferred into an energy store that is wanted.

Wasted energy: energy that is not transferred to a useful energy store.

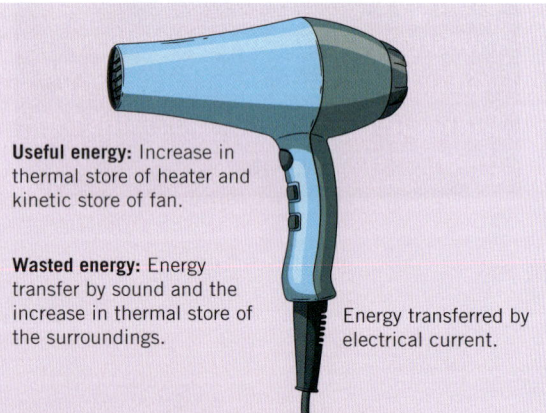

Useful energy: Increase in thermal store of heater and kinetic store of fan.

Wasted energy: Energy transfer by sound and the increase in thermal store of the surroundings.

Energy transferred by electrical current.

Figure 1 The energy transferred by a hairdryer.

In the hairdryer, energy is transferred to the thermal store of the heater and the kinetic store of the fan. Some of this energy is transferred by the hot air from the fan to the thermal store and kinetic store of your hair to dry it. This is a useful energy transfer.

Energy is also transferred to the thermal store of the plastic case and the surroundings, and is transferred as sound. This energy is wasted.

The energy that is spread out into the surroundings is **dissipated energy**. It is not being transferred in a useful way.

> **A:** What is meant by a wasted energy transfer?

Friction

Friction happens between the moving parts of a device. Friction causes energy to be transferred to the thermal store of the parts of the device and its surroundings. This means that not all of the energy supplied to the device is being usefully transferred. Some of it is wasted.

In Figure 2, the friction acts between the drill bit and the wood. The drill spins and rubs against the wood. This increases the thermal store of the wood, the drill, and the rest of the surroundings.

The energy transferred by friction is not always wasted. For example, car brakes increase the friction acting on the wheels of a car to slow it down.

Figure 2 Friction in action.

Reducing waste energy

The effects of friction can be reduced. Through a microscope, even a very smooth surface seems rough. If you can separate the surfaces, this will reduce the friction. Placing oil between the surfaces can reduce the friction. This is called **lubrication**. The oil is a lubricant.

If you want to reduce energy transferred by heating from a hot object then **insulation** can be used. A hot water tank is a store of thermal energy. To slow down the transfer of energy to the thermal store of the surroundings, the hot water tank is covered in insulation.

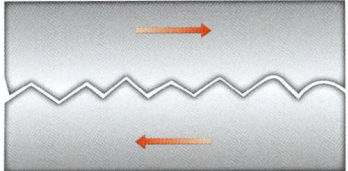

A surfaces moving across each other

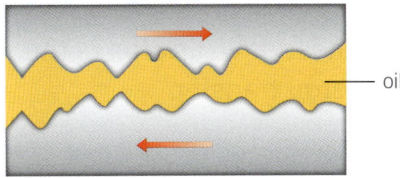

— oil

B same surfaces with lubrication

Figure 3 *Reducing the effects of friction using a lubricant.*

1   Choose the correct words from the box to complete the following sentences.

> **created   destroyed   useful   wasted**

Energy cannot be _____ or _____. The kinetic store of the moving bristles of an electric toothbrush is an example of a _____ energy transfer and the noise is an example of _____ energy.   [4 marks]

2   Complete the table below by choosing the correct energy store. You may need to use some options more than once.

> **heating   kinetic   sound**

Device	Useful energy transfer	Wasted energy transfer
television	light and sound	
headphones		
car		

[5 marks]

3   When you drop a bouncy ball, the first bounce is always lower than the height that the ball is dropped from.

a   How is the energy stored before the ball is dropped?
[1 mark]

b   What useful energy store is energy transferred to as the ball falls?   [1 mark]

c   Some of the ball's energy is tranferred as wasted energy during the fall. What type of energy is wasted during the fall?
[1 mark]

15.3 Energy transfer by heating

Learning objectives

After this topic, you should know:

- which materials are the best conductors
- which materials are the best insulators
- how thermal conductivity affects the rate of energy transfer
- how thickness of walls affects the rate of energy transfer.

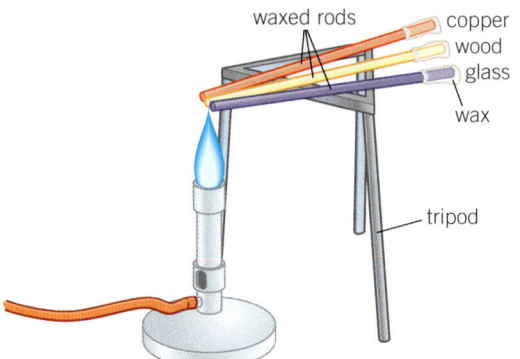

Figure 1 *Comparing the thermal conductivity of materials.*

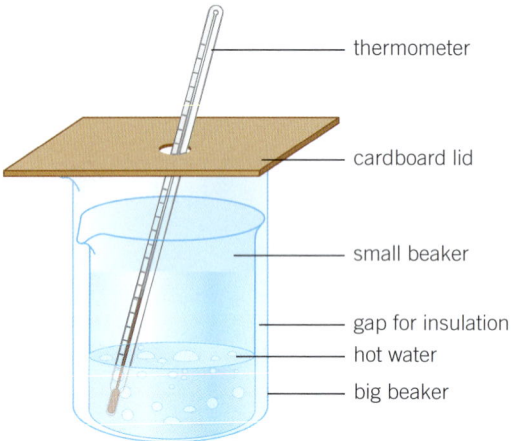

Figure 2 *Equipment for investigating different materials as insulators.*

Testing rods of different materials as conductors

Thermal conductivity is a measure of how quickly energy is transferred by conduction through a material.

You can carry out a simple experiment to compare the thermal conductivity of different materials. Each rod shown in Figure 1 has a small blob of wax at one end and is heated at the other end. The wax melts when it gets hot enough. The first rod on which the wax melts is the best conductor. It has the **highest** thermal conductivity.

Materials can be called **conductors** or **insulators**. A conductor transfers energy at a higher rate than an insulator.

A: What is thermal conductivity?

Investigating different materials as insulators

Step 1: Put a small beaker inside a larger beaker.

Step 2: Pour 100 ml hot water into the small beaker.

Step 3: Use a piece of cardboard as a lid for the large beaker. The cardboard must have a hole for a thermometer.

Step 4: Record the temperature of the water and start the stopwatch.

Step 5: Record the temperature of the water in a table every 3 minutes for 15 minutes.

Step 6: Repeat steps 1–5 using different materials each time to fill the space between the small and large beaker.

The slower the water cools down, the better the material is as an insulator.

B: What is one control variable that should be kept the same when you repeat the experiment?

Investigating the effect of thickness of insulators

Step 1: Put 100 ml hot water into a small beaker and add a lid with a small hole for the thermometer.

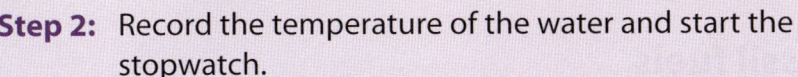

Step 2: Record the temperature of the water and start the stopwatch.

Step 3: Record the temperature of the water in a table every 3 minutes for 15 minutes.

Step 4: Repeat the experiment. This time wrap two layers of insulating material around the beaker, holding it in place with a rubber band.

The thicker the insulation, the slower the water will cool.

C: How will you know from your results how thickness of insulating material affects the thermal insulation?

Using insulation

Figure 3 shows insulating material being fitted in a loft. The material has a low thermal conductivity. It is a good insulator. Several layers are used to reduce the heat energy transferred through the roof and keep the house warm in winter.

Houses are designed so that the walls have low thermal conductivity. Older houses often have very thick walls to help reduce the transfer of energy by heat.

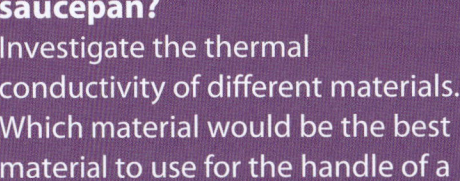

What is the best material for the handle of a saucepan?
Investigate the thermal conductivity of different materials. Which material would be the best material to use for the handle of a saucepan?

How quickly does a hot drink cool down?
Investigate the factors that affect the rate of cooling down of a container of hot water. What factors do you expect to have an effect?

Figure 3 Insulating a loft with fibreglass. The air trapped between the fibres makes fibreglass a good insulator.

---

1 Choose the correct words from the box to complete the following sentences.

high   layers   low

Materials that are good conductors of heat have _____ thermal conductivity. Good insulators have _____ thermal conductivity. Adding more _____ of an insulating material reduces energy transfer by heating.   [2 marks]

2 Sort the following materials into materials that are good conductors and materials that are good insulators.

copper   iron   plastic   wool
[4 marks]

3 A student is investigating two materials to find out which is the better insulator. She recorded the change in temperature of identical beakers of hot water insulated with felt and polystyrene. The temperature of the felt-covered beaker fell by 15 °C and the temperature of the polystyrene-covered beaker fell by 10 °C.

  a Which of the materials is the better insulator?   [1 mark]

  b Which material has the highest thermal conductivity?   [1 mark]

15.4 Energy resources

Learning objectives

After this topic, you should know:

- what is meant by a renewable energy resource
- what is meant by a non-renewable energy resource
- examples of renewable and non-renewable energy resources.

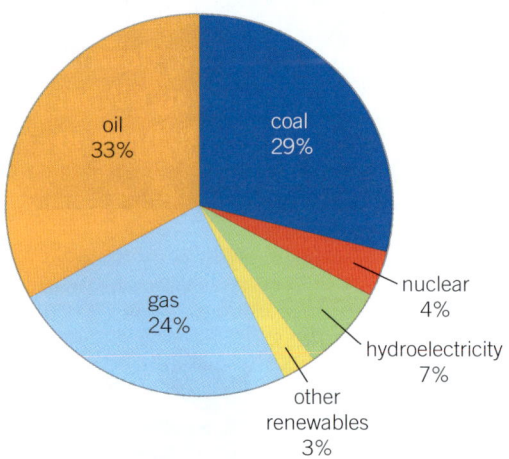

Figure 1 *World use of energy resources in 2015.*

Fossil fuels

Most of the energy you use probably comes from burning fossil fuels. Coal, oil, and gas are all fossil fuels. These fuels are burnt in engines for cars, ships, and aeroplanes, and to heat your house. Fossil fuels can also be burnt to generate electricity. They are used to boil water to produce steam. The steam turns a turbine which spins a generator. This generates electricity.

One problem with fossil fuels is that they will run out. They are **non-renewable**. They were formed from the remains of plants and animals that died hundreds of millions of years ago. This means they cannot be replaced. Figure 1 shows how much the world relies on these non-renewable energy resources.

> **A:** What is meant by a non-renewable energy resource? Give one example.

Nuclear power

A nuclear power station works in almost the same way as a fossil fuel power station. However, in a nuclear power station, the thermal energy used to make the steam is released from atoms that are being split. Nuclear power is a non-renewable source.

Renewable energy resources

The world needs to find **renewable** energy sources. These are sources of energy that will not run out, because they can be replaced. The table below shows some examples of renewable energy resources.

	**Wind** Wind turns the blades of a turbine, which turns a generator to generate electricity.
	**Water** Water generates electricity in several ways. • Hydroelectric – water flows through a gap in a dam and turns a turbine, which turns a generator to generate electricity. • Waves – the movement of the waves can be used to generate electricity. • Tidal – water from high tide is trapped behind a barrier. As it is released it turns a turbine, which turns a generator.

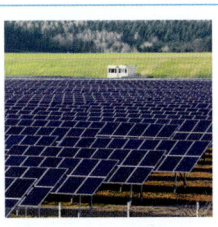	**Solar** Solar radiation transfers energy from the Sun. There are two ways this can be used: • to heat water directly – water flows through solar heating panels on the roof of a house. These absorb solar radiation, heating the water the panels. • to generate electricity using solar cells.
	**Geothermal** Water is pumped underground where there are hot rocks. The water becomes steam that turns turbines, which turn a generator.
 	**Biofuels** These are fuels made from living things or their waste products. For example, methane gas can be made from animal waste, and ethanol can be made from sugar canes.

B: What is meant by a renewable energy resource? Give one example.

1 Choose the correct words from the box to complete the following sentences.

> biofuels   fossil   non-renewable   renewable

Most of the electricity we use is generated by burning _____ fuels. These fuels are _____. This means they will eventually run out. The world is starting to use more _____ sources of energy such as _____.   [3 marks]

2 Which **two** of these energy resources are non-renewable?

biofuel   coal   geothermal
hydroelectricity   oil   [2 marks]

3 Sort the sentences into the correct order to describe how electricity is generated in a fossil fuel power plant.

A Electricity is generated.

B Steam turns a turbine.

C Fuel is burnt to heat water.

D A turbine turns a generator.   [3 marks]

15 Checkpoint

1. Choose the correct words from the box to complete the following sentences.

conduction	faster	high	insulation	low	lower

   In houses that are insulated, the walls are filled with materials that have a _____ thermal conductivity. This stops the _____ of energy through the walls. Materials with a _____ thermal conductivity allow a _____ rate of energy transfer through them. [4 marks]

2. Draw one line from each type of energy store to the correct example.

   Energy store   **Example**

   chemical store   a flying bird

   kinetic store   a spring

   thermal store   a battery

   elastic store   a cup of tea   [3 marks]

3. Complete the table to decide whether each energy source is renewable or non-renewable. One has been done for you.

Energy source	Renewable	Non-renewable
coal		✓
biofuel		
hydroelectric		
oil		
geothermal		

   [4 marks]

4. A car slows down to a stop at some traffic lights. Complete the sentence to describe one of the energy transfers that takes place.

   Energy from the **chemical / kinetic** store of the car is transferred to the **elastic / thermal** store of the car brakes and the surroundings. [2 marks]

5. Draw one line from each energy resource to the correct energy store that energy is transferred from to generate electricity.

   Resource   **Energy store**

   wind turbine   gravitational

   hydroelectric dam   kinetic

   biofuels   chemical   [3 marks]

6. a Which of the following is a **useful** energy transfer of a vacuum cleaner?

   A   chemical   C   kinetic

   B   gravitational   D   thermal   [1 mark]

   b Which of the following is a **wasted** energy transfer of a vacuum cleaner?

   A   chemical   C   kinetic

   B   gravitational   D   thermal   [1 mark]

7. Which energy store always increases whenever energy is transferred between stores? [1 mark]

15 Vocabulary builder

1   Choose the correct words to complete the following sentences.

Some energy sources will run out. These are called **non-renewable / renewable** resources, for example **coal / solar**. Energy sources that will never run out because they can be replenished are called **non-renewable / renewable** resources, for example **biofuels / nuclear**.　　　[4 marks]

2   Draw one line from each energy store to the correct definition and example.
One has been done for you.

Energy store	Definition	Example
gravitational potential	Stored by any moving object.	A cup of tea.
chemical	Energy due to an object's height above the ground.	A book on a shelf.
kinetic	Energy transferred by chemical reactions.	A bow and arrow before it is fired.
elastic	Energy related to the temperature.	A battery.
thermal	Stored by a springy object when it is squashed or stretched.	A jogger.

[4 marks]

3   Choose the correct term from the list to identify the renewable energy resource that is being described.

a   The up and down motion of the sea.

   solar　　　　**tidal**　　　　**wave**　　　　　[1 mark]

b   The energy transferred from the Sun.

   geothermal　　　　**nuclear**　　　　**solar**　　　　[1 mark]

c   Using hot rocks beneath the ground to heat water.

   geothermal　　　　**nuclear**　　　　**solar**　　　　[1 mark]

d   Using the gravitational potential store of water behind a dam.

   geothermal　　　　**hydroelectric**　　　　**wave**　　　　[1 mark]

4   Draw one line from each key term to the correct definition for a torch.

Key term	Definition
useful energy	The chemical store of a battery.
efficiency	The light transferred by a torch.
input energy	The heat transferred by a torch.
waste energy	The measure of how much energy was usefully transferred.

[4 marks]

15.5 Energy efficiency

Learning objectives

After this topic, you should know:

- how to identify the input energy to a device
- how to identify the useful output energy transferred from a device
- what is meant by efficiency
- how to calculate the efficiency of a device.

Useful energy output

All devices are designed to transfer energy from one store to another. The energy supplied to an appliance is the called the **input energy**.

The useful energy transferred by the appliance is the **useful output energy**. Some energy is always wasted.

The percentage of the input energy that is transferred to the useful energy output is called the **efficiency** of the appliance. The higher the percentage of energy that is transferred usefully, the more efficient an appliance is.

Calculating energy efficiency

To calculate efficiency you can use the equation:

$$\text{efficiency} = \frac{\text{useful output energy}}{\text{total input energy}} \times 100\%$$

A: What is the equation for calculating efficiency?

Worked example

An electric fan is supplied with 80 J of energy by an electric current. The fan transfers 20 J as kinetic energy. Calculate the percentage efficiency of the fan.

Step 1: Write down what you know.

Useful output: fans transfer kinetic energy.

useful output energy = 20 J

Input energy: supplied by an electric current

total input energy = 80 J

Step 2: Write down the equation for calculating efficiency.

$$\text{efficiency} = \frac{\text{useful output energy}}{\text{total input energy}} \times 100\%$$

Step 3: Put numbers in the equation and solve.

$$\text{efficiency} = \frac{20 \text{ J}}{80 \text{ J}} \times 100\% = 25\%$$

B: What unit is efficiency measured in?

The efficiency can never be more than 100%. This is because you can never get more energy out of a device than you put in.

Sometimes it is harder to identify the energy input and useful output energy. Here is another example.

Worked example

The electric motor in Figure 1 is supplied with 200 J of energy. It transfers 60 J of this energy to the gravitational potential store of the object being lifted.

Step 1: Write down what you know.

Useful output: the motor is designed to lift objects, so to the gravitational potential store.

useful energy output = 60 J

Input energy: electric current

Total input energy = 200 J

Step 2: Write down the equation for calculating efficiency.

$$\text{efficiency} = \frac{\text{useful output energy}}{\text{total input energy}} \times 100\%$$

Step 3: Put numbers in the equation and solve.

$$\text{efficiency} = \frac{60 \text{ J}}{200 \text{ J}} \times 100\% = 30\%$$

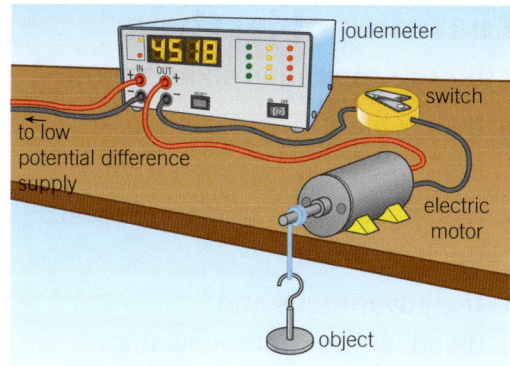

Figure 1 *An electric motor being used to lift an object.*

1   Choose the correct words from the box to complete the following sentences.

| efficiency | in | input | more | out | output |

To calculate the _____ of a device you have to identify the _____ energy and the useful _____ energy transferred. A device can never be _____ than 100% efficient. This is because you can never get more energy _____ than you put _____.   [5 marks]

2   Choose the correct words to complete the table. You may need to use some options more than once.

chemical   elastic   electric   kinetic   light   sound

Device	Input energy	Useful output energy
torch	chemical	
motor		
radio		

[5 marks]

3   A student is deciding which lightbulb to use in their desk lamp. They are comparing a filament lightbulb and an LED lightbulb. Both lightbulbs are supplied with 80 J of energy. The filament lightbulb transfers 4 J as light. The LED light bulb transfers 68 J as light.

   a   Calculate the efficiency of the filament lightbulb.   [2 marks]

   b   Calculate the efficiency of the LED lightbulb.   [2 marks]

   c   Explain which lightbulb they should choose.   [2 marks]

15.6 Energy and the environment

Learning objectives

After this topic, you should know:

- the problems with using fossil fuels
- why people are concerned about nuclear power
- the advantages and disadvantages of renewable energy resources.

We need energy resources for transport, heating, and generating electricity. However, there are problems with transferring energy to useful outputs.

Fossil fuels

When coal, oil, and gas are burnt, greenhouse gases such as carbon dioxide are released. The amount of carbon dioxide in the atmosphere is increasing. This is one cause of **global warming**.

Carbon capture is a way to stop carbon dioxide being released from fossil fuel power stations.

Burning fossil fuels can also produce sulfur dioxide, which causes **acid rain**. The sulfur can be removed from the fuel before it is burnt.

Fossil fuels will eventually become too expensive to get out of the ground. We will have to find alternatives.

> **A:** Give two reasons why we should find alternatives to burning fossil fuels.

Nuclear power

To slow down global warming, people need to use fewer fossil fuels. Could nuclear power be the answer?

Advantages

- It does not produce greenhouse gases, like carbon dioxide.
- More energy is transferred per kilogram of fuel than other energy sources.

Disadvantages

- Used fuel rods contain radioactive waste which has to be stored for centuries.
- An accident at a nuclear power station could affect a very large area.

> **B:** Suggest why people might not want a nuclear power station near their town.

Renewable energy resources

Here are some of the advantages and disadvantages of renewable energy resources.

Advantages

- They will never run out.
- They do not produce greenhouse gases, like carbon dioxide.
- They can provide electricity anywhere.

Disadvantages

- Not enough energy is produced to be able to meet all the world's energy needs.
- Wind turbines are noisy.
- Tidal barriers and hydroelectric dams destroy the habitats of plants and animals.
- Solar cells and wind turbines need large areas of land to generate lots of power.
- They can be unreliable – for example, it isn't always windy or sunny.

Transport

Oil is running out faster than coal. It is becoming more expensive. As a result, people are finding new ways to supply energy for vehicles. Some engines have been converted to run on vegetable oil.

There are also more electric cars on the roads. You can now find charging points at motorway service stations.

C: Why are there more electric cars on the road?

1 Draw one line from each energy resource to the correct problem associated with that energy resource.

Energy source	Problem
nuclear	noisy
wind	produces radioactive waste
tidal	causes global warming
coal	destroys habitats [3 marks]

2 Give **three** reasons we need energy resources.   [3 marks]

3 Name two possible energy sources that could be used to generate electricity for a remote flat island in a cold climate.   [2 marks]

15 Practice questions

01 Choose the correct word to complete the following sentences.

Metals are good **conductors / insulators**. They have a **high / low** thermal conductivity. Insulating materials have a **high / low** thermal conductivity. If you want to improve the insulation you can make it **thicker / thinner**. [4 marks]

02 Figure 1 shows three different renewable resources numbered 1 to 3.

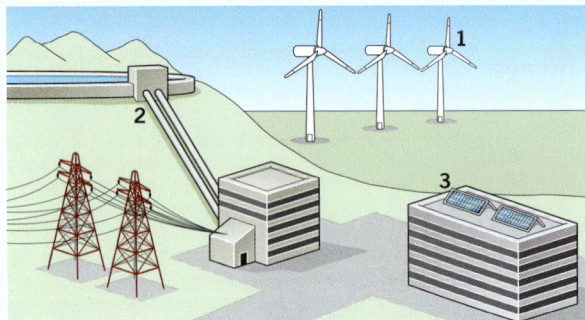

Figure 1

02.1 Choose the correct name of each energy resource from the list below.

hydroelectricity

solar

wind [2 marks]

02.2 What is meant by a renewable energy resource? [1 mark]

03 Draw one line from each electrical device to the correct energy it is designed to output.

Electrical device	Energy
toaster	sound
fan	thermal
torch	kinetic
headphones	light

[3 marks]

04 Figure 2 shows a geothermal power station.

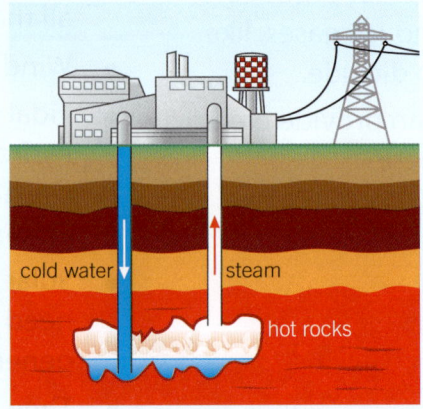

Figure 2

Choose the correct words from the box to complete the following sentences.

> **generator   motor   non-renewable**
> **renewable   Sun   turbine   wind**

Cold water is pumped down to the hot rocks. The water turns to steam. The steam drives a _____ which then turns the _____. This is one of the few energy resources which does not need energy from the _____. It is a _____ energy supply. [4 marks]

05 Figure 3 shows the label on a dishwasher. The dishwasher has an efficiency rating of A.

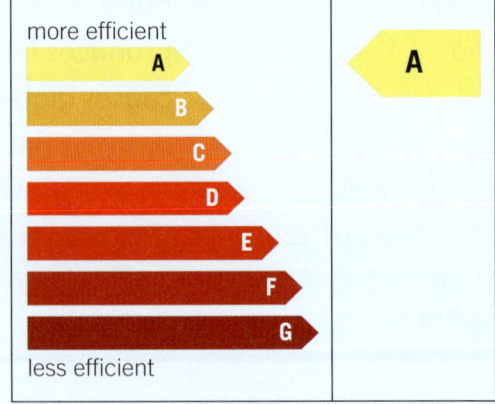

Figure 3

How would a dishwasher labelled D compare with this one? Choose the correct answer from the options below.

A   Dishwasher D would not clean the dishes as well.

B   Dishwasher D would use less electricity.

C   Dishwasher D would waste more energy.

D   Dishwasher D would waste less energy.   [1 mark]

06   A student is investigating thickness of insulation. She used 100 ml of water at a temperature of 80°C in each experiment and recorded her results in Table 1.

Table 1

Number of layers of insulation	Temperature after 10 mins in °C	Temperature change after 10 mins in °C
0	65	
1	68	
2	72	

06.1   Give one variable the student should control in her investigation.   [1 mark]

06.2   Name the independent variable in her investigation.   [1 mark]

06.3   Calculate the temperature change in each investigation.   [3 marks]

07   An energy-efficient light bulb is supplied with 400 J by an electrical current. 320 J of energy is transferred by light.

07.1   What is the energy input to the light bulb?   [1 mark]

07.2   What is the useful energy transferred by the light bulb?   [1 mark]

07.3   Calculate the percentage efficiency of the light bulb.   [2 marks]

07.4   Determine the amount of energy wasted.   [1 mark]

08   A car's fuel is a store of one form of energy. As the car moves energy is transferred from one store to another. Describe how stores of energy change as a car slows down.   [3 marks]

16 Forces and work
16.1 Forces

Learning objectives

After this topic, you should know:

- what a force is
- how to represent forces using arrows
- what is meant by contact forces and non-contact forces
- how to identify contact and non-contact forces.

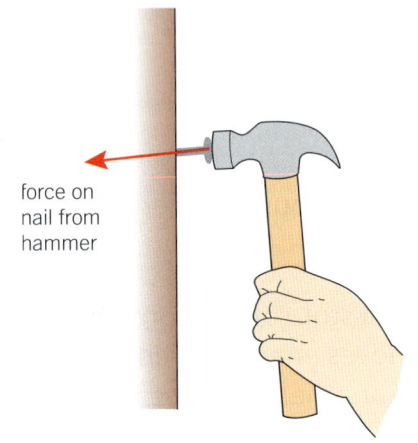

Figure 1 *The force from the hammer is acting on the nail.*

force on nail from hammer

What is a force?

A **force** is a **push** or a **pull** that acts on an object because of another object. For example, in Figure 1, the hammer is **pushing** on the nail.

> **A: What is a force?**

Representing forces

You can show forces with arrows. The arrow shows the direction in which a force is acting. A longer arrow shows a bigger force. Figure 2 shows the forces acting on a plane at take-off.

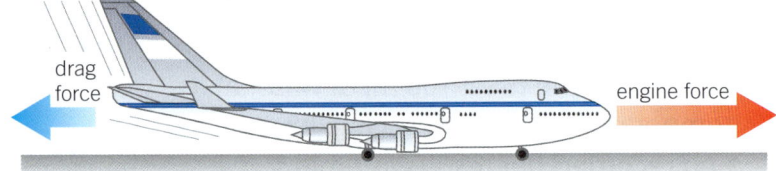

drag force

engine force

Figure 2 *A passenger plane taking off.*

> **B: Look carefully at the diagram in Figure 2. Which force is bigger? How can you tell?**

Types of forces

Forces can be sorted into **contact** and **non-contact** forces.

Contact forces

For a contact force to act, objects must be touching each other. Contact forces include friction, air resistance, tension, and normal contact force.

Normal contact force is a force that supports an object in contact with a surface. For example, when a book is on a table, the table supports the book with an upward force. This is a normal contact force.

Non-contact forces

Non-contact forces act at a distance. The objects need not be touching. Non-contact forces include gravitational force, magnetic force, and electrostatic force.

Gravitational force is the force you feel on Earth that keeps you on the ground.

Skydivers know all about forces. **Gravitational force** pulls them down towards the Earth. **Air resistance** pushes upwards against them and their parachutes and slows them down. This allows them to land safely.

> **C: Name one contact force and one non-contact force experienced by a skydiver.**

Measuring forces

Forces are measured in **newtons**, **N**. You can use a force meter or **newton meter** to measure forces.

> **D: What units are forces measured in?**

1   Choose the correct words from the box to complete the following sentences.

> **contact   pull   weight**

A force is a push or a _____. For example, when you sit on a chair your _____ pushes down on the chair. The chair pushes back up. This is called the normal _____ force.

[2 marks]

2   Which of the following forces are contact forces?

air resistance   electrostatic

friction   weight   [2 marks]

3   The diagram shows a trampoline.

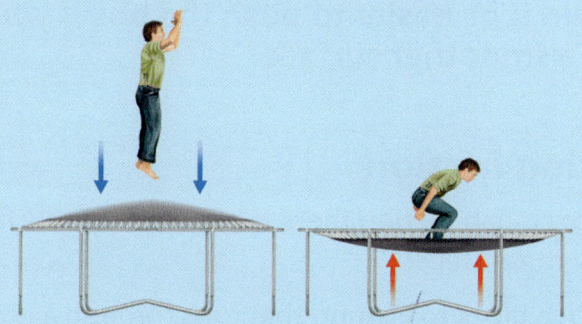

   a   What is the name of the force acting upwards?

[1 mark]

   b   What is the name of the force acting downwards?

[1 mark]

Figure 3 Both gravitational force and air resistance act on a skydiver.

How do forces act on objects?

Investigate how forces act on objects in your classroom. Use a newton meter to measure the forces being applied. What happens to each object when a force is applied?

16.2 Work done

Learning objectives

After this topic, you should know:

- what work means in science
- how energy transfers take place when work is done
- how to investigate friction
- that work done against friction causes a temperature rise.

Work done

When a force makes an object move, we say that **work** is done on the object. Work is measured in joules, J. One joule is the work done when a 1 newton weight is raised by 1 metre.

When you lift a box, you transfer energy to the box's gravitational potential energy store. The amount of energy transferred is equal to the work done.

$$\text{energy transferred} = \text{work done}$$

Work is done because you have moved the box. The larger the weight of the box, the more work you have to do. The further you move the box, the more work you have to do.

A: What is meant by work done?

Friction

When you push a box across the floor, friction acts on the box because it is touching the floor. It acts in the **opposite direction** to your pushing force.

As you do work against the frictional force, the bottom of the box gets hotter. This always happens when you do work **against** friction. If you rub your hands together quickly, they become warm. This is because you are doing work to overcome the friction between your hands.

You need friction to be able to move or change direction. Friction between the sole of your shoe and the ground is what stops you from slipping or sliding.

B: Why would it be easier to push the box if you put it on a smoother surface?

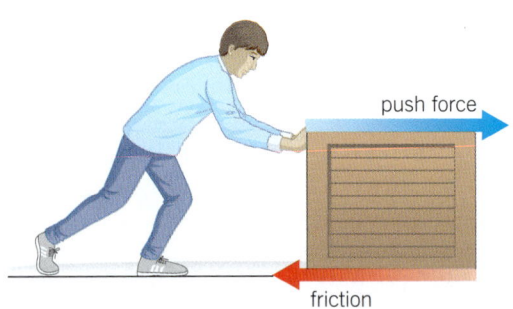

Figure 1 *The forces acting when you push a box.*

How do different surfaces affect friction?

Investigate how different surfaces affect the amount of friction acting on a block that is moving over the surface. What types of surfaces have the greatest effect?

Investigating friction

To measure how much friction there is between two surfaces you can follow these steps:

Step 1: Attach a block to a string that runs through a pulley. Add a hanger to the other end of the string to apply a force to the block, as shown in Figure 2.

Step 2: Add more weights to the hanger until the block slides across the surface.
Record how much weight you added in a table.

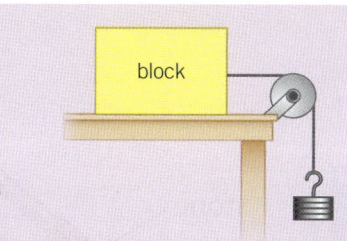

Figure 2 *Equipment for investigating friction.*

Step 3: Change the type of surface that the block is sliding on. Then repeat step 2.

Surface	Weight added to make the block move in N
bench	0.5
cloth	1.2
sandpaper	2.0

Step 4: You could repeat the whole experiment to check the results are similar each time. This would make the experiment more reliable.

C: Look at the table. Which surface has the most friction?

1 Choose the correct words from the box to complete the following sentences.

force   increases   move

When a _____ causes an object to _____, work is done. When you do work against friction, the temperature of the surfaces where the friction acts _____.   [2 marks]

2 Put the following statements in the correct order to describe how to investigate the friction between a block and different surfaces.

A Add weight to the hanger until the block slides across the surface.

B Put the block on a different type of surface and repeat the experiment.

C Record how much weight you added to the hanger.

D Set up the apparatus.   [3 marks]

3 A student does work pushing a trolley up a steep slope. As work is done, energy is transferred.

a What is one energy store that has increased as the trolley moves up the hill?   [1 mark]

b What is one factor that will affect how much work the student has to do?   [1 mark]

16 Checkpoint

1 Figure 1 shows a catapult.

Choose the correct words from the box to complete the following sentences.

> distance   force   friction   transferred
> weight   work done

When you pull back a catapult you do work stretching the elastic. This is because you apply a _____ and stretch the elastic through a _____. The _____ on the elastic of the catapult is equal to the energy _____ to the stone.

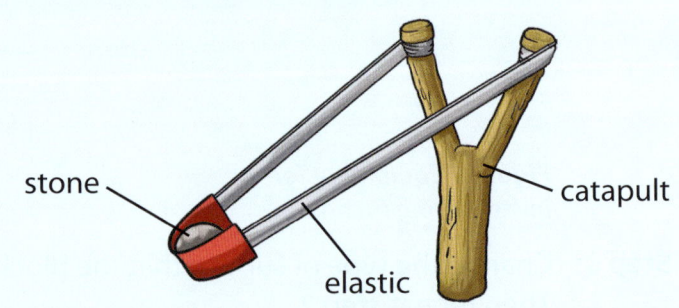

Figure 1

[4 marks]

2 Sort the following forces into **contact** and **non-contact** forces.

weight   friction   magnetic   air resistance   normal contact

[4 marks]

3 A student investigates friction using a newton meter. They record the force needed to pull the box along the table. They then change the friction on the block by attaching rubber bands round it.

The student's results are shown in Table 1.

Table 1

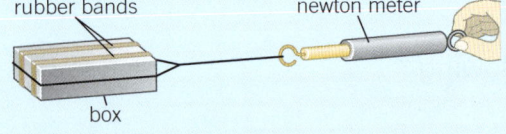

Figure 2

Number of rubber bands	Force needed to pull the box in N
0	4
1	7
2	11
3	17

a Draw one line from each type of variable to the correct variable in the experiment.

Type of variable	Variable
control	number of rubber bands
dependent	mass of box
independent	force needed to pull box

[2 marks]

b What is the relationship between the number of rubber bands and the friction?   [1 mark]

4 When a car slows to a stop the brakes do work.

a What force does work on the wheels to stop them from turning?   [1 mark]

b What is the energy store that the car has when it is moving?   [1 mark]

c What is the energy store that has increased when the car has stopped?   [1 mark]

d If the car is moving faster, does more or less work need to be done to slow it down?   [1 mark]

5 A skydiver is falling through the sky.

a What is the force that is acting downwards on the skydiver?   [1 mark]

b What is the force that is acting upwards against the movement of the skydiver?   [1 mark]

c Which force is a contact force and which force is a non-contact force?   [1 mark]

16 Vocabulary builder

1   Draw one line from each key term to the correct definition.

Key term	Definition
force	a force that acts at a distance
work done	a force that acts when objects are touching
non-contact force	a force moves an object through a distance
contact force	a push or a pull

[3 marks]

2   Choose the correct words from the box to answer the following questions.

arrows   joules   newton meter   newtons

a   What unit is force measured in?   [1 mark]

b   What unit are work done and energy transfer
measured in?   [1 mark]

c   What equipment is used to measure force?   [1 mark]

d   What is used to show the size and the direction of
a force in a diagram?   [1 mark]

3   Choose the correct words to complete the sentences below.

When you lift weights you are doing **energy / work**. You can increase
the work done by lifting **heavier / lighter** weights a **longer / shorter**
distance. When you do work against friction the temperature
decreases / increases.   [4 marks]

4   Complete the words to answer the questions about forces.

a   This force acts when two moving surfaces are in contact.

f _ _ c _ _ _ n   [1 mark]

b   This non-contact force pulls you downwards.

we _ _ h _   [1 mark]

c   If this contact force didn't exist, you could run much faster.

a _ _ r _ _ i _ t _ _ c _   [1 mark]

d   When you compete in a tug of war, the rope experiences this
contact force.

t _ _ s _ _ _   [1 mark]

16.3 Weight

Learning objectives

After this topic, you should know:

- what weight is
- the difference between mass and weight
- how you calculate weight.

Figure 1 *The force called weight is acting on the ball as it falls.*

If you drop a ball, it falls. This is because there is a force pulling it towards the Earth. This force is called **weight**.

What is weight?

Your weight is due to the gravitational force of attraction between you and the Earth. Since the weight depends on this gravitational attraction your weight can change. Table 1 shows your weight on different planets in the Solar System if you have a mass of 60 kg.

Table 1 *Your weight will change on different planets of the Solar system.*

Planet	Your weight in newtons
Earth	600
Mars	220
Jupiter	1500
Neptune	840

A: Using Table 1 identify which planet has the largest gravitational force of attraction.

Mass and weight

You don't really get slimmer if you visit Mars. Your weight is less, but your mass stays the same.

- The **weight** of an object is the force acting on it due to gravity. It is measured in **newtons**, **N**.
- The **mass** of an object depends on the number of atoms in it. It is measured in **kilograms**, **kg**.

Your mass stays the same on Mars because the number of atoms you have doesn't change.

B: Give the unit of weight and the unit of mass.

Calculating weight

If you know the mass of an object you can calculate the weight using the equation:

weight (N) = mass (kg) × gravitational field strength (N/kg)

The gravitational force acting on a 1 kg object is the **gravitational field strength**. You will always be given the gravitational field strength in a question.

Worked example

A dog has a mass of 10 kg. Calculate its weight. The gravitational field strength is 10 N/kg.

Step 1: Write down what you know.

mass = 10 kg

gravitational field strength = 10 N/kg

Step 2: Write down the equation.

Weight = mass × gravitational field strength

Step 3: Put the numbers into the equation and solve.

Weight = 10 kg × 10 N/kg = 100 N

C: Give the equation to calculate weight.

1 Choose the correct words from the box to complete the following sentences.

| gravitational   kilograms   mass   newtons |

The mass of an object is measured in _____. Weight is measured in _____ as it is a force. Weight depends on the _____ force of attraction. The weight can be calculated by multiplying the _____ by the gravitational field strength. [3 marks]

2 A rock has a mass of 60 kg. Calculate the weight of the rock on Mercury if the gravitational field strength is 3.8 N/kg. [2 marks]

3 The gravitational field strength on Earth is 10 N/kg and on the Moon is 1.6 N/kg.

   a Identify whether Earth or the Moon has the largest gravitational force on an object. [1 mark]

   b Calculate the weight of a 70 kg person on Earth. [2 marks]

   c Calculate the weight of a 70 kg person on the Moon. [2 marks]

4 The spacecraft Phoenix landed on Mars in 2008. On Earth it weighed 3500 N and had a mass of 350 kg. Explain whether the weight and mass will be the same or have changed on Mars. [4 marks]

16.4 Work done and power

Learning objectives

After this topic, you should know:

- how to calculate the work done by a force
- the factors affecting how much work is done
- what power is in science
- how to calculate power.

When a force is applied to an object and it moves, energy is transferred to the object and work is done.

The work done on an object by a force depends on the size of the force and how far the object is moved in the direction of the force. One joule of work is done when a force of 1 newton causes an object to move 1 metre in the direction of the force.

A: Give the unit that work is measured in.

Calculating work done

To calculate how much work is done by a force, you can use the equation:

$$\text{work done (J)} = \text{force (N)} \times \text{distance moved in the direction of the force (m)}$$

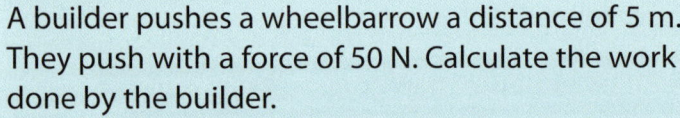

Worked example

A builder pushes a wheelbarrow a distance of 5 m. They push with a force of 50 N. Calculate the work done by the builder.

Step 1: Write down what you know.

distance = 5 m

force = 50 N

Step 2: Write down the equation that has these values in it.

work done = force × distance moved

Step 3: Put in the numbers and solve the equation.

work done = 50 N × 5 m = 250 J

B: Identify which information you need to know to calculate work done.

Power

You do the same amount of work running up the stairs as if you walked up. This is because the force and the distance are the same. But it is harder to *run* up the stairs. This is because you are transferring energy more quickly. The **power** tells you the rate of energy transfer and is measured in watts, W.

C: Who has the greatest power: the person who walked up the stairs or the person who ran up them?

Calculating power

You can calculate power using the equation:

$$\text{power} = \frac{\text{work done}}{\text{time}}$$

Worked example

The work done climbing the stairs in a building is 2800 J. Calculate the power if it takes 10 seconds to reach the top of the stairs.

Step 1: Write down what you know.

work done = 2800 J

time = 10 s

Step 2: Write down the equation that has these values in it.

$$\text{power} = \frac{\text{work done}}{\text{time}}$$

Step 3: Put in the numbers and solve.

$$\text{power} = \frac{2800\,\text{J}}{10\,\text{s}} = 280\,\text{W}$$

D: Calculate the power if 800 J of work is done in 5 seconds.

1   Choose the correct words from the box to complete the following sentences.

distance	joules	transferred	watts

To calculate the work done you need to multiply the force by the _____. Work done is equal to the energy _____ and is measured in _____. Power is the rate of work done and is measured in _____. [4 marks]

2   An electric motor is used to lift a car weighing 10 000 N a distance of 2.5 metres.

  a Calculate the work done when lifting the car 2.5 m. [2 marks]

  b It takes 40 seconds to lift the car. Calculate the power of the motor. [2 marks]

3   In a strength competition a plane is pulled 30 m in as short a time as possible. The winner has the shortest time. One competitor completes the pull in 30 seconds. Another takes 35 seconds.

Compare the work done and the power of the two competitors. [2 marks]

16.5 Forces and elasticity

Learning objectives

After this topic, you should know:

- what is meant by elastic
- how to measure the extension of an object when it is stretched
- how the extension of a spring changes with the force applied to it.

Elastic or inelastic?

You have to pull on both ends of an elastic band to stretch it. To bend, squash, or stretch an object you **always** have to apply more than one force.

Materials like an elastic band are called **elastic** because they return to their original length when the forces are removed.

Materials like polythene are called **inelastic**. This is because they do not return to their original shape. If you put heavy shopping in a plastic bag it will stretch and stay stretched after you unpack it.

Investigating stretching

To investigate how easily a material stretches, follow these steps:

Step 1: Use a clamp stand to hold a spring and a ruler next to it (Figure 1).

Step 2: Use the ruler to measure the length of the spring when there are no weights attached. Measure from the top of the top loop to the bottom of the bottom loop. Record this length in a table like the one below.

Weight in N	Length in mm	Extension in mm
0	50	0
1	90	40
2	130	

Step 3: Hang a 1 N weight on the spring and record the new length of the spring.

Step 4: Repeat step 3 with a 2 N weight hanging off the spring.

Step 5: Repeat the experiment for each weight.

Figure 1 *Equipment for investigating stretching.*

(labels: spring under test, length, original length, extension, weights, stand, metre rule)

You can calculate the extension of the spring from your results using this equation:

$$\text{extension} = \text{new length} - \text{original length}$$

> **A: Calculate the extension of the spring when a 2 N weight was hung from the spring.**

When you finish your investigation, you can plot your results on a scatter graph. Put weight in newtons on the *y*-axis and extension in mm on the *x*-axis.

Do all materials behave in the same way?

Figure 2 shows a graph of how a polythene strip, a rubber band, and a steel spring behave when they are stretched.

The steel spring gives a straight line through the origin. This type of graph is special. It shows the force is **directly proportional** to the extension. Doubling the force doubles the extension.

B: Describe what directly proportional means.

In your investigation, you may have found that the spring did not return to its original length. This is because you put too many weights on the spring. When this happens we say the spring was stretched beyond its **limit of proportionality**.

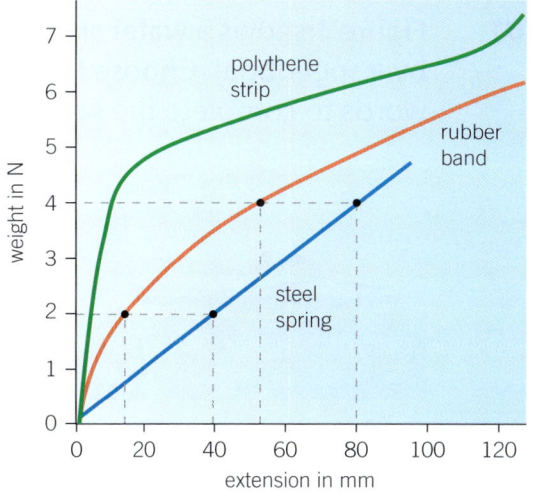

Figure 2 *Extension versus hung weight for different materials.*

1   Choose the correct words from the box to complete the following sentences.

> **bend   elastic   inelastic   two**

To stretch, _____, or squash an object you need at least _____ forces. A material like clay is _____ because it does not return to its original shape when the forces are removed. A rubber band is _____ because it does return to its original length.   [3 marks]

2   Use the graph in Figure 2 to answer these questions.
   a   Give the extension of the steel spring when the weight is 2 N.   [1 mark]
   b   Give the extension of the steel spring when the weight is 4 N.   [1 mark]

3   The table shows the results achieved when a student stretched a spring.

Weight in N	Length in mm	Extension in mm
0	50	0
2	100	50
4	150	100
6	200	
8	250	

   a   Complete the table by calculating the missing extensions.   [1 mark]
   b   Draw a graph of the results with weight on the *y*-axis and extension on the *x*-axis.   [3 marks]
   c   Describe the relationship between weight added and extension.   [2 marks]

16 Practice questions

01 Figure 1 shows a water skier being pulled by a speedboat. Choose the correct words to complete the sentences.

Figure 1

The name of the force in the rope is **normal contact / tension**. This is a **contact / non-contact** force. There is also the **contact / non-contact** force of friction acting on the skier and the non-contact force **air resistance / weight**.

The speedboat does work on the skier. The **bigger / smaller** the engine force and the **bigger / smaller** the distance the more work is done. [6 marks]

02 Figure 2 shows an iron bar hanging from a newton meter. The newton meter reads 1.6 N.

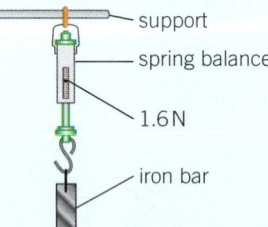

support

spring balance

1.6 N

iron bar

Figure 2

02.1 What is the weight of the bar? [1 mark]

02.2 In which direction does the weight of the iron bar act? [1 mark]

03 A space vehicle has a mass of 200 kg.

03.1 Calculate the weight of the vehicle on the Earth.
Gravitational field strength = 10 N/kg.
Use the equation:
weight = mass × gravitational field strength [2 marks]

03.2 Calculate the weight of the vehicle on the Moon.
Gravitational field strength = 1.6 N/kg. [2 marks]

04 Draw a labelled diagram to show the forces and their direction acting on:

04.1 a book resting on a table [2 marks]

04.2 a car speeding up. [4 marks]

05 A student carried out an experiment to measure how a material behaves when it is stretched. Their results are shown in Table 1.

Table 1

Weight in newtons	Length of material in mm	Extension in mm
0	20	0
2	60	40
4	105	
6	150	130
8	188	168

05.1 Calculate the extension when 4 newtons was added to the material. [1 mark]

05.2 Plot a graph with the extension on the *y*-axis and weight on the *x*-axis. [3 marks]

05.3 Describe the relationship shown by the graph. [2 marks]

05.4 The material returns to its original length when the weights are taken off. Is the material elastic or inelastic? [1 mark]

06 A model car with an engine moves along a 1000 m track. The driving force of the engine is 5 N. Calculate the work done by the engine. [2 marks]

07 A student hangs an object from a spring. The spring stretches as shown in Figure 3.

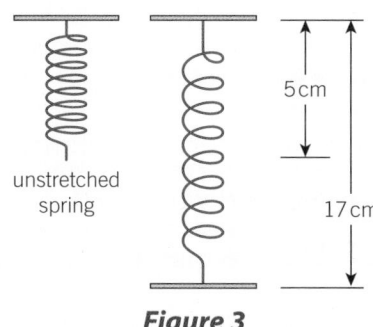

unstretched spring

5 cm

17 cm

Figure 3

07.1 Determine the extension of the spring in metres using Figure 3. [2 marks]

07.2 Calculate the weight acting on the spring if the object's mass is 1.5 kg. Gravitational field strength = 10 N/kg. Use the equation:

weight = mass × gravitational field strength [2 marks]

07.3 Estimate the extension if the student hung 3 kg (twice the mass) from the spring. [1 mark]

08 On a building site, an electric winch is used to lift bricks. The winch can lift 500 N of bricks through a height of 3 m.

08.1 Write down the equation that links work done, force, and distance. [1 mark]

08.2 Calculate the work done by the winch. [2 marks]

08.3 The winch can lift the bricks in 15 seconds. Calculate the power of the winch. [2 marks]

09 A teacher uses an electric motor to lift a 1 kg mass a distance of 1.5 m.

09.1 Calculate the weight of the mass. Gravitational field strength = 10 N/kg. [2 marks]

09.2 Calculate the work done lifting the mass. [2 marks]

09.3 45 J of electrical energy were transferred to the motor during the demonstration. Calculate the efficiency of the motor. Use the equation:

$$\text{efficiency} = \frac{\text{useful energy output}}{\text{total energy input}}$$

[2 marks]

17 Speed and stopping distance
17.1 Speed

Learning objectives

After this topic, you should know:

- what speed is
- the unit of speed
- how to calculate average speed.

How fast are you?

Speed is a measurement of how fast an object is moving. To calculate speed, you have to time how long you take to travel a set distance and then use the equation:

$$\text{speed (m/s)} = \frac{\text{distance (m)}}{\text{time (s)}}$$

In science, the standard unit of speed is metres per second. We sometimes also use kilometres per hour or miles per hour. The units can help you remember the equation. Notice that the units are all a measurement of distance per time. The per means divided by.

Converting units of time

Seconds, minutes, and hours are measures of time.

- To convert seconds to minutes divide by 60.

$$\frac{360 \text{ seconds}}{60} = 6 \text{ minutes}$$

- To convert minutes to seconds multiply by 60.

$$5 \text{ minutes} \times 60 = 300 \text{ seconds}$$

- To convert minutes to hours divide by 60.

$$\frac{90 \text{ minutes}}{60} = 1.5 \text{ hours}$$

A: What is the standard unit of speed?

Worked example

A student ran a 100 m race in 12 seconds. Calculate the speed of the student.

Step 1: Write down what you know.

distance = 100 m

time = 12 s

Step 2: Write down the equation.

$$\text{speed} = \frac{\text{distance}}{\text{time}}$$

Step 3: Put in the numbers and solve.

$$\text{speed} = \frac{100 \text{ m}}{12 \text{ s}} = 8.3 \text{ m/s}$$

B: What is the equation used to calculate speed?

When you calculate speed you are actually finding the **average speed**. For example, a car journey of 120 kilometres might take 2 hours. The average speed for the journey is 60 kilometres per hour. The car probably didn't travel at exactly 60 km/h the whole time. It might have been driven slower than 60 km/h in towns, but then faster than 60 km/h on motorways.

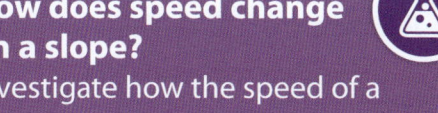

How does speed change on a slope?
Investigate how the speed of a trolley changes as it rolls down a slope. Will the speed stay the same? Increase? Or decrease?

1 Choose the correct words from the box to complete the following sentences.

> **average   distance   time**

Speed is calculated by dividing the _____ by the _____. The speed calculated is always an _____.   [2 marks]

2 Which of these are units of speed?

joules per second

kilometres

km/h

metres per second

miles per hour

seconds   [3 marks]

3 Using the equation $\text{speed} = \dfrac{\text{distance}}{\text{time}}$, calculate the speed for each part of this journey to school.

  a It takes 150 seconds to walk 300 m to the bus stop.   [2 marks]

  b it takes half an hour (0.5 hours) to drive 15 kilometres to school.   [2 marks]

  c It takes 60 seconds to walk 90 m to the school gates.   [2 marks]

17.2 Braking distance

Learning objectives

After this topic, you should know:

- what braking and thinking distance are
- what stopping distance is
- how speed affects thinking and braking distance
- factors that affect thinking and braking distance.

A moving car has lots of energy in its **kinetic energy** store. It needs **friction** from car brakes to stop.

When a car stops, car brakes do **work** to transfer energy from the kinetic store to the **thermal energy** store of the surroundings. The brakes apply a force over a distance.

A fast car has more energy in its kinetic store than a slower car. More work has to be done to stop a car with more kinetic energy. This means the **braking distance** increases.

A: What force does work to stop a moving car?

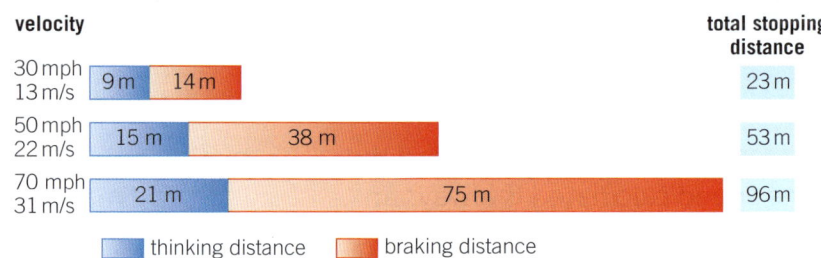

Figure 1 Stopping distances for different speeds.

Stopping distance

The distance it takes for a vehicle to stop is called the **stopping distance**. Figure 1 shows some stopping distances from the Highway Code.

The stopping distance is the **thinking distance** and the **braking distance** added together.

stopping distance = thinking distance + braking distance

B: What happens to the stopping distance if the speed increases?

Thinking distance

Thinking distance is the distance a car travels whilst the driver reacts. The thinking distance depends on:

1 The driver's reaction time.

The slower the reaction time, the further the car moves before the brakes are pressed. Anything that increases reaction times will increase the thinking distance.

2 The speed of the car.

If the car is moving faster, the car will have moved further whilst the driver reacts.

Do you think it is reasonable to ban using mobile phones whilst driving?

It is now illegal in the UK to use your mobile phone whilst driving. Investigate how talking to someone affects your reaction time.

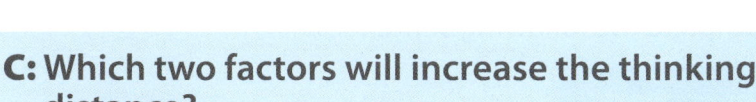

C: Which two factors will increase the thinking distance?

Figure 2 *Braking distances increase if the road is icy.*

Braking distance

Braking distance is the distance the car travels whilst braking. The braking distance depends on:

1   The speed of the car.

A faster moving car needs more force to slow it down. Therefore, it takes a longer distance to stop.

2   Friction.

The braking distance will be shorter when there is more friction. There is less friction on wet or icy roads. This means the braking distance will be longer.

3   The mass of the car.

It takes more force to stop a heavier car. This increases the braking distance.

4   The condition of the brakes and tyres.

Worn brake pads or tyres will increase the braking distance because there is less friction force.

D: What are two factors that will increase braking distance?

1   Choose the correct words from the box to complete the following sentences.

> **friction   greater   kinetic**

A car needs _____ to stop. Brakes transfer energy from the car's _____ energy store. The _____ the kinetic energy the more work has to be done.   [2 marks]

2   All of these factors will increase the stopping distance of a car. Do they affect the **braking distance** or the **thinking distance** or both?

   a   using a mobile phone   [1 mark]

   b   icy road surface   [1 mark]

   c   worn tyres   [1 mark]

   d   tired driver   [1 mark]

   e   driving at a higher speed   [1 mark]

3   What is stopping distance?   [1 mark]

17 Checkpoint

1   Choose the correct words from the box to complete the following sentences.

> **braking   friction   thinking   weight   work**

A moving car has lots of energy in its kinetic energy store. When a car stops the brakes do _____ to stop the car. The force needed to stop a car is _____. The distance a car moves whilst the brakes are applied is the _____ distance.   [3 marks]

2   Which one of these units is a unit of speed?

   h/km   J/s   m/s   s/cm   [1 mark]

3   Which **two** of the following factors increase reaction time?

   A   drinking alcohol
   B   speed of the car
   C   the road surface
   D   tiredness   [2 marks]

4   Figure 1 shows how stopping distance is calculated.

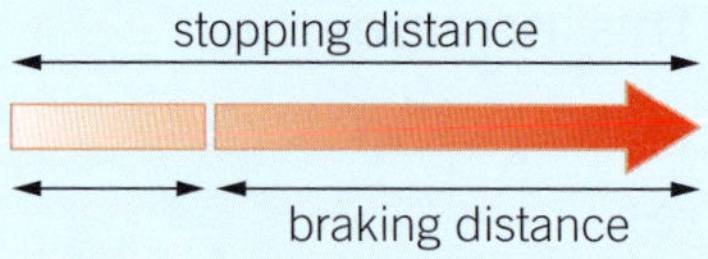

Figure 1

What is the missing label in the diagram?   [1 mark]

5   Sort the following four factors that affect the stopping distance of a car into factors that affect **braking distance** and factors that affect **thinking distance**.

   alcohol

   carrying extra luggage in the car

   rain

   the condition of the brakes   [4 marks]

6   The Highway Code lists the stopping distance for different speeds.

   stopping distance = thinking distance + braking distance

   a   What is the thinking distance?   [1 mark]
   b   What is the braking distance?   [1 mark]
   c   Would a worn tyre on a car affect the thinking distance or braking distance?   [1 mark]
   d   What is one factor that affects both thinking and braking distances?   [1 mark]

7   **a**   What is the equation for calculating speed from distance and time?   [1 mark]
   b   Calculate the speed of a car if it travels 200 miles in 4 hours.   [1 mark]

17 Vocabulary builder

1 Draw one line from each key term to the correct definition.

Key term	Definition
thinking distance	Time it takes to react.
braking distance	Distance it takes for a car to stop.
stopping distance	Distance travelled while you react.
reaction time	Distance travelled while brakes are applied.

[3 marks]

2 Choose the correct units from the box to complete the following sentences.

| cm/s | km/h | mph | m/s |

A car drives 150 miles in 3 hours. The average speed of the car is 50 _____.

A wolf travels 20 km in 2 hours. The average speed of the wolf is 10 _____.

A snail travels 2 cm in 20 seconds. The average speed of the snail is 0.1 _____.

[3 marks]

3 A student wants to investigate how changing the mass of a toy car changes the distance it travels before stopping.
Choose the correct words to answer each question.

a What type of variable is the mass of the car?

control

dependent

independent [1 mark]

b What type of variable is the distance the car travels before stopping?

control

dependent

independent [1 mark]

c What type of variable is the initial speed of the car?

control

dependent

independent [1 mark]

4 Complete the missing words in the sentences below.

a The average value of r _ _ _ _ _ _ _ time in humans is 0.2 to 0.9 seconds. [1 mark]

b A car's b _ _ _ _ _ _ distance would increase if it was icy. [1 mark]

c F _ _ _ _ _ _ _ is the force that stops a car. [1 mark]

d If a driver had been drinking alcohol, their t _ _ _ _ _ _ _ distance would increase. [1 mark]

17.3 Distance–time graphs

Learning objectives

After this topic, you should know:

- how to draw a distance–time graph
- how to use a distance–time graph to determine whether an object is stationary or moving at a constant speed
- how to determine speed from a distance–time graph.

Distance is a **scalar** quantity. This means it tells you how far something has moved, but not the direction that it is moving in. If an object moves in a straight line, you can show the distance it travels using a **distance–time graph.**

A: What is distance a measure of?

The distance–time graph in Figure 1 shows a runner's journey. The runner starts off fast, slows down to a walking pace, and finally stops. You can follow their journey by looking at the shape of the graph.

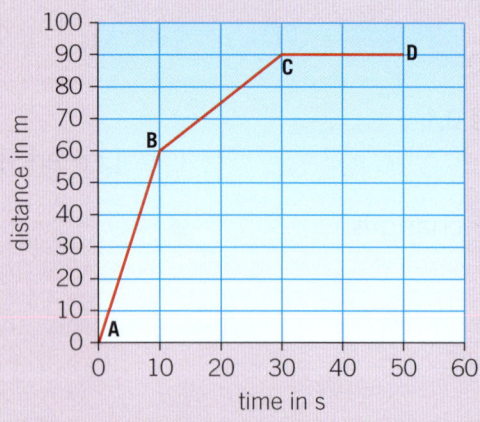

Figure 1 A distance–time graph of a runner's journey.

A to B: Running

The runner has sprinted 60 m in just 10 seconds.

B to C: Walking

The runner is moving more slowly. Notice the graph is not as steep between B and C. They walked 30 m in 20 seconds.

C to D: Resting

The runner has not moved for 20 seconds. They stay the same distance from their starting point.

Interpreting a distance–time graph

A distance–time graph tells you whether an object is moving or not, and how fast it is moving.

- A **horizontal** line means the object is **not moving**.
- A **diagonal** line means it is moving at a **constant** speed.
- The **steeper** the slope of the line, the **faster** the speed.

You can calculate the speed using values from the distance–time graph. Each axis of a graph tells you information. The *x*-axis of a distance–time graph tells you how much time has passed and the *y*-axis tells you the distance travelled.

Calculating speed from a distance-time graph

To find the speed you need to work out the steepness of a graph, known as the gradient. You divide the *y*-axis by the *x*-axis, or distance by time. This is the same as the equation for speed.

For example between A and B on figure 1 they ran 60 m in 10 s

$$\text{speed} = \frac{\text{distance}}{\text{time}} = \frac{60\,\text{m}}{10\,\text{s}} = 6\,\text{m/s}$$

B: How far did the runner go in 30 seconds? Calculate their average speed for the first 30 seconds.

1   Choose the correct words from the box to complete the following sentences.

> **diagonal   distance   horizontal   steeper**

A _____ time graph is a useful way of describing the motion of an object. If the object is moving at a constant speed the line is _____. If the object has stopped moving the line is _____. The faster the object, the _____ the slope of the line.   [4 marks]

2   The diagram is a distance–time graph of a journey. Describe the motion:

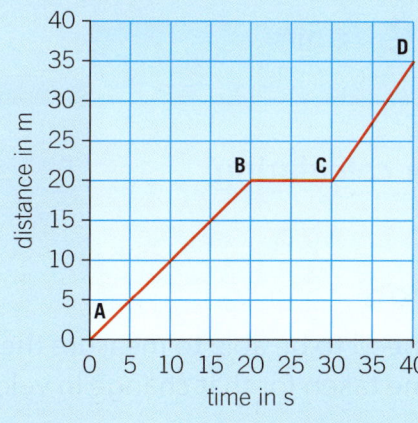

a from A to B   [1 mark]
b from B to C   [1 mark]
c from C to D.   [2 marks]

Figure 2

3   Use Figure 2 to calculate:

a the total distance travelled.   [2 marks]

b the *average* speed for the 40 s journey.
Give the units.   [3 marks]

17.4 Investigating acceleration

Learning objectives

After this topic, you should know:

- what is meant by acceleration and deceleration
- how to calculate acceleration.

Speed is how fast you are moving. **Velocity** is speed in a certain direction. **Acceleration** is how quickly you change velocity or direction. Any quantity that has a direction is called a vector. Force is a **vector**.

Calculating acceleration

To calculate the acceleration of an object you need to know how big the change in velocity is, and how much time it takes to change. You can then use the following equation to calculate the acceleration:

$$\text{acceleration} = \frac{\text{change in velocity (m/s)}}{\text{time (s)}}$$

The unit of acceleration is m/s². If an object slows down, this is called **deceleration**.

Worked example

A cheetah takes 3 seconds to accelerate from 0 m/s to 24 m/s. Calculate the acceleration.

Step 1: Write down what you know.

time = 3 s

change in velocity = 24 − 0 = 24 m/s

Step 2: Write down the equation.

$$\text{acceleration} = \frac{\text{change in velocity}}{\text{time}}$$

Step 3: Put in the numbers and solve.

$$\text{acceleration} = \frac{24 \, \text{m/s}}{3 \, \text{s}} = 8 \, \text{m/s}^2$$

A: Give the equation for calculating acceleration.

Measuring acceleration

To measure acceleration you need to be able to measure the change in velocity and the time taken for that change in velocity.

Investigating acceleration

Use the following steps to measure how the acceleration of a trolley changes as you increase the pulling force.

Step 1: Set up the apparatus as shown in Figure 1. Start with 0.2 N on the hanger.

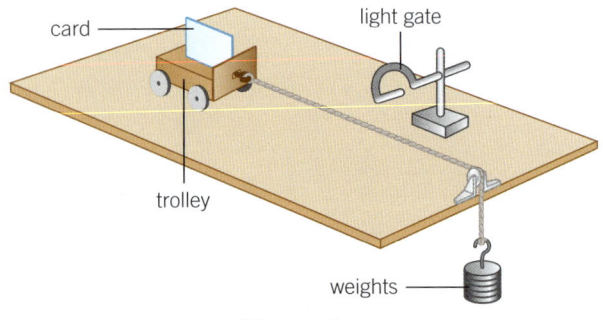

Figure 1

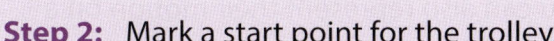

Step 2: Mark a start point for the trolley.

Step 3: Release the trolley.
Use a stopwatch to time how long it takes to reach the light gate. Record this time.
This is the time taken for the velocity to change.

Step 4: Record the velocity measured by the light gate and data logger.
You will have to measure the length of the card on the trolley.
Input the length into the data logger so it can calculate the final velocity of the trolley.

Step 5: Repeat the experiment, increasing the weight by 0.2 N each time.

Weight pulling the trolley in N	Time from start to light gate in s	Velocity through light gate in m/s	Acceleration in m/s²
0.2	1.8	1.2	0.7
0.4	1.2	1.7	1.4

Step 6: Calculate the acceleration for each falling weight.

$$acceleration = \frac{velocity\ through\ the\ light\ gate}{time\ taken\ to\ the\ light\ gate}$$

Step 7: Plot a graph to show how increasing the pulling force changes the acceleration.

B: Describe how the acceleration changes when you increase the pulling force.

1 Choose the correct words from the box to complete the following sentences.

   acceleration   change   speed   time

   The _____ of an object is how fast it is moving. The _____ is how quickly it is changing velocity. To calculate acceleration you need to know the _____ in velocity and the _____ taken for that change. [4 marks]

2 Explain why you used a light gate to measure the final velocity of the trolley. [2 marks]

3 Calculate the acceleration of a sprinter if they accelerate from 0 to 11 m/s in 1.2 seconds. [2 marks]

17.5 Velocity–time graphs

Learning objectives

After this topic, you should know:

- how to interpret a velocity–time graph
- how to calculate acceleration from a velocity–time graph.

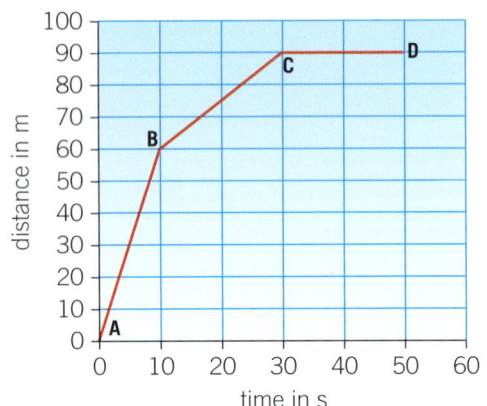

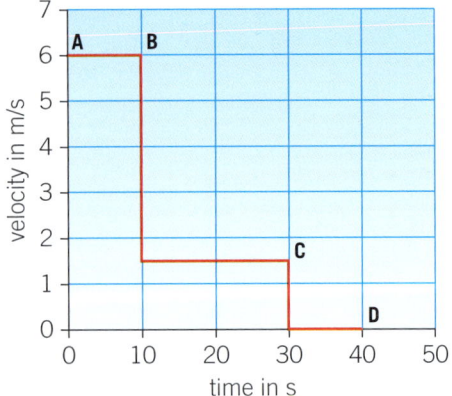

Figure 1 *The distance–time graph and the velocity–time graph of a runner.*

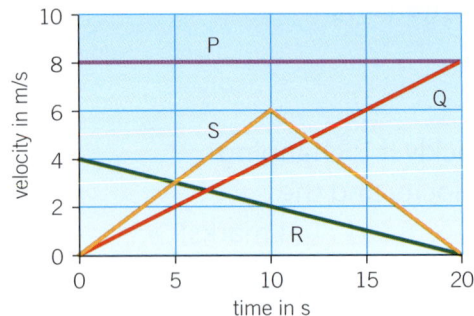

Figure 2 *Velocity–time graph for different moving objects.*

Remember the runner who started fast, slowed to a walk, and then stopped? You can also represent their motion on a **velocity–time** graph.

The velocity–time graph looks very different from the distance–time graph. This graph shows how their velocity changed with time, instead of how far they travelled.

A to B: Running

The runner is running at a constant velocity.

B to C: Walking

The runner has slowed down and is now walking at a constant velocity.

C to D: Resting

The runner has stopped. Their velocity is 0 m/s and is not changing.

A: Give the runner's velocity for the first 10 seconds.

Interpreting a speed–time graph

A velocity–time graph can tell you how the velocity of an object is changing.

- A horizontal line on a velocity–time graph means constant speed.

- A diagonal line sloping up shows constant acceleration.

- A diagonal line sloping down shows constant deceleration.

Figure 2 shows the velocity–time graphs for four different objects.

Object P is moving at a constant velocity.

Object Q has a constant acceleration

Object R has a constant deceleration.

Object S accelerates and then decelerates.

Calculating acceleration from a speed–time graph

You can calculate acceleration from a velocity–time graph. Figure 3 shows how the velocity of a car changes over 50 seconds.

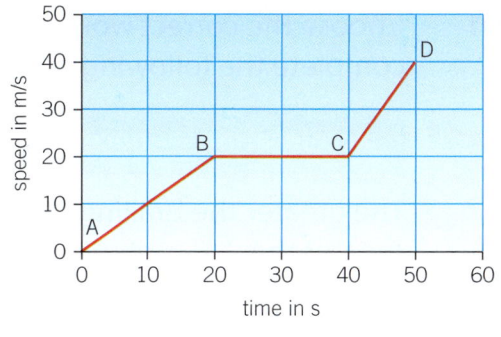

Figure 3 *Velocity–time graph for a car.*

Worked example

Calculate the acceleration between C and D in Figure 3.

Step 1: Write down what you know.

The change in velocity = 40 − 20 = 20 m/s

time = 50 − 40 = 10 s

Step 2: Write down the equation.

$$\text{acceleration} = \frac{\text{change in velocity}}{\text{time taken}}$$

Step 3: Put the numbers into the equation and solve.

$$\text{acceleration} = \frac{20 \,\text{m/s}}{10 \,\text{s}} = 2 \,\text{m/s}^2$$

B: Calculate the acceleration between A and B.

1 Choose the correct words from the box below to complete the following sentences.

> **acceleration   diagonal   horizontal   velocity**

A _____–time graph is a useful way of describing how an object is moving. If the object is moving at a constant velocity the line is _____. If the object has a constant acceleration the line is _____. You can use the graph to calculate the _____ of the object.   [3 marks]

2 The diagram shows a velocity–time graph for a cyclist.

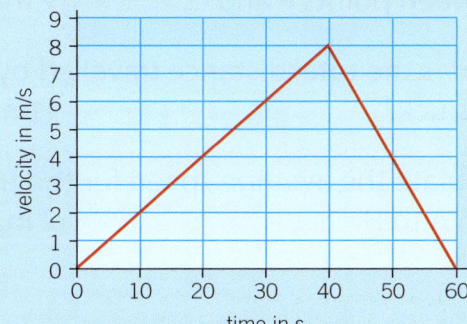

Describe how the velocity of the cyclist changes:

a   over the first 40 second   [1 mark]

b   from 40 to 60 seconds.   [1 mark]

3 Using Figure 3, calculate the average acceleration of the car over the whole 50 seconds.   [4 marks]

17 Practice questions

01 Choose the correct word from the box to complete the following sentence.

> acceleration   deceleration   speed

The greater the braking force on a car the greater the _____ of the car.   [1 mark]

02 Choose the correct words to complete the sentences below.

The stopping distance consists of the **reaction time / thinking distance** and the braking distance added together. If the speed of a car increases the stopping distance **decreases / increases**. If the tyres of a car are worn the thinking distance **increases / stays the same** and the braking distance **increases / stays the same.**   [4 marks]

03 A car has an oil leak. Every 2 seconds an oil drop falls and leaves a mark on the road. Figure 1 shows the pattern left by the car on the road.

Figure 1

Choose the answer below that describes the motion of the car.

A The car is slowing down.

B The car is accelerating.

C The car is moving at a constant speed.

D The car accelerates and then slows down.   [1 mark]

04 Draw one line from each situation to the correct reason why the stopping distance increases.

Situation	Reason stopping distance increases
The road is wet.	The reaction time increases.
The driver is tired.	There is less friction acting on the car.

[1 mark]

05 A truck is used to deliver parcels to different locations in a warehouse. The distance–time graph shows the journey taken by the truck.

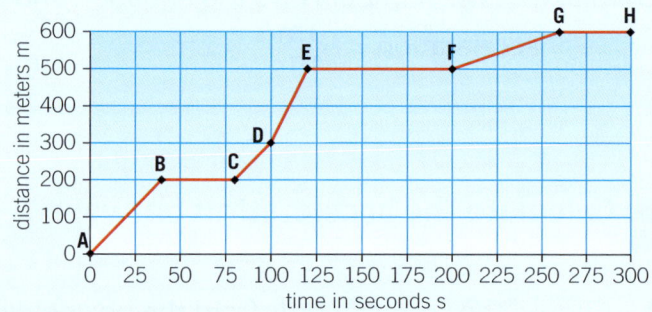

Figure 2

05.1 Describe the motion of the truck between points A and B.   [1 mark]

05.2 Describe the motion of the truck between points B and C.   [1 mark]

05.3 Describe the motion of the truck between points F and G.   [2 marks]

05.4 What is the total distance travelled by the truck?   [1 mark]

05.5 Calculate the average speed for the truck from A to H.   [2 marks]

06 A motorbike travelled 150 m in 3 s.

Calculate the average speed of the motorbike. Use the equation:

$$\text{speed} = \frac{\text{distance}}{\text{time}}$$

[2 marks]

07 A student investigated how the pulling force on a trolley affected the acceleration of the trolley between two points. A and B The apparatus he used is shown in Figure 3.

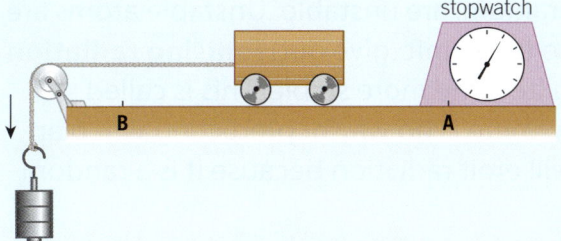

Figure 3

The trolley was held at position A and weights placed on the hanger. The trolley was then released and the time taken to travel between A and B was recorded.

A light gate and data logger were used to determine the speed of the trolley at B. From this speed and the time recorded, the acceleration was calculated.

07.1 Give one control variable in this investigation. [1 mark]

07.2 The results of the student's investigation were recorded in Table 1.

Table 1

Force in N	100	200	300	400	500
Acceleration in m/s²	0.25	0.50	0.75	1.00	1.25

Plot a graph of the results. [4 marks]

07.3 What is the pattern shown by the results? [2 marks]

08 Figure 4 is a velocity–time graph of the journey of a rocket.

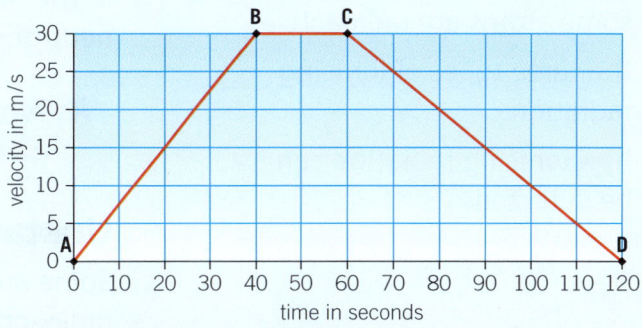

Figure 4

Choose the correct words from the box to complete the following sentences.

> accelerating   decelerating
> stationary
> travelling at a constant velocity

08.1 The rocket is _____ between A and B. [1 mark]

08.2 The rocket is _____ between B and C. [1 mark]

08.3 The rocket is _____ between C and D. [1 mark]

08.4 Calculate the average acceleration between 0 and 40 seconds. Use the equation:

$$\text{acceleration} = \frac{\text{change in velocity}}{\text{time}}$$

[2 marks]

09 A water skier started from rest and accelerated steadily to 12 m/s in 15 seconds. Calculate their acceleration. [3 marks]

18 Atoms and nuclear radiation
18.1 Atoms and radiation

Learning objectives

After this topic, you should know:

- some atoms are radioactive
- the three types of ionising radiation
- how ionising radiation can be detected.

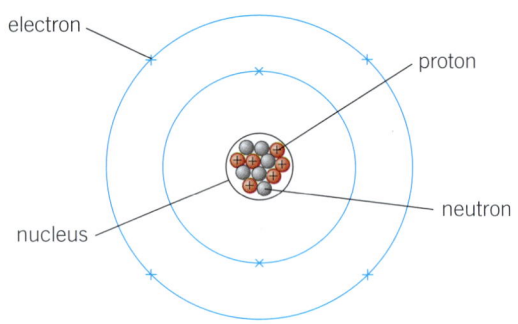

Figure 1 *The structure of an atom.*

The atom

An atom is made up of a nucleus with electrons orbiting around it. The nucleus contains two types of particle – protons and neutrons.

> **A:** Which two types of particle are found in the nucleus of an atom?

Unstable atoms

Some atoms, like uranium, are unstable. Unstable atoms are radioactive because they emit (give out) **ionising radiation** from their nuclei to become more stable. This is called **radioactive decay**. There is no way of predicting when an unstable nucleus will emit radiation because it is a random event.

> **B:** What is meant by radioactive decay?

Types of ionising radiation

Radiation emitted from the nucleus is called nuclear radiation. There are three types of nuclear radiation – **alpha**, **beta**, and **gamma**.

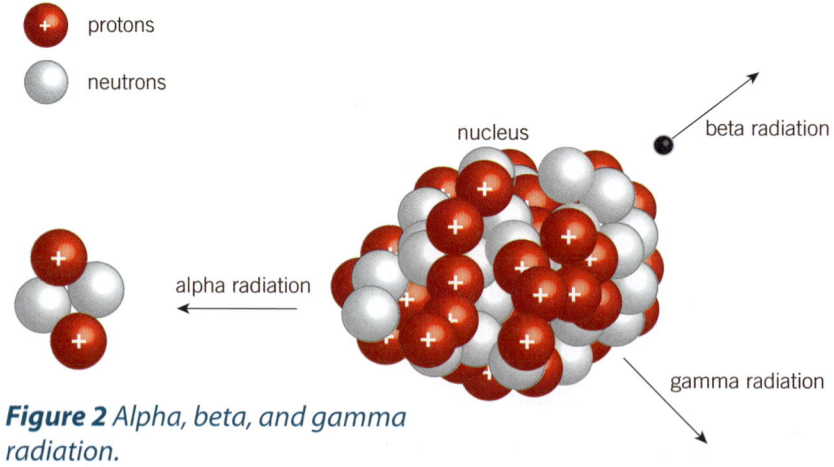

Figure 2 *Alpha, beta, and gamma radiation.*

> **C:** What are the three types of ionising radiation that can be emitted by a radioactive nucleus?

Detecting radiation

You cannot tell that an atom is radioactive by looking at it. However, we can detect ionising radiation in other ways.

Radioactivity was discovered by accident. A packet of uranium salts was left on top of some photographic film. It turned the film black. We still use photographic film to check how much radiation people are exposed to. People who work with radioactive materials wear film badges.

You can use also use a Geiger counter to detect radioactivity. An electronic counter clicks each time a particle of ionising radiation enters the Geiger tube.

A Geiger counter will always detect a low level of radiation, even if it is not near a source of radiation. This is called **background radiation**. Background radiation comes from space and from rocks and soil.

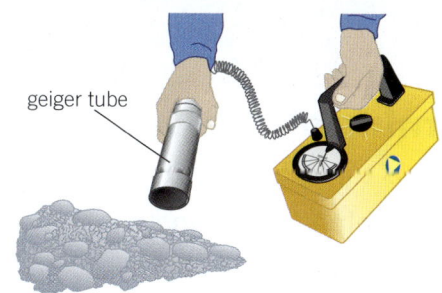

geiger tube

Figure 3 *Using a Geiger counter to measure ionising radiation.*

D: What are two ways we can detect radiation?

1   Choose the correct words from the box to complete the following sentences.

> beta   radiation   unstable

Some atoms are _____. To become more stable they emit ionising _____. This is called radioactive decay. There are three types of radiation alpha, _____, and gamma.   [3 marks]

2   Carbon-14 is an example of an unstable atom. It emits beta particles to become stable. Which of the following statements are true, and which are false?

  a Carbon-14 is radioactive.   [1 mark]

  b Carbon-14 is a stable atom.   [1 mark]

  c The beta particle came from inside the nucleus.   [1 mark]

  d Carbon-14 is a type of radiation.   [1 mark]

  e Beta is a type of ionising radiation.   [1 mark]

3   A student suggests that their mobile phone is radioactive. They use a Geiger counter to decide. Here are the measurements recorded.

count rate with phone switched off   30 counts per minute

count rate with phone switched on   28 counts per minute

count rate when the phone is not in the room   29 counts per minute

  a Is the phone radioactive?   [1 mark]

  b What is your reason for your answer to part a?   [1 mark]

18.2 Alpha, beta, and gamma radiation

Learning objectives

After this topic, you should know:

- how far alpha, beta, and gamma radiation can travel in air
- how alpha, beta, and gamma radiation are absorbed by different materials
- the dangers of each type of radiation.

Radioactive atoms emit radiation, but how far can the radiation travel? What will stop it?

Scientists are able to find out by placing a source of radiation in front of a Geiger tube.

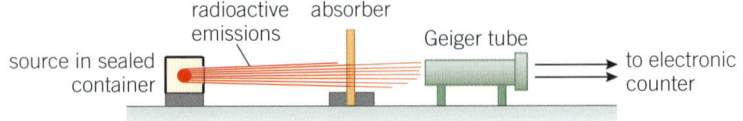

Figure 1 *Testing how far radiation can travel.*

Table 1 *How far the different types of radiation can travel in air.*

Type of radiation	Range in air
alpha	about 5 cm
beta	about 1 m
gamma	unlimited

Range

The distance that radiation can travel is called its **range**.

To find the range of different types of radiation, a Geiger tube is placed in front of the radioactive source. As the distance between the radioactive source and Geiger tube increases, the count decreases until no radiation is detected.

A: Which type of radiation can travel the furthest?

Table 2 *The materials that stop the different types of radiation.*

Type of radiation	Absorbed by
alpha	a thin sheet of paper
beta	5 mm thick aluminium
gamma	thick sheet of lead or 1 metre of concrete

Absorption

Different types of radiation are stopped by different materials. If a material stops radiation, it has **absorbed** it.

To find out whether radiation can pass through a material, the material is placed between the Geiger tube and the radioactive source (Figure 1). If the count rate due to the source is the same as background the material has absorbed the radiation.

B: How would you stop beta radiation?

Dangers of radiation

Ionising radiation can knock electrons out of atoms. The atoms become charged because they lose electrons. The atom has been **ionised**. If an atom in a living cell is ionised it may be damaged or even killed. If the atom is part of the DNA of a living cell then there is a small probability that this will cause mutations. These mutations can increase the chances of cancer or kill cells.

C: What can ionising radiation do to living cells?

Alpha radiation is the most ionising radiation. An alpha radiation source is most dangerous if it is **inside** your body. This is because alpha radiation can be stopped easily, for example, by paper, so it can be stopped by your skin if it is outside.

Beta and gamma radiation sources are dangerous inside **and** outside your body, because they can pass through skin. Gamma radiation can travel the furthest and is hardest to stop, but it is the least ionising.

Reducing the risk

Ionising radiation is very useful. This means some people work with ionising radiation everyday.

Workers who use ionising radiation reduce the risk by:

- staying as far away from the source as they can
- using special tools with long handles
- spending as little time as possible in 'at-risk' areas
- shielding themselves using thick lead plates or concrete barriers
- monitoring how much radiation they are exposed to.

D: What is one way someone who works with radiation can protect themselves?

Figure 2 *The radiation warning symbol.*

1   Draw one line from each type of radiation to the material that can stop it.

Type of radiation	Material that stops the radiation
alpha	concrete
beta	paper
gamma	aluminium sheet

[2 marks]

2   A radioactive source emits radiation that can travel 90 cm in air and is stopped by thick aluminium sheet. Is it alpha, beta, or gamma radiation?

[1 mark]

3   Medical physicists use radioactive sources every day. What is one way that they can protect themselves from the radiation? [1 mark]

18.3 Using radiation

Learning objectives

After this topic, you should know:

- how radiation can be used
- how the radiation is suited to the task.

The different properties of alpha, beta, and gamma radiation make them useful for different jobs.

Alpha is the most ionising. This means it can cause the most damage to living cells but it is also the easiest to stop. Gamma is the hardest to stop but it is the least ionising type. A low dose (small amount) of gamma radiation will do the least damage to living cells.

A: Which type of nuclear radiation is the least ionising?

Use of alpha radiation

Figure 1 *Smoke alarms use alpha radiation to detect smoke.*

Smoke alarms work using alpha radiation. The alpha radiation helps make an electric circuit. Smoke absorbs the radiation so the electric circuit breaks, and the alarm is triggered.

Alpha radiation is the best choice because it is strongly ionising, is absorbed by the smoke, and it cannot pass through the plastic case. This means that it is safe to have an alpha source in your home (in a sealed container).

B: Why is alpha radiation safe to use in smoke detectors?

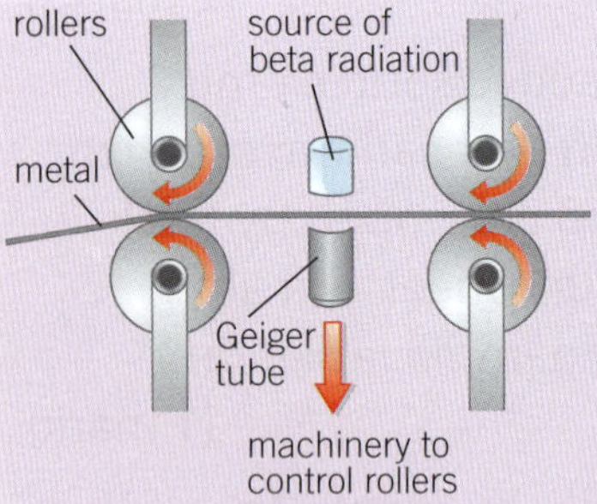

Use of beta radiation

Figure 2 *Thickness monitoring using a radioactive source.*

Beta radiation can be used to monitor the thickness of metal foil as it is produced in a factory. A beta source is placed above the sheet and a Geiger tube below. The amount of beta radiation passing through the foil will change if the thickness of the foil changes.

If the foil is too thick, the Geiger tube reading decreases. This tells the machine to increase the pressure on the rollers. This makes the foil thinner.

If the foil is too thin the Geiger tube reading increases. This alerts the machine to reduce the pressure on the rollers. This makes the foil thicker.

No alpha radiation would pass through the foil at all. Gamma would pass straight through the foil – even if it was very thick.

Use of gamma radiation

Gamma radiation is used in medicine. Gamma radiation can pass through the body and is weakly ionising, so is the safest type of ionising radiation.

Gamma radiation can be used as a medical tracer. A patient is injected with a gamma source. A machine that can detect gamma radiation, called a gamma camera, is used to detect where the radiation source is and allows doctors to see how your body is working.

A larger dose of gamma radiation can be used to kill cancer cells.

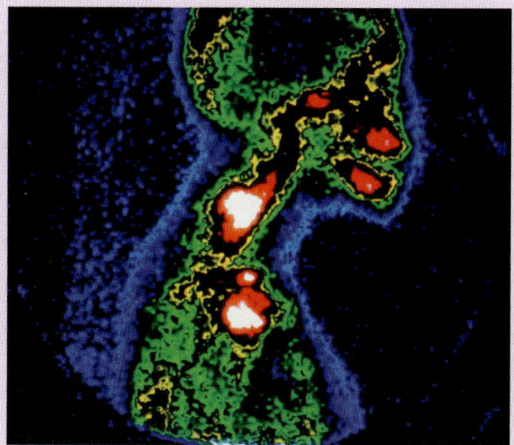

Figure 3 An image from a gamma camera. The red and white areas show where cancer is growing.

D: Why is gamma radiation the best choice for a medical tracer?

1 Draw one line from each type of radiation to the correct use of the radiation. [2 marks]

Type of radiation	Use of radiation
alpha	imaging the body
beta	smoke alarm
gamma	detecting thickness of foil

2 Which **two** of the following are uses of gamma radiation?

measuring the thickness of foil   smoke alarm

medical tracer   treating cancer

[2 marks]

3 When there is a problem in an underground pipe, a radioactive source is put into one end of the pipe. The movement of the radioactive source is then tracked above the ground.

   a Would you use an alpha or a gamma source of radiation? [1 mark]

   b Why would you use this type of radioactive source? [1 mark]

18 Checkpoint

1. Choose the correct words from the box to complete the following sentences.

| alpha | beta | emit | gamma | radioactive | range |

Some atoms are unstable. To become more stable, they _____ radiation. These atoms are _____.
There are three types of radiation. They each have a different _____ in air. The radiation with the
greatest range is _____ radiation.   [4 marks]

2. Draw one line from each type of radiation to the correct material that stops it.

Radiation	Material
alpha	aluminium sheet
beta	metre of concrete
gamma	paper or skin

[2 marks]

3. a Which three of these are properties of alpha radiation?

   A greatest range in air   C stopped by lead

   B most ionising   D stopped by aluminium sheet   [3 marks]

   b Which two of these are properties of beta radiation?

   A greatest range in air   C stopped by lead

   B most ionising   D stopped by aluminium sheet   [2 marks]

   c Which three of these are properties of gamma radiation?

   A greatest range in air   C stopped by lead

   B least ionising   D stopped by aluminium sheet   [3 marks]

4. Draw one line from each type of radiation to the correct use.

Radiation	Use
alpha	monitoring foil thickness
beta	sterilising medical instruments
gamma	smoke alarm

[2 marks]

5. What is one way we can detect radioactivity?   [1 mark]

6. People who work with ionising radiations wear film badges. These badges are replaced and
checked regularly. Why do people wear the film badges?   [1 mark]

7. The results of an experiment to decide what type of radiation is being emitted from sample X
are shown below. The count rate when sample X is not in the room is 2 counts per second.

	Count rate next to the source (counts per second)	Count rate at a distance of 6 cms
sample X	120	2

   a How do we know sample X is radioactive?   [1 mark]

   b What type of radiation is sample X emitting?   [1 mark]

18 Vocabulary builder

1 Draw one line from each key term to the correct definition.

Key term	Definition
radioactive	Causing an atom to become charged.
radiation	When a radioactive nucleus emits radiation.
ionise	When a nucleus is unstable.
radioactive decay	What a radioactive nucleus emits to become stable.

[3 marks]

2 Choose the correct word from the box to complete the sentences.

absorption   emission   range

The distance that radiation can travel is called the _____. [1 mark]

3 Sort these words into types of radiation and parts of an atom.

alpha   **beta**   **electron**

gamma   **neutron**   **proton** [6 marks]

4 Choose the correct term from the list to identify the key word being described.

a Equipment used to detect radioactivity.

gamma counter

Geiger counter

general counter [1 mark]

b Gamma radiation cannot penetrate thick lead. This is because the radiation is

absorbed

reflected

transmitted [1 mark]

5 Complete the missing words to complete the sentences.

An unstable atom releases i _ _ _ _ _ _ _ radiation from its n _ _ _ _ _ _.
There are three types of radiation
a _ _ _ _ _ , b _ _ _ , and g _ _ _ _ radiation. [5 marks]

18.4 Half-life

Learning objectives

After this topic, you should know:

- what is meant by the activity of a radioactive source
- the units of activity
- what half-life is.

Activity

The radiation emitted by a radioactive source decreases with time. Even though radioactive decay is a random process we can predict how the radiation will change.

We can monitor how the **activity** changes with time.

In a radioactive source, the number of unstable nuclei that decay each second is called the activity. The activity is measured in becquerels (Bq).

1Bq = 1 decay per second

A: Define what the activity of a radioactive source is.

Measuring radioactive decay

If you measure the activity of a radioactive source over time, you will find that it decreases. Figure 1 shows the activity of a radioactive source over time.

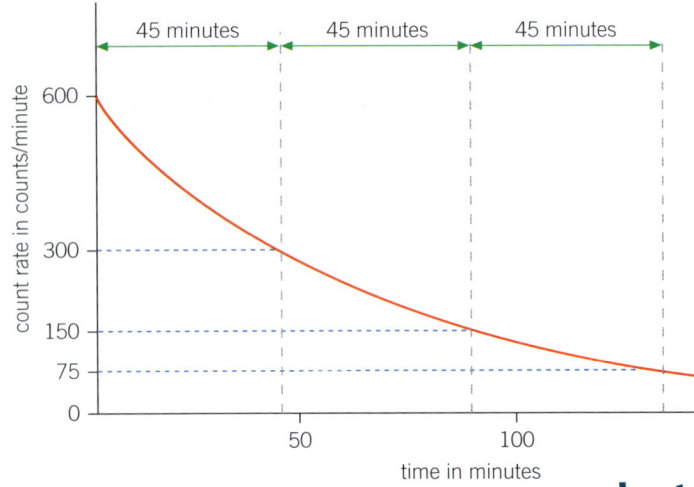

Figure 1 *A graph of count rate against time.*

The activity of this radioactive source halves every 45 minutes.

- The time for taken for its activity to go from 600 to 300 counts per minute is 45 minutes.

- The time for taken for its activity to go from 300 to 150 counts per minute is 45 minutes.

Half-life is the time it takes for the activity to fall to half its initial value.

Isotopes

Elements can exist in different forms called **isotopes**. Isotopes are atoms of the same element with the same number of protons and electrons, but a different number of neutrons. For example, carbon-12 has six protons and six neutrons. The unstable isotope carbon-14 has six protons and eight neutrons.

Different radioactive isotopes have different half-lives. You can use a graph of activity against time to measure the half-life. Look at the graph to see how long it took for the activity to halve. In Figure 1 the substance has a half-life of 45 minutes.

B: What is meant by the half-life of a radioactive substance?

Worked example

A radioactive substance has a half-life of 8 days. The activity is 200 counts per second. Determine the activity of the sample after 8 days and after 24 days.

8 days: Calculate the number of half-lives.

$$\text{Number of half lives} = \frac{\text{(Number of days)}}{\text{(Half life)}} = \frac{\text{(8 days)}}{\text{(8 days)}} = 1 \text{ half-life}$$

$\frac{1}{2}$ of 200 = 100

Answer is 100 counts per second.

24 days: Number of half lives $= \frac{\text{(Number of days)}}{\text{(Half life)}} = \frac{\text{(24 days)}}{\text{(8 days)}} =$ 3 half-lives

$\frac{1}{2}$ of 200 = 100, $\frac{1}{2}$ of 100 = 50, $\frac{1}{2}$ of 50 = 25

Answer is 25 counts per second.

---

1 Choose the correct words from the box to complete the following sentences.

> activity   half-life   halve   random

Radioactive decay is a _____ process. If you monitor the _____ of a radioactive source over time you can plot a graph. You can use the graph to work out the _____ of the source. This is the time taken for the activity to _____.   [3 marks]

2 A radioactive isotope has a half-life of 15 hours. The initial count rate is 400 counts per second. Calculate the count rate:

   a after 15 hours   [2 marks]

   b after 60 hours.   [2 marks]

3 A student monitored how the activity of a radioactive source changed with time. The results are shown in the table.

Activity in counts per second	160	80	40	20	10	5
Time in hours	0	4	8	12	16	20

   a Plot a graph of the results.   [4 marks]

   b Determine how many hours it took for the activity to go from 160 to 80.   [1 mark]

   c Calculate the half-life of the radioactive source.   [1 mark]

18.5 Radioactive contamination

Learning objectives

After this topic, you should know:
- what is meant by contamination
- what is meant by irradiation.

Contamination

Radioactive contamination is the presence of radioactive materials where they should not be.

This is a risk because as the radioactive materials **decay** they expose the area around them to radiation. The level of risk depends on the half-life of the source and the type of radiation it emits.

> **A:** Define radioactive contamination.

Nuclear accident

In 2011 there was an earthquake in Japan. During the earthquake, radioactive iodine and caesium were released from a nuclear power station into the air and water. An area up to 20 km away was evacuated and the radioactivity monitored.

Radioactive iodine has a half-life of 8 days and caesium has a half-life of 30 years. People will only be allowed to return to their homes when the radioactivity has reached safe levels. People were only allowed to return to the town of Namie in April 2017. It took six years for the area to be decontaminated. Seven years after the disaster, thousands of people from other affected areas were still unable to return home.

> **B:** Identify whether iodine or caesium was responsible for the radioactivity that lasted six years.

Irradiation

Irradiation is exposure of an object or person to ionising radiation.

The object or person does not become radioactive. The irradiation stops as soon as the source of ionising radiation is removed.

> **C:** Define irradiation.

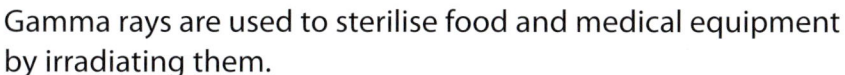

Gamma rays are used to sterilise food and medical equipment by irradiating them.

Microorganisms and insects can cause food to decay. Gamma radiation kills microorganisms and insects that might be on the food. This means the food stays fresh for longer. The food does not become radioactive as it is not contaminated. Food that has been irradiated always has the symbol in Figure 1 displayed on the packaging.

> **D:** Describe why food is not radioactive after being sterilised with gamma radiation.

Contamination will always cause irradiation. Irradiation can also happen without contamination because irradiation does not leave radioactive material on the object.

Figure 1 *This symbol is displayed on food that has been sterilised using gamma radiation.*

1   Choose the correct words from the box to complete the following sentences.

> **contaminated   decays   half-life   irradiation**

If you breathe in a radioactive substance you will be _____. This is dangerous because as the radioactive substance _____ it will expose you to radiation. This is called _____. How dangerous this is depends on the type of radiation and the length of its _____.   [3 marks]

2   Decide which of these is an example of contamination.

   A   A plant absorbing radioactive minerals from the soil.

   B   Having an X-ray taken.

   C   Irradiating food.

   D   Sterilising medical instruments.   [1 mark]

3   **a**   Suggest why gamma radiation is used to sterilise food, rather than alpha radiation.   [3 marks]

   b   Is it safe to eat irradiated food? Give a reason for your answer.   [2 marks]

01 Choose the correct words to complete the following sentences.

Some atoms emit **radiation / radioactive** from their **atom / nucleus**. These atoms are called **radiation / radioactive** atoms. There are three types of radiation. Alpha is the **least / most** ionising. Gamma is the **least / most** ionising. All types of radiation can be stopped by thick **aluminium / lead**.

[6 marks]

02.1 Draw one line from each type of radiation to the correct range in air.

Radiation	Range in air
alpha	unlimited
beta	1 m
gamma	5 cm

[2 marks]

02.2 Draw one line from each type of radiation to the correct material that can be used to stop it.

Radiation	Material that can stop it
alpha	5 mm aluminium
beta	sheet of paper
gamma	1 m concrete

[2 marks]

03 Choose the correct words from the box to complete the following sentences.

> alpha   beta   detected
> gamma   thickness

Radiation is used by engineers to monitor the _____ of metal sheet in factories. They cannot use _____ because it would not pass through the metal. They cannot use _____ because the metal would not absorb it. Instead they use _____. This will be _____ on the other side, but the amount will depend on the thickness of the sheet.

[4 marks]

04 An alpha radiation source is used in smoke alarms. When smoke fills the smoke alarm it absorbs the alpha radiation. This triggers the alarm.

04.1 Why would a gamma radiation source not be a good choice for a smoke alarm?

[1 mark]

04.2 Ionising radiation can cause damage to cells. Why is an alpha radiation source safe to use in a smoke alarm?

[1 mark]

05 A radioactive sample is placed in front of three different absorbers. Figure 1 shows how far the radiation got through.

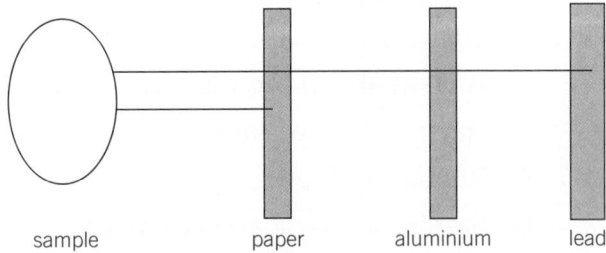

sample   paper   aluminium   lead

Figure 1

Name the two types of radiation emitted by this sample.

[1 mark]

06 An experiment was carried out to find out what type of radiation is emitted by an unknown radioactive source. Table 1 shows the results that were recorded.

Table 1

Source at 20 mm from tube	Average count rate in counts per minute
no source present	29
no absorber present	385
sheet of paper between source and tube	384
thick aluminium plate between source and tube	32

06.1 Why was a reading taken with no source present? [1 mark]

06.2 What type of radiation is being emitted by the source? [1 mark]

06.3 Explain how you reached your answer to **06.2**. [2 marks]

07 Table 2 shows how the count rate of a radioactive source changes with time.

Table 2

Time in hours	Count rate in counts per minute
0	300
2	240
4	190
6	150
8	110
10	90

07.1 Plot a graph of count rate (on the *y*-axis) against time (on the *x*-axis). [3 marks]

07.2 Determine how long it takes for the count rate to halve. [1 mark]

07.3 What is the half-life of this radioactive source? [1 mark]

08 A radioactive source has a count rate of 800 counts per minute. It has a half-life of 4 hours.

08.1 Determine the count rate after 4 hours. [2 marks]

08.2 Determine the count rate after 12 hours. [2 marks]

08.3 This radioactive source emits gamma radiation and is injected into a patient to monitor their kidneys with a gamma camera.

Why do doctors use a gamma source for this purpose? [1 mark]

08.4 Determine the count rate after 24 hours. [1 mark]

Physics

Current is the movement of charge. It is the same everywhere in a series circuit. In a parallel circuit, the current divides between the different loops of the circuit.

Voltage is the amount of energy per unit charge through a circuit. In a series circuit it is shared between components. In a parallel circuit all the components have the same voltage.

Q **What is the definition of current and voltage?**

Magnets have magnetic fields around them that exert a force on other magnets and on magnetic materials. The stronger the magnet and the smaller the distance from it, the greater the force experienced.

When a current flows through a coil of wire, the coil becomes an electromagnet.

Q **What is an electromagnet?**

There are two types of waves: longitudinal waves and transverse waves.

Sound is a longitudinal wave. Light is a transverse wave.

Q **Name another example of a transverse wave.**

Component 6
Electricity, magnetism, and waves

▶ Electric current

Electric current is a flow of electrical charge and is measured in amps. The size of the current depends on the resistance of the circuit.

We use electricity in our homes to transfer energy. The amount of energy transferred by an appliance depends on the power of the appliance and how long it is switched on for.

▶ Magnets and electromagnets

Magnets exert forces on other magnets and on magnetic materials like iron. This force acts over a distance and is a non-contact force. There are permanent magnets and electromagnets.

An electromagnet is made when a current flows through a coil of wire.

▶ Waves

Waves transfer energy from one place to another. There are two types of waves: transverse and longitudinal. The speed of a wave can be calculated using the frequency of the wave and its wavelength.

Electromagnetic waves are a type of transverse wave. They have many uses, including being used to send information.

19 Electrical current
19.1 Electrical current

Learning objectives

After this topic, you should know:

- what an electrical current is
- how to measure current
- how to measure voltage in a circuit
- that the resistance of a component affects the current.

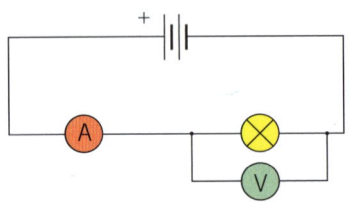

Figure 1 *Using an ammeter and a voltmeter. Connect the ammeter and bulb to the battery first. Always add the voltmeter last. This is because it is connected across the bulb.*

What is current?

Electrical **current** is the flow (movement) of **electrical charge**. The size of the current is how much charge is flowing per second. We call this the **rate** of flow of electrical charge.

A: What is an electrical current?

Making measurements in electrical circuits

A circuit diagram shows how to build a circuit. The black lines represent the electrical leads or connectors. The parts of the circuit connected by the leads are called components. Each component, like a lightbulb or a battery, has a symbol.

Figure 1 shows a battery connected to a bulb. The battery is transferring energy to the bulb. Notice there are two cells in the battery. You can measure the current and **voltage** in a circuit.

Current is measured in amps using an **ammeter**.

Voltage is measured in volts using a **voltmeter**.

B: What are the correct symbols for an ammeter, a voltmeter, and a bulb?

Investigating current

You can use the simple circuit in Figure 1 to investigate the factors that affect the current through different components.

Table 1 *How changing voltage affects current.*

Voltage in volts	Current in amps
6.0	0.20
4.5	0.15

How does the voltage affect the current?

Keep the components, e.g. the bulb, the same throughout this experiment.

Step 1: Switch on the circuit and measure the current and voltage. Record your readings in a table.

Step 2: Change the voltage and measure the current and voltage. Record your new readings in a table.

Step 3: Repeat until you have at least three readings.

C: Does increasing the voltage increase or decrease the current?

How do the components affect the current?

Keep the voltage the same throughout this experiment.

Step 1: Switch on the circuit and measure the current. Record your readings in a table.

Step 2: Swap the bulb for a resistor and measure the current. Record the result.

Step 3: Repeat using different components.

Table 2 *Current through different components.*

Component	Current in amps
bulb	0.20
motor	0.60
buzzer	0.02

> **D:** Which component allows the biggest current to flow: the bulb, the motor, or the buzzer?

Factors affecting current

From your experiments you will have seen that both the voltage and the component affect the current.

Increasing the voltage across the component **increases** the current through it.

The **resistance** is how difficult it is for a current to pass through a component. Different components have different resistances. **Increasing** the resistance in a circuit **decreases** the current through it.

> **E:** How does increasing the voltage affect the current through a bulb?

Which materials are the best electrical conductors?
Investigate which materials are good conductors of electrical current. Good conductors will have a lower resistance to the electrical current than a poor conductor.

1   Choose the correct words from the box to complete the following sentences.

> ammeter   amps   charge   rate

Electrical current is the flow of electrical _____. The size of the current is the _____ of flow of charge. Current is measured in _____ using an _____.

[3 marks]

2   Table 2 shows the currents when different components are connected to a battery.

   a Which component has the lowest current?   [1 mark]

   b How can you tell that the motor will have the lowest resistance?   [1 mark]

3   How does increasing the voltage across a component affect the current flowing through it?   [1 mark]

319

19.2 Types of current

Learning objectives

After this topic, you should know:

- that cells and batteries supply a direct current
- that mains electricity is an alternating current supply
- the difference between ac and dc
- that mains electricity has a frequency of 50 Hz and is 230 V.

Current is the rate of flow of charge. In a metal wire, the charge is made of negatively charged electrons moving along the wire.

Electric charge is measured in **coulombs** (C). One coulomb is the charge that flows in one second when the current is one amp.

Charge cannot flow unless there is a **complete circuit**. This means that all of the components in the circuit are connected.

Direct current (dc)

In a circuit powered by a battery, electrons are attracted to the positive end of the battery and are repelled (pushed away) by the negative end. This is called **direct current** or dc because the charge keeps moving in the **same direction**. Batteries and cells supply direct current, see figure 1.

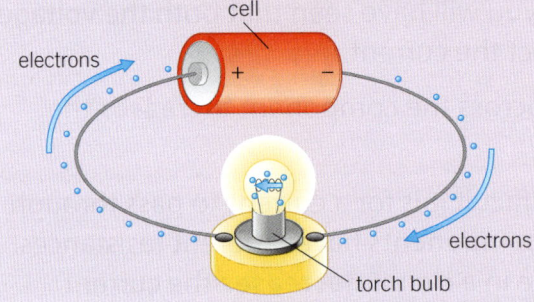

Figure 1 Electrons moving in a circuit.

A: What type of current is supplied by batteries?

Alternating current (ac)

Many electrical appliances, like lamps and computers, need to be plugged in to complete the circuit. These appliances **use mains electricity**. Mains electricity in the UK is usually 230 V.

When you use mains electricity you are using an **alternating current**, or ac, supply. The current **constantly changes direction**. Electrons flow one way and then the other. The number of times the current changes direction in a second is called the **frequency**. The frequency of mains electricity is 50 Hz.

B: What type of current is supplied by mains electricity?

Comparing alternating current and direct current

Figure 2 shows you what you would see if you were to look at ac and dc using an oscilloscope.

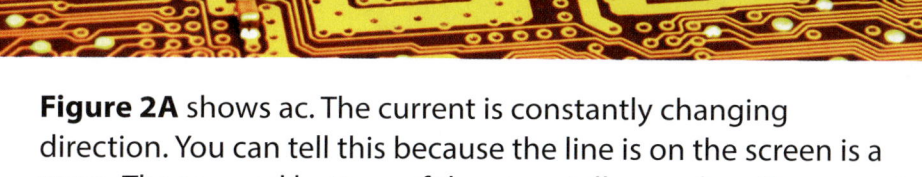

Figure 2A shows ac. The current is constantly changing direction. You can tell this because the line is on the screen is a wave. The top and bottom of the wave tell you when the current is largest in each direction.

Figure 2B shows dc. The current is always in the same direction. You can tell this because the line is constant.

A
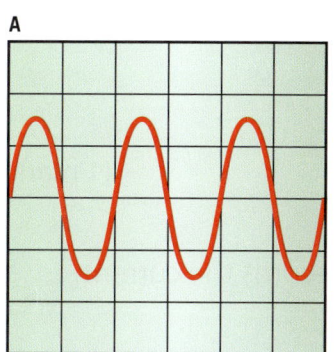

B
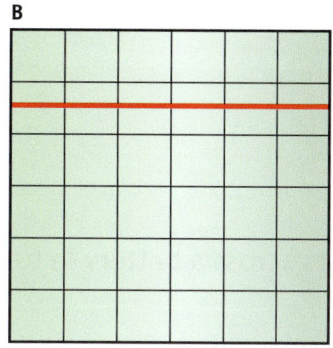

Figure 2 An oscilloscope screen showing: A – the voltage from ac, and B – the voltage from dc.

How are different current supplies different?
Investigate the differences between ac and dc using an oscilloscope. Does changing the size of the current or voltage make a difference?

C: How can you tell that Figure 2B shows dc?

1   Choose the correct words from the box to complete the following sentences.

> **alternating   constantly changes**
> **direct   stays the same**

Batteries supply _____ current. The direction of the current _____. Mains electricity is _____ current. The direction of the current _____.   [3 marks]

2   Which of the following statements are true and which are false?

   a   dc stands for digital current.   [1 mark]

   b   The UK mains supply is 230 V ac with a frequency of 50 Hz.   [1 mark]

   c   The current from an ac supply always flows in the same direction.   [1 mark]

   d   ac stands for alternating current.   [1 mark]

3   Which **three** of these devices use ac?

   calculator   camera   hairdryer
   toaster   TV   [3 marks]

19 Checkpoint

1   Choose the correct words from the box to complete the following sentences.

| bigger | complete | resistance | smaller | voltage |

A circuit must be _____ for a current to flow. The current depends on the _____ of the supply and the _____ of the components.   [3 marks]

2   Which of the following correctly describes UK mains electricity?

   A   50 V and 230 Hz

   B   120 V and 60 Hz

   C   230 V and 50 Hz

   D   230 V and 100 Hz   [1 mark]

3   A student connects three different components across a battery in turn and records the current through each. His results are shown in Table 1.

Table 1

Component	Current in A
bulb	0.5
motor	0.3
resistor	0.1

   a   Which of the three components has the highest current through it?   [1 mark]

   b   Which of the three components has the highest resistance?   [1 mark]

4   Are the following statements about electricity true or false?

   a   A complete circuit is needed for a current to flow.   [1 mark]

   b   Mains electricity is dc.   [1 mark]

   c   Batteries always supply direct current.   [1 mark]

   d   The current depends on the resistance only.   [1 mark]

5   Sort the following devices into those that use ac and those that use dc.

   fridge   **mobile phone**   **washing machine**   **watch**   [4 marks]

6   Which **two** of these factors will increase the size of the current flowing in a circuit?

   A   decreasing the resistance

   B   decreasing the voltage

   C   increasing the resistance

   D   increasing the voltage   [2 marks]

19 Vocabulary builder

1 Choose the correct terms from the list to identify the key term being described.

   a The rate of flow of electrons in a wire

      charge

      circuit

      current [1 mark]

   b How difficult it is for a current to pass through a component

      resilience

      resistance

      resistor [1 mark]

2 Draw one line from each key term to the correct definition.

Key term	Definition	
alternating current	how regularly the flow of charge changes direction	
direct current	electrical charge that is constantly changing direction	
frequency	the flow of electrical charge in a single direction	[2 marks]

3 Complete the key term being described.

   a Different components have different values of this.   r _ s _ _ t _ _ _ e   [1 mark]

   b Increasing this increases the current.   v _ _ _ _ _ _   [1 mark]

   c This measures the current in a circuit.   a _ _ _ t _ _   [1 mark]

   d This measures the voltage across a component.   v _ _ _ m _ _ _ _   [1 mark]

   e Batteries supply this type of current.   d _ _ _ _ _   [1 mark]

   f Mains electricity supplies this type of current.   a _ _ _ _ n _ _ _ _ g   [1 mark]

19.3 Resistance

Learning objectives

After this topic, you should know:

- how to calculate resistance
- how to investigate how length of wire affects resistance.

Calculating resistance

Resistance is a measure of how difficult it is for a current to flow through a component.

Resistance can be calculated using this equation:

$$\text{resistance } (\Omega) = \frac{\text{potential difference (voltage) (V)}}{\text{current (A)}}$$

Resistance is measured in **ohms** or Ω.

> ### Worked example
>
> The voltage across a bulb is 12 V and the current flowing through it is 2 A. Calculate the resistance of the bulb.
>
> **Step 1:** Write down what you know.
>
> voltage = 12 V
>
> current = 2 A
>
> **Step 2:** Write down the equation that links these values.
>
> $$\text{resistance} = \frac{\text{voltage}}{\text{current}}$$
>
> **Step 3:** Put the numbers into the equation and solve it:
>
> $$\text{resistance} = \frac{12\ \text{V}}{2\ \text{A}} = 6\ \Omega$$

A: What is the equation used to calculate resistance?

Investigating the resistance in a wire

Step 1: Build the circuit shown in **Figure 1**. Crocodile clip B is free to slide along the length of wire.

Step 2: Measure a distance of 10 cm between A and B. Switch on the circuit. Record the voltage and the current. Turn the power off.

Take care as the wire may get hot. Only leave the circuit on for short times.

Step 3: Increase the distance between A and B to 20 cm. Switch on and record the voltage and current.

Step 4: Repeat until you have reached 70 cm.

Step 5: Calculate the resistance of each length of wire.

Step 6: Plot a graph of resistance against length of wire.

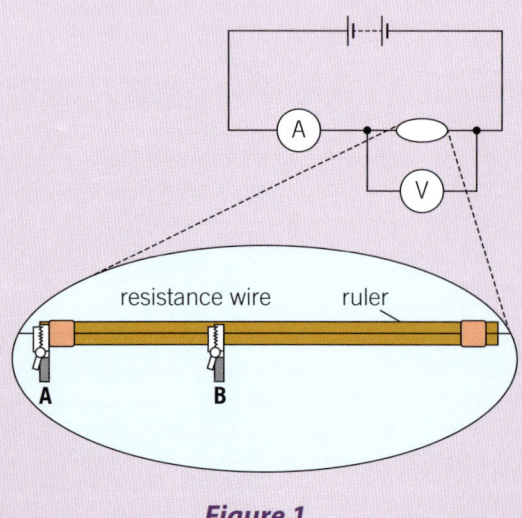

Figure 1

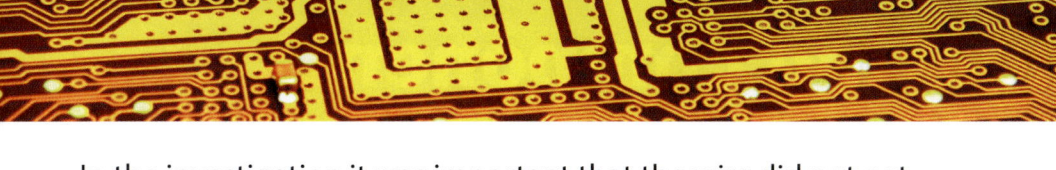

In the investigation it was important that the wire did not get hot. This is because the temperature of the wire affects its resistance. The hotter the wire the greater the resistance.

1 Choose the correct words to complete the following sentences.

> **bigger   current   resistance   smaller   voltage**

_____ is a measure of how difficult it is for a _____ to flow through a component. To calculate the resistance of a component you must divide the _____ by the current. The larger the resistance of a component the _____ the current for the same potential difference. Temperature changes the resistance of a wire. The hotter the temperature the _____ the resistance.   [4 marks]

2 The current through a wire is 0.5 A when the voltage across it is 4 V.

   a Calculate the resistance of the wire. Use the equation:

$$\text{resistance } (\Omega) = \frac{\text{voltage (V)}}{\text{current (A)}}$$ [2 marks]

   b The length of the wire is increased.

      Explain what would happen to the current.   [2 marks]

3 A student investigates how the resistance of a wire changes with length. Her results are shown below:

Length of wire in cm	10	20	30	40	50
Resistance in Ω	0.8	1.4	2.0	2.6	3.2

   a Name the independent variable in this investigation.   [1 mark]

   b Name the dependent variable.   [1 mark]

   c Name one control variable.   [1 mark]

   d Plot a graph of the results.   [4 marks]

   e When the length of the wire is zero there is still a resistance of 0.2 Ω. Suggest a reason for this. [1 mark]

19.4 Investigating components

Learning objectives

After this topic, you should know:

- how to investigate the current–voltage characteristics of a bulb, a resistor, and a diode.
- how the resistances of a bulb and a resistor change with increasing voltage
- what happens to the resistance of
  - a light-dependent resistor as light level increases
  - a thermistor as temperature increases.

Investigating the resistance of different components

To investigate the resistance of different components you need to use a variable resistor. A variable resistor will allow you to change the voltage across the component.

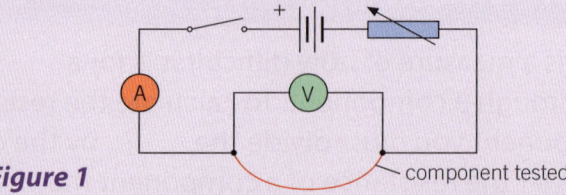

Figure 1

Step 1: Connect the circuit and place a filament lamp in the space labelled 'component tested' in Figure 1.

Step 2: Record the voltage and current.

Step 3: Move the dial on the variable resistor to a new position and record the new voltage and current.

Step 4: Repeat until you have six results for that component.

Step 5: Repeat steps 1 to 4 with a resistor and then a diode.

A: Explain why you need a variable resistor to investigate the resistance of different components.

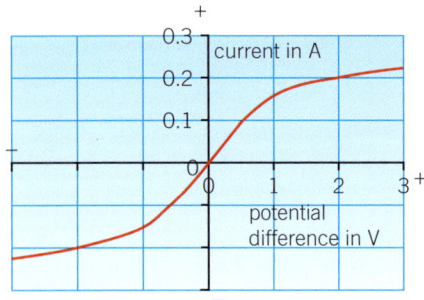

Figure 2 *The results for a filament lamp.*

Filament lamp

Figure 2 shows some results for a filament lamp. Notice that after a certain point when you increase the voltage the current stops increasing by as much. This is because the filament lamp gets hotter as you increase the voltage. The resistance increases as the lamp gets hotter, so less current is able to flow.

B: Describe how the resistance of a bulb changes as the temperature increases.

Resistor

Figure 3 shows the results for the resistor. The resistance of a resistor stays constant when you change the voltage. The current is **directly proportional** to the voltage. This means that

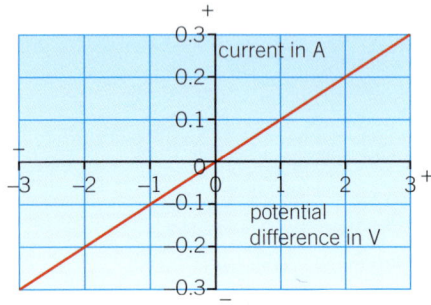

Figure 3 *The results for a resistor.*

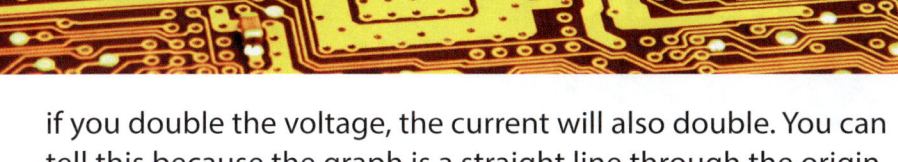

if you double the voltage, the current will also double. You can tell this because the graph is a straight line through the origin (0 on both axes).

> **C:** Describe how the resistance of a resistor changes as you increase the voltage.

Diode

A diode only allows the current to flow in the opposite direction. This is because the diode has a really high resistance in the opposite direction.

> **D:** How does the resistance of a diode compare in each direction?

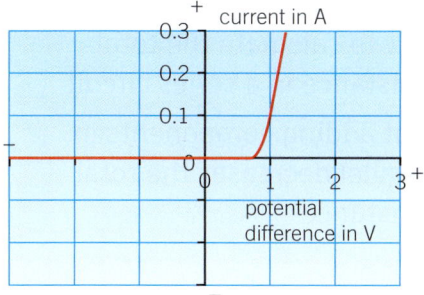

Figure 4 *The results for a diode.*

Thermistors and light-dependent resistors (LDR)

Thermistors and LDRs are used in lots of circuits.

The resistance of an LDR decreases as light intensity increases. Security lights that only come on at night have an LDR in them.

The resistance of a thermistor decreases with increasing temperature. Fire alarms that come on when it is very hot have a thermistor in the circuit.

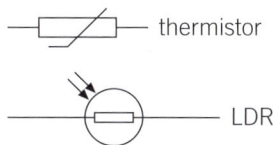

Figure 5 *The symbols for a thermistor and LDR.*

1 Choose the correct words from the box to complete the following sentences.

> **decreases   increases   LDRs   one   resistors**

Some components like _____ have a constant resistance. The resistance of bulbs, diodes, thermistors, and _____ is not constant. The resistance of a bulb _____ as temperature increases. The resistance of a thermistor _____ as temperature increases. Diodes only allow the current to flow in _____ direction. **[4 marks]**

2 Identify the component that has a resistance that:

  a stays constant as you increase the potential difference **[1 mark]**

  b increases as you increase the temperature **[1 mark]**

  c decreases as temperature increases. **[1 mark]**

3 Using the graph in Figure 3 calculate the resistance of the resistor when the current is 0.1 A. **[3 marks]**

19.5 Series and parallel circuits

Learning objectives

After this topic, you should know:

- about current and potential difference in series and parallel circuits
- how to calculate the total resistance in a series circuit
- that adding components in parallel decreases the total resistance.

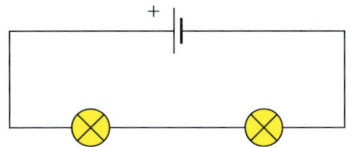

Figure 1 *A series circuit.*

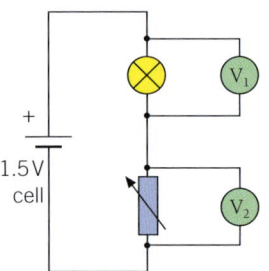

Figure 2 *A series circuit including a bulb and variable resistor.*

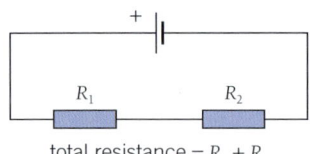

total resistance = $R_1 + R_2$

Figure 3 *The total resistance in a series circuit is the sum of the resistance of the components.*

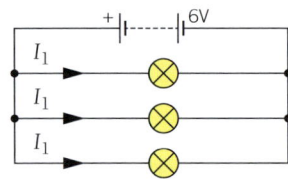

Figure 4 *A parallel circuit.*

Series circuits

Figure 1 shows a simple series circuit. You can tell it is a series circuit as there is **only one** route for the electrical current.

In a series circuit:

- the same current flows through both bulbs
- the voltage of the power supply is shared between the components.

A: What is a series circuit?

Investigating voltage in a series circuit

Step 1: Build a circuit using a bulb and a variable resistor connected in series (Figure 2).

Step 2: Record the voltage across the variable resistor and the bulb.

Step 3: Change the resistance of the variable resistor and record the new voltages across the two components.

Step 4: Repeat step 3 until you can spot a pattern in your results.

B: If the voltage of the resistor increases, what will happen to voltage across the bulb?

In a series circuit, adding more components increases the total resistance. The total resistance is equal to the sum of all the individual resistances.

C: A 10 Ω resistor is connected in series with a 20 Ω resistor. What is the total resistance?

Parallel circuits

Figure 4 shows a simple parallel circuit. The three bulbs are all connected in parallel. You can tell it is a parallel circuit because there is **more than one** route for the electrical current.

Since each bulb is in its own loop with the power supply they have the same voltage as the power supply. For components in parallel the voltage is the same.

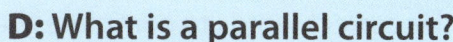

D: What is a parallel circuit?

Investigating current in a parallel circuit

Step 1: Build a circuit using one variable resistor, two bulbs and three ammeters (Figure 5).

Step 2: Record the current through each of the ammeters.

Step 3: Change the resistance using the variable resistor and record the new currents through each of the ammeters.

Step 4: Repeat until you spot a pattern.

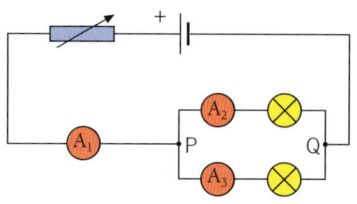

Figure 5 *Investigating a parallel circuit.*

In a parallel circuit the total current through the whole circuit is the sum of the current in each of the separate routes.

The resistance in a parallel circuit decreases as you add more components in parallel. In fact the total resistance is always less than the smallest resistance.

1   Draw one line from each circuit to the correct name of the circuit.

Circuit   **Name**

series circuit

parallel circuit

[1 mark]

2   In Figure 1 the voltage of the cell is 2.0 V. If the voltage across one bulb is 0.5 V, determine the voltage across the second bulb.   [2 marks]

3   A 15 Ω resistor is placed in parallel with a 10 Ω resistor. The voltage across the 15 Ω resistor is 6 V.

   a   What is the voltage across the 10 Ω resistor?   [1 mark]

   b   What is the total resistance in the circuit
      A 10 Ω   **C** 6 Ω
      B 25 Ω   **D** 15 Ω   [1 mark]

19 Practice questions

01 Choose the correct words from the box to complete the following sentences.

> ac   current   dc   higher
> resistance   smaller

_____ is a rate of flow of charge. The size of the current depends on the voltage or potential difference and the _____. The _____ the potential difference, the bigger the current. The bigger the resistance, the _____ the current, There are two types of current, _____ and dc. Batteries supply _____ and mains electricity is ac.

[5 marks]

02 A TV uses mains electricity. Which of the following shows the frequency of a mains supply?

A   230 V

B   140 W

C   0.6 A

D   50 Hz   [1 mark]

03 Draw one line from each component to the correct circuit symbol.

Component	Circuit symbol
bulb	—(A)—
ammeter	—/▭—
diode	—▭—
thermistor	—⊗—
resistor	—▷|— [4 marks]

04 Choose the correct words to complete the sentences.

Current is measured using an **ammeter / voltmeter** connected in **parallel / series**. The unit of current is the **amp / ohm**. Potential difference is measured using an **ammeter / voltmeter** connected in **parallel / series**. The unit of potential difference is the **amp / volt**.   [6 marks]

05 Draw one line from each component to the correct description.

Component	Description
diode	Component has a constant resistance.
filament lamp	Component only allows current to flow in one direction.
resistor	Resistance decreases as temperature increases.
thermistor	Resistance increases as temperature increases.

[3 marks]

06 Which two of the following statements about series and parallel circuits are true?

A   In a series circuit the total resistance is equal to the sum of each individual resistor.

B   In a parallel circuit the potential difference across each component is shared.

C   In a series circuit the current changes as it enters different components.

D   In a parallel circuit the total resistance is always less than the smallest resistor.

[2 marks]

07 Figure 1 shows two circuaits, A and B. The bulbs are all identical.

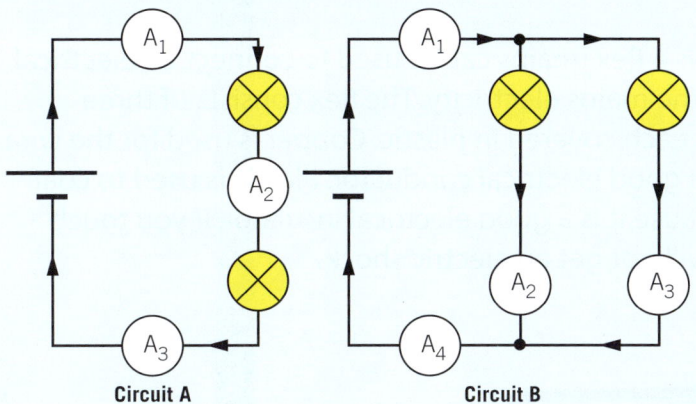

Circuit A   **Circuit B**

Figure 1

07.1 Which circuit shows two bulbs connected in series? [1 mark]

07.2 Which circuit shows two bulbs connected in parallel? [1 mark]

07.3 Explain which circuit would have the greater resistance. [2 marks]

08 A student investigates how the current changes in a circuit as they increase the potential difference. Table 1 shows the results the student recorded.

Table 1

Potential difference in V	Current in A
1	0.30
2	0.40
3	0.50
4	0.55
5	0.60

08.1 Plot a graph of the results shown in Table 1. [4 marks]

08.2 Calculate the resistance when the potential difference is 3 V. Use the equation:

$$\text{resistance} = \frac{\text{potential difference}}{\text{current}}$$

[2 marks]

08.3 Calculate the resistance when the potential difference is 5 V. [2 marks]

08.4 Describe how the resistance of this component changes with increasing potential difference. [2 mark]

09 A circuit contains three identical 10 Ω resistors connected together in series.

09.1 Calculate the total resistance of the circuit. [1 mark]

09.2 The total potential difference of the circuit is 12 V. Determine the potential difference across each resistor. [1 mark]

10 The current flowing through a car headlight bulb is 4 A and the potential difference across it is 12 V. Calculate the resistance of the bulb. Use the equation:

$$\text{resistance} = \frac{\text{potential difference}}{\text{current}}$$

[2 marks]

20 Domestic electricity
20.1 Wiring a plug

Learning objectives

After this topic, you should know:

- what the casing of a plug is made from and why
- what is inside a flex
- how to identify the live, neutral, and earth wire.

Cables

Figure 1 shows a flex (mains cable) used to connect an electrical appliance to the mains electricity. The flex consists of three copper wires, each covered in plastic. Copper is used for the wire because it is a good electrical conductor. Plastic is used to coat the wires because it is a good electrical insulator. If you touch the flex you will not get an electric shock.

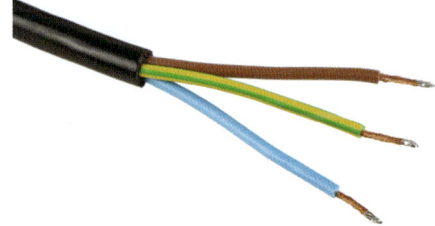

Figure 1 *An electrical mains cable (flex). and its three wires.*

Each of the three wires is colour coded so that they can be quickly identified:

- brown – **live wire**
- blue – **neutral wire**
- green and yellow stripes – **earth wire**.

> **A:** What are the names and colours of the three wires in the flex?

Plugs

The flexes are attached to plugs that can be pushed into sockets. The plugs and the sockets are made from plastic. This is because plastic is a good insulator.

Plugs have three pins – the live pin, the earth pin, and the neutral pin. These are made of brass. This is because brass is hard, a good conductor, and does not rust.

> **B:** Why are the cables and plugs covered with plastic?

Figure 2 *The earth pin of a plug is longer than the other pins. It opens shutters so that the live and neutral pins can be inserted.*

Figure 3 shows the inside of a plug.

The plug contains a **fuse** between the live wire (brown) and the live pin. If too much current flows through the live wire, the fuse melts and cuts off the electricity supply.

The brown wire (live) is connected to the live pin.

The blue wire (neutral) is connected to the neutral pin.

The green and yellow striped wire (earth) is connected to the earth pin.

The cable grip holds the flex firmly in place.

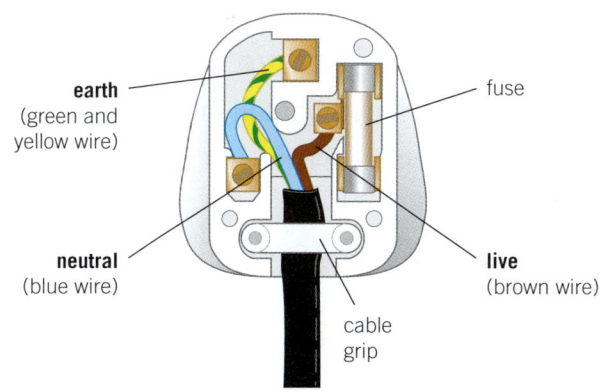

Figure 3 *Inside a three-pin plug.*

C: Which wire is the fuse connected to?

1   Draw one line from each colour of wire coating to the correct type of wire.

Colour of wire coating	Type of wire
brown	earth
blue	neutral
green and yellow stripes	live

[2 marks]

2   Choose the correct words from the box to complete the following sentences.

> blue   brown   conductor   copper
>
> green   insulator   plastic   three

Most appliances are connected to the mains using a cable with _____ wires in it. The inner core of each wire is made from _____ because it is a good _____. Each wire is covered in _____ because it is a good _____.   [5 marks]

3   The diagram shows the inside of a plug.

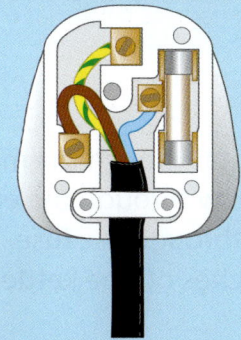

a   What is wrong with this plug?   [1 mark]

b   How would you fix it?   [1 mark]

20.2 Fuses and earth wires

Learning objectives

After this topic, you should know:

- what happens to a fuse when the current is too high
- how to identify the correct fuse for an appliance
- why some appliances don't need an earth wire.

Earth wire

The live wire carries alternating current from the mains electricity supply and the neutral wire completes the circuit. What does the earth wire do?

The earth wire is a safety wire to stop the appliance becoming live. This stops people being electrocuted.

In Figure 1, the earth wire is connected to the metal casing of the kettle. If there was no earth wire, the live wire could touch the metal casing and the whole kettle would become live. If you touched the kettle you would be electrocuted. The earth wire stops that happening.

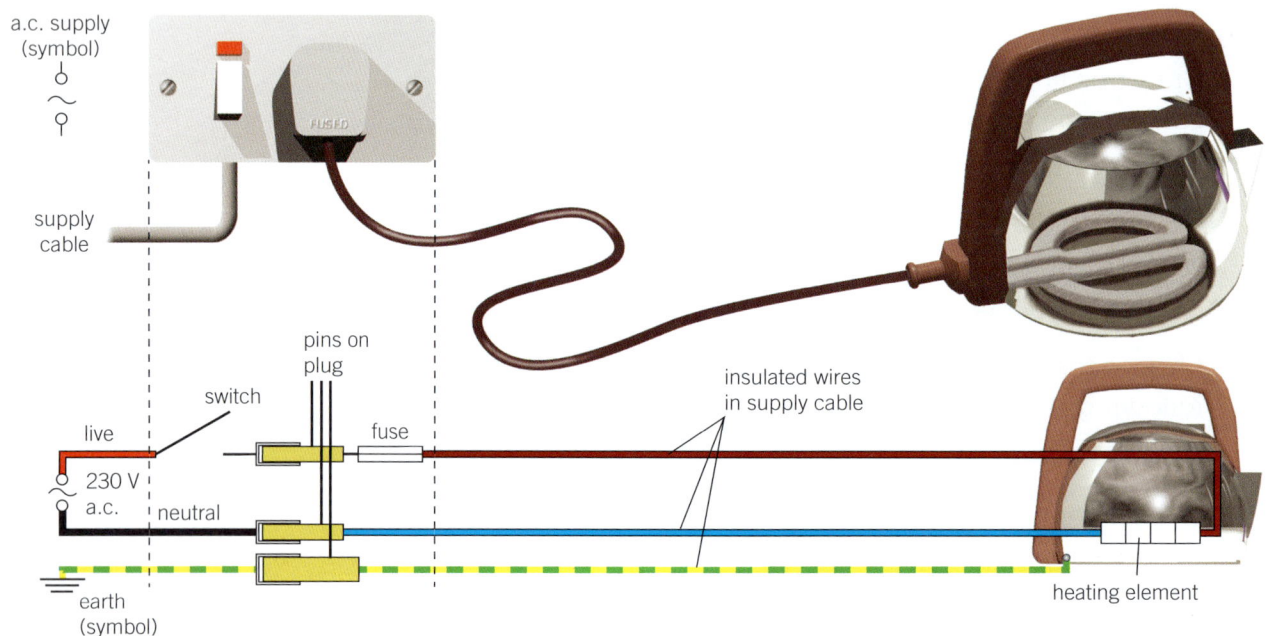

Figure 1 *The earth wire stops this metal kettle from becoming live and being dangerous to touch.*

A: What part of the kettle is the earth wire connected to?

Fuses

If the live wire does accidentally touch the metal case of the kettle, a large current will flow through the earth wire. The large current will also flow through the fuse. The fuse melts and breaks the circuit. This switches off the kettle at once. Figure 2 shows several fuses.

Figure 2 *Electrical fuses contain a piece of thin wire.*

B: Describe what happens to a fuse when the current is too big.

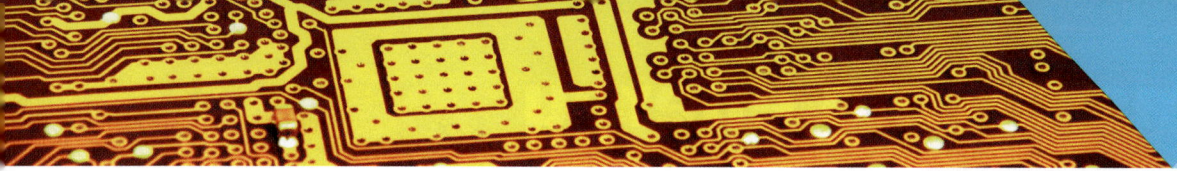

Using the correct fuse

There are several different fuse values. You can buy a 3 A, 5 A, or 13 A fuse. The fuse is designed to melt and break at that current. How can you know which fuse to choose?

A lamp has a maximum current of 0.25 A. The correct fuse value is 3 A.

A kettle has a maximum current of 10 A. The correct fuse value is 13 A.

The fuse value has to be higher than the maximum current but not too high. For example, with a 13 A fuse in the lamp a current of 3 A could flow and the fuse would not melt. The lamp might overheat and start a fire because it is not designed for such a high current. Using the right fuse prevents fires.

> **How does the size of a current affect a fuse?**
> Investigate what happens when you increase a the current in a fuse.

> **C:** A microwave has a maximum current of 6 A. Should you use a 3 A, 5 A, or 13 A fuse?

Double insulation

Some double-insulated appliances do not need an earth wire. They may have an insulating lining that stops the live wire from touching the metal casing. This means the casing can never become live. Or they may have a plastic casing.

> **D:** Why do double-insulated appliances not need an earth wire?

1   Complete the sentences using the words below.

> breaks   fuse   live   safety

The earth wire is the _____ wire. It stops the appliance from becoming _____. The _____ contains a thin piece of wire which melts and _____ if the current is too high. This switches off the appliance.   [3 marks]

2   Which **two** of these appliances would not be safe to use?

   A   double-insulated hairdryer   **C**   3 A lamp with a 15 A fuse
   B   metal kettle without an earth wire   **D**   3 A lamp with a 5 A fuse   [2 marks]

3   Choose the correct fuse, 3A, 5A, or 13 A, for the following appliances.

Appliance	Maximum current in A
kettle	11.0
TV	0.5
microwave	5.0

[3 marks]

20.3 Transferring energy

Learning objectives

After this topic, you should know:

- the units in which electricity is sold
- what affects how much energy an appliance transfers
- how to calculate the energy transferred by an appliance.

Power

Appliances in your home are designed to transfer energy.

The amount of energy an appliance transfers depends on the **power** of the appliance and how long it is left on for. Table 1 shows power ratings for some common household appliances.

Table 1 Power ratings for common household appliances

Appliance	Power rating in watts (W)
refrigerator	200
hairdryer	2000
microwave	950
tumble dryer	2500
television	120
iron	2800
mobile phone charger	10

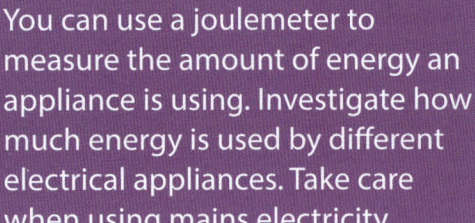

How much energy is being used?

You can use a joulemeter to measure the amount of energy an appliance is using. Investigate how much energy is used by different electrical appliances. Take care when using mains electricity.

A: Which **three** appliances have the highest power ratings? What do they have in common?

How much energy is transferred?

Whenever you plug in an appliance, you are transferring energy from mains electricity to the appliance. Electricity meters in homes measure the energy transferred in **kilowatt hours** (kWh). You can calculate how much energy is transferred using the equation below

$$\text{energy transferred (kWh)} = \text{power (kW)} \times \text{time (h)}$$

Converting watts to kilowatts

Kilo means 1000.

To convert watts to kilowatts, simply divide by 1000.

1000 W = 1 kW

200 W = 0.2 kW

B: What is 2000 W in kW?

Worked example

A 2500 W tumble dryer is used for 2 hours. Calculate the amount of energy transferred.

Step 1: Write down what you know (remember to convert power into kW).

power = 2500 W = 2.5 kW

time = 2 hours

Step 2: Write down the equation.

energy = power × time

Step 3: Put the numbers into the equation and solve.

energy = 2.5 kW × 2 h = 5 kWh

C: What equation would you use to calculate the energy transferred to an appliance?

1   Choose the correct words from the box to complete the following sentences.

energy	power	thermal	time

Appliances transfer _____. A kettle transfers energy to the _____ store of the heating element. How much energy is transferred depends on the _____ of the appliance and the _____ it is left on for.   [3 marks]

2   Complete the table to show what energy transfer each appliance is designed for.

Appliance	Energy transfer it is designed for
lamp	
heater	
electric toothbrush	
radio	

[4 marks]

3   A 200 W electric blanket is left on for 4 hours. Calculate the energy transferred. Use the equation:

energy (kWh) = power (kW) × time (h)   [1 mark]

20 Checkpoint

1 Choose the correct words from the box to complete the following sentences.

Appliances are connected to the mains through a three-core flex. The _____ wire is brown, the _____ wire is blue, and the _____ wire has green and yellow stripes.

The amount of energy an appliance transfers depends on the _____ of the appliance and the _____ it is on for.   [5 marks]

2 Draw one line from each material that a part of a plug is made from to the correct reason why that material is used.

Material

The core of each wire is made from copper

The cable wires are covered in plastic

The cable wires are colour coded

The pins of the plug are made from brass

Reason

because it is a hard material and good conductor.

because it is a good electrical conductor.

because it is a good electrical insulator.

to make it easy to identify each wire.   [3 marks]

3 Give the names for the parts of the plug labelled A, B, C, and D.   [4 marks]

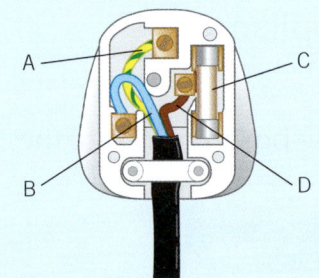

Figure 1

4 Table 1 shows the maximum current of some appliances. For each one, choose the correct fuse that should be fitted to each appliance.

3 A   5 A   13 A

Table 1

Appliance	Maximum current in amps (A)
fan heater	9.0
lamp	0.3
iron	7.0
microwave	4.5

[4 marks]

5 Convert the following powers in watts to kilowatts.

A 2000 W   [1 mark]   **C** 800 W   [1 mark]

B 3500 W   [1 mark]   **D** 20 W   [1 mark]

6 A 2000 W tumble dryer is on for 7 hours. Calculate the energy transferred. Use the equation:

energy transferred = power × time   [2 marks]

20 Vocabulary builder ✏

1 Draw one line from each wire to the correct colour.

Wire	Colour
earth	brown
live	blue
neutral	green and yellow stripes

[2 marks]

2 Choose the correct words to complete the following sentences.

Appliances are designed to transfer **energy / power**. The longer an appliance is left on the **less / more** energy is transferred. The lower the power of the appliance the **less / more** energy is transferred. To calculate the energy transferred in kilowatt-hours the power must be in **kilowatts / watts** and the time must be in **hours / seconds**.

[5 marks]

3 Which of the following key terms is being described below?

appliance   double-insulated   earth

fuse   live   power

a It does not need an earth wire. [1 mark]

b It melts and breaks when the current is too high. [1 mark]

c It prevents the metal case from becoming live. [1 mark]

d The fuse is connected to this wire. [1 mark]

e It is a device designed to transfer energy. [1 mark]

f It is measured in kilowatts or watts. [1 mark]

4 Identify the missing words using the clues below.

a L _ _ _ wires carry the alternating current to the mains. [1 mark]

b The e _ _ _ _ wire is the safety wire. [1 mark]

c The _ _ u _ r _ l wire completes the circuit. [1 mark]

d Plastic is used to make sockets and plugs because it is an i _ _ _ _ _ _ _ r. [1 mark]

e The inner core of the wire is made of copper because it is a c _ _ d _ _ _ _ _ _ . [1 mark]

20.4 Power

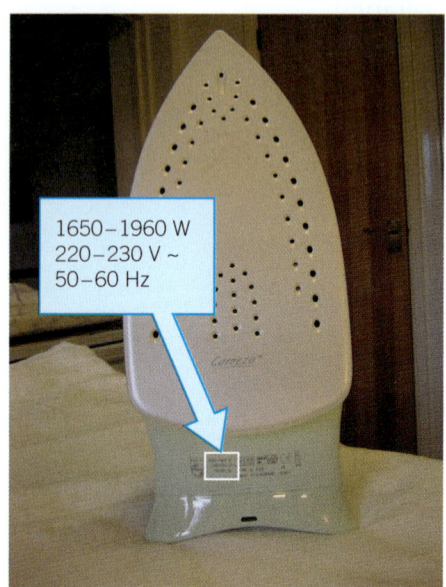

1650–1960 W
220–230 V ~
50–60 Hz

Figure 1 *The power of an iron.*

Power or energy?

People often confuse power and energy. The power of an appliance is the energy transferred per second.

The maximum power of the iron in Figure 1 is 1960 W. This means that on its maximum setting, the iron transfers 1960 joules of energy every second.

> **A:** Give the power of a microwave if it transfers 950 joules of energy every second.

Calculating power

You can calculate the energy transferred by an appliance using the equation:

$$\text{energy transferred (J)} = \text{power (W)} \times \text{time (s)}$$

To calculate power, you can rearrange this equation:

$$\text{power (W)} = \frac{\text{energy transferred (J)}}{\text{time (s)}}$$

Worked example

A lamp transfers 400 J of energy in 10 seconds. Calculate the power of the lamp.

Step 1: Write down what you know.

energy = 400 J, time = 10 s

Step 2: Write down the equation.

$$\text{power} = \frac{\text{energy transferred}}{\text{time}}$$

Step 3: Put the numbers into the equation and solve.

$$\text{power} = \frac{400 \text{ J}}{10 \text{ s}} = 40 \text{ W}$$

> **B:** A charger transfers 240 joules in 40 seconds. Calculate the power of the charger.

Calculating power

If you know the current through an appliance and the potential difference (the voltage) across it, you can calculate the appliance's power using the equation:

$$\text{power (W)} = \text{potential difference (V)} \times \text{current (A)}$$

Worked example

The potential difference of a laptop battery is 16 V and the current is 3 A. Calculate the power of the laptop.

Step 1: Write down what you know:

potential difference = 16 V, current = 3 A, power = ?

Step 2: Write down the equation:

power = potential difference × current

Step 3: Put the numbers into the equation and solve:

power = 16 V × 3 A = 48 W

C: Calculate the power of a TV connected to mains potential difference of 230 V when the current is 2.5 A.

Which equation should I use?

You now know two equations for calculating power. How do you decide which one to use?

Look carefully at the information in the question.

- If the question tells you the energy transferred and the time, use: $\text{power} = \dfrac{\text{energy}}{\text{time}}$

- If the question tells you the current and the potential difference, use:
power = potential difference × current.

1   Choose the correct words from the box to complete the following sentences.

| energy | joules | power | watts |

The _____ of an appliance is the _____ transferred per second. Power is measured in _____ and energy is measured in _____.

[3 marks]

2   Identify which appliance transfers more energy each second:

200 W electric blanket   **2 kW fan heater**   [2 marks]

3   Calculate the power of each of these appliances.

a   a toaster that transfers 96 000 J in 120 seconds   [2 marks]

b   a TV that transfers 24 000 J in 600 s   [2 marks]

4   Calculate the power for each of these appliances.

a   a 12 V, 5 A light bulb   [2 marks]

b   a 230 V, 12 A heater   [2 marks]

20.5 The National Grid

Learning objectives

After this topic, you should know:

- what the National Grid is
- what step-up and step-down transformers do
- why the National Grid is an efficient way to transfer energy.

The **National Grid** is a system of cables and **transformers** linking all the power stations in the UK to homes and businesses. Some of the power stations generate electricity all of the time and others are used only when they are needed. This means customers' electricity demands can be met.

Figure 1 shows the National Grid.

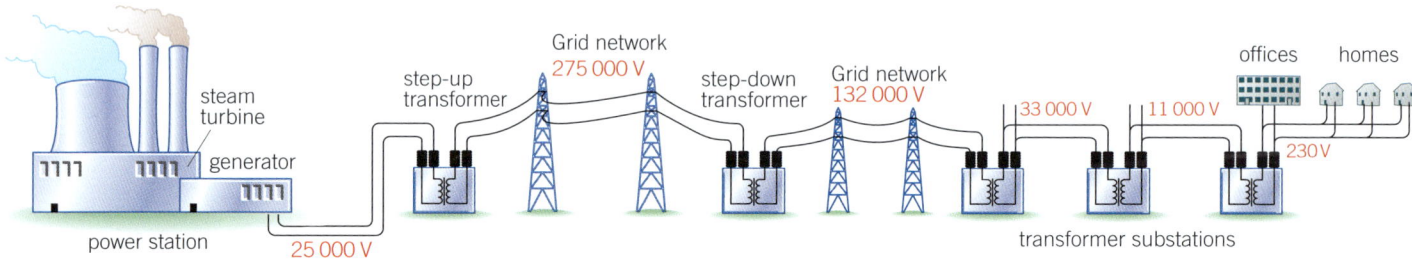

Figure 1 The National Grid.

Figure 2 Electricity pylons.

Figure 3 Step-down transformers change a high potential difference to the 230 V supplied to your house.

Power stations

Power stations generate electricity at 25 000 V.

Step-up transformers

Step-up transformers are used at power stations to increase the potential difference from the power station to the cables. They increase it from 25 000 V to 132 000 V.

Transmission cables

You may have seen electricity pylons like those in Figure 2. In towns and cities many of the cables are hidden under ground.

Step-down transformers

Step-down transformers are used to supply electricity from the National Grid to the buyers. They decrease the potential difference to 230 V for homes. Factories need higher potential differences so the potential difference is decreased to 100 000 V or 33 000 V.

A: What does a step-up transformer do?

Efficient transfer

Transformers allow very high potential differences to be used in the National Grid. This means that a much smaller current is needed to transfer the same amount of energy per second. A large current would cause the wires in the cables to get very hot. Using a smaller current means less energy is wasted by being transferred to the thermal store of the cables. Transformers allow the National Grid to transfer energy in an efficient way.

B: When you step up the potential difference what happens to the current?

1   Choose the correct words from the box to complete the following sentences.

> cables   decreased   down   high
> increased   low   up

The National Grid is a system of _____ and transformers that link power stations to customers. The potential difference is _____ by a step- _____ transformer as it leaves the power station. Power is then transmitted at very _____ potential differences and _____ currents across the country. Before it reaches homes the potential difference is _____ by a step- _____ transformer.   [6 marks]

2   Sort the parts of the National Grid into the correct order. The first one has been done for you.

[B] → [ ] → [ ] → [ ] → [ ]

A   step-down transformer

B   power station

C   homes

D   step-up transformer

E   cables   [3 marks]

3   Explain why the potential difference is stepped up to such high potential differences in the cables that cross the country.   [3 marks]

20 Practice questions

01 Choose the correct words to complete the following sentences.

Most appliances have a **two / three** core cable. The **live / neutral** carries the alternating potential difference and the **earth / neutral** completes the circuit. The **earth / neutral** is there to stop the appliance becoming live. Some appliances have a **two / three** core cable. This is because they are **double / triple** insulated. This means they have a **metal / plastic** case. [7 marks]

02 Draw one line from each part of a three-pin plug to the correct materials they are made of.

Part	Material
cable insulation	brass
case	copper
pin	plastic
wire	stiff plastic

[3 marks]

03 Which two equations can be used to calculate power?

A power = potential difference × current

B power = energy × time

C power = $\dfrac{\text{energy}}{\text{time}}$

D power = $\dfrac{\text{potential difference}}{\text{current}}$

[2 marks]

04 Table 1 shows the maximum working current of some household appliances.

Table 1

Appliance	Maximum working current in amps (A)
iron	9.0
fan	0.5
food mixer	3.0

04.1 For each appliance listed in Table 1, choose the correct useful energy output it has been designed for from the box.

> **chemical energy**
> **gravitation potential energy**
> **kinetic energy**   **thermal energy**

[3 marks]

04.2 Draw one line from each appliance to the correct fuse you should use.

Appliance	Fuse
iron	5 A
fan	1 A
food mixer	13 A

[2 marks]

05 Figure 1 shows the National Grid.

05.1 Name the place where the potential difference is highest. [1 mark]

05.2 Name the type of transformer X. [1 mark]

05.3 Name the type of transformer Y. [1 mark]

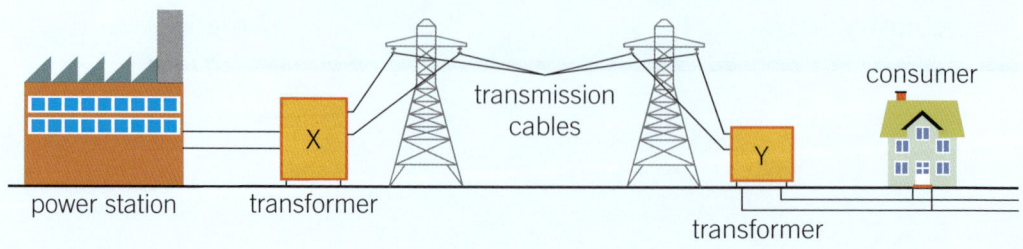

Figure 1

06 Figure 2 shows the inside of a plug.

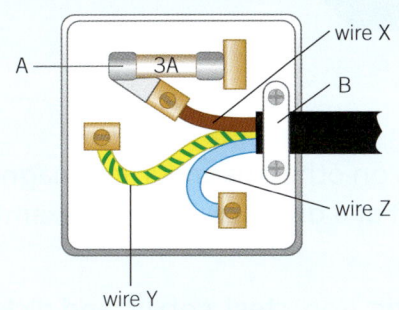

Figure 2

06.1 Name wires X, Y, and Z. [3 marks]

06.2 Name part B. [1 mark]

06.3 Give a reason why a mains appliance with a metal casing is unsafe if the case is not earthed. [1 mark]

06.4 Name part A. [1 mark]

06.5 Describe what part A does. [1 mark]

07 A rating plate for an electric toaster states 230 V, 50 Hz, 800 W.

07.1 What is the frequency of the mains supply? [1 mark]

07.2 What is the power rating of the toaster? [1 mark]

07.3 What useful energy output is the toaster designed for? [1 mark]

07.4 The toaster is left on for 300 s. Calculate the energy transferred by the toaster. Use the equation:

energy transferred = power × time [2 marks]

08.1 Write down the equation that links power, potential difference, and current. [1 mark]

08.2 A kettle has a current of 10 A flowing through it and a potential difference of 230 V across it. Calculate the power of the kettle. [2 marks]

09 Calculate the energy transferred by a 5 W torch lamp left on for 15 minutes. Use the equation:

energy transferred = power × time [3 marks]

10 When the potential difference is increased by a step-up transformer the current is decreased. A flow of an electric current causes the wires to heat up.

Explain why the National Grid is an efficient way to transfer energy. [3 marks]

21 Magnetism and electromagnetism
21.1 Magnetic fields

Learning objectives

After this topic, you should know:

- how to draw the magnetic field around a magnet
- how to identify where the magnetic field is strongest
- what happens when the poles of magnets are brought close to each other.

Magnets

Magnets can exert forces on other magnets and magnetic materials. These forces act at a distance. They are examples of **non-contact forces**.

Not all metals are magnetic. Iron, steel, cobalt, and nickel are all magnetic metals. If you put them near a magnet, they will experience a force. The force of attraction is stronger closer to the magnet.

> **A: What type of force is magnetic force?**

Magnetic fields

Iron filings are small pieces of iron. They are so small and light that they can be used to show the **magnetic field** around a magnet. Any magnetic material placed in this magnetic field will feel a force.

In Figure 1, iron filings show the magnetic field around a magnet. They form lines. These lines are called **magnetic field lines**. Figure 2 shows a diagram of these field lines.

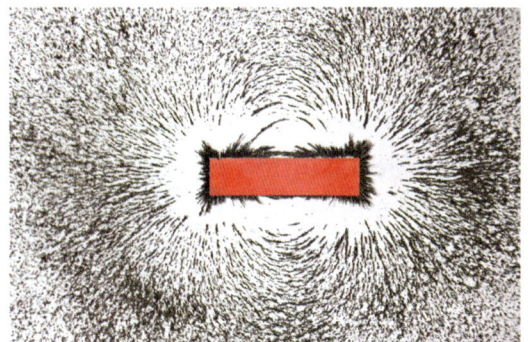

Figure 1 *The magnetic field of a bar magnet shown using iron filings.*

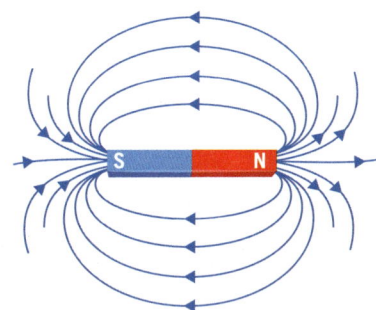

Figure 2 *The magnetic field around a bar magnet.*

The field lines are much closer together at the ends of the magnet. This is because the force is stronger here. These are the **poles** of the magnet. The field lines point from the north pole of the magnet to its south pole.

> **B: Where is the magnetic field strongest?**

Attracting and repelling

When you put the poles of two bar magnets near each other, two things can happen. The two poles might **attract** (pull) each other or they might **repel** (push) each other.

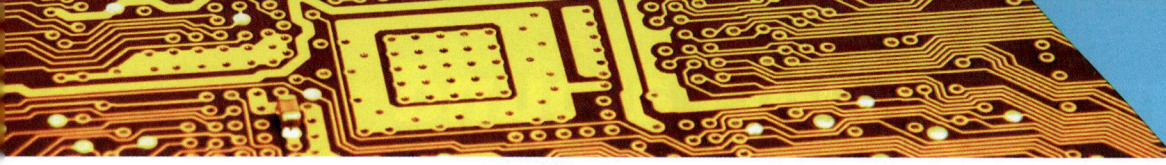

The outcome depends on which poles are next to each other. Like poles will **repel** each other. Unlike poles will **attract** each other. The force attracting or repelling the poles is a non-contact force.

Figures 3 and 4 show what is happening to the magnetic field when the poles of two bar magnets are next to each other.

How do magnets attract or repel?
Investigate what happens when you put a magnet near another magnet. Is this the same as what happens when you put a magnet near a magnetic material? Investigate the attraction of magnetic materials to a magnet.

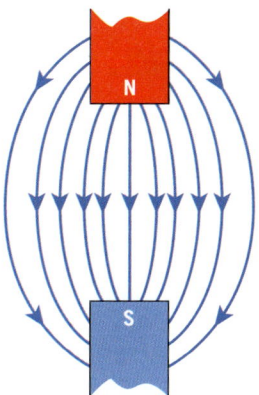

Figure 3 *The shape of the magnetic field between a north pole and a south pole.*

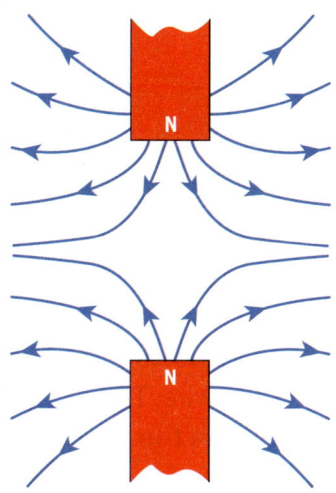

Figure 4 *The shape of the magnetic field between two north poles.*

C: **What happens when the south pole of a bar magnet is brought near the north pole of another magnet?**

1 Choose the correct words from the box to complete the following sentences.

attract   non-contact   poles   repel

The magnetic force is strongest at the _____. If you bring a north pole near another north pole the magnets will _____. If you bring a south pole near a north pole the magnets will _____. Magnetic forces are an example of _____ forces.   [3 marks]

2 Choose the correct word to complete the sentences.
If you bring a north pole and a south pole together, they will **attract / repel**.
If you bring a south pole and a south pole together, they will **attract / repel**.
If you bring a north pole and a north pole together, they will **attract / repel**.

[3 marks]

3 **a** Draw the magnetic field pattern around a single bar magnet.   [1 mark]
 b Mark with a cross one of the points where the magnetic field is strongest.   [1 mark]
 c How do you know the force is strongest here?   [1 mark]

21.2 Magnetic fields around an electric current

Learning objectives

After this topic, you should know:

- how to draw the magnetic field around a current-carrying wire
- the factors affecting the strength of the magnetic field around the wire
- what a solenoid is.

Magnetic field near a current-carrying wire

When an electric current flows through a wire it produces a magnetic field around the wire.

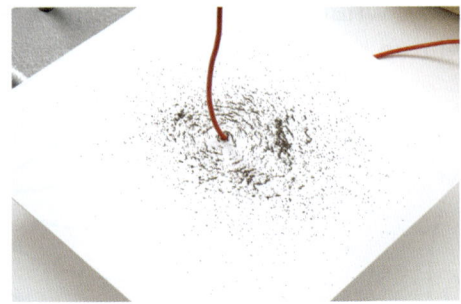

Figure 1 *The magnetic field lines around a wire are circular.*

Figure 1 shows the magnetic field pattern around a current-carrying wire. The magnetic field pattern is a series of circles. centred on the wire.

A: How are we able to see the magnetic field pattern in Figure 1?

Strength of a magnetic field around a wire

The strength of the magnetic field around a wire depends on:

- the current – **increasing** the current **increases** the strength of the magnetic field around the wire
- the distance from the wire – **increasing** the distance from the wire **decreases** the strength of the magnetic field.

B: What are the two factors that determine the strength of the magnetic field around a current-carrying wire?

You can create a stronger field by making the wire into a coil. The magnetic field lines go through the coil and round the outside. Figure 2 shows this. If the current in the coil is reversed, the field direction is also reversed.

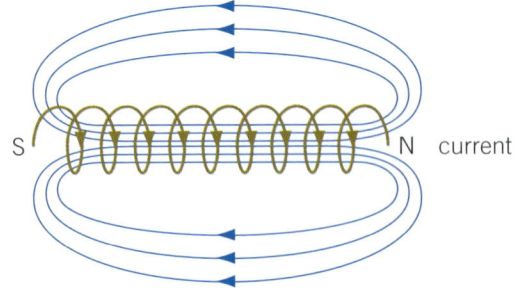

Figure 2 *The magnetic field around a coil of wire carrying a current.*

Solenoids

A **solenoid** is a long coil of insulated wire. This coiling increases the strength of the magnetic field around a wire. A solenoid's magnetic field pattern looks the same as that of a bar magnet.

Solenoids are often used when a strong magnetic field needs to be produced.

Adding an iron core increases the magnetic field strength of a solenoid even more. A solenoid with an iron core is called an **electromagnet**.

C: What is a solenoid?

1   Choose the correct words from the box to complete the following sentences.

| current   distance   magnetic |

When a current flows through a wire a _____ field is produced around the wire. The strength of the magnetic field depends on the _____ in the wire and _____ from the wire.   [2 marks]

2   Choose the correct word to complete the sentences.

Increasing the current in a wire **decreases / increases** the strength of the magnetic field.

Decreasing the distance from a wire **decreases / increases** the strength of the magnetic field.

Decreasing the current in a wire **decreases / increases** the strength of the magnetic field.   [2 marks]

3   Does this magnetic field pattern show the pattern around a solenoid or a single wire?

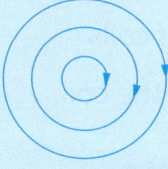

[1 mark]

4   a   What is a solenoid?   [1 mark]
    b   Why would you use a solenoid rather than
        a single wire?   [1 mark]

21.3 Electromagnets

Learning objectives

After this topic, you should know:

- what an electromagnet is
- how to investigate the factors affecting the strength of an electromagnet
- some uses of electromagnets.

An **electromagnet** is a solenoid wrapped around an iron bar. When a current is passed along a wire, a magnetic field is created around the wire. Because of this the iron bar is magnetised. When it is switched off the iron bar loses its magnetism.

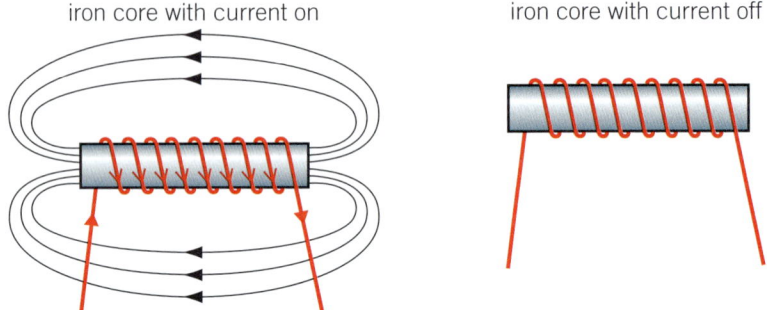

iron core with current on   iron core with current off

Figure 1 *An iron bar wrapped in wire when the current is flowing and when it is not.*

A: What is an electromagnet?

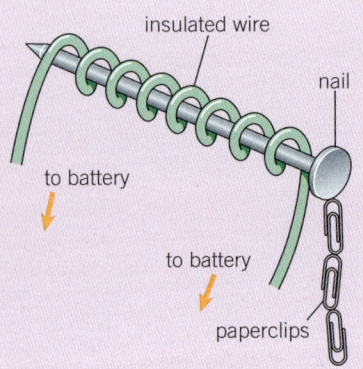

insulated wire

nail

to battery

to battery

paperclips

Figure 2 *A simple electromagnet.*

Investigating electromagnets

Step 1: Take an iron bar (or nail) and wrap insulated wire around it. Connect the wires to a battery.

Step 2: Use this simple electromagnet, pick up metal paperclips.
Count how many paperclips your electromagnet can hold. Record this number in a table.

Step 3: Increase the number of coils and repeat step 2.

Step 4: Repeat five times until you can see a pattern between the number of coils and the number of paperclips.

The strength of an electromagnet can be increased until the iron is fully magnetised by

- increasing the number of coils
- increasing the current in the coil.

Using electromagnets

Car scrapyard

In a scrapyard, the crane has a large electromagnet attached. To pick up the cars the electromagnet is switched on. When the crane has to drop the cars the electromagnet is switched off.

Figure 3 *An electromagnet attached to a crane in a scrapyard.*

B: Why use an electromagnet rather than a permanent magnet in the scrapyard?

Relay

A relay is an electrical switch that is opened and closed by another circuit. The first circuit contains an electromagnet.

- When the electromagnet turns on, it attracts the iron armature towards it. This pushes the second switch closed, which turns on the second circuit.

- When the first circuit is switched off, the electromagnet turns off, and the iron armature is released. This switches off the second circuit.

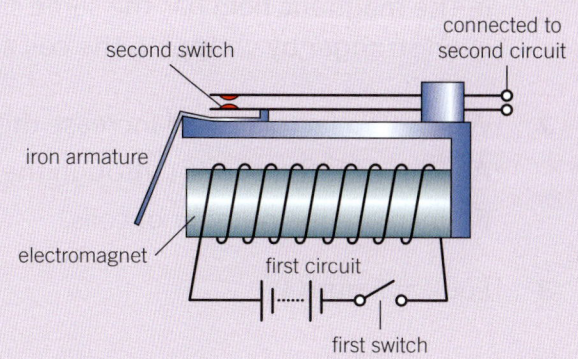

Figure 4 *A relay.*

C: Which part of the relay is attracted to the electromagnet?

1 Choose the correct words from the box to complete the following sentences.

| current | electromagnet | increase | solenoid |

An _____ is a _____ wrapped around an iron bar. To increase the strength of an electromagnet you can increase the _____ or _____ the number of coils. [3 marks]

2 What is one advantage of using an electromagnet instead of a permanent magnet? [1 mark]

3 A student investigates how changing the current changes the strength of an electromagnet. The table and graph shows his results.

Current in amps (A)	Number of paperclips
1	2
2	4
3	
4	8
5	10

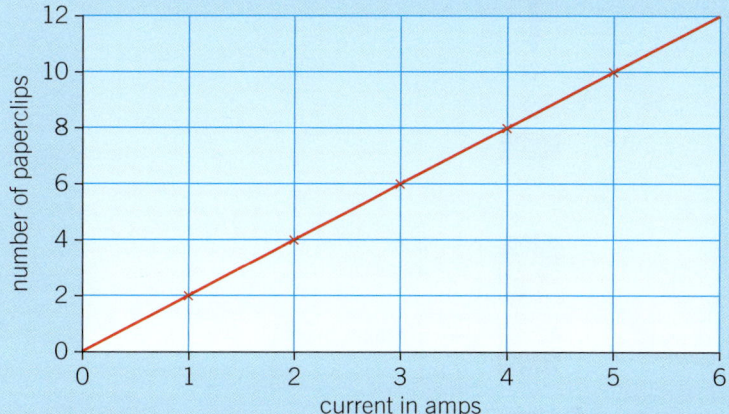

a How many paperclips were picked up when the current was 3 A? [1 mark]
b What pattern is shown by the student's results? [1 mark]
c What is one control variable in this experiment? [1 mark]

1 Choose the correct words from the box to complete the following sentences.

> current   electromagnet   magnet   magnetic   solenoid

A _____ is a long coil of wire. When a _____ flows through the wire, a _____ field is produced around it. The magnetic field has the same shape as that of a bar _____. You can make the magnetic field even stronger by wrapping the coil around an iron core. This is called an _____. [4 marks]

2 Which **two** factors could increase the strength of an electromagnet?

  A Decrease the current through the wire.   **C** Use a copper core.

  B Increase the number of coils.   **D** Use an iron core. [2 marks]

3 Look at Figure 1.

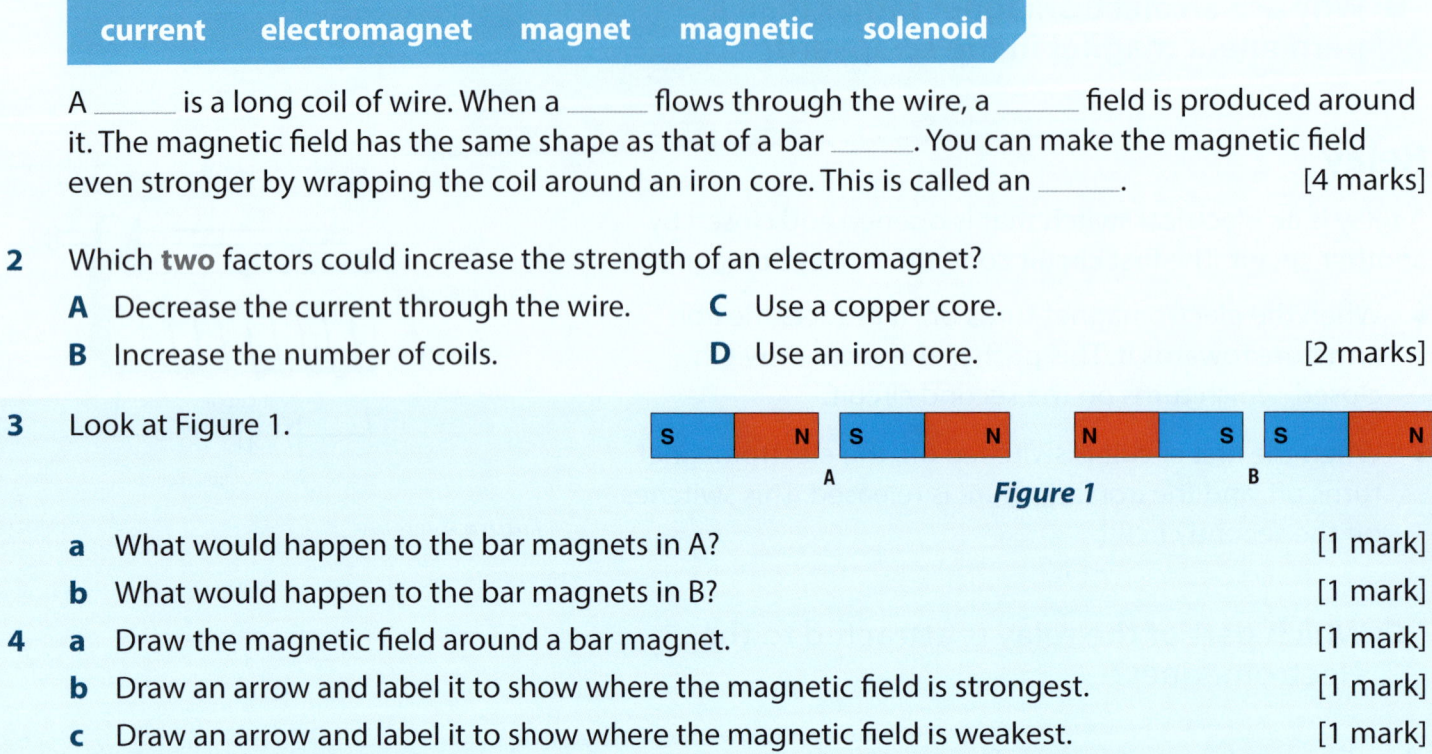

Figure 1

  a What would happen to the bar magnets in A? [1 mark]

  b What would happen to the bar magnets in B? [1 mark]

4 **a** Draw the magnetic field around a bar magnet. [1 mark]

  b Draw an arrow and label it to show where the magnetic field is strongest. [1 mark]

  c Draw an arrow and label it to show where the magnetic field is weakest. [1 mark]

5 A student investigates how the strength of an electromagnet varies with distance from it. Her apparatus is shown in Figure 2. The electromagnet attracts the iron disc and the spring balance measures the force. Her results are shown in the table below.

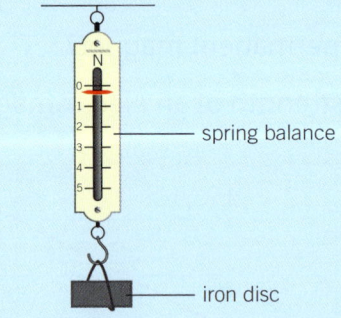

spring balance

iron disc

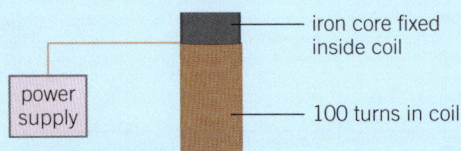

iron core fixed inside coil

power supply

100 turns in coil

Figure 2

Distance from electromagnet in cm	Force of attraction in N
1.0	10.0
1.5	3.0
2.0	1.3
2.5	0.6
3.0	0.4

  a What is one control variable in this experiment? [1 mark]

  b What is the relationship between distance from electromagnet and strength of an electromagnet? [1 mark]

21 Vocabulary builder

1 Draw one line from each key term to the correct definition.

Key term	Definition
solenoid	area where the magnetic field is strongest
electromagnet	area where a magnet or magnetic material feels a force
magnetic field	a coil of insulated wire
poles	a coil of wire wrapped around an iron core

[3 marks]

2 Choose the correct key word that is being described.

a Magnetic force is strongest in this area of a magnet.

ends

points

poles

[1 mark]

b A coil of wire that increases the strength of a magnetic field around a wire.

electromagnet

solenoid

solid

[1 mark]

c The area affected by a magnet.

field

force

plane

[1 mark]

3 Choose the correct word from the box to complete the following sentence.

| current   power   strength |

Increasing the number of coils in an electromagnet, increases
the _____ of the electromagnet.

[1 mark]

4 Complete the key words being described.

a Magnetic force is an example of this type of force.

n _ _ - c _ _ t _ _ _ _

[1 mark]

b Like poles do this.

r _ _ _ _

[1 mark]

c Unlike poles do this.

a _ _ r _ _ _

[1 mark]

21.4 Plotting magnetic fields

Learning objectives

After this topic, you should know:

- the shape of the Earth's magnetic field
- how to plot a magnetic field using a plotting compass
- how to describe the magnetic field strength using the magnetic field lines
- what induced magnetism is.

A magnetic field is the space around a magnet where a force will act on another magnet or on a magnetic material.

Earth's magnetic field

The Earth has a magnetic field. A compass has a tiny magnetic needle balanced at its centre. Due to the Earth's magnetic field one end of the compass always points north, and the other always points south. The end of the compass that always points north is called the 'north seeking pole' or north pole. The other end is called the south seeking pole or south pole.

The Earth's magnetic field is like the field round a bar magnet.

A: Describe why a compass points north.

Using a plotting compass

A plotting compass placed in a magnetic field will line up with the magnetic field lines. The needle will point away from the north pole of the magnet and towards the south pole of the magnet.

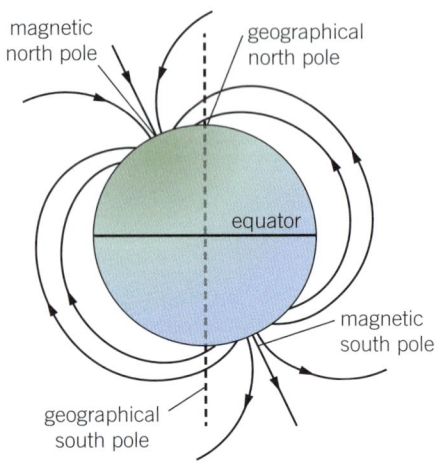

Figure 1 *The Earth's magnetic field. The Earth has a magnetic north pole near to its geographic south pole.*

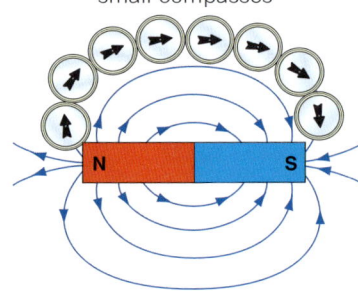

Figure 2 *The field around a bar magnet shown by a plotting compass.*

You can use a plotting compass to accurately plot magnetic field lines.

Step 1: Place the plotting compass on a piece of paper next to the north pole of the magnet.

Step 2: Put a dot on the paper to show where the needle points.

Step 3: Move the compass forward, lining up the end of the needle with the previous dot. Put a dot where the needle points.

Step 4: Repeat steps 2 and 3 until the compass is next to the magnet.

Step 5: Repeat this until you have plotted several of the magnetic field lines for your magnet.

Magnetic field lines are closer together at the poles of the magnet and further apart as you move away from the magnet. This shows that the magnetic field is strongest at the poles. It also shows that magnetic field strength decreases with distance from the magnet.

B: Describe how you can tell the magnetic field strength from the magnetic field lines.

Induced magnetism

Some materials that are not magnets can be made into temporary magnets by placing them into a magnetic field. We say that the magnetic field **induces** magnetism in the material. This only works with materials that are attracted to permanent magnets such as iron.

In Figure 3, the paperclips have been magnetised. This means the paperclips have become magnets. The second paperclip is attracted to the first one. The force is always **attractive**. If you take the magnet away, the paperclips lose their magnetism.

C: Describe how you can induce magnetism.

1   Choose the correct words from the box below to complete the following sentences.

> compass   field   force   line
> magnet   north   south

A magnetic _____ is a space round a magnet where another _____ or a magnetic material feels a _____. The direction of a magnetic field is always from the _____ pole towards the _____ pole. A _____ consists of a small magnet balanced at its centre. Compass needles _____ up with magnetic fields.   [6 marks]

2   A bar magnet labelled XY is hung horizontally on a piece of thread so that it is free to turn. The end marked X points north, and the end marked Y points south.

   a   Which end of the magnet is the north pole, X or Y?   [1 mark]

   b   The north pole of a second magnet is brought near to end X. Describe what would happen to magnet XY.   [2 marks]

3   Describe what happens to unmagnetised magnetic material in a magnetic field.   [2 marks]

4   Draw a diagram to show the magnetic field of the Earth.

[2 marks]

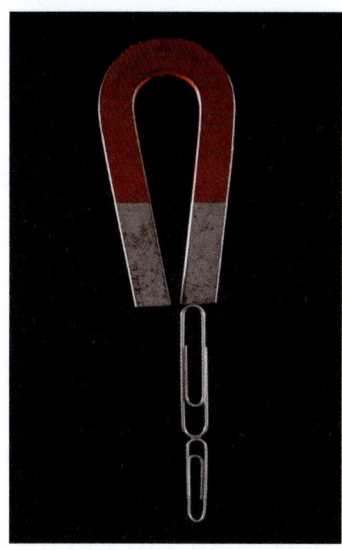

Figure 3 Induced magnetism.

21 Practice questions

01 Choose the correct words to complete the sentences.

The direction of a magnetic field is from the **north / south** pole to the **north / south** pole. The **closer / further apart** the magnetic field lines are the stronger the field. The force between a magnetic material and a magnet is always one of **attraction / repulsion**. [4 marks]

02 Identify which **three** materials in this list are magnetic.

aluminium   **copper**   **iron**

nickel   **steel**

[3 marks]

03 Figure 1 shows five situations A, B, C, D, and E where bars of different materials are placed next to each other. Some of the bars are magnets and some of them are non-magnets.

Sort them into whether the bars are attracted, repelled, or not affected. The first one has been done for you.

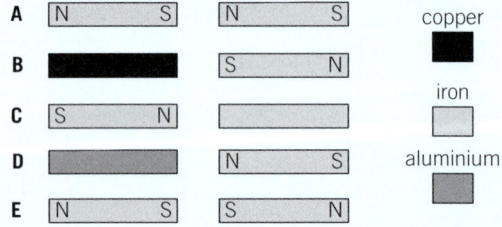

Figure 1

Attracted	Repelled	No effect
A		

[4 marks]

04 Figure 2 shows a solenoid.

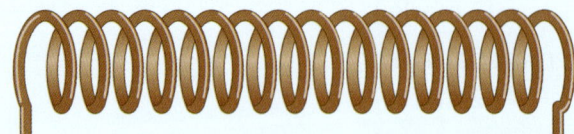

Figure 2

04.1 Draw the magnetic field around the solenoid when a current flows through it. [1 mark]

04.2 Describe how the magnetic field strength of a solenoid varies with distance from the solenoid. [1 mark]

04.3 Solenoids increase the strength of the magnetic field due to the current. Give **two** other ways the magnetic field could be increased. [2 marks]

05 Figure 3 shows an overhead view of a plotting compass near a vertical wire. When a current flows in the wire the compass points in the direction shown.

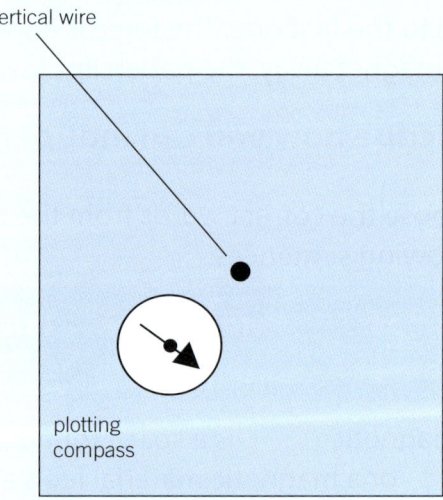

Figure 3

05.1 Draw two magnetic field lines near the wire. [2 marks]

05.2 What would happen to the plotting compass if the current direction was reversed? [1 mark]

06 A student demonstrates how changing the current in a solenoid affects the magnetic force. He used the equipment shown in Figure 4.

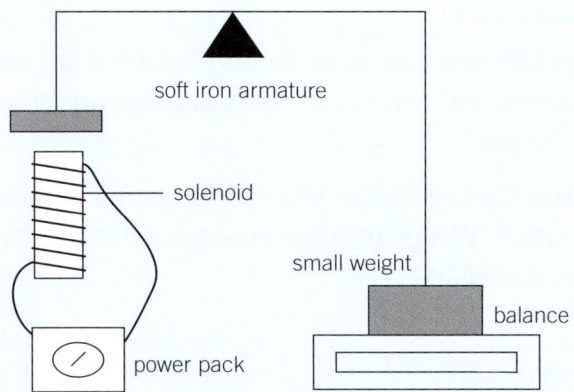

Figure 4

The electromagnet attracts the iron armature, which is attached to a small mass, lifting the small mass off the balance.

The results of the student's demonstration are shown in Table 1.

Table 1

Current in A	Weight on balance in N
0	5.0
2	2.5
4	1.2
6	0.8
8	0.5

06.1 Plot a graph of the student's results.
[4 marks]

06.2 Name the independent variable.
[1 mark]

06.3 Name the dependent variable.
[1 mark]

06.4 Give **two** variables the student would control in this experiment. [2 marks]

07.1 What is an induced magnet? [1 mark]

07.2 How is an induced magnet different from a permanent magnet? [1 mark]

08 Figure 5 shows an electric bell.

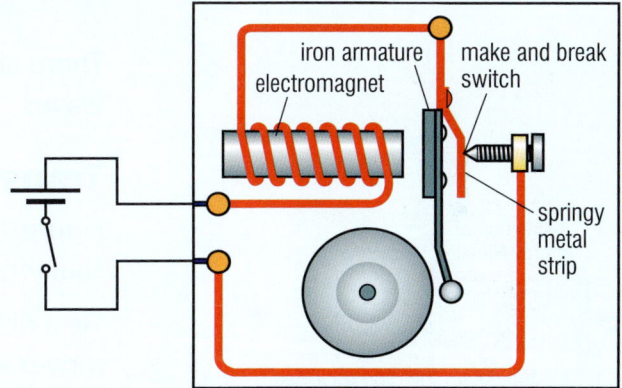

Figure 5

08.1 What happens when the circuit is switched on that makes the bell ring?
[2 marks]

08.2 Why does the iron armature hitting the bell switch off the electromagnet?
[1 mark]

22 Different types of waves
22.1 Longitudinal and transverse waves

Learning objectives

After this topic, you should know:

- what longitudinal waves are
- what transverse waves are
- how to identify longitudinal and transverse waves.

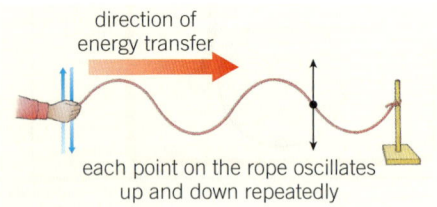

Figure 1 *Transverse waves.*

What are waves?

There are many different waves, including light waves, sound waves, water waves, and waves on ropes and springs. What do they have in common?

Waves involve **oscillations** (vibrations) and transfer energy from one place to another. Waves transfer energy without moving matter from place to place.

> **A:** What is a wave?

There are two types of waves – **transverse** and **longitudinal** waves.

Transverse waves

Figure 1 shows how to make a transverse wave on a rope by shaking one end up and down.

Tie a ribbon to the middle of the rope. You will see that the wave moves along the rope but the ribbon just moves up and down. The ribbon is oscillating.

- The oscillations of a transverse wave are **perpendicular** (at right angles) to the direction of energy transfer.

Water waves and light waves are examples of transverse waves.

> **B:** How do the particles of water move as a wave moves across the surface of a pond?

Longitudinal waves

Figure 2 shows how to make longitudinal waves using a long slinky.

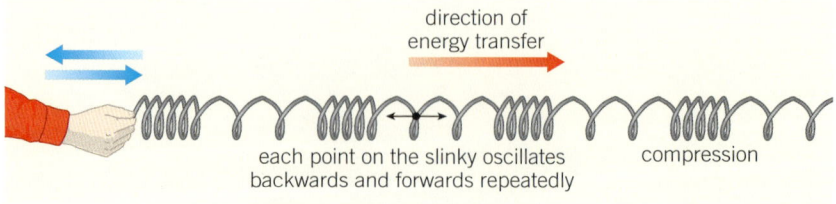

Figure 2 *Longitudinal waves.*

Tie a ribbon to the middle of the slinky. You will see the ribbon move backwards and forwards.

- The oscillations of a longitudinal wave are **parallel** (along the same line) to the direction of energy transfer.

Notice that the coils are squashed together in some places and stretched apart in others. The areas where the coils are squashed are called **compressions**. The areas where the coils are stretched apart are called **rarefactions**.

Sound waves are an example of longitudinal waves.

C: How do air particles move as a sound wave travels through a room?

1   Choose the correct words from the box to complete the following sentences.

| energy | longitudinal | matter | transverse |

Waves transfer _____ without transferring _____. There are two types of waves. In _____ waves the oscillation of the particles is perpendicular to the direction of energy transfer. In _____ waves the particles oscillate parallel to the direction of energy transfer.   [3 marks]

2   Which of these statements are true and which are false?
   a   Water waves are transverse waves.   [1 mark]
   b   Sound waves are longitudinal waves.   [1 mark]
   c   Light waves are longitudinal waves.   [1 mark]

3   Two students use a long rope to demonstrate a wave. One student makes a wave by rapidly moving their hand up and down. The second student holds the other end still.
   a   Which type of wave are they demonstrating?   [1 mark]
   b   What is the direction of the energy transfer?   [1 mark]
   c   How will a ribbon tied half-way along the rope move?
                [1 mark]

22.2 Properties of waves

Learning objectives

After this topic, you should know:

- what is meant by amplitude, wavelength, and frequency of a wave
- how to identify amplitude and wavelength on a diagram of a wave
- how to use the wave equation to calculate the speed of a wave.

There are many different types of waves, but you can use the same key words to describe them.

Amplitude is the maximum displacement of a point on a wave away from its undisturbed position. Amplitude is measured in metres. The bigger the amplitude of a wave, the more energy it is transferring.

Wavelength is the distance from a point on the wave to the same point on the next wave. Wavelength can be measured in metres, centimetres, or millimetres.

Frequency is the number of waves passing a point each second. Frequency is measured in hertz or Hz.

Figure 1 shows a diagram of a wave. The amplitude is the distance between the peak of the wave and the middle, or the distance between the trough and the middle. The wavelength is shown as the distance between two peaks, or two troughs.

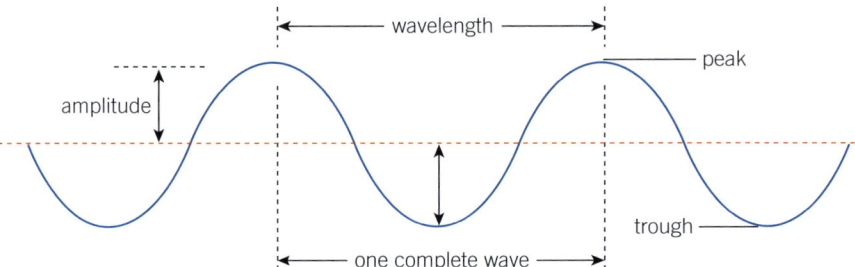

Figure 1 *Measurements of a wave*

A: Which key word means the number of waves that pass a point in a second?

Wave speed

The speed of a wave is the distance travelled by each wave per second. You can calculate the speed of a wave from its frequency and wavelength using this equation:

$$\text{wave speed (m/s)} = \text{frequency (Hz)} \times \text{wavelength (m)}$$

How do changes in frequency and amplitude affect a wave?

Using an oscilloscope, investigate how changing the frequency or amplitude of a wave changes the shape of a wave. How is frequency related to the pitch of a sound wave? How is amplitude related to the volume of a sound wave?

Worked example

Waves are generated in the ripple tank in Figure 2 at a frequency of 8 Hz. The waves have a wavelength of 5 cm. Calculate the speed of the waves in the ripple tank in cm/s.

Step 1: Write down what you know.

> frequency = 8 Hz
>
> wavelength = 5 cm

Step 2: Write down the equation that links these values.

> wave speed = frequency × wavelength

Step 3: Put the numbers in the equation and solve.

> wave speed = 8 Hz × 5 cm = 40 cm/s

Figure 2 *A ripple tank.*

B: What do you need to know to calculate wave speed?

1   Draw one line from each key word to the correct definition.

Key word	Definition
amplitude	The number of waves passing a point each second.
frequency	The distance from a point on a wave to the same point on the next wave.
wavelength	The maximum displacement of a wave from its undisturbed position.

[2 marks]

2   Choose the correct word to complete the following sentences.

The bigger the amplitude of a wave, the **less / more** energy the wave transfers.

Frequency is measured in **hertz / metres**.

[2 marks]

3   Figure 3 shows a wave travelling from left to right along a rope.

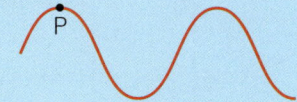

Figure 3

In what way does point P move when the wave peak at P moves along a distance of one wavelength?

[1 mark]

4   A speedboat on a lake sends waves travelling across the lake at a frequency of 2 Hz and a wavelength of 3.0 m.

Calculate the speed of the wave. Use the equation:

wave speed = frequency × wavelength

[2 marks]

22 Checkpoint

1 Choose the correct words from the box to complete the following sentences.

| energy | longitudinal | matter | oscillate | parallel | transverse |

Waves transfer _____ without transferring _____. There are two types of waves, _____ where the particles _____ perpendicular to the direction of energy transfer, and _____ where the particles move _____ to the direction of energy transfer.

[6 marks]

2 Which of the following is an example of a longitudinal wave?

light   sound   water

[1 mark]

3 Figure 1 shows a wave.

Figure 1

a On the wave, label a compression. [1 mark]

b On the wave, label a rarefaction. [1 mark]

c Is the wave in Figure 1 a longitudinal wave or a transverse wave? [1 mark]

4 Figure 2 shows a wave.

a On the wave, label the amplitude. [1 mark]

b On the wave, label the wavelength. [1 mark]

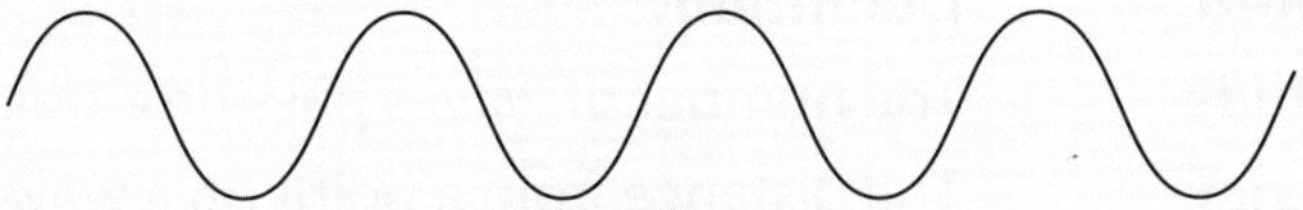

Figure 2

5 Figure 3 shows a diagram of a wave over time.

a What is the wavelength of this wave?

5 cm   10 cm   20 cm   25 cm [1 mark]

b What is the amplitude of this wave?

5 cm   15 cm   20 cm   25 cm [1 mark]

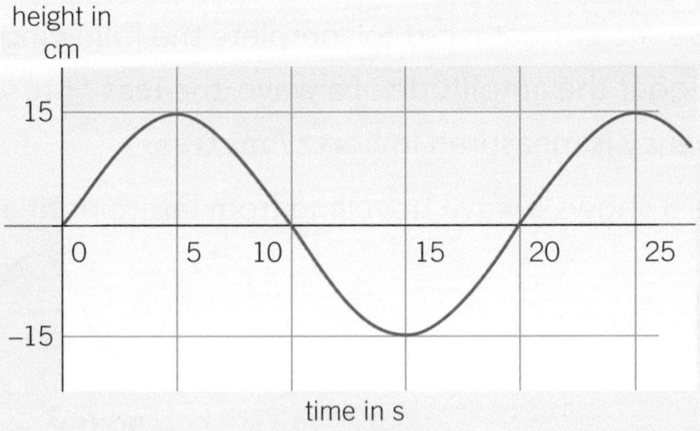

Figure 3

6 A sound wave has a frequency of 5 Hz and a wavelength of 66 m.

Calculate the speed of the sound wave. Use the equation:

wave speed = frequency × wavelength

[2 marks]

22 Vocabulary builder

1   Draw one line from each key word to the correct definition.

Key word	Definition
wavelength	The number of waves passing a point each second.
amplitude	Distance from a point on the wave to the same point on the next wave.
frequency	Distance from the rest position for a point on a wave.
displacement	The maximum displacement of a point on the wave.

[3 marks]

2   Choose the correct words from the box to complete the following sentences.

longitudinal   parallel   perpendicular   transverse

A wave in water is a example of a _____ wave. The particles oscillate _____ to the direction of energy transfer.

A sound wave is an example of a _____ wave. The particles oscillate _____ to the direction of energy transfer.

[3 marks]

3   Choose the correct term from the list to identify the key term being described.

a   This is measured in hertz.

   amplitude   frequency   wavelength   [1 mark]

b   This is the maximum displacement of a point on a wave.

   amplitude   frequency   wavelength   [1 mark]

c   This is the distance between two peaks of a wave.

   amplitude   frequency   wavelength   [1 mark]

4   Complete the key terms being described.

a   Area in a longitudinal wave where particles are squashed together.

   c _ _ _ _ _ _ _ _ _ _   [1 mark]

b   Area in a longitudinal wave where particles are further apart.

   r _ _ _ _ _ _ _ _ _ _   [1 mark]

c   Calculated using the equation frequency × wavelength

   s _ _ _ _   [1 mark]

d   Name given to the movement of the particles in a wave.

   o _ _ _ _ _ _ _ _ _   [1 mark]

22.3 Wave measurements

Learning objectives

After this topic, you should know:

- how to calculate frequency from the period of a wave
- how to measure the wavelength and frequency of a wave in a ripple tank
- how to calculate the speed of a wave in a ripple tank
- how to measure the speed of sound in air.

Period

The **period** of a wave is the time taken for one complete wave to pass a fixed point.

If a point on a transverse wave takes 5 seconds to oscillate up, down, and back to where it started, then the time period of the wave is 5 seconds.

Calculating frequency

The period and the frequency of a wave are linked.

To calculate the frequency of a wave you divide 1 by the period.

$$\text{frequency (Hz)} = \frac{1}{\text{period (s)}}$$

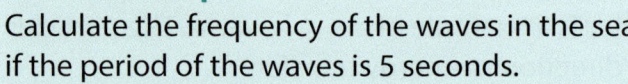

> **Worked example**
>
> Calculate the frequency of the waves in the sea if the period of the waves is 5 seconds.
>
> **Step 1:** Write down what you know.
>
> $$\text{period} = 5\text{s}$$
>
> **Step 2:** Write down the equation.
>
> $$\text{frequency (Hz)} = \frac{1}{\text{period (s)}}$$
>
> **Step 3:** Put in the numbers and solve.
>
> $$\text{frequency} = \frac{1}{5\text{s}} = 0.2 \text{ Hz}$$

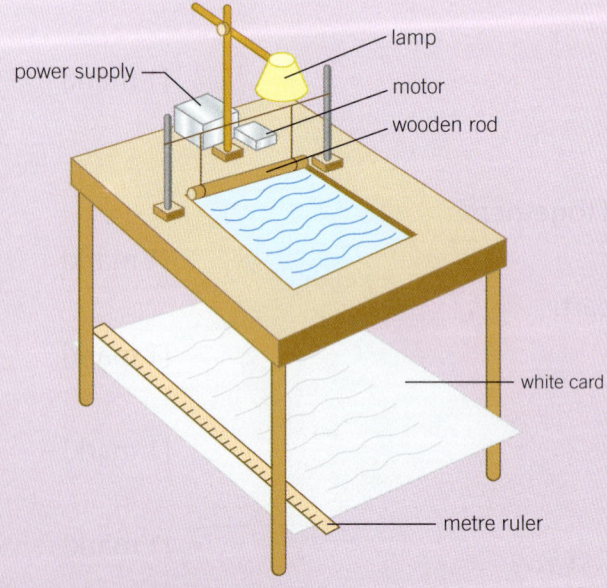

power supply, lamp, motor, wooden rod, white card, metre ruler

Figure 1 *A ripple tank.*

Investigating wave speed

Step 1: Set up the ripple tank as shown in Figure 1.

Step 2: Place a ruler and stopwatch on the white card.

Step 3: Take a photo of the waves moving along the card.

Step 4: To calculate the wavelength, measure the distance between five peaks on the photo. Divide this distance by 4. This gives you the wavelength for one wave.

Step 5: To measure the frequency, video the waves and the stopwatch. Play the film in slow motion and record the time it takes for 10 waves to pass a fixed point. Then divide 10 by the time you recorded. This gives you the frequency of the waves.

Step 6: Change the frequency and repeat.

Measuring the speed of sound in air

You will need two people for this. You and your partner should stand about 200 m apart. Record the distance between you.

If your partner crashes two cymbals together you should hear the sound a bit later than you see them crash. This is because sound travels much slower than light.

Use a stopwatch to time the interval (delay) between seeing them crash and hearing them.

This is the time it takes the sound to travel the distance between you. Repeat this so you can calculate an average time.

You can calculate the speed of sound in air using the equation:

$$speed = \frac{distance}{time}$$

A: Calculate the speed of sound in air if it takes 0.59 s for the sound to travel 200 m.

1 Choose the correct words from the box to complete the following sentences.

| film | frequency | period | photograph | ruler | stopwatch |

To measure the wavelength of ripple tank waves you should take a _____ of the waves with a _____ in clear view. To determine the _____ you will need to _____ the waves in slow motion with a _____ in clear view. This allows you to measure the time _____.   [5 marks]

2 The table shows some results for the experiment in Figure 1.

Distance between 5 peaks in cm	Wavelength in cm	Time for 10 waves in s	Period in s	Frequency in Hz	Wave speed in cm/s
10	2.5	1	0.1	10	25
20	5	2	0.2	5	25

Describe what happened to the wave speed and wavelength when the frequency was decreased.   [3 marks]

3 In an experiment to find the speed of sound in air, two students stand 150 m apart. They time how long it takes from seeing cymbals crash to hearing them. Their results are shown below.

Time interval in s	0.42	0.48	0.52

a Calculate the average time interval in seconds.   [1 mark]

b Calculate the speed of sound from these results.   [2 marks]

c The actual speed of sound in air is 340 m/s. Why is their answer different?   [1 mark]

22 Practice questions

01 Sound travels in waves. Which **two** statements describe sound waves?

    A Sound waves are longitudinal.

    B Sound waves are transverse.

    C Sound wave oscillations are parallel to the direction of energy transfer.

    D Sound wave oscillations are perpendicular to the direction of energy transfer.   [2 marks]

02 Figure 1 shows two types of waves.

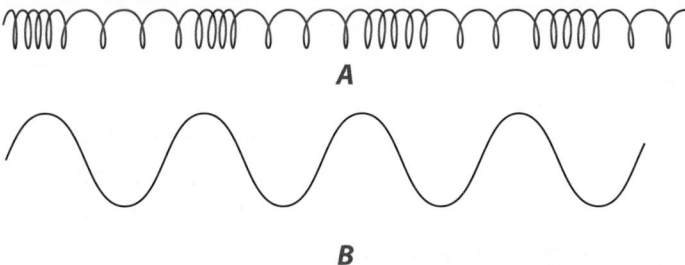

A

B

Figure 1

02.1 What type of wave is Figure 1A?   [1 mark]

02.2 Give an example of the type of wave shown in Figure 1A.   [1 mark]

02.3 What type of wave is Figure 1B?   [1 mark]

02.4 Give an example of the type of wave shown in Figure 1B.   [1 mark]

03 Draw one line from each key term to the correct definition.

Key term	Definition
amplitude	Number of waves passing a point each second.
period	Maximum displacement of a wave.
wavelength	The distance between two peaks.
frequency	The time take for each wave to pass a point.

    [3 marks]

04 Figure 2 shows some waves in a ripple tank.

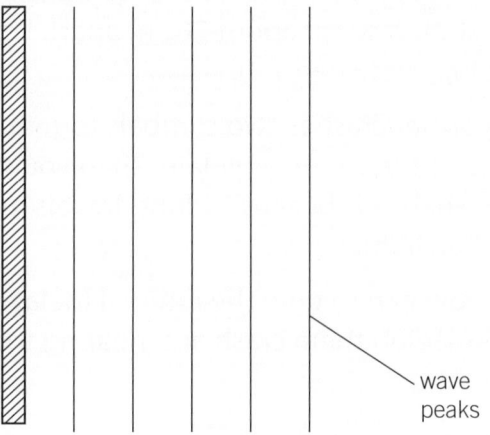

wave peaks

Figure 2

The distance between 5 peaks is 8 cm. Calculate the wavelength of one wave. Use the equation:

$$\text{wavelength} = \frac{\text{distance}}{\text{number of wavelengths}}$$

    [2 marks]

05 A wave on a slinky has a wavelength of 20 cm and a frequency of 4 Hz.

Calculate the speed of the wave. Use the equation:

wave speed = frequency × wavelength

    [2 marks]

06 A surfer observes 5 waves in 25 seconds.

06.1 Calculate the period of the waves.   [2 marks]

06.2 Define the frequency of a wave.   [1 mark]

06.3 Write down the equation that links wave period and frequency.   [1 mark]

06.4 Calculate the frequency of the waves.   [2 marks]

07 In an experiment to measure the speed of the wave in a ripple tank, a student times how long it takes a wave to travel from one end of the tank to the other end and back. She repeated her experiment three times and achieved these results:

2.3 s   2.5 s   2.5 s

07.1 Calculate the average time for the wave to travel from one end to the other and back. [2 marks]

07.2 The length of the tank is 60 cm. Determine the distance travelled by the wave. [1 mark]

07.3 Calculate the speed of the wave. [2 marks]

08 A student observes a large stone falling into a pool of water. A ripple forms on the surface of the pool. Figure 3 is a diagram of one point on the surface over time.

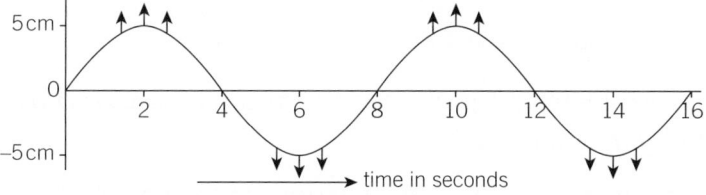

Figure 3

08.1 Was the wave transverse or longitudinal? [1 mark]

08.2 What was the amplitude of the wave? [1 mark]

08.3 What was the period of the wave? [1 mark]

08.4 Calculate the frequency of the wave. [2 marks]

08.5 Calculate the speed of the wave if the wavelength was 28 cm. [2 marks]

09 Two students carry out an experiment to determine the speed of sound in air. One holds cymbals and the other has a stopwatch. They stand on opposite sides of a field.

09.1 Describe what the student with the stopwatch will observe when the other student clashes the cymbals. [2 marks]

09.2 Give **two** measurements the students will need to record to calculate the speed of sound. [2 marks]

23 Electromagnetic waves and matter
23.1 Electromagnetic spectrum

Learning objectives

After this topic, you should know:

- what an electromagnetic wave is
- the order of the groups in the electromagnetic spectrum
- the similarities and differences between the groups
- hazardous effects of some electromagnetic waves on human tissue.

Electromagnetic waves are transverse waves that transfer energy from a source to an absorber. For example, microwaves are electromagnetic waves. In a microwave oven energy is transferred to food by microwaves. The energy heats up the food.

A: What is an electromagnetic wave?

Figure 1 shows all the groups of electromagnetic waves. They form a continuous spectrum called the **electromagnetic spectrum**.

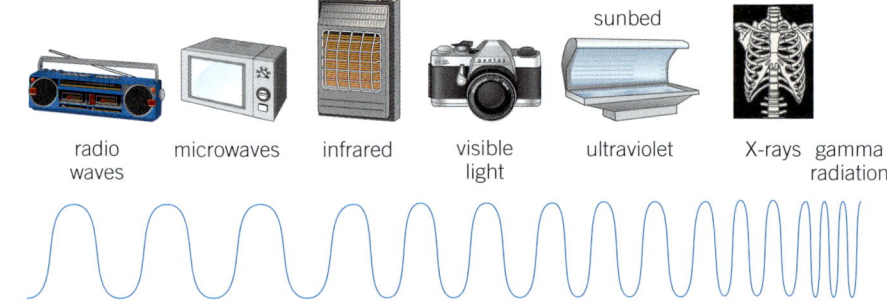

Figure 1 *The electromagnetic spectrum.*

The groups of the electromagnetic spectrum can be ordered by wavelength or by frequency (Figure 2).

All electromagnetic waves travel in a vacuum at the speed of light, which is 300 000 000 m/s. They also all travel at the same speed in air.

B: Which group of the electromagnetic spectrum has the longest wavelength?

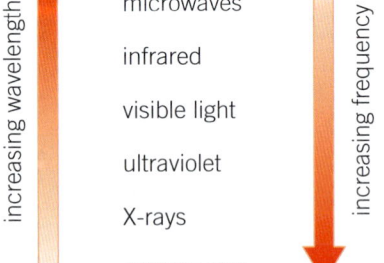

Figure 2 *Comparing frequency and wavelengths of groups of waves in the electromagnetic spectrum.*

Visible light

Visible light is made up of many colours.

Figure 3 *Colours of visible light.*

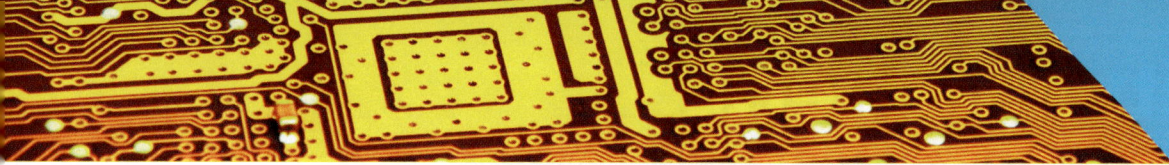

Red light has the longest wavelength. It is next to infrared in the electromagnetic spectrum. Violet light has the shortest wavelength, and is next to ultraviolet in the electromagnetic spectrum.

C: **Which colour of visible light has the shortest wavelength?**

How well can humans see in different coloured light?
Investigate how the frequency of visible light used in a room affects the ability of a person to see different objects.

The dangers of electromagnetic waves

Gamma radiation is dangerous. It is a type of **ionising radiation** and can cause mutations in living cells. X-rays and ultraviolet radiation can also harm living cells. The level of danger depends on the frequency of the radiation and the size of the dose.

D: **Which three groups of the electromagnetic spectrum can harm living cells?**

1   Put the groups of the electromagnetic spectrum in order of increasing frequency.

gamma rays	infrared	microwaves
radio waves	ultraviolet	visible light
X-rays		[6 marks]

2   Complete the sentences below.

   a   The parts of the electromagnetic spectrum are grouped together in terms of their _____ and frequency.   [1 mark]

   b   All the waves of the electromagnetic spectrum are _____ waves.   [1 mark]

3   Gamma rays, X-rays, and ultraviolet are hazardous to human health.

   a   What does the level of danger depend on?   [1 mark]

   b   What do you notice about their position in the electromagnetic spectrum?   [1 mark]

23.2 Electromagnetic waves 1

Learning objectives

After this topic, you should know:

- uses for radio waves, microwaves, infrared, and visible light.

How far can Bluetooth signals travel?

Investigate the range of a Bluetooth signal. How far can a Bluetooth signal travel and still be effective at transmitting data?

Figure 1 *A mobile phone mast.*

Radio waves

Radio waves are used to carry radio, TV, and mobile phone signals. Bluetooth devices communicate using radio waves.

Microwaves

Microwaves have a shorter wavelength than radio waves. Microwaves can be used for communications in the same way as radio waves. They are used for satellite TV and mobile phone signals.

Microwaves are also used to heat food in microwave ovens.

A: What is one use of microwaves and one use of radio waves?

Infrared

All objects emit (give out) infrared radiation. The hotter the object, the more infrared radiation it will emit. Electric heaters use infrared radiation to heat rooms and ovens use it to cook food.

Figure 2 *Image of a kangaroo taken by an infrared camera.*

Infrared cameras can detect infrared radiation. They can be used to find people and animals in the dark.

B: Which group of electromagnetic waves can a thermal camera detect?

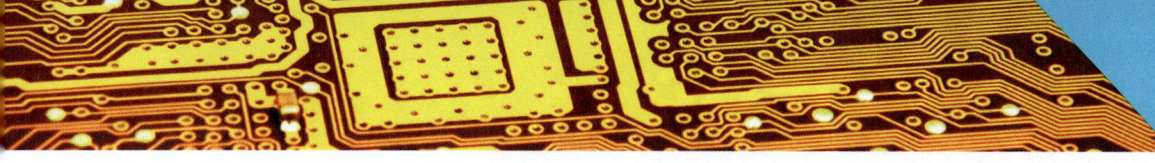

Visible light

Visible light is the only part of the electromagnetic spectrum that our eyes can detect.

- Cameras use visible light to capture an image.

- Fibre optic communications use visible light as well as infrared.

A rainbow shows the colours of the visible light part of the spectrum.

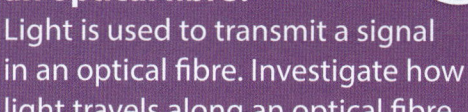

How does light travel in an optical fibre?
Light is used to transmit a signal in an optical fibre. Investigate how light travels along an optical fibre.

C: What are two uses of visible light?

1 Choose the correct words from the box to complete the following sentences.

| information | microwaves | mobile | visible |

Radio waves, _____, infrared, and _____ light are all used in communications. These waves carry _____. Radio and microwaves are used in _____ phone, and infrared and visible light are used in fibre optic cables.   [3 marks]

2 Choose which **two** parts of the electromagnetic spectrum can be used to cook food.

gamma rays	infrared	microwave
radio	ultraviolet	visible light
X-rays		[2 marks]

3 Choose the correct type of electromagnetic waves to answer the following questions.

| gamma rays | infrared | microwave | radio |
| ultraviolet | visible light | X-rays | |

a Which type of wave is detected by an aerial of a radio?   [1 mark]

b Which type of wave is emitted from a TV screen?   [1 mark]

c Which type of wave carries signals to and from a satellite?   [1 mark]

23.3 Electromagnetic waves 2

Learning objectives

After this topic, you should know:

- uses for ultraviolet, X-rays, and gamma rays
- dangers of using ultraviolet, X-rays, and gamma rays.

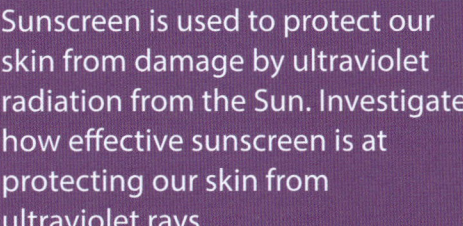

How effective is sunscreen?

Sunscreen is used to protect our skin from damage by ultraviolet radiation from the Sun. Investigate how effective sunscreen is at protecting our skin from ultraviolet rays.

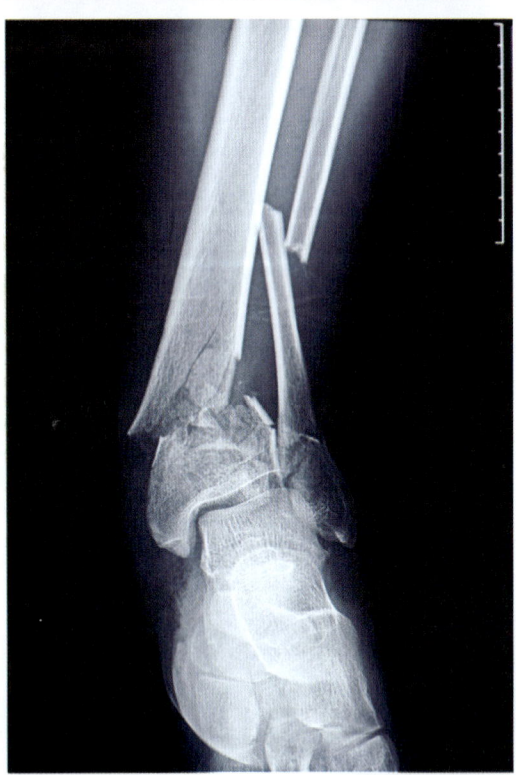

Figure 1 *X-rays are used to find broken bones.*

Ultraviolet, X-rays, and gamma rays can all harm living cells. The amount of damage done depends on the type of radiation and the size of the dose.

Ultraviolet

Ultraviolet radiation is between violet light and X-rays in the electromagnetic spectrum.

Uses of ultraviolet

Some chemicals absorb ultraviolet waves and then emit visible light. Security markers use ink that contains this kind of chemical.

Dangers of ultraviolet

Ultraviolet waves are harmful to your eyes and can cause blindness. They are also harmful to your skin. Too much ultraviolet from the sun or a sunbed can cause skin cancer.

A: What is one use of ultraviolet waves?

X-rays

X-rays can travel straight through many materials. You need a thick plate of lead to stop X-rays.

Uses of X-rays

X-rays are often used to detect cracks in metal objects. They are also used in medicine to create images of broken bones. X-rays pass through the soft tissue in the body but are absorbed by the bone. The white parts of an image show where the X-rays were absorbed by the bone.

Dangers of X-rays

X-rays are ionising radiation. This means they can damage or kill living cells. X-ray operators have to stand behind a concrete or lead screen to take X-ray images so they are not exposed to too much radiation. Lead aprons cover other parts of your body during an X-ray to avoid damage to your cells.

B: Why do the operators of X-ray machines stand behind a screen whilst a patient is having an X-ray?

Gamma rays

Gamma rays have the shortest wavelength of all the groups in the electromagnetic spectrum. Gamma rays are very useful in medicine.

Uses of gamma rays

Gamma rays are used to sterilise surgical instruments. The gamma rays kill harmful microorganisms on the instruments, making them safe to use.

Gamma rays are also used to kill cancer cells. The gamma rays are aimed at the cancer cells. This means the cancer cells get the maximum dose and healthy tissue is given the smallest dose possible.

Dangers of gamma rays

Exposure to gamma radiation can damage or kill cells. Workers have to wear radiation badges so that the amount of radiation that they are exposed to can be monitored.

Figure 2 *A film badge shows how much ionising radiation the wearer has received.*

C: What is one use of gamma radiation?

1   Choose the correct words from the box to complete the following sentences.

electromagnetic	size	type	wavelengths

The three groups of the _____ spectrum that have the shortest _____ are the ones that can cause harm to living cells. The amount of harm depends on the _____ of radiation and the _____ of the dose.   [3 marks]

2   Put the following parts of the electromagnetic spectrum in order of decreasing wavelength (increasing frequency).

  gamma   **ultraviolet**   **X-rays**   [2 marks]

3   Why is gamma radiation used to treat cancer?   [1 mark]

23 Checkpoint

1   Choose the correct words from the box to complete the following sentences.

| bones | continuous | properties | tissue |

Electromagnetic waves form a _____ spectrum. They have different _____ that make them useful for different things. For example, _____ absorb X-rays but the X-rays can pass through soft _____.   [3 marks]

2   Which **one** of these types of electromagnetic wave can our eyes detect?

   A infrared

   B radio

   C visible light   [1 mark]

3   Which **two** of these properties do infrared and radio waves share?

   A longer wavelength than visible light

   B not visible to the human eye

   C shorter wavelength than visible light

   D visible to the human eye   [2 marks]

4   Place the five types of electromagnetic radiation listed below in order of decreasing wavelength.

   gamma   infrared   microwaves   radio waves   ultraviolet   [4 marks]

5   Draw one line from each electromagnetic wave to the correct use.

Electromagnetic wave	Use
visible light	to send signals to and from satellites
microwaves	thermal imaging
ultraviolet	fibre optic communications
infrared	security markers

                                                                                                                  [4 marks]

6   A student investigates the infrared radiation emitted from a TV remote control. They place paper between the remote and the TV.

   They discover that when there are seven pieces of paper between the remote and the TV, the remote does not work.

   a What is the independent variable in this investigation?   [1 mark]

   b What is the dependent variable in this investigation?   [1 mark]

   c What is one control variable in this investigation?   [1 mark]

   d Why did the remote stop working when there were seven pieces of paper between the remote and the TV?   [1 mark]

7   A radio wave has a wavelength of 3 m and a frequency of 100 000 000 Hz.

   a What is the equation that links wave speed, frequency, and wavelength?   [1 mark]

   b Calculate the speed of the radio wave.   [2 marks]

   c Give the speed of a radio wave with wavelength 5 m.   [1 mark]

23 Vocabulary builder

1 Draw one line from each key word to the correct definition.

Key word	Definition
wavelength	The number of waves passing a point each second.
frequency	Waves with oscillations that are perpendicular to the direction of energy transfer.
transverse	Distance from a point on the wave to the same point on the next wave.

[2 marks]

2 Choose the correct word from the box to complete the following sentence.

electric   electromagnetic   magnetic

The _____ spectrum is made up of groups of different waves. [1 mark]

3 Choose the correct terms to identify the key term being described.

a This type of wave is used for cooking and heating rooms.

infrared

microwave

ultraviolet [1 mark]

b This type of wave is used to sterilise surgical instruments.

gamma

infrared

microwave [1 mark]

c This type of wave is used to communicate with satellites.

infrared

microwave

X-rays [1 mark]

4 Complete the sentences with the missing words.

The groups of electromagnetic waves form a c _ _ _ _ _ _ _ _ _ spectrum. Radio waves and microwaves have l _ _ _ _ _ wavelengths than ultraviolet, X-rays, and gamma rays. All the waves travel at the same s _ _ _ _ in a vacuum. [3 marks]

23.4 Density

Learning objectives

After this topic, you should know:

- what is meant by density
- how to measure the density of a solid
- how to calculate density.

What is density?

A concrete block is much heavier than a wooden block that is the same size. This is because the **density** of the concrete is much greater than the density of wood.

Density is how much mass a substance has in a certain amount of space.

Calculating density

You can calculate density using the equation:

$$\text{density} = \frac{\text{mass of object}}{\text{volume (the space the object takes up)}}$$

Density can be measured in kg/m³ or g/cm³.

- When the mass of the object is given in kg and the volume is given in m³, then the unit of density is kg/m³.

- When the mass of the object is given in g and the volume is given in cm³, then the unit of density is g/cm³.

Table 1 shows the of density of some common materials.

Table 1 *Densities of some common materials.*

Material	Density in kg/m³	Density in g/cm³
concrete	2400	2.4
water	1000	1.0
air	1.3	0.0013

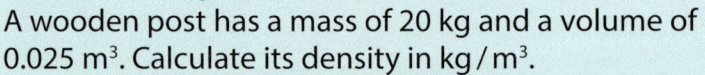

Worked example

A wooden post has a mass of 20 kg and a volume of 0.025 m³. Calculate its density in kg/m³.

Step 1: Write down what you know.

mass = 20 kg,   volume = 0.025 m³

Step 2: Write down the equation.

$$\text{density} = \frac{\text{mass}}{\text{volume}}$$

Step 3: Put the numbers into the equation and solve.

$$\text{density} = \frac{20\,\text{kg}}{0.025\,\text{m}^3} = 800\,\text{kg/m}^3$$

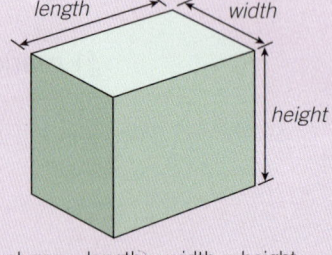

length   width

height

volume = length × width × height

Figure 1 *The volume of a cuboid.*

Measuring the density of a regular-shaped object

Step 1: Measure and record the length, width, and height of your object in centimetres and record in a table.

Step 2: Calculate the volume of the object using the equation

volume = length × width × height

Step 3: Measure the mass of the object in grams using a digital balance and record in your table.

Step 4: Calculate the density in g/cm³.

Measuring density of an irregular-shaped object

Step 1: Measure the mass of your object in grams and record in a table.

Step 2: Fill a displacement can with water until water comes out of the spout.
When the dripping stops place a measuring cylinder under the spout.

Step 3: Tie a piece of thread round the object and carefully lower it into the displacement can.

Step 4: Measure the volume of the water collected in the measuring cylinder. This is equal to the volume of the object. 1 ml = 1 cm³

Step 5: Calculate the density of the object.

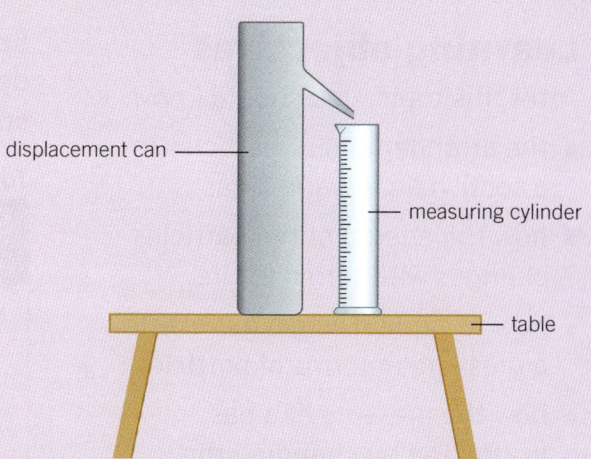

Figure 2 *Equipment to measure the density of an object with an irregular shape.*

A: A 65 g stone displaces 25 ml of water. Calculate the density of the stone.

1   Choose the correct words from the box to complete the following sentences.

| density   g / cm³   mass   volume |

_____ is the mass per unit volume. It can be calculated by dividing the _____ by the _____. If the mass is in g and the volume is in cm³, the units of density are _____.   [3 marks]

2   The table shows some data about blocks of aluminium and wax.

Object	Length in cm	Width in cm	Height in cm	Volume in cm³	Mass in g	Density in g / cm³
aluminium	6	2	2		64.8	2.7
wax	8	3	7	168	151.2	

   a Calculate the volume of the aluminium block.   [1 mark]
   b Calculate the density of the wax.   [2 marks]

3   An empty beaker has a mass of 50.0 g. 15 cm³ of vegetable oil is poured into the beaker. The total mass of the beaker and oil is 63.5g.
   a Calculate the mass of the vegetable oil.   [1 mark]
   b Calculate the density of the vegetable oil.   [2 marks]

23.5 Kinetic theory of matter

Learning objectives

After this topic, you should know:

- the arrangement of particles in a solid, a liquid, and a gas
- how the energy of the particles changes with temperature
- how to explain why a gas exerts a pressure in terms of particles
- how the pressure of a gas is affected by changing the temperature.

Solids, **liquids**, and **gases** are made of particles. Table 1 describes how the particles are arranged in each of these three **states of matter**.

Table 1 How the particles are arranged in solids, liquids, and gases.

State of matter	Particle diagram	Description
solid		particles vibrate in fixed positions
liquid		particles are in contact with each other but can move about randomly
gas		particles are much further apart than in liquids and move randomly at much faster speeds

- Particles in a gas state have more energy than particles in a liquid state.

- Particles in a liquid state have more energy than particles in a solid state.

A: Give **one** similarity and **one** difference between the arrangement of particles in a solid and a liquid.

Internal energy

The energy stored by the particles in a substance is called **internal energy**. Internal energy is the total energy in the kinetic energy and potential energy stores of the particles that make up a substance.

Heating a substance increases the internal energy of the particles. Heating can:

- increase the temperature of the substance – increasing the temperature increases the energy in the kinetic energy store of the particles

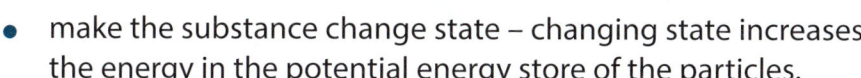

- make the substance change state – changing state increases the energy in the potential energy store of the particles.

Gas pressure

The particles in a gas have a lot of energy in their kinetic energy store. They move at high speed in random directions.

The particles collide with each other and the sides of the container. Each of these collisions with the container exerts a force. These forces add up over the area of the sides to cause a **pressure** on them.

When a gas is heated, energy is transferred to the **kinetic energy** store of the particles and they move faster. This causes the pressure of the gas to increase because the particles collide with the sides more often and with more force.

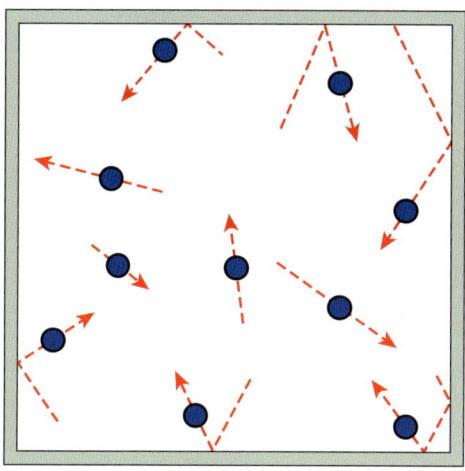

Figure 1 *Gas molecules in a box.*

1   Choose the correct words from the box to complete the following sentences.

> collide   force   internal
> kinetic   pressure   random

The energy stored by a substance is called the _____ energy. It is the total energy in the _____ energy store and the potential energy store. The particles in a gas move at high speeds in _____ directions. As they _____ with the walls of the container, they exert a _____. This causes _____.   [5 marks]

2   Which particles have the most internal energy – the particles in a solid, the particles in a liquid, or the particles in a gas?   [1 mark]

3   When a gas is heated in a sealed container, describe how each of the following properties of the gas changes:

   a   the pressure of the gas   [1 mark]

   b   the number of collisions the particles make per second with the walls of the container.   [1 mark]

379

23.6 Changes of state

Learning objectives

After this topic, you should know:

- that mass is conserved in a change of state
- definitions of the melting and boiling points of a substance
- how to use a temperature–time graph.

A substance can change from one state to another.

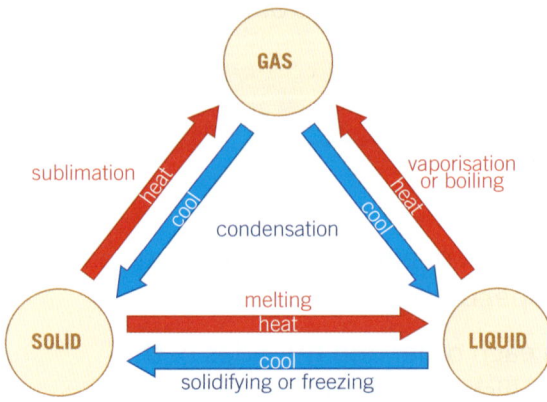

Figure 1 *Changes of state.*

A change of state is called a physical change because the changes can be reversed. For example, when a kettle boils, water becomes steam. If that steam touches a cold surface, it becomes water.

The temperature at which a solid changes into a liquid or at which a liquid changes into a solid is called the **melting point**.

The temperature at which a liquid turns into a gas or at which a gas turns into a liquid is called the **boiling point**.

Table 1 *Changes of state.*

Change of state		Temperature at change called
melting	solid to liquid	melting point
freezing	liquid to solid	
boiling	liquid to gas	boiling point
condensation	gas to liquid	

A: Name the change of state that occurs when a liquid becomes a gas.

Conservation of mass

During a change of state mass is **conserved**. This means the total mass stays the same. This is because the number of particles does not change as the substance changes state.

For example, when an ice cube melts, there are the same number of particles in the liquid water as there were in the solid ice cube. This means the mass of the water is the same as the mass of the ice cube.

B: Explain why the mass is conserved during a change of state.

What happens during a change of state?

The temperature of a substance stays the same when it changes state. This is because energy is needed to change its state. This energy is called **latent heat**.

Figure 2 shows how the temperature of water changes as you slowly heat ice until it boils.

The melting point is at 0 °C. This is when the solid ice becomes liquid water. The temperature does not change until all the ice has melted.

The boiling point is at 100 °C. This is when the liquid water becomes the gas steam. The temperature does not change until all the water has boiled away.

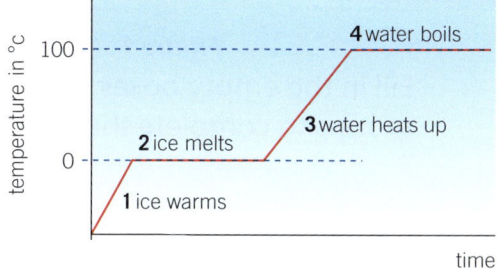

Figure 2 *Changes and states of Melting and boiling water.*

C: Describe how you can tell the water is changing state in Figure 2.

---

1 Choose the correct words from the box to complete the following sentences.

> boiling   mass   physical   reversed   temperature

A change of state is a _____ change because it can be _____. In a change of state, the _____ is always conserved. When a substance changes state, the _____ remains constant. By plotting a graph of how the temperature changes with time you can find the _____ point of a substance.   [4 marks]

2 Name the change of state that occurs when:

a steam from a shower turns to water on a bathroom mirror   [1 mark]

b snowflakes turn into water.   [1 mark]

3 A student heated a solid substance in a boiling tube. They measured the temperature every 30 seconds. Their results are shown in the table below.

Time in seconds	0	30	60	90	120	150	180	210	240	270
Temperature in °C	20	35	49	61	71	79	79	79	86	92

a Plot a graph of the results with temperature on the *y*-axis and time on the *x*-axis.   [3 marks]

b Use your graph to find the melting point of the substance.   [1 mark]

23 Practice questions

01 Figure 1 shows the electromagnetic spectrum.

radio waves	microwaves		light	ultraviolet		gamma rays

Figure 1

Fill in the empty boxes with the missing groups to complete the spectrum.

[1 mark]

02 Choose the correct words from the box to complete the following sentences. Each word can be used once, more than once, or not at all.

> energy   faster   higher   longer
> lower   shorter   sound   the same

Radio waves have a _____ wavelength and _____ frequency than any other electromagnetic wave.

Radio waves have _____ speed in air compared with microwaves.

Radio waves transfer _____ from place to place.

[4 marks]

03 Draw one line from each part of the electromagnetic spectrum to the correct use.

Electromagnetic spectrum	**Use**
microwave	Kills cancer cells.
ultraviolet	Transmits mobile phone signals.
gamma rays	Sunbeds.

[2 marks]

04 Give the scientific name for the following changes of state. Choose from the words in the box.

> boiling   condensation   freezing
> melting   sublimation

04.1 The windows in a bus full of people mist up. [1 mark]

04.2 An ice cube thaws out. [1 mark]

04.3 Water in a freezer turns to ice. [1 mark]

05 Table 1 lists the properties of the particles in three different substances.

Table 1

	Distance between the particles	Particle arrangement	Movement of the particles
A	close together	not fixed	move about
B	far apart	not fixed	move about
C	close together	fixed	vibrate

Draw one line from each substance to the correct state.

Substance	**State**
A	solid
B	liquid
C	gas

[2 marks]

06 The following four statements are about electromagnetic waves. Decide if each statement is true or false.

A Electromagnetic waves are transverse waves.

B Only two types of waves cause harm to living tissue.

C There are seven different groups of electromagnetic waves.

D Human eyes can detect ultraviolet light. [4 marks]

07 A microwave oven produces microwaves with a wavelength of 12 cm and a frequency of 2 500 000 000 Hz.

07.1 Write down the equation that links wave speed, frequency, and wavelength. [1 mark]

07.2 Use the equation to calculate the speed of the microwaves. [2 marks]

08 A student is finding the density of different materials. He measures a metallic block and finds the length is 10 cm, the width is 4 cm, and the height is 2 cm.

08.1 Calculate the volume of the block in cm³. [1 mark]

08.2 The block has a mass of 880 g. Calculate the density of the block. Use the equation: $\text{density} = \dfrac{\text{mass}}{\text{volume}}$ [2 marks]

09 A teacher demonstrates heating some naphthalene in a fume cupboard. The temperature of the naphthalene is measured every 2 minutes.

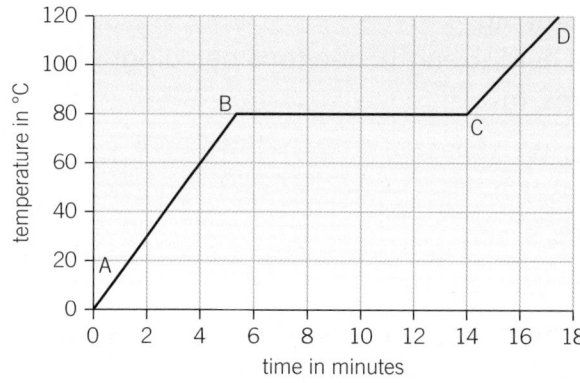

Figure 2

09.1 Identify the melting point of the naphthalene. [1 mark]

09.2 Describe what is happening to the particles of the naphthalene between A and B. [2 marks]

09.3 Describe what is happening to the particles of the naphthalene between B and C. [1 mark]

09.4 Describe what is happening to the particles of the naphthalene between C and D. [2 marks]

10.1 Explain what is meant by internal energy. [2 marks]

10.2 In which state do the particles have the most internal energy? [1 mark]

11 In an investigation into how pressure of a gas changes with temperature, a student obtained the results shown in Table 2.

Table 2

Temperature in °C	Pressure in kPa
20	100
30	103
40	107
50	110

11.1 Name the independent variable and the dependent variable in this experiment. [2 marks]

11.2 Plot a graph with temperature on the *x*-axis and pressure on the *y*-axis. [3 marks]

11.3 Explain how a gas can exert a pressure on the sides of its container. [2 marks]

11.4 Describe and explain what happens to this pressure when the gas is heated. [4 marks]

Physics equations

If you are studying AQA GCSE Combined science: Trilogy, there is a list of equations that you need to be able to remember or apply for your physics assessment.

Not all of these equations have been covered in this book.

Equations to remember

You need to be able to **remember** all of the following equations.

Equation	Units
weight = mass × gravitational field strength	weight: newtons, N mass: kilograms, kg gravitational field strength: newtons per kilograms, N/kg
work done = force × distance	work done: joules, J force: newtons, N distance: metres, m
force = spring constant × extension	force: newtons, N spring constant: newtons per metre, N/m extension: metres, m
distance travelled = speed × time	distance: metres, m speed: metres per second, m/s time: seconds, s
$acceleration = \dfrac{change\ in\ velocity}{time\ taken}$	acceleration: metres per second squared, m/s^2 velocity: metres per second, m/s time: seconds, s
resultant force = mass × acceleration	force: newtons, N mass: kilograms, kg acceleration: metres per second squared, m/s^2
kinetic energy = 0.5 × mass × (speed)^2	kinetic energy: joules, J mass: kilograms, kg speed: metres per second, m/s
gravitational potential energy = mass × gravitational field strength × height	energy: joules, J mass: kilograms, kg gravitational field strength: newtons per kilogram, N/kg height: metres, m
$power = \dfrac{energy\ transferred}{time}$	power: watts, W energy: joules, J time: seconds, s
$power = \dfrac{work\ done}{time}$	power: watts, W work done: joules, J time: seconds, s

Equation	Units
$\text{efficiency} = \dfrac{\text{useful output energy transfer}}{\text{total input energy transfer}}$	
$\text{efficiency} = \dfrac{\text{useful power output}}{\text{total power input}}$	
wave speed = frequency × wavelength	wave speed: metres per second, m/s frequency: hertz, Hz wavelength: metres, m
charge flow = current × time	charge flow: coulombs, C current: amperes, A time: seconds, s
potential difference = current × resistance	potential difference: volts, V current: amperes, A resistance: ohms, Ω
power = potential difference × current	power: watts, W potential difference: volts, V current: amperes, A
power = (current)^2 × resistance	power: watts, W current: amperes, A resistance: ohms, Ω
energy transferred = power × time	energy: joules, J power: watts, W time: seconds, s
energy transferred = charge flow × potential difference	energy: joules, J charge flow: coulombs, C potential difference: volts, V
$\text{density} = \dfrac{\text{mass}}{\text{volume}}$	density: kilograms per metre cubed, kg/m^3 mass: kilograms, kg volume: metres cubed, m^3

Equations to apply

You need to be able to apply these equations. You will be given them as an equation sheet in your assessment, but you will need to remember the correct SI units.

Equation	Units
$(\text{final velocity})^2 - (\text{initial velocity})^2 =$ $2 \times \text{acceleration} \times \text{distance}$	velocity: metres per second, m/s acceleration: metres per second squared, m/s^2 distance: metres, m
elastic potential energy = $0.5 \times \text{spring constant} \times (\text{extension})^2$	energy: joules, J spring constant: newtons per metre, N/m extension: metres, m
change in thermal energy = mass $\times$ specific heat capacity $\times$ temperature change	energy: joules, J mass: kilograms, kg specific heat capacity: joules per kilogram per degree Celsius, J/kg °C temperature: degrees Celsius, °C
$\text{period} = \dfrac{1}{\text{frequency}}$	period: seconds, s frequency: hertz, Hz
thermal energy for a change of state = mass $\times$ specific latent heat	energy: joules, J mass: kilograms, kg specific latent heat: joules per kilogram, J/kg

Glossary

acceleration	Change of speed per second.
acid	A chemical that has a pH value of less than 7.
acid rain	Rain that is more acidic than normal because of the gases dissolved in it.
activation energy	The amount of energy needed for a chemical reaction to start.
active site	The part of an enzyme that the substrate binds to.
active transport	The movement of substances from an area of low concentration to an area of high concentration, against a concentration gradient.
activity	The number of unstable atoms that decay per second in a radioactive source.
activation	The minimum amount of energy needed for particles to react.
adaptation	A special feature that makes an organism well suited to the environment that it lives in.
addiction	When a person becomes dependent on a drug.
aerobic respiration	Chemical reaction in which glucose is broken down using oxygen to produce carbon dioxide and water. Energy is transferred to the cells.
alkali	A base that dissolves in water.
alkane	A compound made only of carbon atoms and hydrogen atoms. All the bonds between the atoms are single bonds.
alkene	A compound made only of carbon atoms and hydrogen atoms. There is at least one double bond between two carbon atoms.
alleles	Different forms of the same gene.
alloy	A mixture containing mainly metals.
alpha radiation	Alpha particles, each composed of two protons and two neutrons, that are emitted by unstable nuclei.
alternating current (ac)	Electric current that constantly changes its direction of flow.
ammeter	A piece of equipment used to measure the current in a circuit.
amplitude	The maximum displacement of a point on a wave away from its undisturbed position.
anaerobic respiration	A chemical reaction in which glucose is broken down in the absence of oxygen.
anode	Positive electrode.
antibiotic	A chemical that kills bacteria within the body.
antibodies	The chemicals produced by white blood cells to destroy a pathogen.
arteries	The blood vessels that carry blood away from the heart.
artificial selection	The process by which humans breed animals and plants with desired characteristics.
asexual reproduction	Involves only one individual and the offspring is identical to the parent. There is no mixing of genetic material.
atmosphere	A layer of gases around the planet.
atom	The smallest part of an element that can exist.
background radiation	Low levels of radiation that come from your environment.
bacteria	Small microorganisms made up of only one cell.
balanced diet	Eating food containing the right nutrients in the correct amounts.

balanced symbol equation	A way of representing a chemical reaction and showing how the atoms are rearranged between the reactants and the products.
base	A chemical that reacts with an acid.
beta radiation	Beta particles that are high-energy electrons created in, and emitted from, unstable nuclei.
biodegradable	A substance that can be broken down by microorganisms.
biodiversity	A measure of the variety of all the different species of organisms in one place.
blood glucose level	The concentration of glucose in the blood.
boiling	Change of state from a liquid to a gas when heated.
boiling point	The temperature at which a liquid changes into a gas or a gas to a liquid.
(chemical) bond	How atoms are attached to each other.
braking distance	The distance travelled by a vehicle during the time it takes for its brakes to act.
breeding programmes	Breeding animals in human-controlled environments.
capillaries	The smallest blood vessels. They run between individual cells and have a wall that is only one cell thick.
carbohydrases	Enzymes that speed up the breakdown of carbohydrates into simple sugars.
carbon capture	A way to collect greenhouse gases and store them in porous rocks.
carbon footprint	A measure of greenhouse gases produced over the lifecycle of a product, event, or service.
catalyst	A chemical that speeds up a reaction by lowering the activation energy.
cathode	Negative electrode.
causal mechanism	Something that explains how one factor affects another.
cell	The smallest functional unit in an organism.
cell membrane	The barrier around the contents of a cell that controls what moves in and out of the cell.
cell wall	The rigid structure around plant cells that holds the shape of the cell.
central nervous system	The part of the nervous system where information is processed. It is made up of the brain and spinal cord.
chemical energy	The stored energy found in food, fuels, and batteries.
chemical reaction	A change in which atoms are rearranged to make new substances.
chlorophyll	The green pigment contained in chloroplasts which absorbs energy transferred by light.
chloroplast	The part of a plant cell where photosynthesis happens.
chromatography	A method to separate mixtures of liquids.
chromosome	A strand of DNA containing genes.
circulatory system	The organ system that transports materials around the body in the blood.
clones	Identical offspring produced by asexual reproduction.
collision	When two particles hit each other.
combustion	Burning.
communicable disease	A disease caused by pathogens that can be passed from one organism to another.
community	The group of interdependent living organisms in an ecosystem.
competition	The process by which living organisms compete with each other for limited resources.

complete combustion	Burning in lots of oxygen.
compound	Two or more elements chemically bonded together.
compression	In a longitudinal wave this is the area where the particles are squashed together.
concentrated	A solution with a large amount of solute.
concentration	A measure of the amount of solute within a solution.
condensation	Change of state from a gas to a liquid.
conductor	A material that easily transfers thermal energy and/or electricity.
conservation	Protecting a natural environment to ensure habitats and organisms are not lost.
consumer	An animal that eats other organisms to gain energy.
contact force	A force that acts when two objects are touching.
contraception	A method used to prevent pregnancy.
correlation	An apparent link or relationship between two factors.
corrode	React with chemicals in the soil or air.
covalent bond	A shared pair of electrons.
cracking	Thermal decomposition of long-chain hydrocarbons to make smaller, more useful hydrocarbons.
crude oil	A mixture of lots of chemicals used to make fuels and oil.
crystallisation	A separation method used to separate dissolved solids from solution.
current	The flow of electrical charge.
cytoplasm	The liquid in which the parts of the cell are suspended and most of the chemical reactions of the cell take place.
decay	The process by which waste materials and dead animals and plants break down.
deceleration	Change of speed per second when an object slows down.
decomposer	A microorganism that breaks down dead bodies and waste materials.
deforestation	The removal of forests from an area.
density	Mass per unit volume of a substance.
diamond	A form of carbon in which each carbon atom is bonded to four other carbon atoms.
diffusion	The spreading out and mixing of particles from high concentration to low concentration.
digestion	The breakdown of large insoluble molecules into small soluble molecules.
digestive system	The organ system in which food is digested and absorbed.
dilute	A solution with only a small amount of solute.
direct current (dc)	Electric current in a circuit that is in one direction only.
directly proportional	A graph shows two variables are directly proportional if the line of best fit is a straight line through the origin.
disinfectant	A chemical used to kill microorganisms in the environment.
displacement reaction	A chemical reaction in which a more reactive element takes the place of a less reactive element in its compound.
dissipated energy	Energy that is stored in less useful ways.
distance–time graph	A graph that plots distance an object has travelled against time.
distillation	A separation method used to separate a liquid from a solution.
DNA	A chemical that contains all the information needed to make an organism.

dominant allele	The form of a gene whose characteristics are always expressed if present in the genotype.
drug	A chemical that affects the way the body works.
dual circulatory system	How blood vessels are arranged in humans – one loop that takes blood from the heart to the lungs and back, and another loop that takes blood from the heart to the rest of the body and back.
earth wire	The wire in a mains cable used to connect the metal case of an appliance to earth.
economical	When, for example, the cost of extracting a metal is less than the amount the metal can be sold for.
ecosystem	All the living organisms and physical conditions present in an area.
effector	A muscles or gland that brings about a response in the body.
efficiency	The useful energy transferred by a device divided by the total energy supplied to the device.
effluent	The liquid part separated from waste water.
elastic	A material is elastic if it is able to regain its shape after it has been squashed or stretched.
elastic energy	The energy stored in an object when it is squashed or stretched. Also called strain energy.
electrode	Made of metal or graphite, and allows an electric current to flow through a solution.
electrolysis	Using electricity to break down an ionic compound into simpler substances.
electrolyte	A liquid, containing free-moving ions, that can be broken down by electrolysis.
electromagnet	An insulated wire wrapped around an iron bar that becomes magnetic when there is a current in the wire.
electromagnetic spectrum	The continuous range of wavelengths of electromagnetic waves.
electromagnetic wave	Electric and magnetic disturbances that transfer energy from one place to another.
electron	The negatively charged particle in an atom.
element	A substance made up of only one type of atom.
endothermic	A reaction that transfers energy from the surroundings.
energy store	The energy that a substance has.
energy transfer	The transfer (passing) of energy between energy stores.
enzymes	Biological catalysts that speed up a reaction without being used up.
equilibrium	When a reversible reaction happens in a sealed container, so that the rate of the forward reaction is the same as the rate of the reverse reaction.
evaporation	Change of state in which a liquid turns into a gas.
evolution	The gradual change in a species over time.
exothermic	A reaction that transfers energy to the surroundings.
extinct	Species which have no surviving organisms left in the world.
extraction	The process by which metals are obtained from rocks and ores.
fermentation	A form of anaerobic respiration performed by plant cells and yeast. Glucose is broken down into ethanol and carbon dioxide, transferring a small amount of energy to the cell.
fibre	A nutrient that provides bulk for food to move through the gut.
filtration	A separation method used to separate solids from liquids.
finite resource	A resource that is used faster than more can be made.

food chain	A diagram that shows the transfer of biomass or energy between organisms.
food web	A diagram that shows a number of linked food chains.
force	A force acts on an object to make it do something.
formulation	A mixture of chemicals that make a useful product.
fossil fuel	A non-renewable fuel that is formed underground from the remains of plants and animals that died millions of years ago. Crude oil, natural gas, and coal are fossile fuels.
fossil	The remains of a plant or animal mineralised, or changed to rock.
fractional distillation	A separation method used to separate a mixture of liquids with different boiling points.
fractions	The parts that crude oil is separated into.
freezing	Change of state from a liquid to a solid.
frequency	The number of wave peaks passing a fixed point every second. Also the number of times an alternating current changes direction.
friction	The force opposing the relative motion of two solid surfaces in contact.
fuel	A store of chemical energy.
fuse	A fuse contains a thin wire that melts and cuts the current off if too much current passes through it.
gall bladder	The small organ where bile is stored.
gamma radiation	Electromagnetic radiation emitted from unstable nuclei in radioactive substances.
gas	A state of matter in which particles are far apart and move at random.
gene	A section of DNA which codes for a characteristic.
genetic engineering	The process by which scientists can manipulate and change the genotype of an organism.
genetic material	The chemical DNA, which contains all the information needed to make an organism.
genotype	The alleles present in an organism.
giant ionic lattice	A large network of ions bonded together.
gland	Any structure in animals which releases hormones.
global dimming	Dust and soot in the atmosphere reflect some sunlight.
global warming	The gradual increase in the average surface temperature of the Earth.
graphite	A form of pure carbon in which each atom is bonded to another three carbon atoms forming hexagonal rings. The rings are joined together in a giant structure and form layers.
gravitational field strength	The force of gravity on an object of mass 1 kg
gravitational potential energy	The energy stored in an object when it has been raised above the ground.
greenhouse gases	Methane and carbon dioxide, which trap energy in the atmosphere to keep the Earth warm.
group	A column of the periodic table.
habitat	The place in which an organism lives.
half-life	The time taken for the activity of a radioactive isotope to halve. Also the time taken for the number of radioactive nuclei in a sample to halve.
herbicide	A chemical used to kill weeds.
heterozygous	An individual with two different alleles for a characteristic.

homeostasis	The regulation of the internal conditions of a cell or organism to maintain optimum conditions, in response to internal and external changes.
homozygous	An individual with two identical alleles for a characteristic.
hormone	A chemical produced in one area of the body of an organism that has an effect on another area.
hydrocarbon	A chemical that contains only carbon and hydrogen.
immune	When a person is no longer able to get a disease.
incomplete combustion	Burning in limited oxygen.
induced magnetism	Magnetisation of a magnetic material by placing it in a magnetic field.
inelastic	A material that does not return to its original shape if it is stretched.
infectious disease	A disease caused by pathogens that can be passed from one organism to another.
infertility	When a person is unable to have a child naturally.
ingestion	The process by which a white blood cell can surround and destroy pathogens.
insoluble	A substance that does not dissolve in a liquid.
insulator	A material that does not easily transfer heat or electricity.
interdependence	The network of relationships between different organisms within a community.
internal energy	The sum of the kinetic and potential energy of all the particles of a substance.
ionic bond	Electrostatic force of attraction between oppositely charged ions.
ionising radiation	Radiation that can cause a charge in the atoms it passes through.
ion	A charged particle formed by the gain or loss of electrons.
irradiation	Exposure of an object or person to ionising radiation.
isotopes	Atoms that have the same number of protons but a different number of neutrons.
kinetic energy	The energy stored in the movement of an object.
large intestine	The organ in which water passes back into the body, leaving a solid waste of undigested food.
latent heat	The energy transferred to or from a substance when it changes its state.
life cycle assessment (LCA)	A way to measure sustainability of a product.
limiting factor	A factor that limits the rate of a reaction.
lipase	Enzymes that speed up the breakdown of lipids into fatty acids and glycerol.
lipids	Fats and oils.
liquid	A state of matter in which particles are close together and move at random.
live wire	The mains wire that has alternating voltage. In the UK this is 230 V.
liver	The organ that produces bile.
longitudinal wave	A wave in which the vibrations are parallel to the direction of energy transfer.
lubrication	The use of a substance that reduces friction between surfaces where they rub together.
magnet	An object that creates a magnetic field.
magnetic field	The space around a magnet or a current-carrying wire where another magnet or a magnetic material feels a force.
magnetic field line	A line drawn to show a magnetic field.
mass	The amount of matter in an object.
melting	The change of state when a solid turns into a liquid.
melting point	The temperature at which a solid turns into a liquid or a liquid to a solid.

menstrual cycle	The monthly cycle that prepares a female for a possible pregnancy.
menstruation	Part of the menstrual cycle, where the lining of the uterus is released through the cervix if a female is not pregnant.
metals	The elements found on the left of the periodic table.
microbe	A microorganism that can cause disease.
microscope	A piece of equipment that is used to magnify objects.
mineral	A nutrient needed for the animals or plants to function properly.
mitochondria	The places where respiration happens in a cell.
mixture	Made of more than one substance not chemically joined.
model	A simplified way to represent a system or process.
molecule	A group of two or more atoms strongly bonded together.
monomer	A small reactive chemical that can join up to make a polymer.
National Grid	The network of cables and transformers used to transfer electricity from power stations to consumers.
natural selection	The processes by which evolution takes place. The organisms most suited to their environment will survive to breed, and pass on their useful characteristics to their offspring.
neutral (solution)	A solution with a pH value of exactly 7. The solution is neither acidic nor alkaline.
neutral wire	The wire of a mains circuit that is earthed at the local substation so its voltage is close to zero.
neutralisation	A type of reaction in which an acid and a base react to produce a solution with a pH of 7.
neutron	A sub-atomic particle found in the nucleus of an atom. It has no charge.
newton	A measure of force.
newton meter	A piece of equipment used to measure force.
non-contact force	A force that acts when two objects are not touching.
non-metals	Elements found on the right of the periodic table.
non-renewable	A resource that is used faster than it can be replenished.
nucleus (of a cell)	The part of the cell that contains the genetic material.
nucleus (of an atom)	The centre of an atom, made up of protons and neutrons. Contains most of the mass of the atom.
ore	A rock that it is economical to extract the metal from.
organ	A collection of different tissues working together to carry out specific functions.
organ system	A group of organs that work together to carry out specific functions.
organism	A living thing.
oscillate	Move to and fro about a certain position along a line.
pancreas	An organ that produces digestive enzymes.
paper chromatography	A separation method in which small amounts of dissolved substances are separated by running a solvent along a piece of absorbent paper.
parallel circuit	Components connected in a circuit so that the potential difference (voltage) is the same across each one.
particles	The tiny parts that all material is made from.
pathogens	Microorganisms that cause disease.
penicillin	A type of antibiotic.

period (menstruation)	Part of the menstrual cycle, where the lining of the uterus is released through the cervix if a female is not pregnant.
period (of a wave)	The time taken for one wave to pass a fixed point.
periodic table	A list of all of the known elements, arranged by atomic number.
permanent vacuole	The space in the cytoplasm of a plant cell that is filled with cell sap.
perpendicular	At right angles.
pesticide	A chemical used to kill pests that eat crops, normally insects.
pH scale	A measure of the acidity and alkalinity of a solution. The pH scale runs from 0 (very acidic) to 14 (very alkaline). A pH of 7 is neutral.
phenotype	How the alleles of an organism are expressed.
photosynthesis	The process by which plants make food using carbon dioxide, water, and light.
plasma	The liquid part of the blood that carries dissolved substances and blood cells around the body.
platelets	Fragments of cells in the blood that are involved in clotting the blood when there is a cut.
pole	The place where a magnetic field is strongest.
pollution	Chemicals that are released into the environment in levels that are higher than what they would naturally be. These chemicals then cause damage to the environment.
polymer	A long-chain molecule made from many repeating units.
population	The number of organisms of a species living in an area.
potable water	Water that is safe to drink.
potential difference	a measure of the energy transfer by electric charge when charge flows
power	The energy transformed or transferred per second. The unit of power is the watt (W).
pressure	The force applied to a surface by the collision of moving particles.
producer	An organism that makes its own food by photosynthesis.
products	The chemicals made during a chemical reaction.
proteases	Enzymes that speed up the breakdown of proteins into amino acids.
protein	A nutrient needed to repair body tissue and grow.
proton	A sub-atomic particle found in the nucleus of an atom. It has a +1 charge.
pure	A substance is pure if no other substances are mixed with it.
quadrat	A sample area used for measuring the abundance and distribution of organisms in the field.
radioactive	An unstable atom that emits ionising radiation from the nucleus to become more stable.
radioactive contamination	The presence of radioactive material where it should not be.
radioactive decay	When unstable atoms emit ionising radiation.
range (of radiation)	The distance that radiation can travel.
rarefaction	In a longitudinal wave this is the area where the particles are stretched apart.
rate of reaction	How quickly the reactants are used up or products are made in a chemical reaction.
reactants	The starting chemicals in a chemical reaction.
reaction profile	A graph that shows the energy of the reactants and the energy of the products.
reaction time	How quickly a human can react to a stimulus.
reactivity	How well a substance undergoes a chemical reaction.

reactivity series	A list of metals from most to least reactive.
receptor	A group of specialised cells that detect a stimulus.
recessive allele	A form of a gene whose characteristic is only expressed if two copies are present in the genotype.
recycling	Purifying used materials then using them in a new product.
red blood cell	A cell that carries oxygen around the body in the blood.
reflex action	An automatic nervous response which occurs very rapidly. These actions do not involve conscious thought.
relative atomic mass	The average mass of the atoms of an element.
relative formula mass	The total relative atomic masses of all the atoms in a compound or molecule.
renewable	A natural source of energy that is always being replenished so it never runs out.
resistance	A measure of how difficult it is for current to flow through a component in a circuit.
respiration	The reaction in which glucose is broken down using oxygen to produce carbon dioxide and water and transfer energy for the cells.
reversible reaction	The reactants make the products and the products make the reactants in a chemical reaction.
ribosome	The place where proteins are made in a cell.
salivary gland	A gland that produces saliva.
scalar	A physical quantity, such as mass or distance, which only has magnitude (unlike a vector, which has magnitude and direction).
secrete	When cells or glands release a hormone.
selective breeding	The process by which humans breed animals and plants with desired characteristics.
series circuit	Components connected in such a way that the same current passes through them.
sewage	Waste water.
sexual reproduction	Involves the joining of male and female sex cells. Produces genetic variation in offspring.
sludge	The solid material separated from waste water.
small intestine	The organ in which small digested molecules are absorbed into the blood stream.
solenoid	A long coil of wire that produces a magnetic field in and around the coil when there is a current in the coil.
solid	A state of matter in which particles are close together and vibrate about in fixed positions.
soluble	Able to dissolve in a liquid.
solute	The substance dissolved in the liquid of a solution.
solution	A mixture in which a substance is dissolved within a liquid.
solvent	The liquid that a substance dissolves in to form a solution.
specialised cell	A cell that is adapted to form a particular function.
speed	The speed of an object (metres per second) = distance moved by the object (metres) divided by time taken to move the distance (seconds).
speed–time graph	A graph that plots the speed an object is moving at against time.
state of matter	Solid, liquid, and gas – the three forms in which a substance can exist.

state symbol	A symbol added to balanced equations to show the state of a substance.
steel	An alloy made of mainly iron with some carbon.
sterilised	Treated to remove or kill microbes.
stimulus	Change in the external or internal environment that can be detected by receptors.
stomach	The organ in which food is churned with digestive juices and acids.
stopping distance	The distance travelled by a vehicle during the time it takes for the driver to react and brake.
substrate	The substance an enzyme acts on.
sustainable	Leaving resources for the future.
target organ	The organ that a hormone will affect on.
thermal energy	The energy stored in an object because of its temperature.
thermal conductivity	A measure of how quickly energy is transferred by conduction through a material.
thinking distance	The distance travelled by a vehicle in the time it takes the driver to react.
tissue	A group of specialised cells with a similar structure and function.
toxin	A poisonous substance.
transect	A measured line or area along which ecological measurements are made.
transformer	Electrical device used to increase or decrease an alternating voltage.
transverse wave	A wave in which the vibration is perpendicular to the direction of energy transfer.
useful energy	Energy transferred to where it is wanted in the way that is wanted.
vaccination	Inserting a small amount of a dead or inactive pathogen into the body to cause an immune response by white blood cells.
vacuum	A space containing no particles.
variation	Differences within a species.
vector	a physical quantity, such as force or velocity, that has magnitude and direction.
veins	The blood vessels that carry blood towards the heart.
velocity	speed in a given direction
velocity–time graph	A graph that plots the velocity of an object against time.
virus	A type of pathogen that can cause disease.
vitamin	A nutrient needed in small quantities for the body to function properly.
voltage	The potential difference across a component.
voltmeter	A piece of equipment used to measure the voltage in a circuit.
wasted energy	Energy that is not usefully transferred.
wave	An oscillation that transfers energy from one place to another without transferring matter.
wavelength	The distance from one peak to the next.
weight	The force of gravity on an object (in newtons, N).
white blood cell	A blood cell that defends the body against disease.
withdrawal symptoms	The unpleasant side effects a person may suffer if they try to stop taking a drug that they are addicted to.
word equation	A way of representing a chemical reaction. The reactants are on the left of an arrow and the products are on the right.
work	The energy transferred by a force.
zone of inhibition	An area on an agar plate where bacteria cannot grow.

Periodic table

1	2												3	4	5	6	7	0
																		4 **He** helium 2
7 **Li** lithium 3	9 **Be** beryllium 4												11 **B** boron 5	12 **C** carbon 6	14 **N** nitrogen 7	16 **O** oxygen 8	19 **F** fluorine 9	20 **Ne** neon 10
23 **Na** sodium 11	24 **Mg** magnesium 12												27 **Al** aluminium 13	28 **Si** silicon 14	31 **P** phosphorus 15	32 **S** sulfur 16	35.5 **Cl** chlorine 17	40 **Ar** argon 18
39 **K** potassium 19	40 **Ca** calcium 20	45 **Sc** scandium 21	48 **Ti** titanium 22	51 **V** vanadium 23	52 **Cr** chromium 24	55 **Mn** manganese 25	56 **Fe** iron 26	59 **Co** cobalt 27	59 **Ni** nickel 28	63.5 **Cu** copper 29	65 **Zn** zinc 30		70 **Ga** gallium 31	73 **Ge** germanium 32	75 **As** arsenic 33	79 **Se** selenium 34	80 **Br** bromine 35	84 **Kr** krypton 36
85 **Rb** rubidium 37	88 **Sr** strontium 38	89 **Y** yttrium 39	91 **Zr** zirconium 40	93 **Nb** niobium 41	96 **Mo** molybdenum 42	[98] **Tc** technetium 43	101 **Ru** ruthenium 44	103 **Rh** rhodium 45	106 **Pd** palladium 46	108 **Ag** silver 47	112 **Cd** cadmium 48		115 **In** indium 49	119 **Sn** tin 50	122 **Sb** antimony 51	128 **Te** tellurium 52	127 **I** iodine 53	131 **Xe** xenon 54
133 **Cs** caesium 55	137 **Ba** barium 56	139 **La*** lanthanum 57	178 **Hf** hafnium 72	181 **Ta** tantalum 73	184 **W** tungsten 74	186 **Re** rhenium 75	190 **Os** osmium 76	192 **Ir** iridium 77	195 **Pt** platinum 78	197 **Au** gold 79	201 **Hg** mercury 80		204 **Tl** thallium 81	207 **Pb** lead 82	209 **Bi** bismuth 83	[209] **Po** polonium 84	[210] **At** astatine 85	[222] **Rn** radon 86
[223] **Fr** francium 87	[226] **Ra** radium 88	[227] **Ac*** actinium 89	[261] **Rf** rutherfordium 104	[262] **Db** dubnium 105	[266] **Sg** seaborgium 106	[264] **Bh** bohrium 107	[277] **Hs** hassium 108	[268] **Mt** meitnerium 109	[271] **Ds** darmstadtium 110	[272] **Rg** roentgenium 111	[285] **Cn** copernicium 112		[286] **Nh** nihonium 113	[289] **Fl** flerovium 114	[289] **Mc** moscovium 115	[293] **Lv** livermorium 116	[294] **Ts** tennessine 117	[294] **Og** oganesson 118

key

relative atomic mass
atomic symbol
name
atomic (proton) number

1 **H** hydrogen 1

*The lanthanides (atomic numbers 58–71) and the actinides (atomic numbers 90–103) have been omitted.

Relative atomic masses for **Cu** and **Cl** have not been rounded to the nearest whole number.

Index

Great Clarendon Street, Oxford, OX2 6DP, United Kingdom

Oxford University Press is a department of the University of Oxford.
It furthers the University's objective of excellence in research, scholarship,
and education by publishing worldwide. Oxford is a registered trade mark
of Oxford University Press in the UK and in
certain other countries

Original AQA GCSE Combined Science: Trilogy text © Jim Breithaupt,
Ann Fullick, Lawrie Ryan 2018

British Library Cataloguing in Publication Data
Data available

ISBN 978-0-19-842883-1

10 9 8 7 6 5

Paper used in the production of this book is a natural, recyclable product
made from wood grown in sustainable forests.
The manufacturing process conforms to the environmental regulations
of the country of origin.

Printed in Great Britain by Bell and Bain Ltd. Glasgow

Acknowledgements

The publisher and authors would like to thank the following for
permission to use photographs and other copyright material:

Cover: PRILL/Shutterstock
All photos © Shutterstock, except: **p6, 16(t)**: DR GOPAL MURTI/SCIENCE PHOTO
LIBRARY; **p11**: ERIC GRAVE/SCIENCE PHOTO LIBRARY; **p16(b)**: JOHN DURHAM/
SCIENCE PHOTO LIBRARY; **p48**: ABERRATION FILMS LTD/SCIENCE PHOTO LIBRARY;
p92: Nigel Cattlin/SCIENCE PHOTO LIBRARY; **p102**: SCIENCE PHOTO LIBRARY;
p103: MARTYN F. CHILLMAID/SCIENCE PHOTO LIBRARY; **p120**: MICHAEL W.
TWEEDIE/SCIENCE PHOTO LIBRARY; **p121(t)**: MICHAEL W. TWEEDIE/SCIENCE
PHOTO LIBRARY; **p124**: EYE OF SCIENCE/SCIENCE PHOTO LIBRARY; **p137**:
ANDREW LAMBERT PHOTOGRAPHY/SCIENCE PHOTO LIBRARY; **p139(l), 149(l)**:
TREVOR CLIFFORD PHOTOGRAPHY/SCIENCE PHOTO LIBRARY; **p139(r), 149(r)**:
TREVOR CLIFFORD PHOTOGRAPHY/SCIENCE PHOTO LIBRARY; **p149(m)**: TREVOR
CLIFFORD PHOTOGRAPHY/SCIENCE PHOTO LIBRARY; **p158**: ANDREW LAMBERT
PHOTOGRAPHY/SCIENCE PHOTO LIBRARY; **p199**: SCIENCE PHOTO LIBRARY; **p200**:
MARTYN F. CHILLMAID/SCIENCE PHOTO LIBRARY; **p230**: PAUL RAPSON/SCIENCE
PHOTO LIBRARY; **p232**: SCIENCE PHOTO LIBRARY; **p234(t)**: CORDELIA MOLLOY/
SCIENCE PHOTO LIBRARY; **p241**: ANDREW LAMBERT PHOTOGRAPHY/SCIENCE
PHOTO LIBRARY; **p249(r)**: GUSTOIMAGES/SCIENCE PHOTO LIBRARY; **p307**: CNRI/
SCIENCE PHOTO LIBRARY; **p340**: OUP; **p348**: TREVOR CLIFFORD PHOTOGRAPHY/
SCIENCE PHOTO LIBRARY; **p373**: MARTYN F. CHILLMAID/SCIENCE PHOTO LIBRARY.

Artwork by Aptara Inc. and Q2A Media Services Inc.

The authors would like to thank the editorial team at OUP for all of their
help and support on this project.

Every effort has been made to contact copyright holders of material
reproduced in this book. Any omissions will be rectified in subsequent
printings if notice is given to the publisher.